The moving finger writes,
and having writ
Moves on; nor all your
piety nor wit
Shall lure it back to cancel
half a line
Nor all your tears wash
out a word of it.

Stanza 71
The Rubaiyat of
Omar Khayyam

1547 – 1577

A HISTORY OF ANCIENT MEXICO

By

FRAY BERNARDINO DE SAHAGUN

TRANSLATED BY FANNY R. BANDELIER

FROM THE SPANISH VERSION

OF

CARLOS MARIA DE BUSTAMANTE

The Rio Grande Press, Inc.

GLORIETA, NEW MEXICO · 87535

First edition from which this edition was
reproduced was supplied by

T. N. LUTHER, Books,

P O Box 6083
Shawnee Mission, Kans. 66206

Library of Congress Cataloging in Publication Data

Sahagún, Bernardino de, d. 1590.
A history of ancient Mexico : 1547-1577.

(A Rio Grande classic)
No more published.
Translation of Books 1-4 of Historia general de las cosas de Nueva España.
Reprint of the ed. published by Fisk University Press, Nashville, in series: Fisk University social science series.
"Bibliography of Fray Bernadino de Sahagun's writings" : p.
1. Aztecs. 2. Indians of Mexico--Religion and mythology. 3. Calendar, Mexican. I. Title.
II. Series: Fisk University, Nashville. Social science series.
[F1219.S1323 1976] 970'.004'97 76-27292
ISBN 0-87380-108-3

A Rio Grande Classic
First Published in 1932

First Printing 1976

The Rio Grande Press, Inc.
GLORIETA, NEW MEXICO · 87535

Publisher's Preface

One of America's richest heritages is the bountiful literature by and about the European Spaniards in the New World—what happened when they came, what they saw as they survived, and what they did as they conquered. It is a voluminous literature, for the Spaniards had an apparently inherent compulsion to record in some manner or other everything they came to know about.

Naturally, all of it was originally written in Spanish. Little by little, through the succeeding generations, the largest part of this literary treasure has been translated into English. Any persistent research into this period of Western Hemisphere history will sooner or later bring the reader into awareness of the work of Fray Bernardino de Sahagún.

We had encountered innumerable citations and references to Fray Bernardino's material in our twenty years' study of the history of New Spain, but until recently, we had never seen the single volume published by Fisk University Press in 1932. We were browsing in one of the very excellent catalogs of rare books offered to the market by our friend and colleague T. N. Luther, of Shawnee Mission, Kansas. We ordered it sight unseen, for we were virtually certain it was a title we would want to reprint.

While this work was 30 years in preparation (1547-1577), it was not published until 1829, in a Spanish language edition edited by the great Mexican scholar Carlos Maria de Bustamente. Even then, what was published was not entire; what we have in this book is the first volume of a projected multivolume translation by Fanny Bandelier. This is all of the project that ever materialized. It was published by Fisk University Press under the somewhat misleading title *A History of Ancient Mexico*, which it is not, really—but we have retained that title for the sake of citation stability and continuity. We have added the subtitle on the cover as a modest clarification of the content: *The Religion and Ceremonies of the Aztec Indians,* which we believe more accurately describes the text than does the primary title.

When The Rio Grande Press publishes a book (all of our books are reprints), we like to include new material which we feel will enhance the usefulness and utility of our edition over the first edition, or preceding editions. We considered that we should have a scholarly introduction here, placing the title in its proper sociological and historic perspective. Via the academic grapevine, we were referred to Professor John Greenway, of the Department of Anthropology at the University of Colorado in Boulder. Dr. Greenway's extensive writings have brought him both scholarly fame and idealogical contumely. When we mentioned to a friend that Dr. Greenway was writing an introduction for our edition of Sahagún, the comment was: " . . . he's controversial, but he's an A-1 first class gold plated scholar."

Dr. Greenway mentions his many *kudos* vaguely, but he likes the slings and arrows of outrageous fortune. He likes especially a remark by Emile Capouya in a *Saturday Review* article: ". . . I would hate to be as sure of anything as Dr. Greenway is of everything." One of his students wrote (after graduation, of course): ". . . Dr. Greenway: You are notorious on this campus; it seems that people who've never taken a course from you are still able to identify you as 'that crazy son of a bitch'. Well, I took your ethnoliterature course, and it's true; you are a crazy son of a bitch, and you're also one of the best professors I've encountered."

All of this leads to a couple of apropos observations made for the occasion, one by George Gordon Lord Byron, in *English Bards and Scotch Reviewers:* " . . . I'll publish, right or wrong; fools are my theme, let Satire be my song", and by Robert Burton in *Anatomy of Melancholy:* ". . . Wit without employment is a disease."

We approached the erudite and "notorious" scholar with considerable apprehension, lest he turn his rapiers on us. But no, he was the very soul of gracious courtesy, and he was interested in our request. Sure, he breezed, he would be delighted to write an introduction for us. Of what length? We gave him carte blanche. Write, we suggested, whatever you wish to say at whatever length is required; we will publish whatever you write. We envisioned the usual 2500 to 3500 words, but when the manuscript was submitted (in beautiful format), it was some 14,200 words.

To read this essay is to savor true scholarship at a high and delightful level; it really is such a remarkable discourse that we felt obliged to categorize it as an "Introductory Essay", and of such merit as to warrant reference to it on the cover of the book. This kind of recognition is new for us—we have never done it before. Many scholars have written introductions to many of our books without their name on the cover of the book, but then, none took advantage of the opportunity they all had as Dr. Greenway did. He wrote, he said, what he thought needed to be written; we believe he did it in an engrossing and entertaining fashion—what he wrote is both informative and interesting. We hope he will do more introductions for us, and he says he will, God willing. We look forward with pleasure to some day meeting Dr. Greenway in person.

This rare title is another of our continuing series which we call The Beautiful Rio Grande Classics—Magnificent Reprints of Distinguished Western Americana.

Robert B. McCoy

LaCasa Escuela
Glorieta, New Mexico 87535
August 1976

Litho by Walsworth Pub. Co., Inc., Marceline, Mo.

Introductory Essay

DISCOVERY

Much have I travell'd in the realms of gold,
And many goodly states and kingdoms seen;
Round many western islands have I been
Which bards in fealty to Apollo hold.
Oft of one wide expanse had I been told
That deep-brow'd Homer rul'd as his demesne;
Yet did I never breathe its pure serene
Till I heard Chapman speak out loud and bold:
Then felt I like some watcher of the skies
When a new planet swims into his ken;
Or like stout Cortez when with eagle eyes
He star'd at the Pacific—and all his men
Look'd at each other with a wild surmise—
Silent, upon a peak in Darien.

In three eerie and lethargic hours between dawn and breakfast after a night made sleepless by reading an equivocal translation of blind Homer's *Iliad,* perhaps the most inopportune time ever chosen by a poet for creative composition, a young man with the hand of death already upon him, the last of the great Romantic poets to be born and the first to die, who left his birthplace only to be buried in an alien land, wrote those fourteen lines that have conveyed to our civilization better than any explorer the nearly incommunicable ecstasy of discovery appreciated. More often than not the exigencies of exploration—of the seas or the skies—demand of the searcher a practicality not compatible with expressed imagination. Balboa's sight of the Pacific was made alone—of course it was not Cortés who made the discovery—and his personal worries that ended with his execution four years later could not have conduced to a romantic mood; so it was that a forgotten scout, one Alonso Martín, wet his feet in the Pacific before Balboa. And he could not have been sure that the comparatively unimpressive fragment of the South Seas he saw from his mountain top was not the eastern ocean he had for weeks watched with some apprehension from the deck of his ship. Sir John Herschel, into whose ken the planet Uranus swam in 1781, was certainly less excited by the discovery than Keats, for that slow-moving pinpoint of light (which our best telescopes and space probes have still not made significantly larger) was at first to him just another comet, of which his sister Caroline had discovered seven. Much have I travell'd in the realms of sand in the great deserts of Australia and placed my foot's imprint where probably no other man has been, and many goodly explorers and discoverers I have known, yet not one of them thought of what he had found as anything more than the product of a day's work. For myself, having more imagination than ability, finding in a dry lake bed a protruding half-inch of iron that my shovel revealed to be the head of a broken hatchet thrown away by Ernest Giles, one of the greatest of the antipodean explorers, nearly a century earlier, was a thrill probably never to be equalled. John Keats travelled his realms of gold only in books and saw his goodly kingdoms in museum urns and sculptures torn from their contexts. He had his Homer not from the Greek but from a translation published two centuries earlier by a journeyman journalist who would scarcely be remembered today had he not inspired Keats's sonnet. The "eagle eyes" of the mistaken Cortés came to him from the portrait by Titian. The "wild surmise" of the absent seamen he remembered from Shakespeare's *Rape of Lucrece,* where Tarquin first sees the tragic lady. His "western islands" were in William Robertson's *History of America,* written the year before America became the United States; Herschel's finding the dim planet Uranus he had from Bonnycastle's *Introduction to Astronomy.* But little history and less legend can stand much scrutiny; what endures is not the prosaic fact but the needful truth, that amalgam of imagery and imagination that can make us feel what Balboa and Herschel should have felt.

The history of Mexico is more fortunate in both aspects in having for its discoverer and chronicler a man equally gifted as a scholar, a linguist, an anthropologist, a polymath of practicality and imagination, a maker as well as a writer of history; the Fray Bernardino de Sahagún, a Renaissance man whose life spanned the Age of Discovery. He was born in Sahagún, Spain—probably with the surname Ribeira—in 1499, as nearly as we can tell, seven years after Columbus discovered America; he was ten years old when Henry VIII ascended the English throne and outlived all of the king's ephemeral wives; he was fourteen when Juan Ponce de León discovered Florida and Balboa discovered the Pacific Ocean; eighteen when Martin Luther began the destruction of Christianity, which Sahagún labored so hard to establish in the New World. Fernando Magellan began his voyage around the world the year Sahagún was twenty; Giovanni da Verrazano nudged his vessel into New York bay when he was a man of twenty-five. What the young Sahagún was doing during these great events we know little of; until he arrived in Mexico in 1529 at the age of thirty his biography is the product of retrograde analysis. The momentous history he lived through as a man—the Biblical translations of Tyndale and Coverdale, the conquest of Peru by Pizarro, Coronado's crossing of the Rio Grande into our own portion of the New World, the protracted religious revolutions on the European continent, the birth and early career of Shakespeare, the ominous conquest of the Conquistadores by the English ravager of the Spanish seas Sir Francis Drake, the disaster of the Armada—all were buried under the events in New Spain which he affected and which nearly destroyed him. Unhappily the winds of destructive change blew strong against Sahagún in his last days, and he died old in 1590 without promise that he or his work would be remembered with nearly universal admiration four hundred years later in an age of even worse spiritual deterioration of the manly virtues his military companions exercised to make the New World safe for expiation of guilt for uncommitted sins.

As Dr. Samuel Johnson interpreted the Spanish proverb "He who would bring home the wealth of the Indies must carry the wealth of the Indies with him" to mean that "in traveling, a man must carry knowledge with him if he would bring home knowledge," so the genius of Fray Bernardino de Sahagún was augmented with acquired knowledge without which his unrivalled ethnographic writings could not have been made. His education at the University of Salamanca, his ordination into the scholarly Franciscans, his fascination with ancient and alien languages, his cyclopedic knowledge of his own religion which made his apprehension of the universal components shared by Aztec beliefs and ritual possible, and his special ministry all fused into an electrum greater than its parts of make him the man we honor here by giving to another generation his monumental *Historia General de las Cosas de Nueva España*. The ministry is explicit:

> *. . . it was ordered me as holy obedience to my superior prelate to write in the Mexican tongue what I thought would be useful for the doctrine, culture, and subsistence of the Christianity of these natives of this New Spain, and for the aid of the workers and ministers who indoctrinate them.*

But he knew that

> *. . . a doctor cannot correctly apply medicines to the ill without first knowing from what disposition and cause the sickness proceeds; therefore a good physician should be knowledgeable in medicines and sicknesses so as to apply correctly to each disease the corrective medicine.*

With that somewhat specious excuse Sahagún exceeded his ordered province, the Mexican religion, with apparent irrelevancies that made his book, as Munro Edmonson observed, "not a single work, but three. It is a picture manuscript; and it is a Spanish ethnography." Hence the seeming awkwardness of his title—*General History of the Things of New Spain*—is revealed as a subtle accuracy. Under that heading he entitled himself to speak at length in that fragment of the *Historia*, the *Florentine Codex*, of such irreligious things as the Aztec view of teeth—their colors and cusps, their length and mass, their specialized functions, their development and diseases, even how one can use them to whistle. In this alone he was superior to Aristotle, who made disquisitions on dentistry that dominated that small science for two thousand years, without ever looking closely into a human mouth.

From his arrival in Mexico in 1529 until the probable inception of the *Historia* in 1547 Fray Bernardino immersed himself in the culture and country of his new land while simultaneously carrying out his religious duties. He explored the topography, climbed the mountains, witnessed—and described—volcanic eruptions, taught Latin at the College of Santa Cruz—and incidentally learned the Nahuatl language.

Characteristic if fortunately not typical of this remarkable man's activity was the work of the year 1545, when along with his pedagogical responsiblities as Superior of the College of Tlaltelolco, he assisted so far as the poor medicine of the time permitted in containing the great plague of that year, burying, according to his own statement, more than ten thousand Indian victims of the disease, contracting in the process his own infection. Unlike Gregor Mendel three centuries later Sahagún did not allow his increasing involvement with religious politics to stop his life work on the *Historia* and ancillary documents, though it certainly interfered seriously with what he was born to do. For fifty years he gathered Aztec drawings and their owners' interpretations of those ambiguous picture records, interviews, questionnaires, and translations in three languages. His work was not accomplished only with the pen; when it was necessary, he restrained his innate sympathies for Indianism and pulled down stone idols to erect crosses—good works then, now become sins of inexcusable conquest, "religious genocide" in the spurious modern term—but he worked his conversion in the manner of that greatest of Popes, Gregory the First, who sent his missionaries into the pagan northwest of Europe nearly a thousand years earlier with instructions to destroy idols and idolatry but to preserve the feasts of the people, to coincide the two so that the good could be retrieved from the bad. Though it would have been too dangerously close to heresy to say so, it is evident that Fray Bernardino recognized that it is the vitality and emotion of a religion rather than its dogma that gets its social necessity done. He tried to make the new religion more reasonable than the old—an anthropological fallacy undeniably, but it would be many centuries before scholars recognized that the less reason in a religion, the more strength. In the view of his superiors he must have done well in his missionary work, for he was made a member of the Governing Board of the Franciscan Order by 1552, and a half dozen years later was assigned to Michoacan as Order Inspector. In that latter year Fray Francisco Toral became Superior of the Order and assigned him to the work for which he was born—the assemblage of Mexican history.

Sahagún's research methods were far ahead of his time. At Tepepulco he put together a consortium of native elders under the aegis of a leading Mexican citizen, Don Diego de Mendoza. The informants were eminently qualified: some had been themselves recorders of pre-Conquest history; most were his own graduates and thereby trilingual in Spanish, Latin, and Nahuatl; and all were members of the presently despised class that makes history. The modern scholarly curiosity of meliorating knowledge with ignorance, of drawing historical interpreters from the "qualifiable" rather than the qualified; from the noisy minorities in poverty, pigmentation, and procacity; from the halt, the blind, and the lame—did not exist in the middle of the sixteenth century, and would not have been countenanced if it had then been spawned. Since non-professional readers of Sahagún's ethnographic history cannot escape the lamentable reality of the new direction in Consensus Anthropology if they consult any contemporary criticism at all, it must be mentioned with regret that Fray Bernardino is coming into a new era of condemnation and in our lifetime will probably be excommunicated from scholarship as he was excommunicated from the Church in 1587 by the odious Fray Alonso Ponce, capriciously sent to Mexico as Commissary General. Professor Munro Edmonson's otherwise commendable study of the work of Sahagún, *Sixteenth-Century Mexico,* is for example infected by a carping article whelped by one Edward E. Calnek, "The Sahagún Texts as a Source of Sociological Information," in which Fray Bernardino is scourged for "utilizing" as informants the oppressive elite rather than the oppressed infestation of what in our days is called "disadvantaged ghetto dwellers." Typically concocted by a professor himself suffering the deprivations of a post at the University of Rochester, the Calnek article, we are assured, represents "an idea whose time has come," the wave of the future, the product of The Most Enlightened Generation Since Creation, and impossible to ignore any more than incipient carcinoma.

Similar social trends in Fray Bernardino's aging years made difficulties having nothing to do with scholarship, but which harried Sahagún, drawing him against his nature into profitless contention, and obstructed the perfected completion of his life work. Indeed, the internecine controversy over the presence and conduct of the Spanish in Mexico, boiling over into religion and research, actually resulted in the confiscation of Sahagún's manuscripts in 1577 and their deliberate dispersion.

Like the manuscript of the first volume of Thomas Carlyle's massive history *The French Revolution,* lent to and carelessly burnt to unintelligible ashes by that celebrated booby John Stuart Mill, much of Sahagún's writing was by one means or other destroyed or lost, so that like Carlyle, he had to recompose from a flagging memory.

The history of the vicissitudes of Sahagún and his manuscripts is a sad and unedifying story, best avoided by those whose need for exhaustive scholarship is not compelling. For others, it is sufficient to know that the *Historia* is now only an arbitrary entity existing for the most part in about a dozen and a half inarticulated works, some in print and some in manuscript, of which the invaluable *Florentine Codex* is archetypical. This precious work, named for its deposition in Florence's Laurentian Library, is a tripartite recension of the *Historia* in Nahuatl, Spanish, and pictographs, explained and thereby vitiated to some degree by deferences to the tumultuous contentions of the last quarter of the sixteenth century. A few other, less comprehensive codices are still extant, named for the repositories of their final sedimentation, but like the *Florentine Codex*, they are now practically inaccessible for the definitive *Historia* so urgently needed.

Fray Bernardino himself died ignominiously of a common cold in 1590, and in the words of Juan de Torquemada, who was there, "great multitude attended the funeral, besides all the students of the College of Tlaltelulco, in cassock and sash, and everyone was bowed in deep sorrow." And, no doubt, in relief; for Sahagún, like our own General George S. Patton, Jr., had lived too long into the days of ingloriousness, and so had become at last only a magnificent anachronism.

HISTORY'S INTRUSION

At the close of the conquering century, a time whose precedent grandeur was wilfully rejected by a new generation unworthy of its forebears, and again in our own time, when even anthropology to be tolerated must acknowledge, confess, and do penance for being one of the manifestations of capitalistic imperialism, three things stand adamantly against a reasoned appreciation of Bernardino de Sahagún: He was a *conquistador;* he was a missionary; and he was a practitioner of honest and objective ethnology.

There are more people of certified education alive today who believe in a flat earth than those who accept *Homo sapiens* as an innately and inescapably violent and aggressive species whose uncontested domination of the planet was achieved by incomparable ferocity—all history, experience, and reason notwithstanding.

There is a biological law, no less unexceptionable for its unpopularity, known as the Competitive Exclusion Principle. It says simply that "In a finite world it is impossible for species that are competitive in every respect to coexist indefinitely." An obvious corollary is that the more alike the competitors, the more lethal the competition. Examples from the lower organisms, both plant and animal, are ubiquitous—but so also are examples from man in his culture. Jews and Arabs kill each other with maniacal enthusiasm because they are racially and historically the same people fighting for the same econiche. Anthropologists who should know better tell us that humanity stands above mere laws of biology, that the imperfect world only temporarily is divided between the peacemakers and the warlike, that one bright day the promise of the Sermon on the Mount will be realized. The only trouble with this notion is their utter inability to find any of the destined inheritors of the earth.

Ruth Benedict's *Patterns of Culture*, the most popular book in anthropology ever written, gives this creation of an unreality its imprimatur—but the only Apollonians she could find for illustration were the Pueblo Indians—whose inclusion among inveterate peacemakers will amuse those who know them. Admittedly the Pueblos were by reason of their isolation flabby in fighting—and that is why the Utes now are being paid in megabucks for white usurpation of land they previously took without compensation or guilt from the Anasazi, but early Anasazi history and prehistory swim in blood.

The Pueblos were marginal, provincial, and comparatively weak relatives of the people we arbitrarily lump together as Mexicans, their natural strength and aggressiveness attenuated by distance and isolation from the hiving ground of Amerindian civilization.

While the Yellow Race was settling down into enjoyment of its millennia of conquest in the East and the White Race was fixing the borders of its expansion, a younger civilization clustered in divisive groups along nearly four thousand miles of the New World's Pacific mountain spine. Named and studied as if they were each in sundered continents, these regional loci of high culture were in fact separated less by space than time, and their differention now by archaeologists rests more upon pottery than people. All had far too much in common than practicality will allow even to be summarized, but what they shared most importantly for what was to occur during the sixteenth century of our reckoning was primitive subsistence patterns, illiteracy, gold, and pagans. The two latter possessions drew the Spaniards; the two former made their conquest inevitable.

In the region we call for convenience Mexico, there were first the nameless people displaced by the immemorial people laboring to rise above their Late Paleolithic existence when the Olmecs made—possibly with suggestions from the farthest East—the transition to the Neolithic in the lowlands of the eastern coast sometime before the seventh century of the pre-Christian era. What happened in succeeding centuries was fundamentally only an evolution of the pattern established by the Olmecs—massive ceremonial centers in stone and functional sculpture, petroglyphs never to advance into writing, an impressive calendar, and gods of supernal virility that were augmented into a pantheon rather than displaced by the deities of succeeding peoples and persuasions.

During the nearly six hundred years between the emergence of the Olmecs and the ascendency of the Aztecs, innumerable social entities traded and fought with one another according to the Law of Competitive Exclusion. It has been anthropologically and archaeologically convenient to name some of these groups—for example the Zapotecs, Maya, Toltecs, and Chichimecs—though it would be more defensible to recognize the contending factions as city states within a geographic continuum, like ancient Greece, and just as arbitrarily call the entire area "Mexico," ignoring the fact that it is a term properly applicable to the Aztecs. One must abandon the quest for factual accuracy in unwritten history, for that way madness lies. Bound by some inner drive to subject human behavior to reason and order, theorists in the study of man have recognized an impossibly long "Time of Troubles" in Toynbee's felicitous phrase and consequently have sought a reason for it. Drought, geological upheaval, invasions, religious schisms, exhaustion of the land by the inefficient *milpa* farming, and more imaginative catastrophes have been posited; to the man uncommitted to secular theology of this sort, the effort seems just as futile as explaining what happened to the United States between the unconditional surrender of the Japanese on the deck of the *U.S.S. Missouri* on the second of September, 1945, and the surrender of the *U.S.S. Pueblo* on the twenty-third of January, 1968. We lived through the quarter century that saw America's wilful downfall, and none of us has the least explanation for our national suicide. As Ernest Hemingway tried to teach us in all his generally misunderstood stories, things just happen.

Setting aside therefore the ingenious theories put forward to account for the collapse of the Aztecs, we can say with certainty that the first substantial, inexplicable thing to happen to their abortive empire was the sighting by an itinerant tax and tribute collector named Pínotl in 1518 of what he could describe only as "winged towers containing men with white faces and heavy beards in the sea." Thus was fulfilled a legend that would be much more attractive to us as an explanation if nearly identical prophecies were not universal from Europe to aboriginal Australia. In Mexico the story was unusually elaborate, in accordance with the complexity of their mythology. It seems that a legendary Toltec chief named Topiltzin, by virtue of hereditary connection with Teotihuacan, ancient Mexico's classic city, and his own inherent dominance, transubstantiated himself toward the end of the tenth Christian century into the god Quetzalcóatl. This was Quetzalcóatl's Second Coming, for he had been around some centuries earlier as a peace and prosperity god, satisfied to receive from his worshippers the sacrifice of butterflies—a benevolent deity of the sort that all religions have found useless for terrestrial functions. His resuscitation at the edge of the historical period was brief, for his old rival on the Mexican Olympus, the bloodthirsty Tezcatlipoca, also returned to displace him. Like King Arthur and Lord Nelson and General MacArthur, Quetzalcóatl faded away, promising to come back one day as a bearded white man.

The *Florentine Codex,* which tells the story of this fateful meeting, records a remarkable establishment of communication in which the frightful apparitions from the eastern sea apprised Pínotl of their determination to have a little talk with the reigning monarch, Moctezuma.

Pínotl delayed the ominous interview by placating the Spaniards with gifts of junk jewelry, but neither he nor the incumbent Moctezuma thought this was the end of the affair.

Moctezuma reminds us of other pusillanimous rulers from olden times to history too close to us for comfort. It did not help his resolution to know that Aztec mythology, reinforced coincidentally by comets and volcanic eruptions, that the Christian year of 1519 was the Aztec year of One Reed—*Ce Acatl*—when Quetzalcoatl was scheduled to reappear. Sahagún's historian elders recalled that Moctezuma wailed on hearing Pínotl's news, "He has come back! He will come here, to the place of his throne and canopy, for that is what he promised when he departed."

It must be said in explanation of Moctezuma's unstable state of confidence that even in the expediently altered history of the Aztecs mutability was the only immutable common denominator. From their invasion of the Valley of Mexico toward the closure of the twelfth Christian century the Aztecs thrived on blood and guts. Like the Vikings who established an island base in the center of the River Blackwater swamps before swooping across to the Saxon mainland a couple of centuries and three thousand miles away in time and space, the Aztecs built up new and unoccupied land in Lake Texcoco and gradually established the magnificent city of Tenochtitlán. At first deferential to the stronger mainland Atzcapotzalco people, the Aztecs under a warrior chieftain named Itzcóatl exploded across their causeways upon their neighbors in the year 1427, just about the time Joan of Arc was fulfilling her own prophecy in the chaos that was France. By acquiring gullible allies for short-term purposes and destroying them over the long run, the Aztecs conquered the whole of the Valley of Mexico in less than no time. In order to accomplish their manifest destiny so quickly, the Aztecs adumbrated Adolf Hitler by making war for little or no reason. If reasons and justification were needed, the Aztecs could invent them, for even in Itzcóatl's time they were burning inconvenient pictographic histories and altering the past to suit the present. There is among us nowadays a quaint rationalization propounded by people who for reasons best known to themselves make an invidious distinction between the lower carnivores and man: that lions and tigers and bears justifiably kill only for their own subsistence. It is puzzling why this has not emerged as a defense for the Aztecs, for the *Florentine Codex* asserts that the disposition of captured merchant spies was dietary—"They were slain . . . and served up with chili sauce." Judging others by himself, Moctezuma could have feared the alien seamen for the possibility that he would meet a prandial end.

But Moctezuma and his subjects had much of a year remaining to pleasure themselves with their traditional pastimes of sodomy, sacrifice, and swilling. Pínotl's Quetzalcóatls were only scouts under Captain Juan de Grijalva, sent by Governor Diego Velásquez of Cuba to investigate information reported by slavehunter Francisco Hernandez de Córdoba a year earlier. Neither of these probing expeditions fared very well, but they brought back to Cuba certification that the mainland abounded in pagans and gold. Governor Velásquez then made one of those unaccountable decisions in assigning command that have so often succeeded far beyond any predictable expectations: he ignored seniority and other factors and appointed as leader of a military expedition a young farmer and notary named Hernando Cortés, whose only martial experience was helping to suppress an Indian rebellion on Hispaniola when he was just a boy, and accompanying Velásquez in his occupation of Cuba in 1511. One is reminded again of Patton, for Cortés pestered Velasquez as Patton pestered Pershing four hundred years later when the old general was organizing his invasion of Mexico. Cortés received his commission and promptly set out with six hundred men (a hundred of whom were sailors) and sixteen horses. Young Hernando, again like Patton, ignored messages of recall from Velásquez and directions to limit his activity to exploration; one might extend the parallel by crediting Cortés with Patton's use of the "reconnaissance in force." His first contacts with the outlying Indians were of course violent if insignificant, mere skirmishes which he won handily enough to terrorize Moctezuma. Among the placatory gifts Cortés received was an Indian slave girl named Malintzin or Dona Marina, known in later history as Malinche, a name that has become the anthropological term for cultural treachery—*malinchismo.* The term has become for militant Spanish Americans as invalid as "chauvinism" for American females-*manquée*—just a convenient stick to beat a convenient dog. Just what people and what culture Malinche was supposed to have betrayed are nebulous. She was not an Aztec to begin with; and she was moreover a slave and therefore somewhat less than human. If Malinche had lived in Tenochtitlán instead of Tabasco, she would have been a member of the cadre pool of potential sacrifice offerings. Human sacrifice more or less spoils a person for other functions, and Cortés had better use for Malinche; she became his mistress, interpreter, and advisor—in fact if not in law, she was more of a wife than the legal consorts of many men.

Cortés needed no advice on how to manage a conquest. He evaded the directives and restrictions of Velásquez by appointing civil officials who under the Spanish tradition of recognizing local autonomy commissioned him captain general with authority to kill Indians at his pleasure. He learned quickly that the Indians he met along the way to Tenochtitlán did not regard the Aztec yoke as empyreal bliss, and after a show of Spanish war technology to aid in enlistment, he gathered these dissident native warriors into his little army. Wary of possible mutiny spawned by fear of the unknown, he dismantled his ships and convinced his men that the best way out of Mexico was through. Had Cortés lived four centuries later he surely would have agreed with the hard philosophy of Don Marquis' typing cockroach archy, who observed,

> *there is bound to be a certain amount of trouble running any country, if you are president the trouble happens to you but if you are a tyrant you can arrange things so that most of the trouble happens to other people*

He arranged decisive trouble for Moctezuma long before he met the king. Moctezuma was a born victim; as soon as he heard Cortés was determined to make an appointment with him in his own Samarra, Moctezuma dispatched ambassadors with literal gifts for the gods. But Cortés received the bribes of gold, silver, jewels, and turquoise with angry dissatisfaction; if he were the returned Quetzalcóatl, as Moctezuma feared to believe, then he was not to be satisfied with butterflies this time around. The Mexicans were for all their elevated civilization, singularly witless in some things; in their architecture, to choose an example irrelevant in this context, they erected massive buildings to facilitate the corbelled arch, a primitive device that ultimately collapses into a true arch, as any modern masonry contractor knows, but no one among the millions in the New World ever noticed the process. We are fairly certain that if the high Amerindian civilization did not come packaged from the Far East, it certainly had continuing contacts with the ancient Old World cultures and their advanced warfare, yet Moctezuma's behavior toward Cortés was a series of mistakes first made by a doomed people when *Pithecanthropus* advanced to *Homo sapiens.* Having tantalized Cortés with treasure, he next entertained comfortable doubts that the Spaniard was an immortal after all, and though some kindly students of Mexican history choose to disbelieve deviousness in Moctezuma, it is almost certain that he persuaded his allies in Cholula to ambush Cortés.

The history of the Conquest of Mexico recalls parallels at every point with other military debacles. Readers of the Rio Grande Press series have access to one example that other people are denied—the true story of the bloody engagement at Sand Creek in 1864. The only accounts generally available make the winner of that conflict, Colonel John Chivington, into one of history's genocidal monsters, and the losers a choir of innocent Indian women and children. William M. Breakenridge's *Helldorado,* the fifty-fourth reissue in Rio Grande's Classic series, gives a convenient first-hand account of the incident that searchers of truth can find elsewhere only by the most diligent and persistent research. If ever any marauders needed killing, it was the Sand Creek affair that produced them: some six hundred Indians on the warpath, killing and scalping outlying settlers during the week and reporting to the government agent on weekends for rations. When Denver was cut off from the rest of the United States for some six weeks, the United States Secretary of War authorized Governor John Evans to commission the Third Colorado Cavalry to put an end to the depradations. Chivington, hero of the battle of Glorieta Pass in 1862, the battle that some military historians consider the turning point of the Civil War (that story is told in another Rio Grande Press Classic, William C. Whitford's *The Colorado Volunteers in the Civil War*), correctly if harshly saw that the only way to put an end to Indian murders was to put an end to the Indians, and in a fair battle at Sand Creek, he put the end, after he learned that the outnumbering Indians were preparing to put an end to all the Colorado settlers.

Cortés similarly discovered the Cholula plot, gathered that city's nobility, priests and governors and warriors, in a closed courtyard, and killed them all. Moctezuma's vacillation continued, alternating between servility and treachery, until after a long siege protracted by commendable bravery of the native warriors, the great city of Tenochtitlán and its three hundred thousand citizens fell to the Spaniards in August of 1521.

Though the *Historia* of Sahagún and its ancillary documents are more valuable than all other contemporary accounts of the Mexican conquest and culture together, we have some half dozen corroboratory sources of information on what it was like to discover not merely an ocean or a planet, but a civilization. The letters of Cortés himself to his king are far more than the self-serving reports of a general who exceeded his authority; they demand comparison with Julius Caesar's *Commentaries on the Gallic War,* the classic history of a campaign that brought Gaul into the Roman Empire as the Mexican conquest won the New World for Spain.

An invaluable accompaniment to the letters of Cortés is the inelegant but eloquent memoirs written half a century after the event by one of his soldiers, Bernal Diáz del Castillo—the last survivor of those glorious days. Blind, deaf, ill, and nearly destitute, Diáz would hardly have composed so large and so moving a work had he not been driven to the effort by intolerable circumstances. Even if we did not have irrefutable evidence of what those circumstances were, we could easily have guessed them, for they are the shamefully inevitable products of a successful war. In his historical play *Henry V,* Shakespeare has Westmoreland before Agincourt wishing that the hopelessly outnumbered English army had "but one ten thousand of those men in England that do no work today." Every country fighting for its existence has such creatures; America, to use the closest example, had in all its wars, from the Revolution to Viet Nam, shirkers with no stomach for battle who fled for craven safety into Canada. The title of Diáz's book implies his reason for writing—*Historia Veradera de la Conquista de la Nueva España.* There would have been no need to certify his account as the "true history" if there had been no false histories—principally those of Gonzalo de Illescas and the sycophant Francisco Lopez de Gómara, the Spanish counterpart of England's villainous liar made saint, Sir Thomas More (who was received into Hell only twenty-five years before Gómara). This precious pair were only the best known of the distorters of the Conquest. Critics of the *conquistadors* proliferated like modern journalists plagiarizing the libels of syndicated gossip column scribblers. Some, like Gómara, subtly implied criticism by denying rumors concocted by themselves; others were more directly honest in their vilifications. There were in the sixteenth and succeeding centuries so many of the latter revisionists that in the consensus view today, Gómara is listed as a panegyrist of Cortés. That greatest of the conquerors had twice to leave his New World for Spain to defend himself, and there he died in 1547 like General Patton—wealthy, titled, but deprived of office and authority by an ungrateful government. And New Spain fell into the bestial hands of men like Nuño de Guzman, Matienzo, and Delgadillo.

The degrading history of the military arm of the Conquest would not be relevant here if the same shameful business did not also besmirch the recorded lives of the religious emissaries, including Sahagún. One little-noticed testament to the success of his detractors is the failure of the massive *Encyclopaedia Britannica* and *The New Columbia Encyclopedia* to give entry to Sahagun—though both repositories of universal information think it proper to immortalize Jesse James.

It is difficult for an irreligious people in an irreligious age to believe there is any acquisition sought with more fervor than wealth. It is true that almost all of us will do anything for money. But we will not die for it. On the other hand, men will die so eagerly for immaterial things like country, love, and religion that the supposed instinct for self-preservation becomes a palpable illusion. Certainly the Spaniards came to the New World for gold—but they just as certainly came for souls. This admission is made by contemporary historians who awkwardly show their own disbelief in its veracity by enclosing the fact in quotation marks. And one looks vainly in modern anthropology textbooks for even a tolerant view of missionaries—a curiosity, since within the memory of living people anthropologists were in point of fact ordained missionaries. *Sic transit gloria coelestis.*

It is a regrettable paradox that while religion has only one universal function—to make human beings behave—it does people more harm than any other institution, including war. As Elihu Palmer, the eighteenth-century American philosopher and ordained Baptist minister flatly wrote in his *Principles of Nature, or a Development of the Moral Causes of Happiness and Misery among the Human Species,*

> . . . *Moses, Mahomet, and Jesus can lay as little claim to moral merit, or to the characters of benefactors of mankind, as any three men that ever lived upon the face of the earth. They were all of them impostors; two of them notorious murderers in practice, and the other a murderer in principle: and their existence united, perhaps, cost the human race more blood, and produced more substantial misery, than all the other fanatics of the world.*

After all the manifest sins of induced religious conversion have been indicted, it must be said for missionaries that no other emissaries of conquering states genuinely intended more good for the vanquished. Often they were the only intruders who sought nothing but to preserve, protect, and promote the conquered—frequently at the cost of their own welfare and existence. They can hardly be blamed for the most unfair of all human contradictions: that there is no evil like doing good. The wickedness created in our own time by liberal benevolence is incalculable; it has so infected the minds even of the conservatives that they have been distracted from the foundation of their philosophy, expressed so well by the great Virginia statesman John Randolph: *Never without the strongest necessity disturb a thing at rest.* But it is easy to misinterpret the advice of Voltaire's Candide—"*Il faut cultiver notre jardin.*" For the Spaniards after Cortés, Mexico was their garden and its cultivation was an inescapable responsibility, if only to eradicate the most noxious of its indigenous weeds. Since unhappy Cain offended God by offering Him in sacrifice the fruits of his field, gardening has never been other than an unrespected and thankless labor. So in sixteenth-century Mexico the tillage of religion's garden was left to the selfless men, of whom the greatest was Fray Bernardino de Sahagún.

THE RELIGION OF ANCIENT MEXICO

Most commentators on Sahagún's *Historia General de las Cosas de*

Nueva España tell us more automatically than accurately that religion occupies exclusively about a third of the "things" making up the culture of his New Spain. But this is religion as seen by the irreligious. Where religion is functional in protecting the whole of society against the instinctively destructive appetites of individuals—in aboriginal Australia today, for example, or in the rest of the world before technology put three billion people on the earth to make culture safe for lawlessness and disorder—it is an integument encompassing everything, and our division of things into the sacred and secular does not obtain. In Old Stone Age Australia a tree or a rock exists simultaneously in two worlds or, more properly, in two dimensions: the tangible, terrestrial we perceive, and the *Tjukurpa,* as the Pitjandjara tribesmen call it, the beautiful concept of "The Dreaming," where the totemic heroes still live and guide the conduct of their mortal progeny. So it was in ancient Mexico; there were literally sermons in stones. The elder Aztec priests explained this with great clarity—though they were not understood by the Spanish priests—when they were called upon to defend the practice of human sacrifice. The priests had long forgotten—if they ever knew at all—that human sacrifice exists only in a culture whose religious belief is at its zenith. When faith weakens, the most valuable of all gifts to the gods—human life—is substituted for by goats and sheep and butterflies; and ultimately even these are displaced by lesser things. Cain's sin was not killing his smarmy brother—that came later—but in giving God vegetables instead of meat. In this diminished age of ecumenical expediency, heaven can be attained by inserting a dime in a church lamp slot to turn on the light for a few minutes. One of the most shocking stories in our literature is Shirley Jackson's *The Lottery* wherein the ritual of human sacrifice in its penitential form of scapegoating is moved from the tedious savage world into rural America. The death of our religion blinds us to the universals so that they become unreal and therefore bearable.

Next to human sacrifice, of which Sahagún gives us uncounted examples, the religious practice that most nauseated the Spanish, missionaries and militarists alike, was ritual cannibalism. It is strange that the priests did not recognize in the eating of the victims the central act of their own religion—deipophagy, god-eating. Protestants and rock-mass "Catholics" believe that the transubstantiated bread wafer, the Host, represents the body and blood of Christ; it was not so before English and ghetto jabber displaced Latin in the Mass. Then, at the moment of the Mass's climax, the bread *became* God, and His body was eaten in another universal religious custom. Even today the Australian natives, who are prohibited absolutely from eating their totemic animal, will take a morsel during their yearly "increase" ritual "to increase the spirit within us," as they express it.

And the blood—the blood. Ancient Mexico swam in human blood. The Spaniards were so disgusted by Aztec blood-letting that they let a great deal more with their swords as an appropriate response. Again, a curiosity of purblindness. Neither in the sixteenth nor the twentieth century did the ministers of the Christian religion in Mexico see any resemblance between Aztec bloodiness and their own preoccupation with life's vital essence. Even today, when inspirational wall-hangings are more likely to be pornographic than pious, traditionalist Catholics display that remarkable old painting of the Sacred Heart, wherein Christ looks upon the house with His heart hanging on rather than in His chest—like the red clock on Oz's Tin Woodsman. And now and then, when the electric guitars are quiet, a congregation can be heard singing "In the Precious Blood of the Lamb." Longer ago, before bibulousness became an escape from an intolerable world, the faithful in the Church at Communion not only ate the corporeal body of Christ in the wafer but drank His blood in the wine. The Aztecs had the same trouble with excessive drinking of holy *pulque.*

Sahagún and his fellow priests lacked the anthropological knowledge that would have made the two religions uncomfortably alike—though they saw enough to put them on the edge of suspicion that God had somehow prepared the Mexican pagans for Christianity (one denomination today, with millions of communicants, believes that Christ visited Yucatan; the cult will be nameless here, for the more liberal and sophisticated members of that church do not overmuch like that excresence of fundamentalism). In religious cultures blood was always the substance highest in *mana* content. The people who still inhabit the remoter regions of Australia's deserts are as bloody as Sahagún's Mexicans; they open male veins and pour pure liquid *mana*—which they call *mapanpa,* a clearly diffusionary cognate term—over boys about to become men. In the holiest of their ceremonies the aborigines draw the ritual blood from their penes. So did the Aztecs.

But the concept of *mana* was not apprehended by Sahagún or the other Spanish priests—or, for that matter, by anybody else until the missionary-become-anthropologist Bishop R. H. Codrington discovered its name and its existence in Melanesia a century ago. Once seen and identified, it was found everywhere: the Amerindian *orenda, wakanda, manitou* (misunderstood even by the Indians as an anthropomorphic "Great Spirit"); the African *elima* or *njomm* or a score of other synonyms; the Japanese *kami;* the Greek *dynamis;* the Muslim *baraka;* the Australian aboriginal *mapana* (as an object containing it, *mapanpa*), and, as university students are astounded to hear, in American religious contexts, *grace* (as in the most moving of all hymns, *Amazing Grace*), and the secular adjective, *lucky.* It is a transcendent, invisible, omnipotent power, very much like electricity, even to its being amoral, running both electric can-openers and electric chairs, flowing from the spirit world to the terrestrial when priests, the ritually insulated custodians, make the proper connections. Some anthropologists, who should know better, erroneously call this aspect of religion "magic." But we do not have space to catalog all the jocose notions of Consensus Anthropology.

A lesser annoyance to the Spaniards Cortés brought to Mexico was the filthiness of the native priests. They never washed their hair, matted from the spouting blood of their sacrificial victims. In their disgust the Spanish missed two or three other manifestations of their own religious beliefs. When *mana* is absorbed by men (and women—when they are menstruating or giving birth) by reason of superhuman religious or social status (Polynesian chiefs and their priests are the most familiar examples), this power usually is concentrated in the hair. So the Aztec priests kept their locks stiff with the dried blood of the surrogate gods whose hearts they plucked out; so Samson lost his strength when Delilah cut his hair. It is a delight of discovery not incomparable to Keats's meeting Chapman's Homer or Balboa sighting the Pacific to find manifestations of universals unnoticed by anyone else. My native police officer companion on several of my anthropological expeditions in desert Australia was thought by the aborigines to be spiritually more powerful than myself. I puzzled over this oddity, since my opinion of my own qualities disagreed with theirs, until I equated the name given him by the aborigines, *Tjumpu,* with his left-handedness and its cognate identity with the Oceanic *tumpu,* which is how "taboo" should be spelled and pronounced.

Many natural objects are nearly everywhere thought to contain *mana,* from the primitives' hematite to university students' "lucky pencils" with which they write unlucky examination answers. Of all earthly sources of religious power, none is more nearly universal in time and place than red ochre, hematite, earthy iron ore. Our maligned predecessors the Neanderthals first proved to modern scholars that they had religion and therefore culture—and brains, presumably—when their unearthed skeletons were found with red ochre permeating their bones. Red ochre is still in some happily remote areas used to anoint corpses — Possibly as a specific to restore the dead blood. Uncharacteristically, the Aztecs made only minimal use of red ochre—Sahagún mentions it only two or three times in his *Historia*—for reasons we can only guess. Perhaps red ochre is scarce in alluvial Mexico; perhaps with so abundant a supply of the real thing from the tens of thousands of human sacrifices the Aztecs saw no need of a less powerful source of *mana.* It has never to my unimpressive knowledge been pointed out before, but the Indian practice of taking scalps persuasively suggests still another ancient appreciation of *mana* acquisition. Contemporary Indianists, who for reasons beyond the understanding of normal people, elevate other races above their own, accuse the early white colonialists of introducing the custom of taking scalps from innocent Indians. But ever-reliable Father Sahagún refutes this absurdity: [On the feast of Tlacaxipeoaliztli sacrificial victims were killed by scalping and] "these captives they called *Ovanti,* and they scalped these in the same way, keeping the scalp locks as trophies or relics."

Another possible parallel of modern and ancient religious practices considered loathsome in Aztec ritual was the wearing by priests of the flayed skin of human sacrifices. Again to my knowledge, no one has seen the resemblance, but the chasuble of priests at Mass compels in my imagination the poncho-like human skin worn by their sixteenth-century Aztec counterparts. If one accepts this hypothesis, the Catholic maniple and the Jewish phylactery also bring to mind Aztec skin-wearing rituals—and of the two, especially the Hebraic, since phylacteries were made of leather.

If Father Sahagún had the ethnographic knowledge available to but little used by modern anthropologists, he would have been profoundly disturbed by more resemblances between his Catholic religion's components—the supernatural concept, myth, ritual, obsessive emotion as a motivating force, dogma manifest in human behavior, ordained practitioners (priests or shamans), the *mana* concept, and regularized means of obtaining power for secular purposes (prayer or magic)—and those of the pagan Aztecs. And not only the Aztec religion, but every other viable religion in the history and prehistory of mankind. It might have affected his own faith, one way or other, for even in his comparative ignorance of alien religious systems, Fray Sahagún had tolerance beyond the ordinary for Aztec beliefs. Some he did see, though he did not perceive their universal essence; of the native Aztec conjurors he recorded "When they lost their power of enchanters, and the time approached to end their evil life, someone would get hold of them and cut the hair off the crown of the head, and by doing so they lost their power of conjuring and they died." He speaks of the Feast of Veytocoztli in honor of the maize god Cinteutl; but with Jews expelled from Spain, he probably did not know that the Hebrews celebrated a feast of corn (amusingly transferred through semantic misapprehension from the original wheat to modern maize); his separation in time from ourselves prevented his acquaintance with the modern Feast of Green Corn in the pueblo of Cochiti, where this ancient festival is required to end in the Catholic chapel! Had he known Cochiti, Sahagún's palpable intelligence would have enabled him to refute Benedict's Pueblo Apollonianism as soon as he saw the two moieties in that remote town trying with all their Dionysiac frenzy to direct the outcome of baseball games by the evil *mana* of witchcraft.

Certainly Sahagún perceived inexplicable resemblances between his own theology and the Aztec practices of baptism by water (a weak source of *mana*); the Feast of Toxcatl ("This was the principal festival of all. It was like Easter, and came very close to the Christian Easter, perhaps a few days later"); the sixth-month festival of Etzalqualiztli wherein the priests played the part of fools (compare with the medieval Church's tradition of the Boy Bishop); the Feast of the goddess Chalchiulicue (on the very day of the Catholic Feast of the Purification of the Virgin Mary); crosses like crucifixes; confessions of sin to the priests, who also observed the sanctity of the confessional; movable as well as calendrically fixed feast days; the Feast of New Fire (found in Christianity's appropriation of the pagan Germanic Yule log ritual at Christmas); and the Aztec Deluge myth, which has not only a surviving ark, but two survivors—a man and his wife—and even a dove.

Some things even Sahagún would not have acknowledged had he been apprised of them, for he was eminently a human being with the human weakness—or strength—of not seeing things harmful to his own organism; but we in our greater accumulation of ethnological knowledge, can see, learn from, and even enjoy in his *Historia* more than was dreamt of in his philosophy. Father Sahagún was happily spared acquaintance with the modern witchcraft of psychiatry, but we cannot miss the identity of psychiatrists and Aztec witch doctors, to whom confessions of the most loathsome sins were made. Nor did he see in the costumed parades of sacrificial subjects the costumed parades of condemned victims of his country's Inquisition. And it would have been sacrilegious for the good Father to recognize in the deity Titlacaoan characteristics of Jesus Christ in His dual role of Trickster and Culture Hero. But he said it if he did not see it:

> *The god called Titlacaoan was, they said, the creator of heaven and earth, and was all powerful, he gave to the living everything they needed, such as food, drink and wealth. . . .*
>
> *Titlacaoan was also called Tezcatlipuca, Moiocoiatzin, Iaotzin, Necociautl, and Necaoalpilli. They called him Moiocoiatzin because he did whatever he wanted to do, and thought about doing, and that no one could interfere with what he did or contradict him, either in heaven or on earth; he could give wealth to whom he pleased; and they said, moreover, that the day it should please him to destroy the heavens and make it fall he would do it, and mankind would disappear. . . .*
>
> *Titlacaoan was the one to invent the first fraud, because he turned himself into an old man with very gray hair, and in this disguise he went to the house of Quetzalcoatl . . .*
>
> *Titlacaoan played another trick, disguising himself as a*

strange Indian and calling himself Tobeyo. . . .

The said necromancer called Titlacaoan, after having thus fought and conquered the said enemies, played another trick . . . .

Christ as our civilization's Culture Hero, bringing down the good but forbidden things from heaven (as the Greek Culture Hero Prometheus stole fire for the mortals, and suffered a worse punishment than Christ's crucifixion for bringing salvation to the reprobate), would have been acceptable to Father Sahagún had he known of the concept, but Christ as Trickster he could not have known, for this aspect of his Saviour had been almost totally explunged from his mythology's canon by early Church Councils; all that escaped from the censorious scrutiny of the Fathers was the Christ Child's disobedience in the Temple. We are in a better position to see this less admirable feature of the universal Culture Hero, now that it no longer means anything. In folklore, notably in the old ballads *The Bitter Withy* and *The Cherry Tree Carol*, the mischievous and malicious tricks of the young Christ have been preserved—*trewe wol out, certyn,* to paraphrase Geoffrey Chaucer. It is intriguing to muse on what Fray Bernardino would have thought had he lived to hear the cycle of San Pedro and Jesucristo Trickster tales told by the descendants of his Aztecs in rural Mexico today. One of these at least is worth the space of telling to make the point:

One time San Pedro and Jesucristo were walking along, Jesucristo sent San Pedro up to a near-by house to get a cooked chicken. On the way back Pedro ate one leg of the chicken.

When Jesucristo saw what San Pedro had brought back, he asked, "Why has this chicken but one leg?"

"It never had another leg," answered Pedro. "All of the chickens around this part of the country have but one leg, Sir."

The two proceeded and came to a big tree under which were sleeping many chickens. All of the chickens had one leg tucked up out of sight under their feathers.

Pedro pointed to them and said, "You see! All of the chickens have but one leg apiece."

Jesucristo took a rock and threw it at one of the chickens. It woke up and stood on both feet.

"Oh," said Pedro, "a miracle!" He then took up a rock and threw it at the rest of the chickens. "You see," he said, "I can perform miracles, too."

And what, we wonder, would Sahagún have made of the borrowing toward the end of his life and era by the pirates who ravaged the Spanish main flying the skull-and-crossbones pennant of the Aztecs before Cortés?

It would have been saddening, too, for Father Bernardino had he known of a virulent religious infection that came to Mexico and the American Southwest through the vector of superstitious sailors and soldiers among the Conquistadors, and which was to persist even longer than the orthodox Catholicism he propagated. That malignancy ironically began with a priest of his own order, the Franciscans, perhaps the most influential of canonized medieval churchmen, born almost precisely three hundred miles in space and three hundred years in time from Sahagún himself, Saint Anthony of Padua. Anthony was possessed of two most dangerous qualities: imagination and eloquence. The first gave him a vision of receiving the Christ Child into his own arms; the second gave him the commission of preaching over a wide region of Europe. It was not his message but the emotion of it that opened the infecting wound. His followers began to whip themselves on the bare flesh with scourges as they walked across Europe like Crusaders. Within a quarter century of Saint Anthony's death his followers, known as the Flagellants, had swarmed over most of northern Italy to the south and Germany to the north. Two endemics reached Rome just before the middle of the fourteenth century—Flagellation and the Black Death, the latter thought to be a providential visitation for an age of sin, the former its penitential cure. Pope Clement VI, seeing more clearly, thought otherwise. He could not extirpate the plague, but he could do something about the heavenly whippers: he declared them heretical and burned as many of them at the stake as he could catch. Death is a most effective cure for diseases and dissidents—but you have to get all of them; killing only some strengthens the survivors. For a hundred years and more the Popes executed the flagellants, but some of them endured long enough to come to the New World in Spanish vessels. The Church and civil authorities assure us that the posterity of the medieval flagellants, known in our time as Penitentes, have been at last eradicated. So we have heard, and so in part believe; but the publisher of the Rio Grande Press books can give testimony of how strong the Penitentes are today in north-central New Mexico. It is not entirely irrelevant in this context to mention that the place of our publication, the tiny settlement of Glorieta, is named for a bower where another importation of the conquering Spaniards, the Virgin of Guadalupe, Our Lady of Conquests, *La Conquistadora,* traditionally slept.

THE CHARACTER OF THE MEXICANS

The Aztecs lived by terror—and died by terror; they were half in love with easeful death. So too their distant posterity. In this last quarter of the twentieth century no other country in this wicked world has so high a murder rate as Mexico. White Americans, bad as they are, distribute candy (though sometimes containing embedded razor blades) to children on Halloween; the Mexicans give one another candy skulls with a space on the forehead for the recipients's name. After the brutal and brutalizing death of the hopeless bull by the *torero's* sword or his assistant's dagger, the animal is dragged around the earthy ring by horses until a decorative bloody circle is inscribed for the edification of an audience which, four hundred years earlier, would have been equally excited by the bloody trail of sacrificed men and women whose knife-opened bodies were tumbled down the steps of those great pyramids. "After the victims had been sacrificed," wrote Sahagún, "they dragged the bodies through the *tlachco,* and the entire floor became tinted red with the blood they shed from being thus dragged."

Without implying any invidious comparison with other peoples, it is fair to say that so far back as history penetrates, Mexicans have fed on *Carpe Diem* with a sauce of *Timor Mortis.* Their morbid necrolatry is shown not only in the gory iconography of the *santos* (Sebastian is a favorite saint, for he was pierced like a pincushion by arrows), but in more subtle things as well—autodenigration, hypermasculinity, phallic obsession, micromania, sentimentality, introversion, indecision, fatalism, the eagerness of medical men to operate, the gallinaceous *pelado* (hilarious as Cantinflas), automobile racing, publishing the exact moment of death in the victims of automobile accidents.

A national character anticipating death is not wholly bad. What one continuously lives with is less to be feared than what one hides. Italians live happily still on the slopes of Vesuvius and look with equanimity upon the dead cities of Pompeii and Herculaneum. The ancient theme of *Timor Mortis* also produces great literature; one of the most poignant of all thanatopses ever composed was made by the greatest poet of the primitive world whose name we know—Nezahualcoytl, king of Texcoco, before the Spaniards ended his civilization:

The fleeting pomps of the world are like the green willow trees, which, aspiring to permanence, are consumed by a fire, fall before the axe, are upturned by the wind, or are scarred and saddened by age.

The grandeurs of life are like the flowers in color and in fate; the beauty of these remains so long as their chaste buds gather and store the rich pearls of the dawn and saving it, drop it in liquid dew; but scarcely has the Cause of All directed upon them the full rays of the sun, when their beauty and glory fail, and the brilliant gay colors, which decked forth their pride, wither and fade.

The delicious realms of flowers count their dynasties by short periods; those which in the morning revel proudly in beauty and strength, by evening weep for the sad destruction of their thrones, and for the mishaps which drive them to loss, to poverty, to death and to the grave.

All things of earth have an end, and in the midst of the most joyous lives, the breath falters, they fall, they sink into the ground.

All the earth is a grave, and naught escapes it; nothing is so perfect that it does not fall and disappear.

The rivers, brooks, fountains, and waters flow on, and never return to their joyous beginnings; they hasten on to the vast realms of Tlaloc, and the wider they spread between their marges the more rapidly do they mold their own sepulchral urns.

That which was yesterday is not today; and let not that which is today trust to live tomorrow.

The caverns of the earth are filled with pestilential dust which once was the bones, the flesh, the bodies of great ones who sat upon thrones, deciding causes, ruling assemblies, governing armies, conquering provinces, possessing treasures, tearing down temples, flattering themselves with pride, majesty, fortune, praise, and dominion.

These glories have passed like the dark smoke thrown out by the fires of Popocatepetl, leaving no monuments but the rude skins on which they have been written.

THE AGONIES OF TRANSLATION

Nezahualcoyotl had a translator equal to his eloquence; not so Fray Sahagún. It is a *fallacia consequentis* to equate a polyglot with a translator, a scholar with a writer. Apart from the mere circumstance that they all deal with words, there is no necessity to suppose they have anything in common. Translations must have poets at both ends of the process. Omar Khayyam's *Rubaiyat* would not be known outside Persia had the poet Edward Fitzgerald not lived next door to a scholar of the Iranian tongue. The greatest work of prosody in the English language,

Beowulf, is closed for appreciation to all except students of Anglo-Saxon because, in spite of a myriad of poetasters, it has never had a poet to convey it to us over a thousand years of evolution in the English language. Keats was inspired to compose an immortal sonnet by a translation of Homer made by a negligible poet in the golden age of Shakespeare, but George Chapman needed his Keats. Others thought little of his effort. William Cowper, himself a poet and translator of Homer, read Chapman's book twenty-three years before Keats encountered it. His judgment did not accord with that of the Romantic poet. In a rather ungracious acknowledgement of a gift of Chapman's book to his friend Thomas Park, he wrote,

> *Within these few days I have received . . . your acceptable present of Chapman's translation of the Iliad. I know not whether the book be a rarity, but a curiosity it certainly is. I have as yet seen but little of it, enough, however, to make me wonder that any man, with so little taste for Homer, or apprehension of his manner, should think it worth while to undertake the laborious task of translating him; the hope of pecuniary advantage may perhaps account for it. His information, I fear, was not much better than his verse, for I have consulted him in one passage of some difficulty, and find him giving a sense of his own, not at all warranted by the words of Homer.*

Cowper's condemnation of Chapman's inaccuracies is equivocal. It has validity only when legalistic accuracy is necessary, and of course no translation can even approximate that dubious ideal. It is commonly but wrongly supposed that the Church in the days of reformational ferment burnt the Bible translators only because it could not exercise the same treatment upon their publications. But the Church had reason beyond unmotivated villainy for the proscription of both the translations and the translators. The Bible is a book of ubiquitous ambiguity, a fault of boundless danger to dogma, one of the universally sacrosanct components of all religions. As Chaucer's libelous characterization of Church officials in his *Canterbury Tales* demonstrates (some of them are so scurrilous that they never have been accurately conveyed into modern English), the Church was not concerned with unfavorable criticism of its practitioners. But Chaucer was given the highest praise of his century as a poet (and, curiously, as a translator, which ability was esteemed well above that of a mere creative composer) while some of his translating acquaintances were burnt with their Bibles chained around their necks. The difference—the literally fatal difference—was that translators fiddled with dogma. The extent of inaccuracy is gauged by the special names by which most of these unauthorized Bibles are known—the *Goose Bible, Bug Bible, Breeches Bible, Ears to Ear Bible, Placemakers Bible, Rosin Bible, She Bible, Vinegar Bible, Wife Bible;* and to the point, the *Wicked Bible* (which gave the Seventh Commandment as "Thou shalt commit adultery," a printers' error that resulted in one of the heaviest penalites ever levied against manual laborers). Though the Church and its priests still say otherwise, the faithful were never encouraged to read even the authorized Bible because of the probability of misinterpretation, on which whole religious denominations have been founded. One sentence in the Authorized Version caused a large segment of fundamental Appalachian Christians to withdraw from the orthodoxy of their established church and run about plucking rattlesnakes out of a black box and throwing them at one another—a whimsical ritual which had the commendable consequence of reducing the number of heretical communicants.

When a translator has only accuracy as his intention, the result tends to be like this excerpt from Leonhard Schultze's rendition of a Hottentot story:

> Girls (*/goati* "daughters") went walking (*sari* narr. pass.) to the (*/ga*) kraal of the Aigamucha woman; and when they got there (*si*, with the personal suff. of the subj.) one (*/gui*) of them ("a persons," *kxol's* fem.) is pregnant (*!gom*); this one is addressed (*mi* "to say) like this by (*/a*) the Aigamucha woman: "Come (*/kxi*), let yourself (literally: 'and *e* [imperative], *Ita*, massage you *-si*') be massaged . . . .

Writing of this sort is not calculated to persuade Hottentots to take up literacy—or students to take up anthropology. The translation of Sahagún's *Historia* which follows this Introduction is the best available, but it is at times not appreciably superior to Schultze's abomination in readability. In plain truth it is generally execrable. Consider as an example this fragmentary paragraph:

> *As they were thrust in, a great cloud of ashes arose (from the*

fire) and wherever anyone of them fell, a deep hole (hollow) was made (by the body) in the fire because it was ablaze with embers and live coal. The poor captives at once began to twist and turn in that fire and to suffer from nausea (have vomiting spells), his[sic] body beginning to squeak (I think sizzle would be better) . . . .

Or, to show how much functional illiteracy can be put into a little room, this sentence.

There certain gods called Tlaloques reside, who look like the ministers (priests) of the idols and who wear long hair (wear their hair long).

Sylvanus G. Morley, that most urbane of all Central American archaeologists, in projecting the translation of the *Florentine Codex*, insisted that above all else that it be put into readable English, a cautionary warning forgotten, ignored, or misunderstood by persons who do not know what readable English is—an occupational handicap among Consensus Anthropologists, as a random reading of the *American Anthropologist* will demonstrate.

Whom to blame? Not Sahagún, though he had a plethora of difficulties to contend with in rendering his Aztec sources even into Nahuatl, for his letters to the king during the seraphic quarrels toward the end of his life show an extraordinary skill at putting a simple message into eloquent rhetoric worthy of the delicate eyes of a monarch. So far as his Nahuatl is concerned, there is no question that only Fray Alonso de Molina approached him in its mastery, and he never flagged in making his perfection doubly perfect. But somewhere, and perhaps everywhere, in the last four hundred years, the accuracy and elegance of Sahagún have been destroyed, like the vital essence of a fly when a thoughtless little boy begins his biological investigations by tearing off its wings. Though they are dutifully praised for their translations of the *Historia*, Carlos Maria de Bustamante in the early nineteenth century and Fanny Bandelier in the early twentieth both laid rough hands on Sahagún's delicate wings. Bustamante we know censored out of Fray Bernardino's book his indecent stories of the Trickster Titlacaoan, exposing thus his ignorance that if there is one universal characteristic of the Trickster, it is obscene behavior. As for Fanny Bandelier, who is inescapably responsible for the final Englishing, nothing in her own writing will ever enter Bartlett's *Familiar Quotations*, though a new edition of Fowler's *Modern English Usage* might well quarry her work for Horrible Examples. But Bustamante and Bandelier are running the only game in town.

Fray Bernardino accepted a frightful responsibility in making the *Historia* out of native sources. The Aztec pictographs alone would have been enough to dissuade any translator with the least fear of censorious critics. "One picture is worth more than ten thousand words," declares an ancient Chinese proverb ascribed to Confucius about the time he was warning the United States never to conduct a land war in China. That is true enough; one picture is worth more than ten thousand words—if your purpose is to deceive, for even the simplest picture contains a thousand ambiguities. Like the Bible, the Aztec historical drawings were to be interpreted only by priests, and while Sahagún employed native artist-translators for this part of his work, they too in time admitted to some incompetency. Yet these highly stylized drawings, which their painters, the *tlacuilo*, had to interpret in pre-Hispanic times, were the only authentic texts he had:

> *These people had no letters or any characters, nor did they know how to read or write; they communicated by means of images and paintings, and all their antiquities and the books they had about them were painted with figures and images in such a way that they knew and had memory of the things their ancestors had done and had left in their annals, more than a thousand years back before the arrival of the Spanish in this land.*

These pictographs immediately began to exhibit contamination after the arrival of the Spaniards. The *Codex Tudela*, commended for its authenticity, shows the infection of Spanish influence. What we can call Ethnographers' Myopia is detectable not only in literary texts, but in drawings—even in the sense of sight itself. The American Indians are still seen literally as "red men" in most countries of the modern world interested in other people than themselves, though no one has seen a *red* Indian any oftener than a *black* Negro or a *white* man. The first Amerindian indigenes to present themselves to European visitors had taken the magical precaution of coloring themselves first with red ochre; hence the inexcusable inference that their epidermal pigmentation was a genetic characteristic.

Another source of confusion—and almost unavoidable errors in transcription—lay in the Aztec illiteracy which made their very words an arbitrary entity. Modern anthropological linguists, who look under flat wet rocks for evidence that the most primitive languages are more expressive than their own, encourage mistakes by uttering such familiar nonsense that the Eskimo vocabulary contains single words to describe the size, weight, texture, shape, water content, drift ability, and color of snow, whereas English, which can claim little more than 600,000 words, can only say "snow." Even the greatest historian of our era, William Hickling Prescott (whose *History of the Conquest of Mexico* is an excellent book to read along with Sahagún's *Historia General de las Cosas de Nueva España*), falls into the logical trap. The Aztec word written as *amatlacuilolitquitcatlaxtlahuitl,* he tells us with some amusement, means in our uneconomical tongue, "the reward given to a messenger who bears a hieroglyphical map conveying intelligence." In Sahagun we have the ejaculation "Oh, how wretched we are" represented by the single word *quwcannelocnenquenolocnen.* Well, fair enough; who is to gainsay it? But even lame English has its resources for breathtaking constructions. The chemical compound known to scientists as C_{1289} H_{2051} N_{343} O_{375} S_{8} can more intelligibly be communicated to laymen by its name

Methionylglutaminylarginyltyrosylglutamylserylleucylphen-
ylalanylalanylglupaminylleucyllysylglutamylarginyllysygultamylgly-
cylalanylphenylalanylbalylprolylphenylalanylbalylthreonylleucylg-
lycylaspartylprolylglycylisoleucylglutamylglutaminylserylleucyllysy-
lisoleucylaspartylthreonylleucylisoleucylglutamylalamylglycylalany-
laspartylalanylleucylglutamylleucylglycylisoleucyltrolylphenylalan-
ylserylaspartylprolylleucylalanylaspartylglycycprolylthreonylisoleu-
cylglutaminylasparaginylalanylthreonylleucylarginylalanylphenyl-
alanylalanylalanylglycylvalylthreonylprolylalanylglutaminylcystein-
ylphenylalanylglutamylmephionylleucylaanylleucylisoleucylarginyl-
glutaminyllysylhistidyltrolylthreonylisoleucylprolylisoleucylglycylle-
ucylleucylnethionyltyrosylalanylasparaginylleucylvalylphenylalany-
lasparaginyllysylglycylisoleucylaspartylglutamylphenylalanyltyrosy-
lalanylglutaminylcysteinylglutamyllysylvalylglycylvalylaspartylseryl-
valylleucylvalylalanylaspartylvalylprollvalylglutaminylglutamylse-
rylalanylprolylphenylalanylarginylglutaminylalanylalanylleucylar-
ginylhistidylasparaginylvalylalanylprolylisoleucylphenylalanylisol-
eucylcysteinylprolylprolylaspartylalanylaspartylaspartylaspartylleu-
cylleucylarginylglutaminylisoleucylalanylseryltyrosylglycylarginyl-
glycyltyrosylthreonyltyrossylleucylleucylserylarginylalanylglycylval-
ylthreonylglycylalanylglutamylassparaginylarginylalanylalanylleucy-
lprolylleucylasparaginylhistidylleucylvalylalanyllysylleucyllysylglu-
tanyltyrosylasparaginylalanylalanylprolylprolylleucylglutaminyl-
glycylphenylalanylglycylisoleucylserylalanylprolylaspartylglutamin-
ylbalyllysylalanylalanylisoleucylaspartylalanylglycylalanylalanylgl-
ycylalanylisoleucylserylglycylserylalanylisoleucylvalyllysylisoleucy-
lisoleucylglutamylglutaminylhhistidylasparaginylisoleucylglutamyl-

prolylglutamyllysylmethionylleucylalancylalanylleucyllysylvalylph-enylalanylvalylglutaminylprolylmethionyllysylalanylalanylphreony-larginylserine.

What all of this nonsense comes down to is the question of where, in transcribing "words" from unwritten languages, one puts the white spaces.

If the Aztecs could not write, they certainly could speak. Such eloquent oratory as Nezahualcoyotl's thanatopsis differed in elevation rather than kind from the generality of ancient Mexican expression. Paradoxically, eloquence—even grandiloquence—seems to be characteristic of illiterate cultures. I once had the embarrassing experience of being welcomed to a native village in Samoa Sisifo by a Polynesian Talking Chief (aboriginal press secretaries to administrative chiefs who did not deign to speak to anthropologists—a custom that might well be adopted by all of us). He spoke for some thirteen minutes, presumably on the unutterable honor I had bestowed upon his people by my visit. All I could think to say in reply was "Hi, Chief," which somehow seemed to lack sufficiency.

The correspondence between Polynesia and Mexico could have been polygenetic, but in light of the other close resemblances between many aspects of Oceanic culture and Mexican civilization, the probability of diffusion is inescapable. In both societies oratory was taught to higher class children from their infancy. Maori lullabies are unapproached for all the oratorical qualities ever conceived, even the Mexican. The Aztecs had formal schools for education in speaking well, restricted, of course, to the social class from which political ministers and priests were drawn. In these colleges conventionalized orations known as *huehuetlatolli* (from *huehue*, "elder," and *tlatolli*, "orations") were taught. Drawing her material from some hundred examples in Sahagún, Thelma D. Sullivan categorizes *huehuetlatolli* into five principal subjects, which comprised the immaterial culture of the people who counted in Aztec society: prayers to the gods, court orations, orations of parents to children, orations of the merchants (who were also unofficial spies and emissaries to autonomous regions the Aztecs planned to incorporate into their burgeoning empire, by peaceful means if necessary), and orations relative to the life cycle.

Fray Bernardino de Sahagún's lavish use of *huehuetlatolli* is a microcosm of the riches among his "things" of New Spain. The variety alone in his monumental book's subjects makes his use of the encompassing word "things" a necessity. He makes a plea for understanding forgiveness from the reader who finds omissions in his compilation, but that is a beneficence not many people will be able to give him. Nearly all the conceivable "things" of the Aztec civilization are in the pages that follow; all that is wanting is felicity—but that is his translators' failing, not his. The lack is not an insuperable obstacle to appreciation; indeed, it is for the creative reader an opportunity. In every work of literature the reader constructs his own imagery and drama; only when he chooses to see the motion picture does he abandon this joyous task to directors and screenplay scribblers and set designers and trendy photographers and other improbable experts. The consequence of relinquishing his own part in the interaction between author and audience is diminishing writing to typing. There is work to reaching to touch the hand of a great observer like Father Sahagún, but the exploring reader will stand at last on his own Darien, "with all the illimitable world of thought and feeling before him."

John Greenway

Department of Anthropology
University of Colorado
Boulder, Colorado
May, 1976

1547 - 1577

A HISTORY OF ANCIENT MEXICO

By

FRAY BERNARDINO DE SAHAGUN

TRANSLATED BY FANNY R. BANDELIER

FROM THE SPANISH VERSION

OF

CARLOS MARIA DE BUSTAMANTE

FISK UNIVERSITY PRESS

1932

PRINTED BY BAIRD-WARD PRINTING COMPANY
NASHVILLE, TENNESSEE

To the Memory

of My

Husband

Foreword

The ancient civilization of Mexico still intrigues the learned world. As yet no satisfactory explanation of its origin is forthcoming, partly because we lack full information as to what manner of life it was that Cortez suppressed. It is true that the literature of the nineteenth century affords some romantic and thrilling reconstructions of this old aboriginal Mexican life, the assumed glory and grandeur of which are now a part of contemporary folk-lore. Specialists in this field have long known that such popular accounts were not to be taken literally, but even the layman of our time appreciates original sources as a means of evaluating such reconstructions. Heretofore these sources were not available to him except in French and Spanish, but even so there was little from which to choose, the main source of information being the writings of a Franciscan monk, Fray Bernardino de Sahagun. Other early Spanish writings there are, but as respects native life, these are fragmentary and casual. We blame our English forefathers for neglecting to record the pertinent facts about Indian life in the Atlantic States, and the invaders of Mexico have been especially execrated for their seemingly heedless destruction of precious historical materials and their indolence in recording observations on native life. This may or may not be just, for there were many important things to do at the time, and Europe was still so close to a pagan past that her Christian leaders regarded any contact with Indian culture as a dangerous temptation. Nevertheless, in all times and places a few scholarly-minded individuals did patiently collect data.

Many of these precious documents have been lost, but fortunately a few survive, most conspicuous of which are the writings of Bernardino de Sahagun, the chief contemporary authority on the civilization of the Aztec. He is usually spoken of as the first great historian in the New World, but we can now recognize him as the first true ethnologist. His method should please even the ultra-modern field-worker, because he gathered about him selected native informants, first writing down in the original language what these informants narrated. Yet, not content with this procedure, other informants were sought out to listen to these texts and comment upon their accuracy. Further, natives were encouraged to sketch and write in their own symbols, and finally, with all these original materials in hand, the good Father sat himself down to write.

The brief sketch of his life to be found in this volume shows us that he often worked under an adverse and at times hostile environment, but fortunately most of his manuscripts were copied and survive, chiefly in the Spanish edition of Carlos Maria de Bustamante, here presented for the first time in English translation. The original being the chief source material for all who specialize in Mexican anthropology, Mrs. Bandelier has herein rendered a signal service to American scholarship. Her splendid linguistic equipment and her familiarity with all that pertains to early Spanish contacts with aboriginal American cultures, combine to make this translation one of the important contributions to contemporary anthropology.

CLARK WISSLER.

New York, June, 1932.

Preface

For the loan of the copy of Bustamante's transcription of Sahagun, I wish to express my sincere thanks to the University of Chicago, and also to Dr. Robert Redfield of the faculty of that university, and Dr. Paul Radin of the faculty of Fisk University for their assistance in procuring that loan.

The translation was made as closely as possible to the Spanish text, irrespective of correct English diction. This will explain the often quite stilted wording and the numerous repetitions. However, in the many years of work with Spanish documents of the 16th and subsequent centuries I have found it best to render a translation as literally as possible.

The frontispiece, a portrait of Sahagun, was obtained from the "Historia Patria," new edition of "Mexico a través de los Siglos" by Luis González Obregón, where it appears on page LXXV of the "Introducción" by Alfredo Chavero, noted Mexican historian.

Sahagun's original signature was copied from a photostatic reproduction in the monumental work entitled "Cartas de Indias" and issued by the Minister of Education of Spain, upon the occasion of the ascension to the Spanish throne of Alfonso XII in 1877. It was affixed to a letter to the Emperor Don Carlos, by Fray Francisco de Bustamante and other Franciscan monks, dated: Mexico, October 20th, 1552.

The geographical sketch of the province of León (p. 2), where the birthplace of Sahagun is located, is taken from publications by the "Comisaria Regia del Turismo" of Spain, of recent date.

On page 172 is an old map of the city and lagune of Mexico or Temistitan, showing the then small Spanish settlement in the midst of the lagune, surrounded by native towns with their temples, palaces and causeways to the mainland. It is from the Italian translation of the "Conquistador Anónimo," (supposedly a companion of Cortes), in "Coleccion de Documentos para la historia de Mexico," (vol. I, pp. 568-98) published by Don Joaquin Garcia Icazbalceta, Mexico 1858.

The bibliography of Sahagun's works was extracted from "Bibliografia Mexicana del Siglo XVI, by Señor Garcia Icazbalceta (Mexico 1886), and will be amplified in vol. II of this translation by additional data not available at present.

Fanny R. Bandelier.

BIOGRAPHY

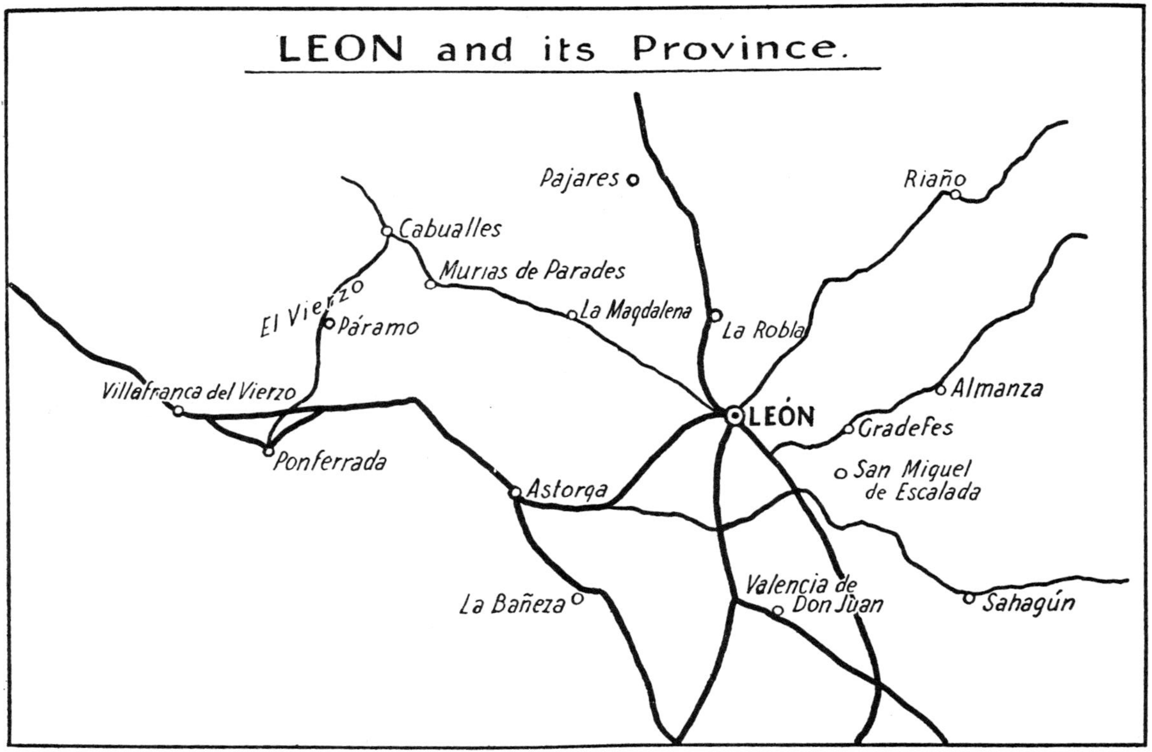
LEON and its Province.
Pajares
Riaño
Cabualles
Murias de Parades
El Vierzo
Páramo
La Magdalena
La Robla
Villafranca del Vierzo
LEÓN
Almanza
Gradefes
Ponferrada
San Miguel
de Escalada
Astorga
Valencia de
Don Juan
La Bañeza
Sahagún

Fray Bernardino de Sahagun[1]

Like many another of his brethren, Fray Bernardino, upon joining the Order of Saint Francis, adopted, or rather was given the name of his native town, Sahagun, as an appellative. He was born about 1499 and the family name was Ribeira,[2] a distinctly Portuguese family name. We have no definite knowledge about what happened at the university of Salamanca to make him stop the course of his studies and enter conventual life at the Franciscan Convent of that city, or what prompted him to forsake scientific studies and become a humble, poor Franciscan monk. It is quite possible that the gay life of the old university town of Salamanca proved too diverting for a mind like his, bent on serious study. All we know is that he was still very young when entering the order and such a fine looking youth that the oldest monks guarded him as zealously as possible to prevent temptations from the outer world. We hear nothing from him until 1529, when he took ship for New Spain (Mexico) as one of the 19 Franciscan monks led thither by Fray Antonio de Ciudad Rodrigo. Herrera[3] tells us that on the same ship with the friars, the Mexican Indians whom Cortés had brought over to Spain to be presented at the Spanish Court, were sent back, by order of the Emperor who recommended them to the special care of Fray Antonio de Ciudad Rodrigo and his companions after they had been provided with adequate clothing and many presents. They naturally traveled as passengers of distinction, being of distinguished lineage, and our Fray Bernardino must have been particularly attentive, for it is said that on this long journey he learned many Aztec words from these men, even entire sentences. He certainly mastered the Indian tongue very quickly, and is considered as one of the foremost students of it, if not the foremost.

A born student, Fray Bernardino was interested in every phase of the ancient history and customs of the people among whom he was to spend the rest of his life; he not only won their entire confidence, but also the sincere affection of his pupils in particular. He was humble, patient, alert,

[1]Joaquin Garcia Icazbalceta, Bibliografia Mexicana del Siglo XVI, Mexico, 1886, p. 253 et seq Alfredo Chavero, in Introduction to Historia Patria, Vol. I, p. 74 et seq.

[2]Sahagun, Estudio por Alfredo Chavero, Secretario perpetuo de la Sociedad de Geografia y Estadistica de Mexico, Mexico, 1877 p. 7. Señor Chavero appears to be the only author to have found Fray Bernardino's family name. It is not mentioned by any of the older sources.

[3]Antonio de Herrera, Descripcion de las Indias Ocidentales, Decada IV, libro 6, end of chapter 4.

learned and easy to get along with, as his chroniclers say. To attain such marked perfection in Nahuatl or Aztec, Sahagun no doubt studied seriously with someone who knew that language perfectly and who also spoke Spanish to give him such a deep knowledge of Nahuatl construction that his contemporaries said of him: "That he acquired such mastery and perfection in the language that only Fray Alonso de Molina surpassed him perhaps." But then this latter was brought to Mexico by his parents very soon after the conquest and as a child naturally learned Nahuatl from the Indian children at play. However, he spoke it so well that the first twelve Franciscan missionaries used the boy as their interpreter, and he also taught the language to several of them. Upon reaching the required age to take the vows, he became a Franciscan monk himself, and for fifty years he preached in Nahuatl in Mexico and other towns and villages, wrote a vocabulary, several catechisms and other religious treatises in that language, all of which were used not only by the clergy but by laymen and Indians as well. He died in Mexico and is buried in the great convent of San Francisco (which is now completely demolished with exception of a small part of its original conventual garden).

Our Fray Bernardino followed the same method; he, too, wrote a vocabulary in Nahuatl or Aztec; he wrote sermons, prayers and other works on Christian lore. While the press in general rather favored Father Molina, Sahagun had the great advantage of a very profound knowledge of ancient Mexican lore which he gathered with utmost patience and never failing interest from his students of the school in Tlaltelulco for presumably quite a number of years. In peace they shared the work among the natives and the love and respect of their charges. In 1555, Fray Bernardino approved the first vocabulary in the Mexican (Aztec or Nahuatl) language, composed by Molina.

To all appearances, his first few years in the New World, that is to say, from 1530 to 1533, were spent by Fray Bernardino in the convent of Tlalmanalco and while there he witnessed a sort of ecstatic rapture or trance of Father Martin de Valencia, when, for the second time, the latter served as Custodian of the convent. It is said that Fray Martin was subject to these religious exaltations.

As the little town of Tlalmanalco lies close to the foot of the two volcanoes, Iztaccihuatl and Popocatepetl, Sahagun made his ascension of both mountains while residing there as he tells us in Vol. III of his "Historia General". He fails to tell us his motive for undertaking these perilous journeys, but it is safe to surmise that his reason was to investigate a report about human sacrifices taking place at certain times of the year in the very craters of both volcanoes. As a matter of fact, the Mexicans held Iztac-cihuatl—the white woman—in great reverence as a powerful goddess whom they worshipped not only in special temples in the various towns, but also in a large cave on the slopes of the mountain bearing her name. So naturally our Fray Bernardino of the inquisitive mind went in search of it, risking his own life in more than one way. Both mountains, Iztaccihuatl and Popocatepetl, were considered to be quite inaccessible, especially the former. The latter had been ascended by three Spaniards, the conquerors Ordaz, Montaño and Mesa, but Sahagun climbed both lofty peaks. His description of the beauty of the mountain itself, referring to Iztaccihuatl, as well as of the view from the summit is short but expressive. " . . . it is grandiose and well worth seeing; I was at the very summit." He goes on speaking of a river formed by the melting snows and which at a certain point disappears under the surface, then comes forth again between the towns of Huexotzinco and Acapetlaoacan, adding: "I saw its source, the place where it becomes lost between boulders, and then again where it flows out from the mountain."

Elsewhere Sahagun speaks of the peak of Orizaba, stating that: "A few years ago its summit commenced to emit fire, but I have seen it covered with snow for many years. When it commenced to burn, the flames could be seen in the daytime as well as at night, from a distance of more than twenty leagues". Orizaba cannot be seen from the valley of Mexico and the eruption of which Fray Bernardino speaks occurred in 1545, according to Muñoz Camargo and as Sahagun is known to have returned to Tlaltelulco some time during that year, he must have left the neighborhood of Orizaba soon after the catastrophe. In all probability he resided at the town or in the valley of Orizaba at two different periods, in one capacity or another, sent by his superiors, because we have no account of his whereabout from 1533 to 1536, and again between the years 1540 to 1545.

In 1536 he was appointed as teacher of Latin at the College of Santa Cruz, founded by Bishop Zumarraga. He remained there until 1540, when possibly the Father Superior of the Franciscan Order recommended him as visiting commissioner to the various Franciscan convents and missions throughout the valleys of Puebla, Orizaba, etc., and thus in the next four or five years we find him traveling. Then, in 1545, he returns once more to Tlaltelulco, recalled possibly to become Superior of that convent, which, as it appears from a royal decree of May 1, 1543, to viceroy Antonio de Mendoza, was to be built or rather enlarged, "because for eight years two Franciscan monks had lived there very humbly and modestly in two cells over the main body of the church and the Indians now offered to build them a house close by so they might live in comfort".

We know that Sahagun had lived in Tlaltelulco previously for about four years, preaching and educating the natives, and it does not seem too far fetched to suppose that it was his influence over the Indians that helped very materially towards the establishment of a regular convent. The first year after his return was a rather tragic one on account of a great plague which raged throughout New Spain, killing Indians by the thousands. Fray Bernardino tells us that he buried "over ten thousand bodies, and that the only way to inhume such a large number was to dig wide trenches in the cemeteries connected with the different churches and to throw eighty to a hundred bodies together into each one of them". He caught the disease himself towards the end of 1546, and was taken to the infirmary of the mother convent in the city proper of Mexico, where he very nearly died.

Before the College of Santa Cruz at Santiago Tlaltelulco—this is its full name—was founded, sons of prominent Mexican Indians received instruction in the Spanish language at the Chapel of San José (St. Joseph) which belonged as a sort of "dependence" to the large convent of San Francisco of Mexico city and their first teacher was Fray Arnaldo Bassario, but no doubt Sahagun began to teach there very soon after his arrival. As we have seen, he showed great interest in the natives already during the crossing from Spain, and this could not fail to establish certain bonds of friendship between him and his charges. His duties kept him during the first years close to the city, and this may be the reason why we hear nothing of his activities, although Mendieta tells us that "in his youth he was Superior of several large convents", which must have been the twenty-five years following his arrival, teaching, we suppose, wherever he was sent to, and especially writing. Later, we are told, for almost forty years he wished to be excused from official duties, although on several occasions during that time he was appointed as "definidor" (among the Franciscan order this meant "member of the governing body in its provinces") and also as "visitador" (surveyor or inspector for the Order) in the province of Michuacan. Such duties, however, were of short duration, and we shall see later how Fray Bernardino improved such trips of inspection.

One of the convents where he acted as Superior was in all probability that of Xochimilco, near Mexico city, and one of the largest the Order had established in New Spain. Sahagun tells us about "a spring of very sweet water" in the above mentioned pueblo of Xochimileo, where, submerged under the water, a stone idol existed to which the Indians offered copal (incense). "I saw this idol and I went down into the spring to take it out, and I erected in its place a stone cross, which is still standing in that spring." In order to trace the existence of such an idol so carefully hidden by the Indians, then to deliberately plunge into the spring to lift it out and replace it by the Christian emblem of the cross, Fray Bernardino not only needed a missionary's zeal and courage, but a certain authority, such as that of Superior of his Order. A simple monk might not have fared so well. He also counted perhaps on the affection the natives had for him, which to a certain extent would help him to persuade them that idolatry was a shallow belief, that idols could not harm him. No doubt he knew that although officially professing Christianity the Indians still clung tenaciously to at least certain idolatrous practices. So he was ever watchful and always found a way to discover the hiding places of such idols. We have seen him climb the summits of the volcanoes to hunt for sacrificial caves, and here in Xochimilco he goes down into a hidden spring to bring forth the idol and replace it by the Cross. And as the natives saw that the former, so greatly feared by them, did not harm the saintly man, they naturally were somewhat shaken in their aboriginal beliefs. It was while he still resided in their midst that they begged him to translate the "Life of St. Bernhard", titular saint of the town, into Mexican.

In 1552, as a member of the Governing Board of the Order, as previously stated, we find his signature affixed to a letter addressed to the Emperor. True, he does not sign as "Definidor", but that was not absolutely necessary; he could not have been a member of the commission without the title. It was a great honor in itself to sign his name with those of men like Fr. Francisco de Bustamante, the great homilist. Fr; Juan de San Francisco, later elected Bishop of Yucatan; Fr. Toribio de Motolinia, Fr. Juan de Ribas and Fr. Antonio de Ciudad Rodrigo, three of the first twelve Franciscan monks sent to Mexico; Fr. Juan Focher, a brilliant Mexican monk and, lastly, the great teacher, Fr. Juan de Gaona.

A few years later, presumably before 1558, Sahagun was sent to Michoacan as inspector of the convents of the Order. He has little to say about the Tarascan Indians in his History, probably because his visit was too short for an intensive study.

From 1558 to 1566 he apparently gave all his time and efforts to the compilation of his "history" which he finished about 1569, and which was presented before a Meeting of the Franciscan Order in Mexico.

Material for this great work had been assembled by Sahagun in the course of fully a quarter of a century, if not more. Perhaps the first idea of writing a history of the Mexicans came to him on the ship sailing to the New World in the company of a few distinguished Aztecs. It is quite certain that while he was teaching Spanish and Latin to Mexican youths he continued studying their customs and especially their language. He no doubt loved history above all, and may have prepared himself already at Salamanca for this chosen field. His biographers only mention that he studied "letras" which in Spanish means science in general; they do not say "bellas letras" which would mean literature, poetry and art, but in his scientific pursuits he probably specialized in history. At all events, he went about it with the thoroughness of the historian, studying primarily the language of the ancient Mexicans.

In 1547, material for book VI of the history of Mexico was assembled, and this certainly is proof sufficient to show that data were gathered very shortly after Sahagun's arrival in Mexico; that while he was one of the teachers of Indians, he also was their historian. He asked questions of his pupils, compiled them, then possibly verified the material by conversing with older men of the tribe. For ten years he appears to have gathered data which he then sorted and put into books, i. e., chapters, but it was only in 1557 when Fray Francisco Toral became "Provincial" (Superior) of the Franciscan Order that positive orders were given to Fray Bernardino to put this vast amount of information into the shape of one or two volumes. To this end he was sent to the pueblo of Tepeopulco, of the jurisdiction of Texcoco, where, with the kind assistance of the native chief and most prominent citizen, Don Diego de Mendoza, he succeeded in assembling ten or twelve Indians, well versed in their ancient lore. Several of these informants were old men, contemporaries of the Aztec empire, while four others were well versed in the Spanish language, having been students of Sahagun's. The latter now resorted to a quite unusual, even unique method, never practiced before. Fully aware of the fact that ancient Mexican history was contained in hieroglyphic signs, many of which had been destroyed, together with the images of the ancient gods, he made a sort of glossary in Spanish in his attempt to reconstruct that part of the ancient lore he was particularly anxious to have explained. The Indians, especially the old men, responded immediately and painted the corresponding glyphs, while the Spanish speaking members of his advisory board explained them to him.

This material was carefully recorded by Sahagun to await the day when it might be published. There can be little doubt as to its authenticity, for, as a matter of fact, it was really composed by the Indians, who drew the pictures and, prompted by clever and pertinent questions on the part of their Spanish historian, explained them to him in Aztec and Spanish.

In 1560, when Fray Francisco Bustamante became the local Superior of the Franciscan Order in Mexico, Sahagun returned once more to Tlaltelulco, where he continued his studies in a similar way. With the assistance of the Indian governor and his staff, he gathered some ten Indians well versed in their past history and three or four trilingual students of the college. Especially helpful in this work were his pupils, Martin Jacobita, Antonio Valeriano, Alonso Vexarano and Pedro de

San Buenaventura, all of whom were thoroughly conversant in Aztec, Spanish and Latin.

"For a little over one year"—he tells us himself—"they remained confined in the school with him and revised all the material gathered at Tepeopulco and rewrote most of it,—in very poor handwriting,—because they were greatly pressed for time."

This third part of the Mexican history was completed in 1561 and was of course mostly composed by the Indians themselves, although, like the previous part written at Tepeopulco, prompted by Sahagun. He now retires into the quiet of the cloisters of the main Franciscan convent of Mexico and, as he says: "I gathered all my notes and papers, and in the course of three years I revised and re-revised them by myself, annotated them, and then divided them into twelve books, each book into chapters and paragraphs." In his introduction to the first book he explains the division according to their various subjects.

The finished product can be called properly Sahagun's own, although even now, while in Mexico he seeks the advice of trilingual students. The manuscript was written in Aztec and was finished in 1566, and, as he himself declares, "after it had run the gamut for fifteen years".

In 1567, when Father Miguel Navarro had been appointed Father Provincial and Fray Diego de Mendoza was General of the Order, the entire work was copied in clear caligraphy, through their endeavours. All the twelve books were copied, the copyists were Diego de Grado, a parishioner of San Martin, and Mateo Severino of Xoohimilco, and the two latter corrected many items and added others as they proceeded.

This copy was finished about 1569 and turned over to Father Rivera, who was then Commissary of the Order. The following year of 1570 Father Navarro took a summary of the "Historia" to Spain, as we shall see later.

Up to this time our historian had been protected by his superiors, as in those times all men interested in similar work were protected, but now came a time of probation for him, quite difficult to fathom, much less to understand.

Fray Bernardino had requested the Commissary, Fray Francisco de Rivera, to appoint a commission consisting of three Franciscan monks to examine his great epic of the ancient Mexicans. While this commission, appearing before the official meeting of the Chapter in 1570, was of the opinon: "that the work was good and should be allowed to be concluded; there were certain members of the governing board who objected to the expenditure this would demand, pretending that such expenditure was contrary to the professed poverty of the Franciscan order." The author was ordered to dismiss his copyists and to finish the copying of whatever remained to be done, in his own hand, as best he could.

Such a truly dishonorable and unjust decision can hardly be explained unless it originated in certain petty rivalries among the Franciscans of Mexico, which, as a matter of fact, motivated the voyage to Spain of Fray Miguel Navarro and Fr. Geronimo de Mendieta. The former, as we have seen, had favored Sahagun in as much as he could. Now that the decision of the Chapter was so decidedly unfavorable, the newly elected Father Provincial, Fray Alonso de Escalona, to emphasize his victory, withdrew the small stipend allowed our historian and thereby forced a man, 70 years old, to copy the pages of his immortal history in his own shaky hand.

Sahagun should not have let it go at that, even for all the sweetness of his nature. He should have protested; instead, he prepared an abstract of his work, however hard this must have been for the poor old hands, and sent it to Spain with his old friend and protector, Fr. Miguel Navarro. He must have written this summary in Spanish, for no doubt Don Juan de Ovando, president of the Council of the Indies, who was very much pleased with it, would not have understood it in the Indian language.

This action, however, of sending an extract of his work to Spain for approval, was considered as an act of insubordination by Escalona and he at once ordained that all the books of the history be taken away from Sahagun and be distributed among the various convents of the province. This was certainly not only a very harsh and undeserved measure, but a very dastardly one, for how easily could one or the other go astray and be lost forever. And Escalona knew that just as well as anyone, possibly did it on purpose to destroy it if possible. This action naturally stopped all further work by Sahagun until 1573, when his good friend Fray Miguel Navarro became Commissary General. The latter at once ordered the books to be collected and turned over to the aged author who in '74, quietly remarks: "Naturally in all that time nothing was done on them, nor was there anyone who offered me his assistance to finish the translation of the work into Spanish." At any rate, Escalona's vengeance was short lived; his plan to destroy the work of a lifetime did not have the desired effect.

In 1576, Fray Rodrigo de Sequera, the new Commissary General, brought orders from the Council of the Indies in Spain, to the effect that the entire work of Sahagun's, in all twelve books, be sent across the ocean. So Fray Bernardino was told to translate it all into Spanish while at the same time means were provided to copy the history anew. The Aztec version was to be put in one column, the Spanish translation in the other. In that same year of '76, the first five books were copied, in 1577 the sixth book was translated and copied, and in 1578 the remaining six were done, and the twelve books were now divided into four volumes, bound and made ready for shipment. This was the eighth time the manuscript had been copied, and in all probability this was the copy consulted by the King's chronicler, Antonio de Herrera, in his "Descripcion de las Indias Ocidentales", although he fails to mention it.

It appears that in 1582, in compliance with a second order from the council of the Indies, other original manuscripts by Sahagun were sent to Spain, among them the one of Tlaltelulco. It is well worth while to treat here of the twelfth book, which is principally speaking of the Conquest of Mexico. When Carlos M. Bustamante published Sahagun's work in Mexico in 1829, he omitted this latter, editing it separately under the title "Historia de la Conquista de Mexico", por el padre Sahagun, (small quarto, 78 pp.)

Fray Bernardino tells us in the prologue of his latest report, "When I wrote the twelve books of the History of this New Spain in this village of Tlaltelulco (for which our Lord King Philip sent and which he has over there now), the ninth book was about the conquest of this country. When this account was written, now more than thirty years ago, it was all written in the Mexican language and later translated into Spanish. Those who helped me in this description were old chiefs, well versed in all things, idolatrous practices as well as their government and its offices and who also were present in the war when this city (Mexico) was conquered.

"In the ninth book, where the conquest is described, several misstatements were made, that is to say, that some passages in the report were badly chosen while others were omitted which ought not to have been omitted. For this reason now in this year of 1585, I amended (corrected) this book, and it is for this reason it appears now in three columns instead of two. The first column is in the Indian language such as they pronounce it and as it was written in those books. The second column is a correction of the first in words as well as phrases. The third column is in Spanish according to the corrections of the second. Any one who should have a copy of this report in Aztec only (without the corrections) must bear in mind that the above mentioned corrections should be included for the sake of exactitude".

This was Sahagun's ninth manuscript on the history of the conquest, which is perhaps the most signal documentary proof of a long suffering soul. For almost thirty years he had preserved, in its original condition, the account of this conquest as given him by contemporary Indians, such as they saw and felt it, and he knew in his heart that it was the truth. However, it suited the victor's convenience to hide certain facts, and these were the ones Sahagun calls distorted or poorly interpreted, and since he appears to have had several copies, they made him change the account of the events. He protested against such violence in his own way, namely, by leaving in the first column his primary account, although only in Mexican or Aztec.

Both Herrera and Torquemada had Sahagun's report before them when they wrote their respective histories, but as one used the original rendering and the other the corrected interpretation, they contradict one another, though they both were supported by the author. Torquemada saw of the eleven books only the notes, commentaries and a few fragments.

This corrected report of the conquest was taken to Spain by Don Juan Francisco de Montemayor, then president of the Royal Audience. Torquemada says on this occasion, referring to the manuscript: "I have a copy of it in my hands, where I find the notice that Señor Don Martin de Villamanrique took away from the author the twelve books and presented them to His Majesty." However, Don Martin de Villamanrique, seventh viceroy of New Spain, governed from October 17, 1585 to February, 1590, and it is therefore quite evident that this manuscript is not the one sent over in 1578, but that the long suffering author had retained one copy of his great work, the tenth, and that even of this one he was cruelly deprived. They could not deprive him of immortality, however, for his great work will live while there are serious minded men who appreciate serious and conscientious historical research, and while there is interest in the ancient history of Mexico.

The revised manuscript of the "Conquest of Mexico" finally turned up in the library of the Royal Academy of History in Madrid, but in 1808, during the French invasion, it was stolen and was bought in 1828 by the Mexican Señor Don José Gomez de la Cortina, from Señor Don Lorenzo Ruiz de Artieda, in Spain. Count de la Cortina loaned it to Don Carlos M. Bustamante, who, as we have seen published in 1829 the twelfth book—on the conquest proper—and later in 1840, published the entire work, which has been used in the translation following this short biography. He preceded it with a dissertation of his own pen, in no way pertinent, and added to each chapter an appendix which he calls "notes," but which he might as well have left out. None of these additions have been rendered in the translation. To follow the fate of the ten manuscripts of Sahagun's masterpiece certainly reads like an Odyssey, and it is well worth recording:

1. The memorandum Fray Bernardino prepared to question the Indians of Tepeopulco. This of course was merely a preparatory work to be used as a sort of note book, and we might suppose that the author did not

preserve it, or else it was left among his loose notes which later on were examined by Torquemada and then were lost.

2. The manuscript of Tepeopulco, which consisted chiefly of hieroglyphs drawn by the Indians, and their interpretation in Aztec. This manuscript is likewise lost apparently, but to find it would be, needless to say, exceedingly valuable.

3. The manuscript of Tlaltelulco, which consists mainly of hieroglyphs, has more extensive explanatory notes and forms, therefore, already a true historical document. Sahagun himself tells us that it was sent to Spain, and there are in effect several important parts of this Mexican Codex in the library of the Royal Academy of History in Madrid.

4. The manuscript in Mexican (or Aztec) already divided into twelve books (or chapters) which remained in Sahagun's hands, but the existence of which is now unknown.

5. A copy of this, with additions which was finished in 1569. Very valuable parts of this copy are in the library of the Academy of Madrid.

6. The abstract of the history which Fray Rodrigo Navarro took to Spain. It is known that it had been taken to the Council of the Indies, and should be in its archive.

7. The history with its Spanish translation, the termination of which had been so cruelly interrupted by Father Escalona. There is little doubt that Torquemada had some fragments of this manuscript and that they are lost.

8. The manuscript in Aztec and Spanish, bound in four volumes and sent to the king. This is really the first manuscript of the entire history. It is known that after it had passed into the hands of Don Juan de Ovando, president of the Council of the Indies, it went to the Franciscans of Tolosa. When these monks were ordered by royal decree to hand it to the chronicler Don Juan Bautista Muñoz, they only gave him a copy in two volumes and—only the Spanish translation. What became of the original during the many political upheavals in Spain, no one knows. Muñoz's copy is preserved at the Academy, and is evidently incomplete as compared with fragments in Mexican.

A copy of this manuscript was used by Lord Kingsborough. Colonel Diego Garcia Panes also made a copy of it and brought it back to Mexico, where Don Jose Miguel Ballido bought it for 100 pesos Mex. and later sold it for the same amount to Bustamante, who published it. Only the last of the twelve books is now in Mexico. Besides, it must not be forgotten that, since the copy turned over to Sr. Muñoz by the Franciscans of Tolosa was not complete, the work of Father Sahagun has never been integrally published, neither in London nor in Mexico.

9. The manuscript of the Conquest is known up to 1840, when it was published, but it is not known who owns it at present.

10. The manuscript which Viceroy Villamanrique took away and of the ultimate fate of which we have no knowledge.

While we know that in Sahagun's lifetime several copies were made of this work, at least of the so-called book of the Conquest, all of them are or seem to be lost.

Since 1702 Llaguno Amirola found part of Sahagun's manuscript; we have a bibliographical notice of the twelve books of Fray Bernardino's work by Señor Gayangos; two descriptions of them by Señor Goycochea, librarian of the Academy of History, one of the Spanish codex by Mr. Buckingham Smith, and notes about it by Señor Ramirez; all of this unpublished. It is to be hoped that with the aid of the above data and more extensive research, an edition of Sahagun's history worthy of his illustrious memory may be published.

Now to return to the life story of Fray Bernardino. We left him upon his return to Tlaltelulco after a long sojourn in Tepeopulco, where he did intensive research work preparatory to writing as true and as complete a history as could be done. From Tlaltelulco he went to the main convent of San Francisco in the city of Mexico, where he was chiefly busy getting his work copied. This went on smoothly enough until 1569, the eventful year when he suffered so keenly under the revengeful actions of Father Escalona.

Fortunately for him, his true friend Father Navarro returned in 1574, but five years of living more or less confined to his cell, forgotten, possibly antagonized, did not give him the necessary inspiration to write. Nothing is known of any literary activities in these years. His heart was well nigh broken, his spirit deeply wounded.

However, Father Navarro at once reinstated him in his old activities, and as early as June 10, 1574, we find him on his return to Tlaltelulco, going over the accounts of Tomé Lopez, mayordomo of the school and convent, together with Father Molina. Once more he lived there, and was in fact principal of the school while Father Molina had become Superior of the convent.

In the codex of Santiago (Tlaltelulco) we find several very interesting and curious annotations of that time. Under June 13th, we find the following footnote: "In this condition were said accounts on this said day and they were signed by the said Judge and Fray Bernardino de Sahagun, Pablo Requena—signed: Fr. Bernardino de Sahagun (his scroll)." On three other occasions we find the signatures of the two friars under similar documents. The second is on occasion of an inventory made of books and other objects, dated September 13, 1574; also several receipts signed by Sahagun alone, which receipts give us an interesting insight into the life of the college. One is for 20 pesos gold for expenses in general, dated Friday, July 23, 1574, but from this receipt we learn just how little money there actually was in Tlaltelulco, because, in order to meet expenses our Father Sahagun demands "the twenty pesos for which a mule had been sold". On folio 84 another receipt states, "The college received a side of bacon which cost two pesos and a half. Today, Wednesday, 28th, July 1574". Then follows an order which gives us an idea of how much was paid in those days to teachers of the college, for here it says: "To Alonso Vexarano, teacher, we order that one peso and a half be given for the four lessons of the week." This Alonso Vexarano was one of the Indians who helped Sahagun in the writing of the history.

The handwriting in the Codex of Santiago is so similar to the one in the manuscript of the "Doctrina" (doctrine) by Fray Bernardino of which we shall speak later, that we surmise they were both copied by the above mentioned Alonso Vexarano. The trilingual Vocabulary was copied by Martin Jacobita, another assistant and former student of Sahagun's; he moreover signed that copy which was made after our historian had become principal of the college, for it is dated 1577, and no doubt executed at Tlaltelulco.

On folio 87 is an entry stating that Bernabé Velazques as proctor of the college paid for a "fanega" (1.60 bushel) of corn, one peso in Xochimileo.

On folio 92 appears the following entry: "This is to entreat your grace to ordain that to the two teachers of the children of the school who are on their way, four pesos and 2 tomins be given each one for the work of four months."

These few extracts present a very touching picture of Sahagun's tender care for the welfare, corporal and spiritual, of his Indian charges, and they also give us an idea of the great poverty of the Tlaltelulco school. In fact, it is often asserted that it was closed in 1578 for lack of funds, which, however, is doubtful. Sahagun presided at Tlaltelulco until at least 1576 and probably part of 1577, when Martin Jacobita replaced him. The former as we know had received orders to copy his history, which work he completed in '78 in the convent of Mexico city. But not only this was accomplished; Fray Bernardino apparently was filled with the joy of work once more, and he had the great satisfaction to publish three of his books prepared years before, to wit:

The "Manual de Cristiano" in 1578; "La Postilla" before the end of 1579, and "La Psalmodia Christiana" in 1583. This latter is the only one of which a copy still exists.

But his happiness was rather short lived. In 1585 dark clouds gathered over the head of the octogenarian, whose only failing was to be too humble and too learned! All the wrath of those in power seemed to break over him. They forced him to alter his original and true report on the conquest; they took the "History" away from him; the first presses that had come to America, after having printed the above mentioned three essays and books, remained inactive as far as his most important work was concerned, and America's most remarkable historian of the sixteenth century returned to Tlaltelulco to end his days in complete oblivion, although almost to the very last he taught, encouraged and cared for his beloved Indian boys, and in this he no doubt found consolation, his charity being strong enough to heal the wounded soul.

In 1590 an epidemic of catarrh infested Mexico city and its suburbs, and Fray Bernardino, the great historian and still greater humanitarian, was one of its victims. Almost half a century before he recovered from a severe attack of the pest which at that time took so many lives and now a simple cold was to be the cause of his death. There seems to be considerable doubt as to the exact date of Sahagun's demise; some historians give February 5, 1590; Betancurt mentions October 23rd of that year; Fray Juan Bautista in the prologue of his "Sermonario" gives 1591 as the fatal date. The safest is probably to accept the date given by one of Sahagun's contemporaries, Fray Geronimo de Mendieta, which is herewith given:

"His death followed an attack of this disease of catarrh (cold) which was so general in the year of 1590. The monks, fearing that he might die at any moment, entreated him to allow himself to be taken to the infirmary in Mexico (evidently attached to the big Franciscan convent in the city of Mexico), to be taken care of and cured, or, should he not care to be restored to health again, at least to be buried among his companions, the saintly old Franciscan fathers, this being a wish he had often expressed. He answered them saying: 'Be quiet, little fools, let me be; my hour has not come yet'. But they were so persistent that, in order not to hurt their feelings or to appear ungrateful of their tender attentions, he went to the conventual hospital in the city where he told the nurse (or orderly), 'These little fools, my brethren, urged me to come here, although it is not necessary'. He was treated for his cold, remaining a few days, then returned to Tlaltelulco, where after a short while he suffered a relapse, and then he said: 'Now my hour has come'. He asked that the young Indians who were being educated at the college and whom he always referred to as his children, be brought to his bedside. He took leave of them all, and then was carried to the convent of Mexico.

After having piously received Extreme Unction, he died and was buried there."

Torquemada, an eyewitness, copies Mendieta in the main and adds that: "a great multitude attended the funeral besides all the students of the college of Tlaltelulco, in cassock and sash, and everyone was bowed in deep sorrow."

BOOK I.

Prologue

All writers endeavor to give to their writings the best authority possible; some do so by means of trustworthy witnesses; others consult other authors who wrote on the same subject before them and whose information is considered as trustworthy; while still others rely on the holy scriptures. I have not had all these fundamentals to prove what I have written in these twelve books, nor do I find other sources to vouch for my assertions; all I can do is to put down here an account of the efforts I made to find out the truth of all there is contained in these books. As I have stated in other prologues of the present work, I was ordered by my Superior to write, in the Mexican language, what to me would seem useful for the culture, support, and teaching of Christianity among these natives of New Spain, and which would at the same time be of assistance to the workers and ministers of the Christian Faith. Upon receiving this order, I at once made out in Spanish a memorandum of all the matters I intended to touch, which was what is contained in the twelve books, in the glossary, and the songs.

This (work) was started in the village of Tepeopulco, in the province of Culhuacán or Tezcoco, and was accomplished in the following manner: In said village I had all the prominent men assemble with the chieftain of the place, whose name was Don Diego de Mendoza, an old man of great dignity and intelligence, well versed in local matters, in warfare and politics, and even in idolatries. Having gathered them all, I told them what I intended to do and begged them to find me intelligent and experienced men with whom I might talk, and who would be able to answer me to whatsoever I should ask them. They replied that they would discuss the matter proposed by me, that the following day they would give me their answer, and with that they took leave. The next day the chief came with the principals and, after having made a very solemn speech as in those times they used to make, they assigned to me about ten of the most prominent old men, and told me that with them I could commune and they would answer whatever I might ask them. There were also present as many as four Spanish-speaking Indians whom I had taught myself a few years previous at the College of Santa Cruz de Tlaltelulco[1]. With these principals and the grammarians, who were also prominent men in the township, I talked for many days in almost two

[1]Tlaltelulco, or Tlaltelolco, both are correct.

years (of my residence there), according to the notes I took at the time. All matters we talked about were given me by them by means of paintings, which was the mode of writing they had in ancient times. The grammarians then explained these paintings in their own language, writing this explanation underneath the pictures. Even now I have the originals of this work. At that time I also dictated the "postilla" (postilla—copy or transcript) and the songs; all this was written by the grammarians—the Indians who had been taught reading and writing, Spanish and Latin, at the college of Tlaltelolco; they wrote it for me right there at Tepeopulco. When I went to attend the Chapter meetings at Mexico at the time Father Francisco de Torál, who had entrusted me with the work, completed his hebdomade, they removed me with all my writings from Tepeopulco, and I went to live at Santiago de Tlaltelolco (again). There I once more assembled all the principal (prominent) men and told them the motive of my writings and demanded to assign to me some able leaders with whose help I might discuss and examine what I had noted down at Tepeopulco. The governor and his aides thereupon pointed out as many as 18 leaders (principals) from among them all who were the best versed in their language and in matters of their ancient culture. With these men and five or six collegians all of whom were trilingual, I worked for a year and a little over, confined in the college. We corrected what we had worked out, and added all the material I had brought from Tepeopulco, and then all of it was copied in very poor writing, because it was all written in a great hurry. Of all the students the one who did most of the work in this scrutiny or investigation was Martin Jacobita, who at that time was principal of the college. He was a citizen of Tlaltelolco, from the city district or ward of Santa Ana.

After having accomplished (finished) all the above mentioned work at Tlaltelolco, I went to live at the convent of San Francisco of Mexico (city), taking with me all my writings (notes) and there for three years I corrected and recorrected them by myself alone; I amended them and then divided them into books, twelve in all, and each book was moreover arranged in chapters and paragraphs. After this was done and while Fray Miguel Navarro was Provincial and Fray Diego de Mendoza, General of the Order of St. Francis in Mexico, they helped me to get the entire work copied in a legible hand, all of the twelve books; also the "postilla" (here it probably means book of annotations or commentaries on the Bible), and the (book of) songs. Also an "Art of the Mexican Language" with a vocabulary appendix was prepared, which the Mexicans corrected, and to which they added a great deal. It was then copied again. Thus, the first advisory council that criticized my work was composed of the men of Tepeopulco, the second of those of Tlaltelolco, and the third by those of Mexico (city), and in all this research work several students of the college who knew Spanish and Latin helped. The principal assistant and the most learned one was Antonio Valeriano, citizen of Aztcapuzalco; another one, little less learned, was Alonso Vegerano of Cuauhtitlan; still another was Martin Jacobita, whom I have already mentioned. There was, moreover, Pedro de San Buenaventura, also of Cuauhtitlan; all these were well versed in three languages: Latin, Spanish and Indian, i.e., Aztec or Mexican. The copyists who copied all the above mentioned books in clear handwriting were Diego Degrado of the city ward of San Martin, Mateo Severino of Xuchimilco, near Ullac. As soon as all this was copied, through the kindness of the two Fathers above mentioned, who spent a good many tomines (pennies) to pay the copyists, the author requested the Father Commissary, Fray Francisco de Rivera, to appoint three or four monks to give their opinion on these manuscripts at the Meeting of the Provincial Chapter, which was soon to take place. These friars came (read the work), and made their report to the "definitorio" of the Chapter. They told the "definitorio" that it was a work of great value and should receive all the help possible to finish it. However, some of the definidores were of the opinion that it was against the (professed) poverty of the Order to spend money for the copy of these writings, and therefore they ordered the author to dismiss his copyists and that he do himself whatever he wanted to with them, copy them in his own handwriting as best he might. But since he was then over seventy years old and his hand trembled, he could not do anything with them, nor was he able to obtain dispensation (on account of that) nor revocation of the order, and thus his work remained absolutely dormant for over five years. Then at the Meeting of the next General Chapter Father Fray Miguel Navarro was appointed custos custodum and as Provincial Father Fray Alonso de Escalona. Meanwhile the author had prepared a summary of all the books, their respective chapters and prologues, giving a short outline of the contents. This summary was taken to Spain by Fray Miguel Navarro and his companion, Fray Geronimo de Mendieta, and so all that had been written up to that time (in abstract) about the things concerning this land remained in Spain. In the meantime the Father Provincial took all the books of the said author and distributed them among all of the convents of the province so that they were, of course, perused by many of the Franciscan monks, who considered them as very valuable and important. After a few years, when Fray Miguel Navarro came back from the Meeting of the General Chapter, where he was appointed as Commissary of the Franciscan Order in New Spain, he ordered the books to be returned to the author upon the latter's petition. After all of them had been gathered once more, within the course of a year, more or less, they were again put into the hands of their author. In all this time nothing had been done on them, nor was there anybody to offer assistance for the translation of what remained into Spanish, until the Commissary General, Fray Rodrigo de Sequera, arrived from Spain. He looked them over and was very much pleased with them, and at once ordered the author to translate what remained into Spanish, facilitating everything necessary for a new and complete copy. In this copy, the Mexican text was arranged in one column and Spanish in the other, and in this shape the work was sent to Spain, because the President of the Council of the Indies, Exmo. Señor Don Juan de Ovando, wished to purchase it, after having had information about it from the summary (abstract) which Father Navarro had taken to Spain as stated above.

All the above stated is to the effect to say that this work was examined and approved by many in the course of many years, and that great suffering and misfortune was endured to get it into the shape it is at present.—*End of the Prologue.*

Chapter I.

The god Vitcilupuchtli was another Hercules, exceedingly robust, of great strength and very belicose, a great destroyer of towns and killer of people. In warfare he was like live-fire, greatly feared by his enemies. His emblem was the head of a very ferocious dragon which emitted fire from its mouth. This god was at the same time a sorcerer of the black arts and a wizard who could change himself into the shapes of diverse birds and beasts. While he lived, the magicians esteemed him very highly on account of his strength and prowess in war; after his death they venerated him as a god, offering him slaves whom they sacrificed in his presence. They endeavored to have these very well cared for and very well dressed and adorned with the well-known ear ornaments and neck-pieces used in these times. All this they did in order to pay him the utmost honor.

Another god very similar to him was worshipped around Tlaxcala. He was called Camaxtle.

The god Paynal was a sort of sub-captain of the first mentioned, who commanded as captain general when war was declared against some province or other. Paynal, as his representative, served when it became necessary to make a sudden attack against the enemy. On such occasions, Paynal, which means the speedy one, had to go personally to summon men so that they might go forthwith to fight the enemy. After his death they honored him with a feast at which one of the "sátrapas," priests, took the image of Paynal, richly bedecked with ornaments like a god's, and carried him thus in a very long procession, all running at top speed, the one who carried the image as well as all the rest of the accompaniment. By so doing they demonstrated the haste which was often necessary to resist enemies who attack before one realizes that they are there, lying in ambush.

Texcatlipoca was considered and held as the true and invisible god who walked all over the heavens and the earth and hell. They were afraid that whenever he trod on earth he caused wars, enmities and discords, all of which meant a great deal of trouble and anxieties. They said that he himself incited the people against one another, causing them to have wars, and for this reason they called him Necocyautl, which means sower of discord on both sides. They called him the only being who ruled the world, and the only one who could grant prosperity and wealth as he was also the only one who could take these away at will.

Tlaloctlamacazqui was the god of rain. They said he gave them the rains to irrigate the earth, and that these rains caused all the herbs, trees, fruits and grains to grow. It was he who also sent hail and lightning and storms on the water and all dangers of rivers and the sea. The name Tlaloctlamacazqui means that he is the god who resides in the terrestrial paradise and gives to man whatever he needs for his physical body. The celebrations held in his honor are cited in Book II among the feasts held in honor of the gods.

Quetzalcoatl, although a man, was held as a god who, they said, swept the road clear for the gods of the water. This they supposed to be a fact because always before the rainy season begins there are heavy winds and dust clouds, and this is the reason why Quetzalcoatl was called the god of the winds who swept the roads for the gods of rain so they might come on with their rain.

The sacrifices and ceremonies with which this god was honored can be found in Book II. The insignia and ornaments with which they adorned Quetzalcoatl are the following: on the head he wore a mitre with a tuft of plumes which are called quetzalli; the mitre was spotted to resemble a tiger-skin; his face and body were painted black. He wore a shirt in the form of an embroidered surplice which reached only as far as the waist; he wore turquoise ear-rings in mosaic; a gold necklace, from which hung some beautiful little sea-shells. As a device he carried on his shoulder a feather arrangement to represent flames of fire. Furthermore, he wore leggings from the knee down of tiger-skin, from which also pended little sea-shells. His feet were clad in sandals dyed black and dipped in margagita.[1] In his left hand he held a shield on which was a painting with five angles, which is called the wind-rose. In the right hand he held a sceptre in the shape of a bishop's crooked shepherd's staff, i. e.: the top of it formed a crook like a bishop's staff, richly adorned with precious stones, but it was not quite as long as a staff. The hilt looked more like the hilt of a sword. Quetzalcoatl was the high priest of the temple.

The first one of the principal goddesses adored by the Mexicans was called Civacoatl, and they say of her that she granted adverse things, such as poverty, mental depression, and sorrows. It is their belief that she frequently appeared, dressed as a lady of rank who visits a palace (frequents royalty); they also said of her that at night she called aloud or howled in the air. Civacoatl means woman of the snake; they also call her

[1]This is probably margajita, or marcasita—marcasite, that is, white pyrite, which the Ancient Mexicans used either pulverized or in small prisms.

Tonantzin, which is "our mother." According to these two items it would seem that they knew what happened between our mother Eve and the snake, who deceived her. The clothes in which she appeared were white, and her hair was done up in such a way that it formed two little horns crossed on her forehead. They also say that she carried a cradle on her back like a woman who carries her child; that she mingled with the other women in the tianquiztli (market) and, suddenly disappearing, she left the cradle behind. When the other women noticed the cradle forgotten there by someone they would look into it to see what was there, and would find a piece of flint like a lance point, which was used by them to kill those they sacrificed to the gods, and they at once knew that it was Civacoatl who had left the cradle in their midst.

The goddess Chicomecoatl was the goddess of food, food that is eaten as well as beverages; and they depicted her as wearing a crown on her head; in her right hand she held a goblet; in the left a shield, on which a large flower was painted, her cuoytl ycipilli (tunic) and her sandals were vermillion in color. She must have been the first woman who made bread and other sweetmeats and stews.

Now follows a goddess whom they called the mother of the gods, heart of the earth (Centeotl or Civeles) and our grandmother. She was the goddess of medicine and medicinal herbs. She was venerated by physicians and surgeons, by those who bled people, and also by midwives and those who gave herbs for abortion; by soothsayers who tell the good or bad fortune children are going to have, according to the date, time or signs of their birth. She was likewise venerated by those who predict the future with grains of corn, the ones who do it by looking into the water in a bowl, as well as those who tell fortunes by means of small strings which they tied together and called the mecatlepouhque and all such who extracted tiny worms from mouth and eyes, and small pebbles from other parts of the body, calling this procedure tetlaquilique. She was also adored by those people who had baths or "temazcalis" in their homes, all of whom placed the image of this goddess in their baths, and they called her Temazcalteci, which means the grandmother of the baths. All these people mentioned above made each year a feast to this goddess, and for this purpose they were wont to buy a woman whom they adorned with ornaments such as behooved this goddess, such as they are represented on pictures they have of her; and every day while her feast lasted they held dances for this woman, entertaining and feasting her greatly to prevent her getting sad or crying on account of her approaching death. They fed her delicately and urged and tempted her with all manner of food, entreating her to eat as if she were a great lady. They played war games before her in those days, and planned many different shows in distinctive devices amid great shouting and rejoicing. They presented prizes to the soldiers who fought before her in order to give her pleasure and amuse her. When the hour of her death had come and after having killed her and two others who had to accompany her in death, they flayed her and a man or sátrapa (priest) dressed himself up in her skin, walking through the whole town and boasting a great deal in this garb. This goddess had her mouth and chin down to the throat dyed with ulli, which is a black gum, and another round mark like a plaster of the same dye on the cheek. On the head she wore a sort of cap or turban made of twisted and knotted cloth, the ends of the knot falling over her back. In the knot itself there was a tuft of feathers with plumes sticking out like flames; these hung over toward the back of the head. She wore a vipilli, which had at its lower end a wide and indented band which, ending in edges and points, looked like a saw. Her skirts were white. She wore sandals on her feet. In her left hand she held a shield with a round gold clasp in the center. In the right hand she held a broom, which is the implement for sweeping.

Another goddess was called Tzaputlatena, because it is said she was born in the town of Tzaputla. She was also sometimes called the mother of Tzaputla, because she was the first one who invented the resin known by the name of vxitl, which is an oil obtained skilfully from pine resin, and which cures many diseases. In the first place, it is very efficient against a sort of pustules or itch (mange) which begins on the head and is called quaxococuixtli; it is also good against another similar outbreak of pustules on the head called chaquachiciuztli; likewise is this oil used for head-itch, for hoarseness, against fissures (cracks) in the skin of the feet and cracked lips and the ringworm on face or hands, as well as against eczema and many other complaints. As this woman must have been the first one who found this oil, she was placed among the goddesses and all these who make or sell that oil, vxitl, celebrate a feast-day in her honor, offering her sacrifices.

The Civapipilti were all the women who died in giving birth to their first child, and thus became canonized as goddesses, according to Book VI, Chapter 28, where the ceremonies celebrated upon their death and their canonization, are described at length. We shall here simply state that it is said that these goddesses are said to always travel together through the air and to appear whenever they chose to those on earth, inflicting boys and girls with sickness such as palsy (paralysis) and entering into human bodies. In order to injure children, they were said to wait on crossroads, and that for this reason parents would forbid their children to leave the house on certain days of the year when these goddesses were supposed to come down to earth. Whenever anyone became ill with paralysis or another sudden disease, or when he became possessed by some demon, they said these goddesses had done it, and for that reason (in order to appease them) they celebrated a feast in their honor, offering in the temple dedicated to them, or on crossroads, bread fashioned into diverse figures; some of these looked like butterflies, others like lightning as it descends from heaven and is called Tlavitequiliztli, or else like large tamales called Xucuichtlamatzxoalli, or toasted corn, izquitl. Images of these goddesses have a whitish face as if it had been painted with some very white paint like titzatl, also the arms and legs; their cars were of gold, the hair was dressed like that of ladies of quality with their little curls or horns. Their vipil was painted with black waves; their skirts were of various colors, and they wore white sandals.

Chalchiuhtliycue was the goddess of water; she is depicted as a woman, for they say that she was the sister of the gods of rain they call Tlaloques. They honored her because they said that she had power over the sea and the rivers, and could drown those who navigated on the waters, causing tempests and whirlwinds that would flood the boats and barges and other vessels happening to be on the water. They made a feast to this goddess in which they call her Etzalqualiztli, which feast is described in Book II, Chapter 7, with all the ceremonies and sacrifices in her honor. Her devotees were all those who derived their livelihood and gain from the water, like men who sell goods from their canoe, and all such that sell things in big earthen jars on the market-place. They represented this goddess with a yellow face, a necklace of precious stones from which hung a gold medal, around the neck. On the head she had a crown made of paper, painted pale blue with tufts of green feathers and certain balls or pellets, some of which hung down toward the back and others toward the front of the crown, all of them light blue. Her ears were made of turquoise mosaic, and she was dressed in a vipil and skirt of pale blue with fringes, from which pended small sea-shells. In the left hand she held a shield with a wide, round leaf on it, which grows in the water and is called atlacuccona; in the right hand she held a cup with a cross on it, which was made just like the cross on the tabernacle in which the holy sacrament is carried by only one man (when the tabernacle is small), this cup and cross represented the sceptre of the goddess. She wore white sandals. This goddess and two others, one Chicumecoatl, goddess of food, and Vixtocivatl, the goddess of the salt, were greatly venerated by lords and kings because these three supported and fed the common people so they might live and multiply. There is more about this goddess in the above-mentioned chapter of Book II.

Now we come to Tlaculteutl, the goddess of carnal matters, who had three different names. First, Tlaculteutl, which means goddess of carnality. The second name was Ixcuina; they called her thus because they said there were four sisters; the first born or oldest was Tiacapan; the second was the youngest and they called her Teicu, the third was the middle one, called Tlaco; the fourth was the youngest of all Xucotzin. All these four sisters were the goddesses of carnality; in these names all women are included who are fit for the carnal act. The third name of the goddess is Tlaclqüani, which means eater of filthy things. This signifies that, according to their sayings, all such carnal men and women confessed their sins to these goddesses, no matter how uncouth and filthy they might have been, and they were forgiven. It is also said that this goddess or these goddesses had the power to produce lust; that they could provoke carnal intercourse and favored illicit love affairs, and that after such sins had been committed, they also held the power of pardoning and cleansing them of the sin, forgiving them if they confessed them to their Sátrapas (priests), who were the soothsayers who kept the books of divination and of the fate of the newly born, of witchcraft and prognostication as well as of ancient traditions, which were transmitted from mouth to mouth from the ancients down to them.

When a penitent was ready for confession, he would at once go in search of one of these priests or divines to whom they were wont to confess, saying to him: "Sir, I want to go to god almighty who is the protector of all (this god almighty is called Yoallichccatlostees-tezcatlipoca) for I wanted to speak in secret of my sins." Hearing this, the Sátrapa would answer: "Be very welcome, my son, for what you say you wish to do is for your salvation and advantage." After saying this he would at once consult his book of divination which was called Tonalamatl, in order to find out by this book what day would be the most opportune for such a deed. As soon as he had found the propitious day, he would say: "Come on such and such a day, for on that day the sign is favorable to do this successfully." When the appointed day had come for the penitent to return he would buy a new mat (petate), white incense which they call copalli, and wood for the fire, over which the copalli was to be burned. If the penitent was a prominent man or invested with some official dignity, the priest would go to his house to confess him (or by chance the penitent man even being a prominent person might choose to go to the house of the priest). Upon arrival (wherever it might be), the place where the new mat was to be spread was very well swept and the confessor seated himself on the mat; the fire was lighted and he, the Sátrapa, threw the incense into it, and addressed himself to the fire, saying to it: "I wish to inform you, oh, lord, who are the father and the mother of all the gods and who are the most ancient god, that there has come today one of your vassals, this your servant, who comes here weeping in deep sorrow; he comes with great suffering; by all this it is clear that he has erred, that he stumbled and met with and found some of the obscenity of sin even with serious crime worthy of death, and he is very sad about it and downcast. Our very merciful lord who are our protector and supporter, accept the penitence and listen to the anguish of your servant and vassal." This prayer finished, the priest then turned to the penitent and spoke to him as follows: "Son, you have come into the presence of god, the helper and supporter of all; you came to tell him your inward shame and rottenness, to disclose unto him the secrets of your heart; be careful not to lead a riotous life nor to throw yourself headlong into it, nor get lost by lying in the presence of our lord. Rid yourself and throw out all your shame and disgrace in the presence of our lord, whose name is Yoallichectla, that is to say, Tezcatlipoca. It is a fact that you are before him (in his presence), although you are not worthy to see him; and even if he doesn't speak to you, because he is invisible and not palpable, mind how you come before him, with what kind of a heart; do not fear to declare your secrets in his presence, tell him your life, tell your (good) deeds in the same way you confessed your excesses and offenses, pour out your evil deeds in his presence, tell them all sorrowfully to our lord god, who is the protector of all, and who holds his arms open and is ready to embrace you and to carry you. See to it that you do not omit anything out of shame or cowardice!" When the penitent had heard all this, he took the oath to tell the truth,—in their own way of taking an oath, which is touching the earth with the hand and licking off whatever had stuck to it. He then threw copal into the fire, which was another way of taking an oath. Then he seated himself opposite the priest and, considering him (in this instance), as god's representative, he began his confession, saying: "Oh, lord, who accepts and helps everyone, listen to my baseness and rottenness. In your presence I disclose myself. I throw out all my shameful acts as many as I have committed, for, to be sure, none of the wickedness I am guilty of is hidden from you, because all things are apparent and clear to you." After this he at once began to tell his sins in the order he had committed them, with entire calm and distinctness, like a person who recites a poem or legend, very slowly and well enunciated, or like one who goes on a very straight road without deviating to one side or the other. After having thus confessed everything he had done, the priest spoke to him and said, "My son, you have spoken before our lord god, telling him of all your wicked acts; now also in his name I shall tell you what you are obliged to do. When the goddesses called Civapipilti come down to earth, or when the feast to the goddesses of carnality whose name is Yxtuiname, is celebrated, you are to fast for four days, punishing your stomach and your mouth, and on the very day of the feast of Yxtuiname, in the morning or at daybreak, you are to make the proper penitence as suits your sins, and that is to pass through your tongue from one side to the other some twigs of what they call teucalcacatl or tlacotl, and if you should wish to do more than that, pass them through the ears, one or the other. This you do as penitence and atonement for your sins; it is not to be as a merit, but as a penitence for your evil deeds. You are to pierce first your tongue in the middle with a maguey thorn and through that same hole you will pass the twigs, passing each one in front of your face and, as you pull them out of the tongue, throw them behind you toward your back. If you should wish to unite (tie) all of them, you may attach one to the other, be there four hundred or eight hundred, in short, just as many as you wish to pass through your tongue; doing this, all the wickedness and filth you committed will be forgiven you." If the penitent has not committed neither very many nor serious sins, the priest to whom he confesses tells him, "My son, you are too fast; tire your stomach by hunger and your mouth by thirst, eating only once a day at noon and repeating this for four days," or he might tell some penitent to go and offer papers at the accustomed places and make images and to cover these images—as many and fashioned as his devotion would command,— with these papers and go through the devotional ceremony of singing and dancing, as is customary in their presence." Or he might say: "You offended god by getting drunk, so you must appease the god of wine, called Totochti, and when you go to comply with your penance you are to go at night, naked with only a paper in front and one at the back to cover your privy parts; when you are ready to return after your prayers are offered, you are to throw the papers that had covered your front and back at the feet of the gods that are there."

Once his confession made and after having received the penance he was to make, the penitent would go home and try never again to incur in the same sins he had just confessed, because it was said that if these same sins were repeated then there was no more absolution.

Confessions of great sins, such as adultery, were only made by old men, and this for the simple reason to escape worldly punishment meted out for such sins; to escape from being condemned to death, which was either having their head crushed or ground to powder between two stones. It must be said that the priests who heard confessions were utterly discreet, never disclosing what they had learned in confession; this was because they considered that it was not they personally who had heard these confessions, but their god, who was the only one before whom sin was revealed, hence it was not supposed that any human heard them, nor had they been told to human ears, only to god (in his representative).

It is well known that even after Christianity had been implanted, they (those Indians) insisted on confessing the most serious and nefarious sins, such as homicide, adultery, etc., and that by carrying out the penitence (penance) imposed in expiation as in times past, the courts of justice also would pardon them. Even now, if one of them kills or commits adultery, he will come to our homes or monasteries and without saying a word about their evil deeds, simply say that they want to do penance. They will work in the orchard, they will sweep the house, or do anything else they are ordered; after a few days they will go to confession, and after that will tell about their crimes, and give the reason why they came to do penance. After confession they ask a statement signed by the confessor with the intention to show it to those in power, be it the governor or the mayors, and thus let them know that they have done penance and have gone to confession, therefore justice has no case against them. Hardly any of the friars (monks) nor of the civil authorities understand this, mainly because they do not know anything about that ancient custom mentioned above, but rather think that the Indians ask for the certificate to show compliance with religious duties (to show that they have confessed that year). We are well aware of this condition on account of the great experience we acquired among them. It is said that the old men confessed their great (serious) sins of the flesh from which fact we may deduce that they probably had greatly sinned in their youth but did not confess until they were old, but that they could continue sinning while young, for it was their belief that once confessed they could not sin again. From the above we may safely deduce that those Indians of New Spain considered it their obligation to go to confession at least once in their lifetime, and that they did this even long before they had any knowledge of the Christian faith.

Now we come to the minor gods. The first one of these is Xiuhtecutli, who has two other names, one being Yxcocauhqui, meaning yellow face; the other is Cuecaltzin, which means flame of fire. He was also called Viveteutl, which is ancient god; he was considered by all as a father according to the effects he caused, because he burns and the flame lights and burns. All these are effects which cause fear, but he has other attributes which call for love and reverence, such as the heat that warms those who are cold, it cooks the food to eat, frying, baking, boiling and toasting it. It (the fire or heat from it) produces the salt (by evaporation of the brine), and the thick honey, coal and lime. It heats the baths for bathing, it makes the oil called Uxitl. With fire we can heat the lye and water to wash soiled and old clothes, so that they will become almost new. The feast to this god was celebrated each year at the end of the month called 13 calli[1] and they dressed his image with all the vestments, ornaments and plumes of the principal lord; in Mochteccusoma's time they dressed this god to resemble him, and even in times of other rulers of the past they were wont to dress him like one of these and place him upon his altar or throne. In his presence they decapitated many quails, sprinkling their blood in front of him, offering him copal (incense) as to a god; also a sort of cakes called quilltamalli made of wild amaranth seed, which they also ate themselves in his honor; in all districts of the town, in every house they offered them, however, first to the fire before eating them, and if they were not first offered, they would not touch them. The priests designated to the service of this god and who were called Ybebeyoban, which means "his old men" danced before him all day, singing as they danced in their own way, playing on conch-shells like horns, beating drums and teponaztli, which are drums made of wood, and in their hands they held rattles to accompany their singing. These rattles are like the toy or baby rattles with which children are quieted when they cry, and also like those used in the fields. On that day they (the Mexican people in general) did not cook bread in comal (the flat earthenware pan in which maize cakes are cooked in Mexico), and they took care that no one should do it anywhere; nor could they cook anything else in comal, to avoid that anyone should touch the fire, since it was the first day of the year on which this kind of tamales were eaten and offered (to the god). On the occasion of this same feast the fathers and mothers of children caught snakes, some caught frogs, or a kind of fish which is called joviles (today juiles) or small water-lizards called axélotl, or birds or any other tiny animal, and these they threw into the home fire, and when they were well toasted the children would eat them, saying, "Our father the fire eats toasted things." That night the old men and women drank uctli, which is wine of the land; before they tasted it themselves, however, they sprinkled some in the four directions (parts) of the house, saying that by so doing they gave the fire a taste of it, humoring it thus as a god in the form of an offering or sacrifice. Every four years a very solemn feast was offered to this god by the lord of the land with all his principal citizens (chieftains), and he arranged a dance in front of the house or temple of that god. At this feast celebrated every four years, not only old men and women, but everybody, youths and maidens, boys and girls, drank wine, or pulque, for which reason this feast was called "pillavano," which means a feast at which children drink wine or pulque. The parents of children this day selected godfathers and godmothers for their children, giving them some presents. These godparents had to carry their god-

[1]That is the feast called Hucy Micailhuitl, or feast of the great deceased.

children on their backs to the temple of the god of the fire, whom they also called Yxcocauhqui; there, in the temple, in front of the god, they perforated the children's ears in the presence of the godparents, who were called Ymavivanyntlavan. After this ceremony all, parents, godparents, and the children, ate together. The image of this god represents a naked man whose chin was dyed black with a resin called ulli, and a bib of red stone in the parting of the chin. On the head he had a crown of paper painted in different colors and with diverse designs; on top of the crown were several green feather tufts imitating flames, on each side hung a few feather balls, looking like pendants over the ears. In the perforations of the ears he wore ear-rings of turquoise mosaic. He carried on his shoulder (or back) a plumage made to look like a dragon's head, fashioned of yellow feathers and small sea-shells; jingles were attached around the ankles; in his left hand he carried a shield with five green stones which are called chalchivites, placed in the form of a cross over a gold plate covering almost the entire shield; in his right hand he held a sort of sceptre consisting of a round gold plate with a hole through the center and at the top of this sceptre as crown or termination there were two globes, one larger than the other, with a point on the smaller one. They call this sceptre Tlachicloni, which means look-out or observatory, because he (the god) hid his face behind it, looking out through the opening in the center of the gold-plate.

Another divinity was called Macuilxochitl, and was also considered as a god, like the god of the fire. He was especially the god of those who dwelt in the houses of lords or in the palaces of the chiefs. The feast celebrated in his honor was the one called Xochilhuitl, which was a movable feast and is described in Book IV under divinatory art. All those who celebrated this feast, men or women, fasted for four days previous, and if during this fast any man had intercourse with a woman or vice versa, they said he or she soiled their fast, and this offended the god terribly, so he gave them dreadful diseases of the privy parts if they did misbehave, such as piles, furuncles, venereal diseases, bubo, etc., and it was understood that all such ailments were punishments meted out by this god for reasons above given, and they made him promises and vows to relieve them and relent his resentment, lifting the scourge off them. When the day of the feast Xochilhuitl, or feast of the flowers, was due, and after they all had fasted during four preceding days on which they did not eat any chillioaxi and only ate once a day at noon and at midnight they drank a sort of pap or gruel called Tlaquilolatulli, which means colored or tinted gruel with a flower placed in the center on top of it; this sort of fast was called the fast of the flowers. Even those who did not leave off eating chilli and other such tasty things only ate them once a day, at noon.

Others fasted, eating unleavened bread (panes acimos),—that is, that the corn of which they make this kind of bread is not mixed with lime before grinding it, thus producing a kind of fermentation, but ground it dry and made their bread with this flour, cooking it in comal (earthenware pan); they did not eat chilli nor anything else with it and also only ate once a day, at noon.

On the fifth day, which was the day of the feast, everyone dressed in the same clothes as the god, as if they were his image or someone who meant the same as the god, and, attired in that way, they held dances and chants accompanied by drums and jingles (rattles-toponaztli). At noon of the same day they cut the heads off of many quails, spilling the blood in front of the god and his image; some bled their own ears in front of him; still others pierced their tongues with maguey thorns, passing a number of straws (twigs) through the opening, bleeding freely; they made many other votive offerings in the temple. One of the ceremonies was to make five tamales of corn, neither very thick nor very round, which they called pan de ayuno (unleavened bread). These loaves were large and had an arrow stuck in the center. These they called xuchimitl, offering of the people. Such individuals as felt like doing so offered five such tamales of small size on a wooden plate, with some chilmolli in a cup; again others offered two cakes called tzoalli, instead of ulli, black gum, which many offered on wooden plates. One of these two cakes was . . . . .[1], the other vermillion. In general people offered many diverse things, toasted corn, toasted corn mixed with honey and flour made of the seeds of wild amaranthus; bread adorned with a certain figure in the shape of lightning as it crosses the skies and which they call Xonecuilli; or bread shaped like butterflies; unleavened bread called yotlaxcalli; cakes of seeds of the wild amaranthus, cakes shaped like shields of that same seed; also shaped like arrows or swords; even dolls they made out of that same dough.

For this same feast, all the chieftains and Calpixques (stewards or rent-gatherers) of the district of Mexico which bordered on the surrounding war-districts, brought the captives they had either made themselves or bought and delivered them to the stewards of Mexico (city) for these latter to keep until the time came to sacrifice them before the idols. If one of these slaves or captives ran away in the meantime the Calpixque in whose care they had been given was obliged to buy another one to replace the one who had fled.

The image of this god looked like a naked man whose skin had been stripped off or dyed with vermillion; his mouth and chin were painted

[1]There is evidently a word left out in Bustamante's copy.

white, black and light blue; the face a bright red; he had a crown dyed a light green, with feather tufts of the same color; a few tassels hung from the crown towards the back; he carried a device or plumage on the shoulders (back) that looked like a flag or banner stuck on a hill; at the top of this banner were green feather tufts. His body was clothed in a bright red mantle which hung to his thigh; this mantle had a fringe, from which hung little sea-shells. His feet were clad in sandals very elaborately made. In his left hand he held a shield, which was white and had four stones in the center, two and two together; lastly also a sceptre, which was shaped like a heart with green feather tufts on top, while from the bottom of it hung other tufts of green and yellow feathers.

Omecatl, which means two canes, is the god of invitations (treats) who, they say, has power (rules) over invitations (festivities) and guests. When, for instance, some prominent men, chieftains or lords, invited all their relatives to give them to eat, present them with blankets and flowers, that they might dance, whirl about and sing in their homes, the one who gave this festivity went to get the image of that god to take it to his house. Some of the priests in the service of this god in his temple would carry the image to the host's house. They said that if they did not do this honor to the god as they should, he would get angry and appear to the host in his dreams to scold and blame him, saying: "You bad man, why did you not honor me as is due me? Do you know that now I shall leave you, I shall forsake you, and you will pay me fully the affront you committed." If he was very angry he showed his anger by mixing animal or human hair with the food and drink in order to sadden the guests and dishonor their host, and when the latter went to communion on the god's feast day, he often would become ill, or when he ate or drank, would choke on the food or beverage, or when he walked, would stumble and often fall. When they celebrated the feast of this god, which took place at night, they communed with their body, that is, by fasting, and for this communion the chiefs and stewards and all those who had charge of the districts, made the figure of a big, thick bone, round like an elbow, and called it the bone of the god. Before communion they ate and drank pulque. At dawn, after having been eating and drinking, they pricked the stomach of the one who represented the image of this god with pins or something of the kind until hurting him. After that they distributed the figure of this dough, which they called Tzoalli, dividing it into three parts and each one ate as much as he could. All those who communed here, had it said and understood that the coming year on the feast of this god they were to contribute toward it providing everything necessary to be spent for it.

The image of this deity was that of a man seated on a bunch of cypress; his face was spotted black and white with a paper crown tightly adjusted around the forehead, with a long and wide scarf, which was tied at the back of the head, laced by something that looked like tassels. Around the crown were wound a few beads of chalchivites (Mex. emeralds). His mantle was like a net; a wide fringe with flowers strewn in it, these latter woven into the same fringe; he had a shield standing close by, from which hung wide tassels at the bottom. In his right hand he held a sceptre which had a round, perforated medallion on it, like a bull's eye (skylight or spy-hole). This sceptre was resting on the edge of a round table, and above it had a pyramidal capital. This sceptre was called tlachialia, which means observatory (watch-tower or lookout), because he covered his face with the medallion and looked through the spy-hole.

To Yxtlilton, which means the little negro, by another name also called Tlaltetecuin, they made a tabernacle of painted boards where his image stood. In his oratory or temple were a good many glazed earthenware tubs and water jars with water, all of which were covered with boards or comales; the water they contained was called tlilalt, meaning "black water". When a child was ill they took it to the temple of god Yxtlilton and, uncovering one of these jars, they gave the sick child some of that water to drink, and it cured it, and if anyone wished to show his devotion to this god by celebrating a feast, he would take his image to his home. This image was neither a statue nor a painting, but simply one of his priests who dressed himself in the insignia, and when they came to take him from the temple they burnt incense or copal in front of him until he reached the house where the celebration was to take place. This consisted of dances and songs, customary among them. Their way of dancing and whirling about is different from ours, and they called these dances macevalistli. For this many got together and paired off in twos and threes, in a large circle, according to their number. They carried flowers in their hands and with their finery they wore plumes. They all made the same motion with body, feet and hands at one time, which was worth seeing, for being very artistic. Their motions were executed to the beating of drums and rattles. They all sang together in chorus, with very sonorous voices, the praise of the god whose feast they celebrated. They have the same custom today, only dedicated to another personality. They govern their motions in posture and dress according to what they sing; they dispose of a great many different movements as as well as a great variety of tunes for their singing, but it is all very graceful and even highly mystical. Idolatry is not uprooted as yet.

As soon as the image reached the house of the man who was offering the god this celebration, they ate and drank first then commenced the dancing and singing with the god whom they so honored. After he had danced with the others a long while, he entered into the house and went to the storeroom where they kept the pulque or wine which they were wont to drink, in many jars all of them covered with boards or comales or earthenware pans, all roughly plastered onto the jugs. These jars had been thus covered for four days, and the god now opened one or many of them, and this opening ceremony was called tlaiacaxapotla, which means "this wine is new". As soon as the jars had thus been opened, the god and these with him drank of that wine, going out into the courtyard of the home where the ceremonies took place. They now went to where the jars of the black water were kept, dedicated to this god, and which had also been sealed for four days. The priest who represented the god opened them and if, after they had thus been opened, there appeared in any of them a bit of dirt, such as a little straw, a human or animal hair or a bit of charcoal, they at once pronounced the host of this festivity a bad man, an adulterer, a thief, or a man given to the carnal sins. They forthwith faced him with the accusation that he was an addict of one of these vices or that he was a sower of discord or corrupting vice, making these accusations in presence of everyone. When the priest who played the part of the god left that house (such a house) they gave him rugs or shawls which they called ixquen, which means opening of the face (of the eyes), because the host of such a festivity felt ashamed if any impurity was found in that black water. The manner of dress of this god will be explained at the end of this book.

The god called Opuchtli was counted among the deities whose collective name was Tlaloques, which means inhabitants of the earthly paradise, although they knew that he was a mere man. They attributed to him the invention of fishing nets as well as of an implement to kill fish and which they call minacachalli, which is like a "fisga"[1] although it has only three points in triangle like a trident with which they injure the fish; they also kill birds with it. Opuchtli also invented the lazoes to kill birds and the oars to row.

When the fishermen and people of the water front who derive their livelihood from that element and who adore him as their god celebrated his feast, they offered him food and wine of the kind they call uctli, by another name, pulque. They also offered him green corn-stalks, flowers, smoke canes which they call yietl, white incense called copalli, an odoriferous herb the name of which is yiauhtli, which they strew in front of him in the same way they spread mats of rattan, rush-rugs, for processions to pass. During this festivity they also used timbrels placed in

[1]Fisga—harpoon.

hollow sticks and which sounded almost like rattles; furthermore, they throw in front of the image toasted corn called mumuchtli, a sort of corn which when toasted opens up and shows the white marrow (popcorn), forming a very white flower. They said this represented hail, which is attributed to the water gods. The old priests, in whose care this god was given, and the old women, sang the songs of praise to him. His image represents a naked man painted entirely black with a grayish face more or less the color of quail-feathers. He wore a paper crown of different colors, fashioned like a rose, one row of petals overlapping the other, and on top there was a green feather tuft which came out of a yellow tassel; large and long tassels hung down towards the back from this crown. He wore a green stole crossed (in front) like the one worn by priests when celebrating mass. Around the waist he wore green paper bands which hung down as far as the knees; his feet were clad in white sandals; in his left hand he held a shield painted red, and in the center of the red field there was a white flower with four leaves which formed a cross, and from these leaves projected again four points which also were leaves (petals) of the same flower. His right hand held a sceptre in the shape of a chalice with something like a socket with arrows (quiver?).

Xipetotec, meaning flayed, was the god honored by all those who lived on the seashore. He was originary of Zapotlan, a town in the state of Xalisco. To this god they attributed the following diseases: small-pox, tumours that form anywhere on the body, itch, also diseases of the eyes such as the soreness of eyes resulting from excessive drinking, and all other eye complaints. Anyone suffering from the above-mentioned diseases made a promise to this god to dress in a (human) skin when his feast was to be celebrated, which feast was called Tlacaxipealiztli, that is, "flaying of men." In the course of this festivity they executed a dance which looks very much like the Spanish "Juege de cañas" namely, a skirmish on horseback, in Spain, with spear-throwing, these spears being made of a light reed (caña). Two bands would be stationed opposite each other, the first one was the band of the image of Totec or the god himself, all his followers dressed in skins of men they had just killed and flayed, all of them still fresh and bleeding. The other band consisted of the daring and courageous soldiers and other martial and fighting men, to whom death meant nothing, and who now, fearless and bold, of their own free-will, stepped forth to fight their opponents in sham battle, pursuing each other close to the enemy line running in full flight back to their own place. After the ammunition was exhausted on both sides the party of the god Totec, dressed in human skins, went through the whole town, entering every house to beg alms, anything, for the love of their god. In the houses they entered the people would make them sit on little bundles of branches of the tzapote tree, throwing about their necks strings of ears of corn and chains of flowers which reached down to their armpits; they adorned them with garlands and gave them pulque to drink, which is their wine.

If a woman fell ill with any of the above mentioned diseases she would present her votive offering on the feast of that god in the way she had promised. The image of this deity represents a naked man with one half of his body painted yellow, the other half tawny; his face is ornamented on both sides by a narrow band which reaches from the forehead down to the chin. On the head he wears a little cap of diverse colors, with tassels that hang down towards the back. He is clothed in the skin of a man; the hair is parted into two braids, the ears are of gold. He wears a short green skirt as far as the knees, with small sea-shells around the bottom. His feet are clad in sandals; he has a yellow shield with a red coping all around. He holds his sceptre with both hands, and it is of the shape of the heart of a poppy with a little quiver stuck straight into it.

It is supposed that Yiacatecutli, god of merchants, was the one who started trading among those people, and that for this reason the guild of the merchants adopted him as their god and honored him in different ways, one being to offer him paper with which they covered his statues wherever they found them. They also venerated the cane (stick) with which they walked, which was a solid cane called utatl (also otate). They have still another kind of cane or walking stick made of a solid light black cane without a knot, and which looks like reed such as is used in Spain.[1] All merchants used that kind of canes on the road. When they reached the place where they were to spend the night, they would gather all their canes and tie them into one bundle, which they then stuck at the head of the sleeping place or camp. They would sprinkle blood in front of this bundle, which blood they obtained by bleeding their own ears, tongue, arms or legs. Then they offered incense by building a fire and burning copal in front of this bundle of sticks, which they considered as the image of the god Yiacatecutli, and by this means they asked him to protect them from all danger. These merchants traveled over the whole land, bartering, trading, buying in some place and selling in another what they had purchased. They also travel through towns, along the seashore, and in the interior. There isn't a place they do not pry into and visit, here buying, there selling; it is neither too hot for them in this place nor too cold in that one. They don't shun a road because it is too rough nor too difficult to search for whatever is there, either pretty or valuable or advantageous to buy and sell again. These

[1]The well known Malacca cane.

traders suffer great hardships and are exceedingly daring; they go anywhere, even if it should be an enemy's domain and they are very sly in their deals with strangers, in learning their languages, as well as in their tactics, attaining through kindness what they want, thus gaining their confidence. They find out where the feathers (plumes) and the precious stones can be had, or the gold; there they purchase them and take them to where they are worth a great deal. They also know where to go to find exquisite and valuable skins of beasts, and where to resell them at high prices. Likewise do they deal in precious cups of many different kinds and material adorned with diverse painted figures, and which are used in all the different districts; some of these cups have covers made of tortoise shell and spoons of the same to stir the cocoa; there are cups with covers painted in different colors and figures, made to resemble a leaf of the "vinarbol"[1] and with various kinds of beautiful sticks with which they stirred their cocoa. If they are forced to enter an enemy's realm, they first learn the language of these people; they adopt their mode of dress so they might not be taken for strangers, but for people of that same country. It often happened that the enemy recognized them, capturing and killing them. If one or two or more were able to escape, they were wont to notify the chief or principal lord of the province, as, for instance, Mocteccuzuma or any of his predecessors, bringing him as an offering some of the treasures of those countries, making a present of these things in remuneration of their sufferings, and in order to be honored by their people and considered courageous. They would give him an amber bib, which is a large, transparent, yellow stone which hangs from the lower lip as a sign that he was brave and noble, too; this bib was highly valued.

Whenever these traders or merchants left for such a voyage to foreign lands they took leave of their relatives amid great ceremonies, in accordance with ancient rites. They remained absent many years, and when they returned they brought back great riches (many treasures). In order to display what they had and to give an account of the countries they had visited and the things they had seen, soon upon their return they would invite all the traders (merchants), especially the principal ones, as well as the chieftains of the town, and arranged a great festivity for them. These festivities they called "washing of feet." The guests did great honor to the cane (walking-stick) with which the traveler had gone and come back; considered it the image of Yiacatecutli, god of the merchants, who had favored them to travel the roads and brought them back safely. In order to do due honor to the cane they placed it in one of the temples they had in the different quarters of the town, and which they call cal-

[1]Probably a name for the grape-vine.

pulli, which means church of the district or parish. In the calpulli to which this particular trader belonged, he put the cane in an honored place, and when the dinner was served to his guests, he first placed food, flowers, and acayietl (small tube containing incense of odoriferous herbs which was burned in front of the stick); and even afterwards, after the invitation was over, each time the trader was about to eat he first placed food and all the other things in front of the stick (cane), which he now kept in his own home, in the private oratory thereof. All these traders, after returning from one of their voyages, as they now were wealthy, would buy male and female slaves, whom they offered to their god on his feast, this generally being Yiacatecutli, who had five brothers and one sister, all being held as deities, and according to the size of their devotion, they would sacrifice slaves to each one of them separately on his personal feast, or to all together, or to the sister alone. One of the brothers was called Chiconquiavitl, the other Xomocuil, the next Nacxitl, another Cochimetl, the fifth Yacapitzaoac; the sister's name was Chalmecacioatl. To each one of these or to one or the other they offered one or more slaves, sacrificing (killing) them in front of these gods, dressed in the insignia of the respective one as if he were his image. There was a regular fair in a town (village) called Azcapotzalco, at two leagues from Mexico where slaves, men and women, were sold. There those who wanted any went to select among a great number of them, for they were very careful that the slave, male or female, should be without blemish of body and free of disease of any kind. After having purchased these slaves, men or women, they were very well treated; they bathed them in hot water, gave them well to eat and drink and in abundance, so that these slaves grew fat, for they were to be eaten and offered to their god. They also feasted them, making them dance and sing at times on the flat roofs of their houses or on the public square; there they sang all the songs they knew until they became tired of singing. They did in no way fear or mind the sort of death awaiting them.

These slaves were killed at the feast called panquetzalistli, and all the time before that feast they were treated to everything, as we have said.

If among these slaves there was a man who appeared to have fair judgment, was quick and intelligent in serving and perhaps could sing well, or if there was a woman among them who was willing and able to prepare food and drink, could embroider or weave, the chiefs or prominent people would buy them for their own service in their homes, and thus these escaped from being sacrificed.

The image of this god represents an Indian who travels with his cane; the face was spotted black and white; in his hair he wore two tassels of the fine feathers (plumes) called quetzalli; these plumes were tied in the center of the head where the hair was gathered like a sheaf at the top (of head). His ears were of gold; he wore a blue mantle, and over the blue was thrown a black net so that the blue shone through the meshes of the net. The mantle had a fringe all around with flowers woven into it. Around the ankles he wore yellow leather straps from which hung diminutive sea-shells. His feet were clad in sandals gracefully made and very elaborate. His shield was yellow with a light blue spot in the center quite plain, without any ornamentation; in his right hand he held a cane such as traders (travelers) carry on the road.

Napatecutli is the god of those who make cypress (rush) mats, and he belongs to the class they call Tlaloques. They say that he is the one who invented the art of making mats, and it is for this reason that the makers of mats "petates," and also those who weave seats for stools, which are called icpales and hurdles, tolqüextli. They said that through the grace of this god cyperus, reed and rush were planted and grew, thus enabling them to work at their trade. At the same time they believed this god to produce rain. They celebrated his feast wherever the above-mentioned things were made, and revered and worshipped him, demanding of him to give them what he was wont to give, namely, water, reeds, or rush for their work, etc. For this feast they bought a slave to sacrifice in front of him, dressing him in the ornaments of this god as if he, the slave, were his image. On the day this slave was to die and after he had been dressed as we just said, they placed a glass with water in his hand, and gave him a branch of willow, and with this he had to sprinkle them all like one who sprinkles holy water. If for devotion anyone wanted to make a feast in honor of this god, he would first go to his (the god's) priests and report; then they all would dress one of their number with the god's vestments to represent his image, and he then would sprinkle water with the willow branch wherever he passed. When they reached the house where the festivity was to be held, they put him in his place (of honor) and performed the reglamentary (usual) ceremonies in his presence, entreating him to grant favors to that house. He who had offered the festivity gave food and drink to the god, those who had accompanied him, and to all he had invited. He did this in gratitude for the prosperity and wealth he was already enjoying, believing that the god had given these to him. They performed dances, sang songs, as is their custom, in honor of Napatecutli, and to have him see how grateful his devotee was, he would spend everything he had, saying: "I do not mind to remain without a thing so long as I have served my god with this celebration. Should he choose to grant me more or leave me without anything, let him do as he pleases." After saying this he would cover the priest, who had come in representation of Napatecutli, with a white blanket, and then this latter would return to the temple with his companions. After they had left, the host and his relatives sat down to eat.

The men who make petates (mats) and whatever else of rush or reed took great care to provide and arrange, sweep and clean and strew cyperus in the temple of their god. They were also mindful to put mats on the floor, stools, icpales, for seats, so that everything would be nice and clean and well furnished, and not even a little straw nor anything else could be seen in the temple.

The image of Napatecutli represented a man dyed all black but for a few white specks among the black in the face. He wore a crown of paper painted black and white, and a few tassels hanging from the crown onto his back; from these tassels came a plume or tuft of three green plumes which rose towards the back of the head. Around the waist he wore a sort of short skirt to the knees painted black and white, and on it were small sea-shells. He had white sandals. In his left hand he held a shield fashioned like a water-lily, which is an aquatic plant, wide and resembling a large plate. In the right hand he held a flowering stalk or cane, the flowers being made of paper. He also wore a wide band like a stole from the right shoulder across the chest crossing under the left arm, black flowers painted on white.

All prominent mountain peaks, especially such around which rain-clouds will gather, they imagined to be gods, therefore they made of each an image according to their idea. They also thought that certain diseases which are due to the cold or inclement weather came from the mountains, and that these mountains had the power to cure them. Therefore, all those who became ill of such diseases made a vow to offer a feast and offering to such and such a mountain closest to which they happened to live, or to which they were most devoted. Similar promises were made by anyone who was in imminent danger of drowning in a river or in the sea. The various diseases for which they made promises to the Tlalocs were the gout (rheumatism) in hands or feet or any other part of the body; also contraction of tendons in any part of the body; for appearance of blotches (stains or spots) on the body (so-called liverspots, et al.), or contraction of any member, limbs or arms, or for paralysis. All those afflicted by any one of these ailments made a solemn vow to make the images of the following tlalocs: the god or tlaloc of the air, goddess of the water, god of rain, as well as the image of the volcano called Popocatepetl and the one of the Sierra Nevada, and of a mountain called Poiauhtecatl, or of any other mountain or hill they wanted to worship. They could make a vow to one or more, and the image or images were made of a dough called tzoalli in human shape; it was not permitted, however, to the worshipper himself to fashion them; he had to go to the different priests of these deities who were experienced in this sort of work, and whose duty it was, besides, to do it. The Satrap in making the image would give it teeth of pumpkin seeds, and for eyes black beans, which are as large as (lima) beans, though of a different shape, and which they call ayecotli. As for their dress and ornaments, they fashioned them according to the image of the tlaloc they represented. Thus they make the god of the wind look like Quetzalcoatl, the one of water like the goddess of the water, rain like the god of rain, and all the mountains according to the paintings they make of them. To these figures they offered the paper they make, consisting of a sheet (of it), onto which they dripped a great many drops of the gum called ulli, which they melted first. This paper they would hang around the neck of the image so that the latter was covered from the chest down, and at the lower end they snatched off the paper. Similar papers dripped all over with ulli they would hang on strings, one alongside the other, in front of the images, and the wind would shake them, for these strings of paper were tied at each end to canes stuck in the ground, the strings or "mecatl" being tied to the upper end. To these images wine—uctli, or pulcre[1], which is the wine of the country, was offered in cups which were made in the following way: there are some pumpkins, smooth, round and mottled between green and white, or else spotted, which they call tzilacayutli, of the size of a large melon. These they cut in halves and emptied the seeds so that they now looked like cups, and these they used for the uctli, or wine they placed in front of the images. To them these gourd cups represented those made of precious stones, called chalchivitl. All this was done by the priests, who knew how to do them, and who were appointed specially for these sacrifices. The rest of the people never made them, even if it were for their own home. After these images were made for the devotional ceremony, the ones who had ordered them invited the priests for the fifth day after their confection, when the celebration was to take place. When that day had come they spent that night (the eve) in wake, singing and dancing in honor of the images and of the gods they represented. During that night they offered tamales, which are a sort of cake made of corn, at four different times, to all those who danced and sang, namely, the priests who had made the images and those invited to partake of the feast. Four times a meal was served to all of them, and as many times they played their musical instruments, the whistling was done by placing the little finger in their mouth; they played on shells and flutes of the kind they used. This was done by jugglers who played that sort of music (at feasts), and to whom they also gave food. At

[1]Pulque, but it is very frequently spelled as above.

daybreak the Sátrapas decapitated all the images they had made of dough, twisting their heads, and they took all that dough and carried it to the house where they, the priests, all lived together, and which is called calmecac, while the hosts, whose vows had caused the images to be made, immediately returned home and joined their guests. They remained together all that day and in the evening toward night all the old men and women drank pulcre (pulque) or uctli, because they all had permission to drink it, and after they all were half or entirely drunk, they went home; some were crying, others made fierce threats like the braves and were dancing and showing off; still others were quarreling with each other. The hosts of such a festivity invited and provided also for the innkeepers, who made (brewed) the pulque, entreating them to make good wine, and the latter did their best to have it as good as possible. In order to attain this, that is, to brew good pulque, they abstained for four days of all intercourse with women, because it was their belief that if in those days they should hold any intercourse with women, the wine (pulque) would turn sour and would spoil. They also refrained during that period from drinking either pulque or the honey (agua miel) of which they brewed it, not even a finger would they dip in it to taste it until on the fourth day, when it would be officially tasted in the ceremony mentioned above. They held the superstition that if anyone drank of that wine, even if it were ever so little, before the official ceremony of the opening of the jugs as mentioned before, his mouth would twist to one side as a punishment of his sin. They also said that if anyone suffered from a shriveled hand or foot, or if the face, mouth or lips would begin to tremble (from palsy) or that he became possessed by some evil spirit, all this happened to him because these tlalocs were angry with him.

The day after the feast, in the morning, the host gathered all his relatives, his friends and those of his parish (city precinct), and everybody of his own household, to finish eating the food left over and to drink the rest of the pulque, and this they called apealo, which means adding to what had been eaten and drunk before; nothing at all would be left for the next day. It was said that if those afflicted with gout or any other disease of those above mentioned, also those who escaped any calamity on river or sea, arranged and celebrated such a festivity, they fulfilled their vows. Once this feast was over, all the papers and ornaments which had adorned the images of the tlalocs, all the vessels that had been used for the guests, were carried to a gutter (sewer) in the lagoon of Mexico, called pantitlan, and there they threw it all into the water.

Even in the past, the wine or pulcre (pulque) of the country was considered as pernicious (bad) on account of the bad effects it caused. Some of those intoxicated by its use would throw themselves from a rock or other height, others would hang themselves, still others would throw themselves into the water, where they would drown, or they would kill one another when drunk. All these calamities were blamed on the god of the wine and on the wine itself, and not on the drunkard who abused it. Furthermore, it was their belief that if anyone spake ill of that beverage or even murmured against it, some disaster (catastrophy) would befall him. The same was said if a drunken man was murmuring against it, insulting it, even if he was simply saying or doing a thousand villainies (in that condition), they were to be punished for it, because, as they said, it wasn't really he who committed or did these things, but the god or, better still, the demon who was in him, and who was Tezcatzoncatl, god of the wine (pulque), or one of the others. Tezcatzoncatl was a relative or brother of the other deities of wine, who were called: Yzyuitecalt, Yiauhteatl, Acolóa, Tlilhóa, Pantecatl, Tultecatl, Papaztac, Tlatecaivoa, Umetuchtli, Tepuztecalt, Chimapalnecatl, and Colhoatzincatl. By the above statement we can clearly see that whatever they did while drunk they did not consider as sin, no matter how serious a misdeed it might be. We might even adduce with good reason that they deliberately became intoxicated in order to commit what they had in mind, and which would not be held against them as sin or crime in that condition, hence he who did it escaped blameless. Even now that they have become Christians, they try to excuse their deeds by saying that they were drunk when they did it. They evidently think that the erroneous conception held by them previous to their Christianization is valid today. Of course, they are very much mistaken, and it is necessary to impress them of their error in confession as well as on other occasions.

BOOK II.

Feasts and Sacrifices With Which the Natives Honoured Their Gods in the Times of Their Paganism.

Chapter I.

The first month of the year was called among the Mexicans Atlacahualco, and elsewhere Quavitleloa. This month began on the second day of the month of February, when we celebrate the Purification of our Lady (the Virgin). On this first day of the month they celebrated a festival in honor (according to some) of the gods Tlaloc, whom they considered as the gods of rain. But, according to others, it was in honor of their sister Chalchiutlicue, the goddess of the water; still others pretended it was in honor of the great priest or god of the winds, Quetzalcoatl, so we may safely say that this feast was probably held in honor of all of them. This month, like all the others, which in all are eighteen, counted twenty days.

CALENDAR

Atlacahualco or Quavitleloa

In this month they killed many children; they sacrificed them in many places on the top of mountains, tearing out their hearts in honor of the gods of rain, so that they might grant them abundant rain.

They adorned the children thus to be sacrificed with many ornaments and carried them on their shoulders in litters. These were adorned with plumes and flowers and they played musical instruments, sang and danced in front of them.

If the children who were to be killed cried a great deal and shed many tears they were glad of it, for they took it as a prognostication of a great deal of rain for that year.

They also killed a great many prisoners in that month in honor of the same gods of water. First they stabbed them with knives, fighting with them as they were tied on to a stone which looked like a mill-stone, from which they routed them by means of knife-thrusts. They then took them to the temple called Yopico, where their hearts were torn out.

When these slaves were to be killed, their owners, who had captured them, danced, magnificently dressed (with plumes on the head) ahead of them, demonstrating their courage. This happened on all the days of this month. A good many ceremonies which took place at this festival are described at length on fol. 15 of their history.

The second month was called Tlacaxipeoaliztli. On the first day of this month they celebrated a festival in honor of the god Totec, who is also called Xippe, when they killed and flayed a number of slaves and captives.

Tlacaxipeoaliztli

> The captives were killed by scalping them, taking the scalp off the top of the head, which was kept by their owners as a relic. The ceremony was performed in the calpul in front of the fire.
>
> When the masters of these captives took their slaves to the temple where they were to be killed, they dragged them by the hair. As they pulled them up the steps of the Cú, some of these captives would faint, so their owners had to drag them by the hair as far as the block where they were to die.

As soon as they had dragged them to the block, which was a stone three spans (3 palmos—24 inches) high, more or less, by almost two in width, they threw them down on their back, five men holding them, two by the feet, two by the arms, and one by the head. Then at once the priest, who was to kill him, would come and strike him a blow on the chest with both hands, holding a flint knife shaped like the iron of an anchor, cutting a hole. Into this hole he would thrust one hand and tear out the heart, which he then offered to the sun; later he put it into a bowl or jar.

After thus having torn their hearts out, and after pouring their blood into a jicara (bowl made of a gourd), which was given to the master of the dead slave, the body was thrown down the temple steps. From there it was taken by certain old men called Quaquaquilti, and carried to their calpul (or chapel), cut it to pieces, and distributed them to be eaten.

Before cutting them up they would flay the bodies of the captives; others would dress in their skins and fight sham battles with other men.

After the above, they would kill other captives, fighting again with them while they were tied around the waist with a rope which ran through the hole in the center of a stone like a millstone. The rope was so long that the men could walk around the stone on all sides. He was given his weapons to fight with; four men, armed with sword and shield, would now come to fight with him until they slew him.

The third month was called Tozoztontli. On the first day of this month they celebrated the festival of the god called Tlaloc, who is the god of rain. At this feast they killed many children on the tops of hills, offering them in sacrifice to this god and his companions, so that they might give them water (rain).

TOZOZTONTLI

On this festival they offered the first flowers that had come out that year at the Cú, called Yopico, and before they were thus offered, no one dared smell of a flower.

The officials (priests or guardians) of the flowers called Sochimanque made the festival to their goddess Coatlycue, or by another name Coatlantona.

In this month also those who were dressed in the skins of the dead they had flayed the previous month went to place them in a cave of the Cú called Topico. They went in procession with many ceremonies, and they smelled bad like dead dogs. After having left the skins there, they went to wash themselves with great ceremony. Some sick persons would make promises to be present at this procession in order to become cured, and they say that some did.

The owners of captives, with their entire household, did penance for twenty days, during which time they neither bathed nor did they wash themselves until (this should be "while") they wore the skins of the dead captives. In the above mentioned cave it is said they did penance for their dead captives.

After this penance was over they bathed and washed themselves, then invited all their relatives and friends, offering them meals, and they performed many ceremonies with the bones of the dead captives.

For all of those twenty days until the beginning of the following month, they rehearsed songs in the houses called cuicatlacalli; they did not dance, but remained seated, singing the praise of their gods. They performed a great many more ceremonies, all of which are described at length in the history of the gods, fol. 27.

The fourth month was called Veytocoztli (according to Clavijero Huytozoztli). On the first day of this month they celebrated the feast in honor of the god Cinteutl, who was regarded as the god of corn (maize). To honor him they fasted four days previous to the festival.

VEYTOCOZTLI

For this festival they put branches of reed-mace by the doors of their houses and sprinkled them with blood from their ears or from the shin-bone. (This might also mean the blackheads which draw blood when dug out). The nobles and also the wealthy adorned their whole houses besides the reed-mace with branches or wreaths which are called acxoatl, and likewise they placed wreaths around the gods each one had in his house, and put flowers before them.

After this they went into the cornfields and brought back some cornstalks (which were still small), arranged them with

> flowers, and then went to put them in front of their gods in the oratory they call Calpulli. They also put food before them.

After having done this in the different city districts (wards) they went to the Cú (temple) of the goddess whom they called Chicomecoatl and there, in front of her, they represented sham battles, and all the girls carried ears of corn of the previous year on their backs and walked in procession up to the goddess to present them to her; then they took them back home with them as blessed objects. From this corn they gathered the seed for the following year's sowing. They also used such ears of corn as "hearts" of the corn bins, because they had been blessed. Of the dough called azoalli they made the image of this goddess in the court-yard of her Cú, and in front of this they placed as offerings all the different kinds of corn, of beans and of chian, the leaves of which are eaten as vegetable and the seeds are used for flavouring, like sesame, because they believed her to be the creator and giver of these things, which are the food-staples of these people.

According to reports of some people, they collected the children they sacrificed in the first month, buying them from their mothers and then killed them at all subsequent festivals until the rainy season came in full force. Thus they killed a few in the first month called Quavitlcoa, others in the second called Tlacaxipeoaliztli, others in the third, Tocoxtontli, and again some in the fourth, Veytocoxtli. As a matter of fact, therefore, they crucified[1] children at all the festivals until the rainy season set in. They celebrated a great many other ceremonies at this feast.

The fifth month was Toxcatl, and on its first day they celebrated a big feast in honor of the god Titlacaoa, known by one other name as Tezcatlipoca, and whom they held to be the god of gods. In his honor they killed on the day of his festival a chosen young man without a blemish on his body and who had been kept in all the delights of life for a whole year, being instructed to play musical instruments, to sing and speak (recite).

TOXCATL

> This was the principal festival of all. It was like Easter, and came very close to the Christian Easter, perhaps a few days later. The youth, educated as told above, was very well grown and chosen from among many. He wore his hair long, as far down as his waist.

When they killed the youth whom they had maintained for a whole year for this purpose, they at once chose another one who, before being sacrificed one year hence, went through the whole town very well

[1]This no doubt should be "sacrificed" and not crucified.

dressed, with flowers in his hand, and accompanied by certain personalities (probably prominent people). He would bow graciously to all whom he met, and they all knew he was the image of Tezcatlipoca and prostrated themselves before him, worshipping him wherever they met him. Twenty days previous to the festival they gave this youth (who was to die) four maidens, well prepared and educated for this purpose. During these twenty days he had carnal intercourse with these maidens. His clothes were changed when they first brought them to him; they cut his hair as for a captain, and gave him some other luxuries of dress.

Five days before he was to die they gave festivities for him, banquets held in cool and gay places, and many chieftains and prominent people accompanied him. On the day of the festival when he was to die they took him to a Cú or oratory, which they called Tlacuchcalco. Before reaching it, at a place called Tlapituoaian, the women (maidens) stepped aside and left him. As he got to the place where he was to be killed, he mounted the steps (staircase) by himself and on each one of these he broke one of the flutes which he had played during the year. Once at the top they threw him down onto the block and tore his heart out, then brought his body down on their hands (arms); down at the foot they cut the head from the trunk and impaled it on a pole called Tzonpantli. Many other ceremonies were celebrated during this festival, all of which are described at length on fol. 53 of the Ms.

The sixth month was called Etzalcualiztli, and on its first day the festival to the gods of rain took place, and in order to honor them, the priests of their sanctuaries fasted for four days before the festival, that is to say, the four last days of the previous month.

Etzalcualiztli

To celebrate this festival, the Sátrapas (priests) of the idols first went to Citlaltepec for cyperus, which grew very tall and very beautiful in a lagoon called Temilco, and from there they brought them to Mexico to adorn the Cús. All along the way nobody else showed himself; travelers on that road would hide for fear of those priests; if they happened to meet anyone they took everything he possessed from him, leaving him naked and should he attempt to defend himself, they so ill-treated him that they left him for dead, even if he was a man who carried the taxes for Mocthecuzoma, which they took from him. For all this they were never punished, because, being the priests (ministers) of the idols, they had complete liberty to do not alone thus, but even worse without fear of punishment. The temple priests celebrated a great many other ceremonies in the four days the festival lasted, all of which are fully described in the account of this celebration.

On the feast of Etzalcualitztli everybody made a sort of delicacy in the way of cooking which is called etzalli (delicate dish to taste) and everybody ate at home and gave to those who came in. A great many crazy things they would do on that day.

It was at this festival that all ministers (priests) of the gods who had committed some fault or other in their service were terribly punished in the waters of the lagune, so much so that they left them almost dead on the bank near the water's edge; their parents or relatives took care of them, carrying them home more dead than alive.

During this month they killed a great many captives and slaves, dressed in the finery of these Tlalocs in whose honor they killed them, in their respective oratories, the Cús. The hearts of thôse they killed they threw into the whirlpool or sewer in the lagune of Mexico, which then was clearly visible.

Many other ceremonies were celebrated.

The seventh month they called Tecuilhiutontli, and its first day was dedicated to the goddess of the salt, whose name was Vixtocioatl; they said that she was the oldest sister of the Tlalocs, and in her honor they killed (sacrificed) a woman dressed in the ornaments of the goddess.

TECUILHIUTONTLI

> On the eve of that festival all the women, old and young, as well as young girls, danced and sang. They were holding on to short cords which they held in their hands, one holding one end and her neighbor the other. These cords were called xochimecatl; they all wore garlands of ascension flowers called iztahyatl, and were led by some old men who also led the singing. In their midst went the woman representing the image of the goddess in her finery and ornaments, and who was going to be sacrificed.

On the eve of the festival the women spent the night with the one that was to be sacrificed, singing and dancing all night. In the morning all the priests dressed in festive garb and performed a very solemn dance, and all those present carried in their hands the flowers called cempoalxochitl. Thus dancing, they led many captives to the Cú (temple) of Tlaloc, and with them the woman who was to be killed, representing the image of the goddess Vixtocioatl. In the Cú they first killed the captives and then the woman.

Many other ceremonies took place at this festival; there also was much drunkenness, all of which is described at length on fol. 76 (Sahagun Ms.).

Veytecuilhiutl was the eighth month, on the first day of which they celebrated a festival in honor of the goddess called Xilonem (goddess of the Xilotes). At this feast they fed the poor, men and women, the old of both sexes, boys and girls, to honor the goddess. On the tenth day of the month they killed a woman arrayed in the finery of the image they painted of Xilonem.

Veytecuilhiutl

They fed men and women, young and old, for eight continuous days previous to the feast. Very early in the morning they gave them to drink a sort of (thin) mush they call chiempinolli. Everyone drank as much as he liked. At noon they placed them all in their order in rows, seated, and then fed them (with) tamales.

The one who distributed these tamales would put into the hand of each one as many as he could hold in one hand, and if anyone misbehaved by taking twice they ill-treated him and took away those he had already taken, leaving him without any. This the lords (wealthy) did to console the poor, because at that time of the year there was generally a shortage of provisions (food staples). During all of these eight days there was general dancing, the men whirling around with the women, all of them attired in their very richest clothes and jewels; the women wore their hair loose, and thus, with it hanging down onto their shoulders, loose, they danced and sang with the men. They began this dance at sunset, dancing continuously until nine o'clock; they carried many torches of candlewood and there were furthermore many fires burning, lighted in the court itself where they were dancing. In this dance they crossed hands or else were in each other's arms, the arm of one around the shoulders of his partner, both, men and women alike. On the day before they killed the woman who was to be sacrificed to honor the goddess Xilonem, the women who attended her in her Cú (temple) and who were called Cioatlamacazque, danced in the court of the Cú, singing the songs in praise of the goddess; they surrounded the victim, who was dressed in the ornaments (insignia) of this goddess. Thus singing and dancing, they spent the night until daybreak of the day when she was to be sacrificed. At early dawn the nobles and the warriors held a dance in the same court, and the woman (victim) danced with them, together with many other women attired like her. The men danced in a group alone, in front, the women following after them. In that manner, dancing, they finally reached the Cú. They lifted her up the steps and once up there they cut her head off, then tore out her heart, offering it to the sun. Many other ceremonies took place at that festival.

The ninth month they called Tlaxochimaco, the first day of which was dedicated to the god of war, Vitzilopuchtli, offering him at that festival the first flowers of the year.

Tlaxochimaco

On the eve of that festival all were busy killing chickens and dogs to use their meat in making tamales and other things to eat. Then, very early on the day of the feast the priests serving the idols adorned the statue of Vitzilopuchtli with a great many flowers, and after that they adorned the statues or images of all the other gods with garlands, wreaths, and necklaces of flowers; then they did the same with the statues in the Calpules and Telpuchcales and in the houses of the Calpixques and of the principals (chieftains) and macehuales; in fact, everybody adorned the statues they had in their houses with flowers.

Once all the statues were thus adorned, they would begin to eat all those viands they had prepared on the previous night, and a little while after eating they commenced a special sort of dance, at which the noble men and women danced together, either holding hands or with their arms around each other's necks. They did not dance in their usual way, nor did they whirl and twist their bodies as in their ordinary dances, but went step by step to the sound of those who played the instruments and sang, and who were all standing a short ways apart from the dancers, near a round altar called mumuztli.

This singing lasted until night, not only in the courts of the Cús, but everywhere in all the houses of chiefs and macehuales they were playing music and singing with great shouts until night. The old men and women drank uctli, but no young man or maiden, and if any one did, they would be punished severely. Many other ceremonies were held which are fully described in their proper place.

Xocohuetzi was the tenth month, and on its first day they celebrated the festival of the god of fire called Xiutecutli, or Ihcocauhui. At this celebration they threw many slaves, their feet and hands tied, alive into the fire, and before they were entirely dead, they pulled them out in order to tear out their hearts in front of the image of the god.

Xocohuetzi

During the festival to Tlaxóchimaco they went into the woods to cut a tree of 25 fathoms (6 feet each) in height and brought it—hauling or dragging it behind them to the court of the Cú of this god; there they pruned it completely and then raised it up and left it standing thus until the eve of the festival of Xocohuetzi, when they again felled it, being very careful that it should not get bruised, using many implements to prevent that. On the eve of the festival, very early in the morning, a number of carpenters would come with their implements, and they peeled it, making it very smooth. After having peeled it, they adorned it with many kinds of paper, then tied ropes and strings to it, raising it with big shouts and great noise, and moored it very well.

As soon as the pole or tree was raised and trimmed with all its ornaments, those who owned slaves whom they were to throw alive into the fire, dressed themselves in their rich vestments and plumes, painted their bodies yellow, which is the livery of the fire, and, taking their slaves with them, performed their dances during that entire day until nightfall.

After having watched over the captives (slaves) throughout the night in the Cú, and having performed many ceremonies with them, they powdered their faces with a powder called yiauchtli to make them lose consciousness and so would not feel their death so much. They now tied their feet and hands and thus tied, carried them on their backs, walking with this load as if they were dancing, around a big fire and a large heap of live coal. While they marched this way they thrust them into the live coal, now one, then another one, and they let each one they had thrown into the fire burn quite awhile, but while he was still alive and nauseated and only partly overcome, they pulled him out with any sort of a pothook or grapple and threw him onto the slaughter-block (or sacrificial stone), and opening his breast, tore out the heart. In this manner all these poor captives died. The tree (or pole) was tied with many ropes at (or near) the top, like the rigging of a ship that is hanging downward from the top (sail?). At the top (of the pole) was fastened, standing up, the image of that god Xiutecutli made of the dough which they call tzoalli. After the sacrifice above mentioned, all the young men attacked (one another) with great impetus. A great many other events took place during this festival, as is described at length elsewhere.

The eleventh month they call Ochpaniztli; on its first day they celebrated a festival in honor of this goddess; they danced in silence and also in silence they killed a woman dressed in the manner of the image of this goddess.

Ochpaniztli

Five days previous to the beginning of this month, they stopped all festivities and rejoicing of the past month. The first eight days of Ochpaniztli they danced without singing and without playing the teponaztli. After these eight days the woman representing the image of Teteuinna appeared dressed in the ornaments of that image. With her came a great number of women, especially the women healers (doctors) and the midwives. They separated into two groups, fighting one another by pelting each other with pellets of pachtli, also tuna-leaves, and pellets made of reed-mace leaves and also flowers called cempoatl-xuchitl. This rejoicing lasted four days.

After these and other similar ceremonies were over, they tried to prevent the woman who was destined to die from knowing it, in order to prevent her from crying or getting sad, for this they considered a bad omen. As soon as the night on which she was to die had come, they dressed her very richly, giving her to understand that she was being taken where a great lord (or chief) was to sleep with her. Amid great silence they took her to the Cú where she was to die. Arrived at the top a man lifted her on his back, her back to his, and they quickly cut her head off, then flayed her, and a strong youth dressed himself in her skin.

At once they took this youth who had put on the skin of the sacrificed woman with great solemnity and in company also of many captives to the Cú of Vitzilopuchtli. There, in front of this god, this youth tore the heart from four captives himself; the rest of them he left for the Sátrapas (priests) to kill.

In this month the chieftain of all the warriors passed muster of all the young men who had not gone to war yet. There were many other ceremonies celebrated at this festival, which can be read elsewhere in this history.

The twelfth month was called Teotleco, which means arrival of the gods. They celebrated this festival in honor of all the gods because they said these had gone to other parts. On the last day of the month they made a great feast because their gods had returned.

Teotleco

> On the fifteenth day of this month the young men and boys enwreathed all the altars and oratories of the gods as well as those within houses and the ones on roads and cross-roads, and for this work they were given corn as reward. Some gave them a chiquivitl full of corn, others a few ears.

On the eighteenth day Tlamatzincatl, the god who had remained a bachelor, also called Titlacaban, arrived. They said that on account of his being a bachelor and strong, he walked faster and therefore arrived first. They at once offered a meal in his Cú, and that night they all ate and drank and rejoiced, especially the old people; men and women drank wine (pulque) on the occasion of the god's arrival, saying that by so doing they washed his feet.

On the last day of this month they celebrated the big festival, for on that day, they pretended the gods were all returning. On the eve (of that day), at night, they placed on a straw mat (petate) a very compact little heap of stacked corn in the shape of a bone. On this heap the gods imprinted the sole of one foot as a sign that they had returned. All night the head-priest kept watch; he would come and go many times during his vigil to see whether the imprint was there.

As soon as he saw the sign of the foot, he would shout: "Our lord has arrived," and at once all the priests of the Cú (temple) would blow cornets (horns), shells, and trumpets, and all other instruments they had then. As soon as the people heard this music, they came to offer food at all the oratories and temples, and again they would rejoice, "washing the gods' feet," as mentioned above.

On the following day the old gods were arriving after all the others for they said that, as they were old, they could not walk quite so fast. For this day they gathered many of their captives to burn them alive. When the fire was so well started that there were heaps of live coal, certain young men, disguised as monsters and thus dancing around it, would throw those unfortunate captives (creatures) into the fire, as stated before. There were a good many other ceremonies to celebrate this day, all of which are fully described elsewhere.

The thirteenth month was Tepeilhuitl, in the course of which they honored all the prominent peaks all over this New Spain, around the summits of which clouds were wont to gather. The images they made of them were human in shape, fashioned of the dough they call tzoalli, and before these images they sacrificed, honoring in them the mountains they represented.

Tepeilhiutl

> In honor of the mountains they made snakes of wood or roots of trees, fashioning the head like a snake's. They also cut thick pieces of wood about a wrist's length, calling them ecatolonti; these, as well as the wooden snakes, they covered with the dough tzoal and shaped them like mountains, making the top in the shape of a human head. Similar figures were made in memory of all those who had drowned or died (otherwise), only so they were not burnt but buried.

After having placed the above-mentioned images on their respective altars, amid great ceremonials they offered to them tamales and other food; furthermore, they sang songs in their praise and drank wine (pulque) in their honor.

When the festival in honor of the mountains commenced they killed four women and one man. The first one of these women was called Tepoxoch, the second one Matlalhue, the third Xochtecatl, and the fourth Mayabel. The man was called Milnaoatl. They dressed these women and the man in many papers covered with ulli (gum) and carried them in litters borne on the shoulders of richly dressed women to the place where they were going to kill them.

As soon as they were killed they would tear the hearts out and then let them slide slowly down the steps, and once down at the foot they cut their heads off and took the bodies to the house called Calpul, where they distributed the pieces of flesh for eating. The heads they impaled. The papers with which they had adorned the images of the mountains, after having broken these to pieces to eat them, they hung up in the Calpul. They celebrated a good many more ceremonies on that occasion, all of which are described at length in the corresponding chapters.

The fourteenth month is Quecholli; in this month the god called Miscoatl was feasted. This also was the month in which they made arrows and darts for their wars; they killed many slaves in honor of this god.

Quecholli

> When they made the arrows and darts during five days, they would also bleed themselves from the ears. The blood they thus squeezed out they smeared on their own temples, saying they did penance in order to hunt deer. They took the blankets away from all those who in that time failed to bleed themselves, as a punishment. No man slept with his wife during that time, nor did the old men and women drink pulque, because they did penance.

When the four (five?) days on which they made arrows and darts had passed they also made some very small arrows, tying them into fours, with every four torches, and thus, having made small bundles of four torches and four arrows each, they offered them on the graves of the dead, at the same time placing two tamales with each such bundle. This was left on the grave for a whole day. At night they then burned them. At this same festival they performed many other ceremonies in honor of the dead.

On the tenth day of that month all the Mexicans and Tlatelulcanos went to the mountain chain they call Cacatepec and which they say is their mother. That day they built xacales (huts) of straw and lodges, and built fires, but did nothing else.

At daybreak the following day they all ate breakfast and then went to the open country (fields), where they formed a great wing (made a wing-like move) and so closed in on a great many animals, deer, rabbits, and other game, closing the circle little by little until they had them all driven into close quarters and now each could attack and kill what he wanted.

After this hunt was over they killed captives and slaves in a Cú called Tlamatzinco, tying them hands and feet, and thus carrying them up the steps of the Cú (as if one carried a deer tied feet and hands to kill it), and then killed them amid great ceremonies. The man and the woman who represented the images of the god Mixcoatl[1] and his wife were also killed, but in another Cú called Miscoateupatl. There were many other ceremonies, at this festival, all of which are described, etc.

Panquetzaliztli they called the fifteenth month, and during this month they celebrated the festival of the god of war, Vitzilopuchtli. Previous to this festival the priests of the idols fasted for forty days and did other heavy (severe) penance, such as to go naked at midnight into the woods to gather bunches of flowers.

PANQUETZALIZTLI

> On the second day of this month they began their dances and to sing the songs of Vitzilopuchtli in the court of his Cú (temple). Men and women danced together. They began these songs in the afternoon and finished about 10 o'clock. These songs and dances lasted for twenty days.
>
> On the ninth day of the month they prepared, amid great ceremonies, all those they were going to kill, painting them in many colors and adorning them with a great many papers, and then danced with them. For this dance there were couples of men and women singing and dancing together.

On the sixteenth day of this month the owners of slaves began to fast and on the nineteenth they began a certain kind of dance in which all held hands, men and women, and in this manner danced winding and twisting about the court of the said Cú; certain old men played and sang while the others danced.

After those who were to die during this festival had gone through a number of ceremonies, Vitzilopuchtli descended from the Cú (temple), that is he, the god, was represented by a man, dressed in the ornaments and insignias of the god Paynal, and he killed four of those slaves (prepared for death) in the ball game which took place in the court called Teutlachtli; he then left and made the circuit of the entire city, running, and in a determined place in each quarter, he killed one slave. After that two parties began to fight sham battles, at which some of the fighters died.

Finally, after performing a number of ceremonies, they killed captives in the temple of Vitzilopuchtli, as well as many slaves. As soon as one had been killed, they played musical instruments; when the music ceased they killed another one, played again, and so forth till all of these poor

[1]This is spelled both ways, Miscoatl and Mexcoatl and evidently both are accepted.

victims had been put to death. Then they started to sing and dance, to eat and drink, and thus the festival ended.

The sixteenth month was called Atemoztli. In this month they celebrated festivals for the gods of rain, because for the greater part of this month thunderstorms came up and the rains began to show. The priests of the Tlalocs commenced to do penance and offer sacrifices to make the rains start.

Atemoztli

> When it started to thunder the priests at the service of the Tlalocs with great activity offered copal (incense) and other perfumes to the gods, and when they had tied their statues, they would say that then the gods are bound to come to give water to the people. They made promises to shape the images of the mountains, which they call tepictli, because those are dedicated to the gods of water. On the sixteenth day all the people prepared offerings to Tlaloc, and for four days they did penance, the men abstaining from intercourse with women, and these latter with men.

When the festival was due, on the last day of the month, they cut strips of paper which they tied or wound around long slender poles from the bottom upwards, and stuck these poles in the courtyards of their houses; they made the images of the mountains of tzoal (dough) with teeth of pumpkin seeds, eyes of a sort of bean called ayecotli, then offered them their offerings (gifts) of food, worshipping them.

After keeping vigil, playing musical instruments and singing, they cut their breasts (of the idols) with a tzotzopaztli, which is an implement used by the women for weaving, almost like a cutlass, and took out their hearts[1], cut off their heads, and then distributed the body among themselves and ate it; the ornaments with which they had bedecked them they burned in the courts of their houses.

After this was done, they gathered all the ashes, all the apparatus (the poles, etc.) with which they had worshipped, to the oratories called ayauhcalco, and then started to eat and drink and rejoice, and thus ended the festivity. Other ceremonies celebrated on this occasion may be found in the corresponding place of their history.

Tititl was the seventeenth month. In this month they celebrated the feast of a goddess called Tlamatecutli[2], and by another name Tona, and still another Coscamiauh. In her honor they killed a woman. After having torn out her heart they cut her head off and held a (special) dance

[1]i.e., the innermost part of the dough-image where the heart would be.

[2]Tlamatecutli, also Ylamatecutli and Yllamatecutli.

with it. The leader (in that dance) carried the head by its hair in his right hand, making the dance steps.

TITITL

> The woman they killed at this festival was dressed in all the ornaments and clothes of the goddess whose image she represented, and whom they called Ylamatecutli[1], by another name Tona, which means "our mother." Donned in all this finery, she had to dance alone to the music some old men played, and while she danced she sighed and cried, remembering that she was to die. After midday the priests, dressed in the ornaments of all the gods, went ahead of her, making her go up to the Cú (temple) where she was to die. They threw her on the stone block (sacrificial stone) and tore out her heart and cut her head off, which at once one of the priests dressed like a god, took by the hair and danced with it at the head of all the rest. And he who thus carried the head in his right hand led the dance, making the dance steps with it in his hand.

On the same day they killed this woman the priests of the idols executed certain skirmishes and rejoicing, running after one another up and down the steps of the temple, performing certain ceremonies at the same time.

On the following day all the people made bags like pouches with cords of an arm's length attached to them. They inflated these bags and filled them with something soft like wool, then took them, hidden under their blanket (manta) and, once on the street and meeting a woman, hit her with this bag in fun; this game was so popular that the boys, too, made their bags and with them then mauled the girls till they made them cry.

As may be seen in the historical part of this work, there were a good many other ceremonies performed on this festival.

The eighteenth month was called Yzcalli, and it was the month dedicated to festivals to the god of fire called Xiuhtecutli Opecauhqui. In his honor they made an image which seemed to throw out flames of fire by itself. Every four years at this same festival they killed captives and slaves in honor of this god, and also perforated the ears of all the children born within these four years, and gave them godfathers and godmothers.

YZCALLI

> On the tenth day of this month, at midnight, they went to obtain new fire in front of the image of Xiuhtecutli, very neatly adorned. Once the fires were all lighted, there came in the morn-

[1]Later on in this work she is called "Tllamatecutli," which is probably the correct mode of writing the name.

> ing young men and boys with diverse animals they had hunted in the past few days, some from the water, others from land, and offered them to the old men whose duty it was to guard this god. These latter threw all the animals into the fire to roast them, and to the young men and boys they gave each a tamal made of wild amaranth, which they called vauhquiltamalli, which all the people offered on that day, and which they all ate in honor of the festival. They ate them very hot; and they drank and rejoiced.

During the usual celebration of this feast of every year they did not kill anyone; they made human sacrifices only on the bissextile years, that is, every four years captives and slaves were sacrificed. The image of Xiuhtecutli was adorned with a great many precious and curious ornaments. Upon the death of these (victims) they performed many and very solemn ceremonies, far more so than at any other festival of the year, as it is explained in their history.

After having killed these slaves and captives and the image of Yzcocauhqui, who is the god of fire, all the chiefs and lords and illustrious personages and even the emperor himself were richly dressed and adorned with precious ornaments, and they held a dance of great solemnity and gravity, which they called netecuitotiliztli, which means "dance of the lords." This dance was only held every four years at this feast. Very early on this same day even before dawn, they started perforating the ears of the boys and girls, and they put a helmet on their heads made of parrot-feathers glued on with ocutzotl, which is pine-resin.

The five remaining days of the year, which are the four last days of January and the first of February, they called Nemontemi, which means "idle" (useless) days, and they considered them as unfortunate (unlucky). It is supposed that they perforated the ears of children every four years on account of these five days of nemontemi, which tally with our bissextile day in leap year.

They said that all who were born in these five days, which they considered unlucky, had to suffer many misfortunes in everything and were (always) poor and miserable; they called them neme; if they were men they were called Nemoquich, if women Nencioatl. They did no work in those days because they were considered unlucky, and they especially refrained from quarreling, because they said that anyone who quarreled in those days acquired the habit; it was also thought bad luck to stumble in those days.

The above mentioned feasts were permanent, that is, they always occurred in the respective month, with a difference of a day or two. The others were mutable, and were celebrated in the course of the twenty signs which completed their circuit of 260 days, and for this reason these feasts would occur one year in one month, another year in another, and if they came together they would somehow shift them around.

About the Mutable (movable) Feasts

1. The first movable feast was celebrated in honor of the sun, when it was in the sign of Ceocelutl, in the fourth house called Naolin. During this feast they offered to the image of the sun quail; they burned incense, and in the center of the house they killed captives in front of the image and in its honor. On that same day they all, big and small, drew blood from their ears, to honor the sun, offering that blood as a sacrifice.

2. Under this same sign, all the painters made their festival in the seventh house, and the washwomen fasted forty days, the painters another twenty in order to attain good luck to paint well or to do good weaving on their blankets or other work in hand. For this purpose they offered quail and incense; the men performed certain ceremonies for the god Chicomexochitl, and the women for the goddess Xochiquetzatl.

3. Under the third sign, cemacatl, they celebrated a festival in the first house, in honor of the goddesses called Cisapitliti, because they said that then these goddesses would come down to earth. They dressed their images with papers and offered gifts.

4. Under the sign called cemecatl they celebrated a great festival in the second house called Ometochtli, in honor of Yzquitecatl, who is the second god of wine, and not only for him but for all the gods of the wine, who were many. They adorned his statue very well in his Cú, offering him all sorts of food, and they sang and played before him. They placed a very large jar of pulque in the court of his Cú (temple), and the innkeepers (also meant for those who brew it) kept on filling it to overflow; all those who wished to went there to drink. The innkeepers had their (own) cups for drinking, and they continued filling the jar so that it was always full. This was especially done by those who had cut the maguey plant anew. The first honey-water (agua miel) which they obtained they carried to the temple of this god as offering of first-fruits.

5. Under the sign called Cexóchitl, the chieftains and lords prepared a great festival in the first house, where they danced and sang in honor of that sign. There were other sorts of rejoicing, and they wore on that occasion the choicest plumes for the dance. During this festival the lord (king or chief) granted favours to the warriors, the singers, and the employees of the palace.

6. Under the sign called Ceacatl the lords and chieftains offered a big feast, in the first house, to Quetzalcoatl, god of the winds. This celebra-

tion was prepared in the house called Calmecac, which is where the priests of the idols lived and where boys were educated. In this house, which was like a monastery, was placed the image of Quetzalcoatl, which they adorned with beautiful ornaments for that festival, offering perfumes and food before it. They said that the sign ceacatl was Quetzalcoatl's sign.

7. Under the sign of Cemiqueztli the chieftains and lords offered a great festival in the first house to Tezcatlipoca, who was the great god and they said that the above was his sign. As they all had their private oratories in their houses, where they also kept the image of this god among many others, on this day they adorned the image and offered to it perfumes and flowers and food, and they sacrificed quail in front of it, tearing their heads off. This was not only done by the chieftains and prominent people, but by everybody who knew about this feast. It was also celebrated in the calpules as well as in the Cús (temples). They all prayed, asking favours of this god, for he was their omnipotent lord.

8. Under the sign of Cequiavitl they celebrated the festival in honor of the goddesses they call Cioapipilli, in the first house. These goddesses were said to be the women who died giving birth to their first child. They became goddesses, they said, and lived in the house of the sun, and that at the time the sign above mentioned came around they descended to earth, and inflicted diverse diseases on all those they found away from their homes. Oratories in honor of these goddesses were erected in all such city wards that had two streets and called them Cioateucalli or Cioateupan. Here they kept the images of these goddesses, which they adorned for their festival with papers which they called amateteuitl. On the feast of these goddesses and in their honor they killed those condemned to death for some crime or other, and who were kept in their prisons.

9. Under the sign called Cequiavitl they killed, in the fourth house, Nauhecatl, which was the house of very bad luck, all criminals (evil doers) who were in prison, and the chieftain also ordered slaves to be killed for the sake of superstition. All the merchants and traders made exhibits of the jewels in which they were dealing, displaying them so that everyone might see them and after this, that same night, they ate and drank. They would take flowers and tubes of perfume, seat themselves in their places, and then begin in turn to brag about their earnings and about the far away places they had reached (in their travel), and at the same time look down upon others who were (timid) and did not have as much as they, nor had traveled to such remote countries. This all gave rise to much fun among them, and lasted the greater part of the night.

10. Under the sign they called Cemallinalli they prepared a great festival in the second house called Umecoatl, because they said that this sign belonged to Tezcatlipoca. For this festival they made the image of Omacatl and anyone who was a devotee of this image carried it to his house, that the latter might be blessed and his property be increased, and if such blessings came to him, he kept the image, and was loath to let it go back (to the temple). To the contrary, if he wished the image to be put back where it belonged, he waited till this same sign came around again, and then carried the image back whence he had taken it.

11. Under the sign called Cetecpatl they took out of the first house all the ornaments of Vitzilopuchtli; they cleaned and dusted them and put them in the sun for, they said, this was his sign and the one of Camaxtle; this was the way the Hacatecos celebrated. Here (in Mexico) they cooked a great many different dishes, deliciously prepared as they are eaten by the chieftains, and they placed them all in front of his image. After they had remained there a little while, the officers (priests) of Vizilopuchtli took them and, distributing them among themselves, they ate them; they also burned incense in front of the image and offered it quail, which they beheaded before it, so that the blood might be spilled before the god. The chieftain or lord offered also all the beautiful flowers which are worn by the lords and chiefs, to the image.

12. They said that under the sign of Ceocumatli the goddesses called Cioapipilli descended to earth and injured the (small) children, boys and girls, afflicting them with palsy, so that if a child fell ill at that time (of the year) they immediately blamed it on the Cioapipilli. They had such great fear of the power of these goddesses that parents would not allow their children to go out during that period, to prevent their meeting them.

13. Under the sign of Ceytzeuintli, which they said was the sign of fire, they celebrated a great festival in honor of Xiuchtecutli, god of the fire, offering him great quantities of copal, and a large number of quails. They adorned his image with many kinds of paper, and with a great deal of rich ornaments. Among the wealthy people and those in power great festivities were held in their own homes, in honor of the fire, and they also prepared reunions and banquets. Under this sign solemn elections of chiefs and consuls were held and were celebrated in the fourth house of this sign with feasts, dances and gifts. After these celebrations were over, they immediately declared war on their enemies.

14. Under the sign called Ceatl they celebrated the feast of the goddess of the water in the first house of that sign. Her name was Chalchiuhtliycue, and festivities in her honor were celebrated by all those who derived their livelihood from the water, either by selling it, or in fisheries

and any other trade they could secure with aquatic products. All such traders adorned her image during this festival, worshipped her, and made offerings in the house (oratory) called Calpulli.

15. The lords and chieftains, the nobles, and the wealthy merchants, were very careful in watching the sign, day and hour, under which a son or daughter was born to them, and they immediately went to inform the judicial astrologers of it, and to ask them about the good or bad fortune the new-born babe might have. If the sign was propitious, they had the child baptized at once, and if it was adverse, they selected the most prosperous house of that sign where to baptize it. To this baptismal feast they invited their relatives and friends to be present at the christening, and gave them to eat and drink, and also asked all the children of the district (ward) where they lived. Baptism took place at sunrise in the house of the parents, and was performed by the midwife pronouncing many orations (prayers) and making a number of ceremonies over the child. This same festival is in usage today when their children are christened as far as it concerns invitations, eating and drinking.

16. As soon as parents considered that their son was of a marriageable age, they informed him that they wished to look for a wife for him, and he would thank them for their thoughtfulness and the care they took in getting him married. They at once spoke to the principal, whom they called Telpuchtlato, who was in charge of the youths, informing him that they wanted to marry their son, and asking him to approve of it. To this end they invited him and all the young men he had in his care, and, after having given them all food and drink, they made a speech. First they placed a hatchet for cutting down trees or splitting fire-wood before him. This hatchet was a sign that the youth was now taking leave of his companions because his parents wished him to marry; and so the Telpuchtlato left fully satisfied. After this, the parents chose the woman they were to give their son, and at once called the marriage-makers (match-makers) who were honest old women arbiters (mediators), and they were to go and speak to the parents of the girl. They went twice or three times to speak, and brought back the answer. In the meantime, the relatives of the girl conferred among themselves whether they were to give her to the youth, and then gave their consent to the marriage-makers. After this they looked for a very lucky day under a propitious sign, i.e., either the sign of acatl, ocumach, cipactli, and quauchtli. When any one of these was chosen the parents of the youth announced the date of the marriage to the girl's parents. They at once began preparations necessary for the ceremony, food and drink as well as blankets and "cañas de humo" (hollow canes with incense in them), and many other things. Then they invited the chieftains and whoever else they wanted to have

at the wedding. After the dinner, at which many speeches and other ceremonials were held, those of the bridegroom's house went to bring the bride from her home; this was done at night. She was conducted amid great solemnity, carried on the back by a matron. Ahead of her were carried two files of lighted torches. Around her, in front and back of her, went a great many people, until she reached the house of the groom's parents. There they placed the couple together close to the hearth, which was always in the center of a hall (large room), with a bright fire, the woman on the left of the man; the mother of the groom now clothed her daughter-in-law in a very beautiful "vipil" (sleeveless blouse), and placed close at her feet some very elaborate skirts, while the girl's mother covered her son-in-law with a very elegant blanket, fastening it on his shoulder, while at his feet she put an elaborate maxtli[1]. This done, certain old women whom they call titici tied a corner of the young man's blanket to the skirt of the girl's garment. Thus ended the wedding ceremonies, with a great many complements of food, drink, dances, executed afterwards, as is fully described in the corresponding chapter.

They had two more festivals which at times were at fixed dates, at times movable. They belonged to the latter class on account of their recurring every so many years, one being celebrated every four, the other every eight years. They could be called fixed because they had year, month and day positively designated; at the festival recurring every four years they perforated children's ears and held the ceremony of what they called "crespa," which means arrange (trim) the hair of children and teach them the handling of fire. The eight-year festival meant fasting for eight days previous with bread and water; they also held a dance at this feast, for which they dressed in the images or likeness of high personages, of birds, or other animals, saying that by so doing they searched for good luck, as we have explained it in the appendix of Book II.

As it happens with us, these movable feasts sometimes occurred on dates of feasts of their calendar.

[1]Maxtli—girdle or belt.

CALENDAR-FESTIVALS

About the festivals and the sacrifices celebrated under the signs of the first month called Atlcaoalo or Quavitleloa

It is not necessary in this second book to try to disprove or discuss the idolatrous ceremonies which are related in it; they are in themselves so cruel and inhuman that they would horrify anyone who heard them, and fill him with terror; I therefore shall simply relate the facts in their proper order.

Under the first signs of the first month of the year called in general Quavitleloa and by the Mexicans proper Atlcaoalo, and which commenced on (our) February the second, they celebrated a great festival in honor of the gods of the water which they called Tlaloques (tlalocs). For this they searched for a great many infants, buying them from their mothers and choosing especially those who had two twisted tufts of hair on the head and were born under a lucky sign, saying that those were a more agreeable sacrifice to the gods to make them grant water at the opportune time. They carried these infants up to the high mountains to kill, where they had made the solemn vow to offer sacrifice. There, on those mountain-tops, they tore out the hearts of some of the infants, while with others they did it in certain places of the lagune of Mexico. One of these places was Tepetzinco, a well known hill in the lagune; another hill in the lagune was called Tepepulco, where they killed a large number of infants each year, and once dead they cooked and ate them.

At this same festival they erected in all the houses and palaces poles on the point of which they fastened papers thickly-sprinkled with ulli (gum) drops. They called these papers amateteuitl, and this was also done in honor of the gods of the water. The places where they sacrificed children were the following: the first one is called Quauchtepetl, which is a prominent mountain chain near Tlaltelulco; the children killed there, boys and girls, received the name of that mountain, Quauchtepetl. All those sacrificed there were adorned with paper dyed red (or flesh color).

The second mountain on top of which they sacrificed children was called Yoaltecatl; this is a prominent height which rises alongside of or near Guadalupe, and they gave the children sacrificed there the same name of Yoaltecatl; they dressed these with papers dyed black with lines drawn in red ink. The third mountain on which children were killed was Tepetzinco, which is that little hillock in the lagune facing the Tlaltelulco; there they killed a girl and called her Quetzalxoch for the reason that the mountain by another name was known as Quetzalxoch. This girl was dressed with papers dyed blue. The fourth hill was called

Poiauhtla, and rises near the border of Tlaxcala and close to Tepetzinco; on its east side they had erected a house (oratory) called Ayauchalli, and it was there they sacrificed children in honor of that mountain, and called them Poiauhtla; they adorned them with papers streaked with ulli (gum) oil. The fifth place of infant sacrifice was the whirlpool or sewer in the lagune of Mexico which they called Pantitlan, and those who died there were called Epecoatl. The finery in which they clothed them was called Epnepaniuhqui. The sixth place of sacrifice was a hill called Cocotl, which is near Chalco Atenco, and the infants sacrificed there were called Cocotl, like the hill; they dressed them in papers one half red and the other half tawny. The seventh place was the hill called Yauhquene, which is near Atlacuioaia (today Tacubaya), and they, too, received the same name as the mountain. Their paper ornaments were tawny in color. Before these poor young victims were taken away to be slaughtered they adorned them with precious stones (jewels), rich plumes, and with blankets and mantles very elegantly made; with very elaborate and highly polished sandals. They furthermore put wings like angel's wings on their shoulders, and dyed their faces with ulli (gum) oil, in the middle of their cheeks they painted small white disks, and placed them in litters which were ornated with rich plumes and other precious jewels. While they bore them in these litters they played flutes and trumpets for them such as they used, and wherever they passed the people were weeping. Upon reaching an oratory close to Tepetzinco on the eastern slope and which was called Tococan, they stopped over night and kept watch over these infants; in order that they might not fall asleep the priests of the idols sang their songs to them. If the children cried very much when they took them to the place of sacrifice, those who were with them were glad, because they considered it as a sign that there would be abundant rain. If they met some hydropic person on the road they thought this to be a bad omen, because a dropsical man or woman prevented the rains. If any one of the ministers (priests) of the temple, and other attendants whom they called quaquavilti, or the old men returned to their houses and failed to reach the place where the children were to be sacrificed, they were considered as scoundrels, unworthy of holding a public office, and from then on they were called mocauhque, which means "dropped one." They foretold rain or frosts from the arrival of certain birds or their song.

During this same festival they committed another cruelty, namely, they took all their captives to a temple called Yopico, belonging to the god Totec. There, after many ceremonies, they tied each one of these captives to a stone looking like a millstone with a rope long enough and in such a way that the man could walk all around the stone; then they gave them wooden swords with dull blades and a shield and put before them pieces of pine wood to throw and the same men who had captured them went to fight with them with swords and shield, and when they had vanquished them would take them at once to the place of sacrifice, where, thrown on their backs over a stone of three or four palms in height by a width of one and a half square, which stone they called techtecatl, they held them, two by their feet and two by the head, while another one with a large flint-knife would cut open the chest with one stroke and, thrusting his hand through the hole, tear out the heart, which he at once offered to the sun and to the other gods, raising it in the four cardinal directions. The body was then thrown down the steps of the temple, and it would fall slowly, bumping against them until reaching the bottom. There the dead man's captor again received it, cut it to pieces, which he distributed, and these pieces were cooked and eaten.

The Ceremonies and Sacrifices Celebrated in the Second Month Called Tlacaxipeoaliztli

On the last day of the said month they celebrated a very solemn feast in honor of the god called Xippetototec, as well as in honor of Vitzilopuchtli. During this festival they killed all the captives they had, men, women and children. Before killing them, however, they celebrated a great many ceremonies, which were as follows: on the eve of the feast after midday they began a very solemn dance, and during the entire night they watched over the captives who were to die, in the house called Calpulco. Here they pulled their hair off the top of the head. This ceremony was performed close to the fire at midnight, when they also drew blood from their own ears to offer it to the gods, a thing they always did at that hour. At daybreak they took their captives to where they were to die, which was in the temple of Vitzilopuchtli. They were killed by the ministers (priests) of the temple in the manner told before, then they flayed them all, and for that reason this festival was called Tlacaxipeoaliztli, which means "skinning of men who, in turn, were called xipeme, or by another name tototecti; the first one of these names means "skinned" or "flayed," the second "dead in honor of the god Totec." The owners of the captives delivered them to the priests at the foot of the Cú, who then dragged them up the steps, each priest his own prisoner, holding them by the hair, toward the sacrificial stone where they were to be killed, tearing out the heart of each one, which then was offered to the sun, as stated before. They then threw them down the steps, where subsequently, other priests flayed them. This all was done in the Cú (temple) of Vitzilopuchtli. The hearts they had thus torn out of the bodies and had offered to the sun and the other gods were thrown into a wooden bowl; these hearts were called quauhnoctli, and those who died after having their hearts torn out were called quauhteca; after the bodies had been flayed by the old men who were called quauquacuilli, they carried them to the calpulco, where the owner of each captive had made his promise or vow, and the body was divided (cut up), and a thigh sent to Mochtecuzoma for him to eat, the rest being distributed to other chieftains or relatives, who went to eat it in the house of the man who had captured the victim. They cooked that meat with corn and gave each one a piece of it with its broth in a bowl with the cooked corn; they called that stew tlacatlaolli; after the meal followed general drunkenness.

The following day, at daybreak, after having spent the whole night awake, they knifed or fought duels rather, with other captives, whom they tied to the round (mill) stone, as told in the preceding chapter. These captives they called oavanti, and they scalped these in the same way, keeping the scalp-locks as trophies or relics. They performed a number of other ceremonies on the same order which are not given in order not to tire the reader, although they all are given in the original text. They also played on the occasion of this festival the following games: a large number of young men dressed themselves in the skins of the sacrificed and they then were called tototecti (like the victims); they seated themselves on hay-beds, benches made of hay, or ticatl, or clay. While they were thus seated other young men would come to incite them to fight either by means of words or by punching them until they ran after their tormentors, who tried to escape. If they reached each other they would arrest one another and be locked into prison, from whence they could only be released by paying a certain amount or making a donation.

As soon as this sham, or playful fight, was over, they would commence to knife such captives as were destined to die stabbed, while tied to the millstone. This time four would fight each of the captives, two who were dressed as tigers and two as eagles. Before the fight commenced they lifted shield and sword towards the sun, and then began fighting man to man. If the captive, tied to the stone, was brave and courageous and if he defended himself well, he would be attacked by two, then by three, and if he was still in a fighting condition, by all four of his tormentors. In this fight the four aggressors were dancing, making a great many turns (and fancy steps). Before the knifing and stabbing began, a very solemn procession took place. From the top of the Cú (temple) called Yopico a large number of priests would appear in their vestments, each representing one of the gods; they appeared in their order, forming a long procession, and were followed by the four fighters, the two tigers and the two eagles. These were strong men, who advanced in a fighting attitude, armed with sword and shield, making motions like fencers. Upon reaching the bottom of the stairway they advanced toward the stone where the captives are stabbed; they all surrounded it and seated themselves in a rather wide circle around it in their ycpales, which they called quecholicpalli, all orderly grouped. The high (chief) priest of that festival who was called Yooallaoa sat in the place of honor, because he was in charge of the tearing out of the hearts of those who were doomed to die there. When all were seated they began at once to play their flutes, trumpets and shells, and to whistle and sing. All those who sang or played any of the musical instruments carried flags (pennants) of white plumes on their shoulders on tall staves and seated themselves in orderly groups around the stone, somewhat removed from the priests. After thus being seated and starting their playing, one of those who owned captives who were to be killed on this occasion brought his victim into the circle, dragging him by the hair to the stone where he was to be stabbed. There they gave him the wine of the country, or pulque, to drink, and as the captive received the bowl of pulque, he raised it to the east, to the north, to the west, and to the south, as if offering it to the four parts of the world and then drank, but not from the bowl itself, but sipping through a hollow cane; then a priest came with a quail, tore its head off in front of the captive, and after that took the captive's shield, raising it on high, then threw the beheaded quail behind him. After this they made the captive stand on the round millstone; one of the priests of the temple dressed in a bear-skin, who acted as a sort of godfather of those who had to die there, came and took a rope which was passed through the opening in the center of the stone and tied it around the captive's waist. He then gave him his wooden sword which, instead of knives (sharp edges) had bird feathers glued along the edge, and he also gave him four pine clubs with which to defend himself, and which he might throw at his aggressors (opponents). The owner of the captive leaving him thus, as stated, on the stone, went to his place and from there looked on to see what happened to his captive dancing there (on the stone). At once those prepared for the skirmish began to fight with their victim, one after the other. Some of these captives being very brave, tired their four combatants, who were unable to make them surrender. In such cases a fifth one, who was left-handed, therefore using his left hand instead of the right, entered the fight, and he conquered him and took his weapons, felling him. Then came at once the one (priest) called Yooallaoa, who cut his breast open and tore the heart out. Some of the captives, after being tied upon the stone, became so faint-hearted that they lost their courage, and since they took arms in such a discouraged condition they allowed themselves to be defeated much sooner, and their hearts were torn out right there upon the stone. Still others became at once terror-stricken to such an extent that, refusing to take their weapons, they begged to be killed at once, so they took the man, in such a case, threw him on his back over the edge of the stone and the functionary called Yooallaoa cut his breast open, tore out the heart, offered it to the sun, and then threw it into a wooden "jicara" (bowl); another priest then took a piece of hollow cane and, inserting it in the opening where the heart had been extracted, dipped and dyed it in the blood, withdrew it, and offered that blood to the sun also. Then the owner of the captive approached and received the blood of the latter in a (jicara) bowl, the border of which was adorned all around with feathers. In that bowl was a small tube also lined (covered) with feathers, and with this bowl of blood he went to make his devotional visits to the statues of all the gods in the temples and the calpules, and he touched each one with the small tube dyed by the blood of his captive, as if he were giving them a taste of it. For this function he was arrayed in all his fine feathers and jewels. After having thus visited all the statues of the town and given each a taste of the blood of his dead captive, he at once went to the royal palace to take off all his regalia. The body of his captive was meanwhile take to the house called calpulco, where he had spent the night before the sacrifice in wake, and there they flayed it. From there the skinned body was taken to the house of its owner, who now dismembered it and divided the meat between his superiors, friends and relatives; he, the owner himself, did not partake of any of the flesh of his captive because from the hour he captured him he considered his captive as his own flesh and blood, calling him son, while the latter called him father, and for that reason he only partook of the flesh of the captives of others. The skin also belonged to the captor, who in turn presented it to someone else to wear and pass through the streets as if he had a wolf's head on, or as if masqueraded or disguised, and everybody gave him who wore such a skin something, all of which he brought forthwith to the owner of it, who in turn divided these gifts among those who wore the skins, as he saw fit.

Once this knifing and killing of captives was over, all those who had witnessed it, priests and chieftains and slave-owners, began their solemn dance around the stone upon which these captives had been sacrificed, the owners of the latter carrying the heads of the victims by the hair, hanging from the right hand or wrist. This dance was called motzontecomaitotia, and the godfather of the captives, called Cuitlachucue, took hold of the ropes by which they had been tied to the stone and raised them successively to the four parts of the world, in reverence and obeisance, and while he did so, they cried and sighed like people who mourn their dead.

This spectacle was secretly watched and attended by the people from the towns of Vexotzinco, Tlaxcala, Nonoalco, Cempoala, and many other places against whom Mochtecuzoma was on the warpath, and the Mexicans feigned not to notice them, in order that they might tell their people at home what happened to their captives. With these ceremonials the festival of the prisoners knifed on the stone ended. During this entire festival they all ate tortillas made like small pies (turnovers rather), which were made of raw corn, and which they called vilocpalli, and all those who went to see the spectacle made provision of them and ate them where the festival took place. The following day they paired off for the solemn dance, which began at the royal houses. For this they dressed in all the robes, devices (insignias) or rich plumes they found in these royal houses, and in their hands they carried, instead of flowers, all kinds of tamales and tortillas; instead of strings (of beads) and garlands they wore (strings of) toasted corn (popcorn) which they call mumuchtli. They also carried red ospreys made of red feathers and corn stalks, with the ears of corn on them. After midday the priests stopped dancing in the temple and all the chieftains and nobles came and, ranged in their corresponding order in front of the royal houses, stood there in line. Mochtecuzoma also appeared at the head of the procession and had on his right side the lord of Tezcoco and on his left the one of Tlacuba, and a very solemn dance was executed, which lasted all afternoon until sunset. After this ceremonial dance they commenced other kinds of dances in which, holding hands, they moved in winding lines, snakelike. In these dances old soldiers as well as cadets and new recruits took part; also old women, if they chose to do it, and prostitutes. These dances lasted until about midnight, and the festival went on for twenty days in this place where the captives had been slain, and until the feast of next month's sign, called Tocoztontli, was due.

Feasts and Sacrifices Celebrated on the Last Day of the Second Month. Called Tlacaxipeoaliztli

On the last day of the second month, Tlacaxipeoaliztli, they celebrated the festival called Ayacachpixolo, in the temple they named Yopico. At this feast all the neighbors of the district belonging to that temple were seated in the latter, singing and sounding rattles for an entire day, also offering flowers. These were offered as the first blooms of the year, and no one dared even to smell of a flower before this votive offering had been made in the temple. For this feast they also made a certain kind of tamales called Tzatzapaltamali of wild amaranth (or white goosefoot). These tamales were especially made by the people living in the Coatlan ward (district), where they offered them in their (Cú) temple at the feet of the goddess they called Coatlyate or Coatlantonan, for whom all these famous for making (artificial) flowers professed great devotion. During this festival they also went to hide in some cave the skins of the captives they had flayed at the past feast, because they were tired of wearing them, and also some of them were ill with the itch (mange) or with eye-trouble. They made a solemn promise (vow) to go and help to hide these skins, for this was done in procession and amid great solemnity. These diseased men went in this procession in order to get well, and it is said that some of them recovered and these attributed their recovery to this procession and their devotion. The festival ended amid great ceremonies, and those who had worn the skins of the captives also cleansed themselves with great solemnity. Owners of captives and their entire households did not bathe nor wash their heads until the conclusion of this festival, thus for almost twenty days. As soon as this feast was over they and all members of their household who had worn the skins washed themselves, and this procedure took place in the Cú (temple), with water mixed with flour or corn-dough (used for tortillas), and from there they went to bathe in ordinary water. They did not wash themselves either but were washed by others, who, however, did not rub or scrub their bodies, but merely patted them with moist hands, saying that in this manner the fat from the skins they had worn would come off. Then the owners of captives and all their household washed and soaped their heads, from which they had abstained for twenty days as a sign of penance for the dead captive. After all this, the master of the dead slave put up a round globe in the court of his house; this globe was made of petate (matting), with three feet, and on top of it he placed all the papers with which the captive had been adorned at the time of his death. He then sought a valiant youth, whom he dressed in them, giving him a shield to carry in one hand and a stick in the other. This youth then had to run through the streets trying to hit (beat) whomsoever he met. All fled from him in great consternation and shouted upon seeing him, "there comes the Tetzonpac!" If he succeeded in hitting anyone, he took that man's blankets away from him, and these he carried along and threw them into the court of the one who had dressed him in the papers. After this, the owner of the dead captive erected in the center of his courtyard a pole-like column, which was a sign that he had captured an enemy, and thus the pole or column signified his bravery in war. Then he took the thigh-bone of the captive after the meat had been eaten, adorned it with papers, and hung it by means of a rope on the pole in his courtyard. For the day when this was to take place he invited his relatives and friends and the people of his district, gave them food and drink, and in their presence hoisted that bone on the pole. They performed certain ceremonies in the preparing of the pulque for that day, and all sang the songs of his house or lineage; all this was done within the twenty days before Veytocoztli.

Feasts and Ceremonials Performed During the Signs of the Fourth Month, Which Was Called Veytocoztli

In the fourth month, Veytocoztli, they celebrated the feast of the god of the grain-fields called Tzintautl, and of the goddess of sustenance (livelihood), Chicomecoatl. Before celebrating this feast, however, they fasted for four days and placed reed-mace close to the images of their gods. This reed-mace had to be very white, very well cut, and the lower part where it is whitest was tinted with blood from their ears or legs. This service was done by the young men and boys in the houses of the most prominent and wealthy merchants. These boys also put before the images clusters of acxoiatl, and they placed before these goddesses or their altars beds (bankings) of hay, the edges of which were woven like straw-mats, while the rest of the hay was just loosely piled by hand. Furthermore, they made many kinds of "mazamorra" (a sort of mush or pap) which, while it was still very hot, almost boiling, was poured into the "cajetes" (flat earthen pulque bowls), in the house called Telpuchcalli. In the morning the young men and the boys visited all the houses where they had adorned the images as above stated and begged for alms, each one for himself, never going with one another. They were given that pap so they might eat. The young men of the Cús (temples) called Tlamaztoton carried theirs to the calmecac to eat it there, and the youths of the common people called Telpupuchtli took their portion to the telpuchcalli and ate it there. Then they all went into the cornfields and into the country and brought back corn-stalks and other herbs called mecoatl, and with these they adorned the god of the grainfields, whose image they all had in their houses; they, moreover, adorned it with papers and placed food before it, which consisted in five chiquiviles with their tortillas, and on top of each chiquivitl a frog roasted in a certain way; then they placed before the same image another chiquivitl of "chian," flour, which they call pinolli, and one of toasted corn mixed with beans. They cut a cane (stalk) of corn and stuffed it with all these viands (different kinds of food), taking a little of each kind, and then placed that tube on the back of the roasted frog, as if it were carrying it on its back.

This all each one did in his own house, and for that reason they called this feast calionaoac. Later, in the evening, they carried all this food to the Cú of the goddess of sustenance, Chicomecoatl, and, snatching it off from one another, they ate it all. At this festival they would also carry the ears of corn they had put aside for sowing, to the Cú of the said Mecoatl and of Cinteutl, that they might be blessed there. This corn was carried on the back by young virgin-girls, wrapped in blankets, never more than seven ears in each bundle, and on each ear they sprinkled a few drops of "ulli" oil, and then wrapped each in paper first. The arms and legs of the young girls were covered with red feathers and on their faces they put melted tar which they call chapopoctli (this might now be chapote, which is black wax), sprinkled with white pyrite-powder. As they went along the road they were surrounded (constantly) by a big crowd, and everyone was looking at them without ever taking their eyes off, but no one dared to speak to them, and if perchance a daring or mischievous young fellow said some flattering words to them one or the other of the old women who accompanied these maidens would promptly answer him, "And you, coward, you undisciplined recruit (fellow) dare to speak? You should speak? Think before you commit any crazy folly, for they might take off that lock of hair off your neck to mark you as a coward and a man of no account, you dastardly villain; you have no right to speak here! You are just as much of a woman as I am; you never got away from behind the hearth!" In this way they tried to encourage young manhood to become good warriors, to be brave in all matters of warfare, and if one of the youths took these remarks personally, he would reply to the old woman, saying, "Very well said, old lady, I receive your words as a favour, and shall do as you command. I shall go where I can do something whereby I shall be considered as a man. Good care of it shall I have; I am sure I appreciate two cocoa beans more highly than I do you and your descendants. Go and smear your belly with dirt and scratch it! Cross your legs and roll in the dust! Over yonder is a rough stone; go get it and hit your face with it and your nose till it bleeds, and if you wish anything else, go make a hole in your throat with a firebrand and spit through that hole! Pray keep quiet and be at peace!" Although they spoke thus rudely to the old woman who had reproved them, it was only to show their bravado, for it hurt them inwardly to be thus spoken to, and later they would say among themselves: "I offer this arrant rogue of an old woman to the devil (may the devil take this knavish old person), and since she has scolded us so cruelly that our very hearts are sore over her speech, friends, it is most urgent that we do some manly act to show who we are!"

After the ears of corn had thus been carried to the Cú, they returned them again to their homes and put them at the very bottom of the troughs, saying that they were like the heart of them, and when sowing time came they used these as seeds. This festival was celebrated in honor of the goddess Chicomecoatl, whom they thought to be a woman who granted them all the necessary elements to preserve life, for they said whoever has not the food he needs to maintain life fails and has to die. They also said that she created all the different kinds of corn, of beans or any other vegetable, as well as the many kinds of "chian," and that was their reason for offering her food during her festival, with solemn dances, songs, and the blood of quails. All the ornaments with which they adorned her on that occasion were bright red and quaintly made. In her hand she held corn-stalks. Thus ended the festivities in honor of that goddess, and then the next festival began with dances.

Festival Held During the Signs of the Fifth Month, Which Was Called Toxcatl

This festival was held under the signs of the fifth month, which they called Toxcatl. In this month they celebrated a paschal festival in honor of the principal god called Tezcatlipoca, or by another name Tlilacaoan, or Yautl, and by still other names Telpuchtli or Tlamatzincatl. At this festival they killed (sacrificed) a youth of great elegance of carriage (great fitness or perfect health and proportion) whom they had maintained for a whole year in constant delight. They said he was (represented) the image of Tezcatlipoca. Once this youth was dead, they immediately put another one in his place, whom they petted and spoiled for another year, and so on, always replacing the one they sacrificed, and they had a great number of them in readiness from which to choose the successor to the one they killed at the festival. They selected for this purpose the best looking men among their captives and kept them in the Calpixques; they took great pains to choose the most intelligent and best suited there might be, without the least physical defect. The youth chosen for the coming year was carefully trained to play the flute very well, to gather and bring in the "smoke sticks" (cañas de humo) and the flowers, as is the custom among chieftains and courtiers; they also taught him how to swallow smoke and smell the perfume of flowers, walking about as do the nobles and people of the court. Even while these young men were still under the care of the calpixques and prior to the announcement of their ultimate destiny, they were carefully instructed by these same calpixques in good manners in speech and behavior, in the correct way to bow to those they met on the street, and all other good habits. The one appointed for the sacrifice at the next festival of this god was greatly venerated by all those who met him, and they kissed the earth in his honour and worshipped him. If, due to the good treatment (good food) he grew stout, they would make him drink salt-water to keep slender.

The young man thus chosen to die at the next feast went through the streets playing the flute, carrying flowers, and smoke-sticks. He was free to be out day and night wherever he chose to go in town; he was always attended by eight pages, dressed like those of the palace, and he himself was given elegant and precious clothing by his master, for henceforth he was considered as a god himself. His whole body and face were anointed; his head was adorned with white chicken-feathers pasted on with resin; his hair was allowed to grow to reach the waist. After he was all dressed they adorned him with a wreath of flowers called izquixuchitl, and a long garland of the same was fastened on both shoulders and hung down to the armpit on both sides. In the ears he carried gold ornaments like ear-rings (pendants). Around the neck he wore a string of precious stones with a large pendant of a beautiful white stone hanging down to the chest. They put around his neck also a long helmet beaver, made of sea-shells; on the back he wore an ornament shaped like a bag, of the size of one square span (eight inches) made of white linen with its tassels and fringe. On the arms above and below the elbow he wore gold rings (armlets), and around the wrists strings of precious stones, which they call macuextli, which covered almost the entire forearm. He was covered with a very rich looking blanket fashioned like a net, with a very fancy fringe around the edges. Close to his body he wore a very odd piece of cloth which they used to cover the lower part of their bodies, called maxtlatl; the lower part of this maxtlatl had a very elaborate border about a span in width, and this border hung down in front as far as the knees. On the legs he wore golden rattles (or jingles), which sounded at every step. His feet were clad in elaborately painted sandals, which they called ocelunacace. Thus the youth was clothed for the first part of the year. Twenty days before the feast these clothes were changed; they washed the dye off his skin, and they married him to four maidens, with whom he lived for these last twenty days of his life. They now cut his hair in the style worn by war-captains, tying it like a tassel on top of the head with a very elaborate fringe and adorned that hair-bundle with two tassels with their buttons, made of feathers, gold and techomitl very oddly made, and which they called aztaxelli.

The four girls they gave him as wives and who had likewise been reared with special care for that purpose were given names of four goddesses; one bore the name of Xochiquetzatl, another the one of Xilonen, the third was called Atlatonan, and the fourth Vixtocioatl. Five days before the sacrifice they worshipped the young man as one of their gods. The lord remained alone in his house while all those of the court followed his example and solemn banquets and dances were held in very elaborate costumes. On the first day they feasted the youth in the district (of the city) called Tecanman; on the second day in the place where they kept the image of Tezcatlipoca; the third on the little hillock; the fourth at what is called Tepetzinco, which is in the lagune called ilquioa, antlalpia, antlalcuya, micontlalpia, itoci; on the fourth day on another hillock, also in the lagune, and called Tepepulco. After this fourth day they placed him in a canoe in which the king was wont to navigate, and which was covered by an awning; with him went his four wives, consoling him. Leaving Tepepulco they navigated towards a place called Tlapizaoaian, which is near the plain of Ixtapalapan, and extends toward Chalco, where rises the little hillock of Acaquilpan or Olcoaltepec. At this place his wives and all the other people left him, returning to the city, and he remained only with the eight pages who had been his followers for the entire year. They took him to a small and poorly decorated temple which stood near the highway (road) outside the city at a distance of almost a league from it. As they reached the foot of the Cú, the young man mounted the steps by himself, and on the first one he broke one of the flutes he had played on during that past year of prosperity; on the second one another, and so successively until he had broken them all, and thus reached the top. There he was awaited by the Sátrapas or priests who were to kill him, and these now grabbed him and threw him onto the stone-block and, holding him by feet, hands and head, thrown on his back, the priest who had the stone knife with a mighty thrust buried it in the victim's breast and, after drawing it out, thrust one hand into the opening and tore out the heart, which he at once offered to the sun. In this manner they killed all those who were offered to Tezcatlipoca, but instead of throwing the bodies down the steps after the sacrifice as they did on other occasions, this young man was carried down these steps by four men into the court, where they cut off his head, which they stuck onto a pole called Tzompantli. Thus ended the life of this unfortunate youth who for an entire year had been petted and honored by everybody. They said that this (sacrifice) signified that those who had possessed riches and pleasures in their lifetime would thus end in poverty and sorrow.

For this feast they also used to make the image of Vitzilopuchtli in dough, called Azoalli, of the size of a man down to the waist and that, in order to place this image in the Cú, which they called Vitznaoac, they would erect a stand the wood of which was carved to resemble snakes, their heads tied on the four sides of the pedestal, head against head, so that on all four sides there were tails and heads. For arms they inserted two sticks of mizguitl, and then inflated the dough in such a way that it resembled the bust of a man. They made this bust in the house (oratory) where the image of Vitzilopuchtli was always kept. After finishing the bust they adorned it with the vestments of the god; a jacket made of embroidered cloth of "besos de hombres" (whatever that may be), they covered the image with a very transparent blanket of "nequen" (probably henequen), and they crowned him with a crown shaped like a basket, very closely fitting to the head and widening at the top where it was elaborated with a plume; over a paper in the center rose a mask also made of feathers, and at the top of the mask a flint knife was inserted like the cross-iron of an anchor (ancon) dipped in blood to the middle of it (one half of it dipped in blood). Another blanket made entirely of elaborate feather-work was thrown over the bust. In the center of this feather-blanket was a round plaque (medallion) of hammered gold. At the bottom were ornaments made of tzoalli in the shape of kisses[1] close to the foot of the image, and these were covered also by the first mantle on which similar kisses had been elaborated, as well as limbs of a cut-up human body. The mantle or blanket thus adorned was called Tlaquaquallo.

They made still another ornament to honor this god, and which consisted of an enormous piece of paper, twenty fathoms (six feet each) long by one in width, and one finger thick. This paper was carried by a number of strong young men in front of the image, holding it on either side. In order to prevent this paper from tearing they mounted it on shafts or darts which they call teumitl, and these shafts or darts were adorned with feathers close to the arrow-head, in the center and at the end. These darts were so arranged that one crossed the width of the paper above, another underneath, so that in order to carry this large paper one youth would hold the two lower ends of the shafts together, another one the points, thus pressing the paper tightly held between them. When this was done, the image (bust of Azoalli) on its pedestal (platform) was raised onto the shoulders of a number of captains and warriors who, grouped on either side, carried it like a litter with the long paper always in front. Thus they proceeded in a procession, singing the songs to the god and dancing before him a solemn dance. Arriving at the foot of the temple steps, they tied ropes to the pedestal or platform in order to mount it up the stairway, and they did this very carefully so as not to tip the statue to either side. Those who carried the large paper again mounted ahead of the statue, and to prevent tearing it, those who climbed first at once began rolling the paper up with great care, pulling out the arrow shafts as they proceeded, and handing them to the one whose duty it was to gather them in a big bunch. As soon as the statue had reached the top they placed it where it belonged on its throne or chair, and they laid in

[1]Besos. In Spain these "besos" are a sort of pastry very much like our "meringues," of white of egg and shaped like lips.

front of the platform the roll of paper securely tied, to prevent its unrolling. Then all but the Sátrapas (priests) left the Cú, and the latter were on duty guarding the idols. This ceremony being over at about sunset, tamales and other kinds of food were placed in front of the image as offerings. The next morning at dawn everyone made this offering of food to the image of Vitzilopuchtli, which he had in his own house, and all of them went to the Cú to offer the blood of quails to the image they had installed there on the previous day. The chieftain or lord came first, pulling off the heads of four quails, which latter he then offered to the image, then followed the priests with their sacrifices, and after them the people. After pulling off their heads they threw the beheaded birds at the feet of the idol, where they fluttered until death felled them. They then were gathered by the shield-bearers and warriors of the king, who had them peeled, roasted and salted, dividing them then among themselves. A certain amount, however, belonged first to the king or lord, to the chiefs, to the priests, and only what was left was of the shield-bearers. They all brought their braziers; a fire was built in the Cú and live coal was produced, for the burning of incense, for they all brought their "copalli" (copal-incense) and their own earthen incense-burners, which look like cups with holes, very ornate, and which they called tlemaitl; they also brought copal (incense) of all kinds, and proceeded with the ceremonies of the service of that god (according to rules). At a certain stage of the ceremonial the priests took live coal from the fire, put it into their incense-burners, and incensed the image of Vitzilopuchtli, which they had brought to the Cú shortly before. This ceremony was not only performed in the Cú, but also in all the homes by the owners who on that occasion incensed all the statues of the different gods they happened to have. After the incensing they threw the live coal left in the incensories into a round hearth of about two spans in height made of clay, which was in the center of the patio, and which they called tlexictli.

At this festival all the young girls painted (beautified) their faces, adorned their arms and legs with red feathers, and carried certain papers flatly stuck (fastened) on sticks which they called tetelvitl; these papers were painted with ink (dye). If they happened to be daughters of chieftains or wealthy people, they wore instead of the paper very thin blankets called "canaoc." The blankets were also painted in black in the shape (or form) of commas, vertically. These papers or clothes on their sticks they carried in their hands on high (like banners), and walked in procession with the other people to honor their god. These girls also danced, holding their paper (or cloth) banners in both hands, around the hearth, upon which stood two shield-bearers with faces dyed with ink, who carried on their back something that looked like cages made of candlewood, around the edges of which small paper flags were stuck. They carried them, not in the fashion (way) men carry their long bundles of firewood, fastened by a strap about the forehead, but in women's way, tied over the breast. These two men, on top of the hearth guided the dance of the women surrounding it, dancing in woman-fashion. At the same time the priests of the temple danced with their companions and these two groups, the men and the women, danced or rather hopped a dance called Toxcachocholoa, which means jumping or dancing on the festival of Toxcatl. The priests wore around their foreheads a sort of paper disks shirred in the shape of roses. All the priests had their heads adorned with white chicken feathers; their faces and lips were bedaubed with honey after they had been painted black, as they always did, and the honey shone on that dark background. As was their custom, they wore under-garments of paper called amasmaxtli; in their hands they carried sceptres of palm leaves, at the top of which was a flower of black feathers; this sceptre was called cuitlacuchtli, after the knot or ball it had at the lower end. The part of the sceptre they held in hand was wrapped in paper painted with black stripes or lines, and when they danced they bent right down to the soil in a certain figure of the dance, resting on the sceptre. Those who furnished the music for dancing were stationed within the house called calpulco, so that dancers and musicians could not see each other; the latter were seated; in their midst was the kettle-drum, and all played jingles and all the other instruments used by them for dancing. All the employees (people of the palace), even the warriors, old and young, danced in other (separate) parts of the courtyard, holding each other by the hand, and winding in and out (wriggling) in snake-fashion, very similar to the popular dances the people of Castilla la Vieja, men and women, dance today. Among these warriors one could also see maidens dancing, very well painted, and their arms and legs adorned with red feathers. On the head they wore small hoods which, instead of flowers, were made of roasted corn (popcorn) which they call momochitl, of which each grain looks like a (very) white flower. These little hoods were very much like the flower-hoods the country girls of Castilla wear in the month of May. They also wore strings of this same popcorn hanging from both shoulders to the armpits. They call this sort of dance tlanaoa, which means embraced; "quinaoain Vitzilopuchtli," to embrace Vitzilopuchtli. All this was done with great circumspection and modesty, and if anyone looked or spoke dishonourably, he was at once punished, for there were people (men) stationed nearby to watch over them. These dances lasted until nightfall.

While after having given him a year of luxury they killed the youth who was supposed to be the image of Tlitacaoan, at the beginning of this festival, they had already begun to educate, together with him, another young man whom they called Yxteucali, by another name Tlacabepan, or also Teicauhtzin. They always were together, although this latter one was not worshipped like the former, nor was he so highly esteemed. As soon as the above-mentioned festival was over with its rejoicing and its ceremonies, they killed Tlacabepan, the image of Vitzilopuchtli, and for this purpose adorned him with papers all painted with black wheels (or circles). On his head they put a mitre of eagle-feathers with many tufts on the top, and in the center of which was a flint-knife, stuck upright, one half of it tinted with blood and adorned with red feathers. On his back he wore an ornament, one span square, made of very thin cloth, and which they call icuechin, tied by means of cotton strings around the breast and over the cuechin there was a small bag called patoxin. On one of his arm's there was an ornament made of the skin of a wild animal, shaped like a maniple such as (in the Catholic church) is used for saying mass. They called this maniple imatacox. His legs were adorned with golden jingles such as are worn by dancers. Thus attired, he danced during the festival and he guided (or led) the plebeian dances, at the head of the dancers. This youth of his own free will and at his own time, delivered himself into the hands of those who were to kill him. The priests who took care of these young men and watched over them until they were to be sacrificed were called Tlatlacaanalti, and they were the ones who cut the respective victim's breast and extracted the heart, later beheading him and sticking the head on a pole in the Tzompantli close to that of the first youth, above-mentioned. On that same day the priests inflicted wounds, with a flint knife, on boys and girls, on the breast, the stomach, on the muscles of the arms or on the wrist. It appears that these wounds were meant to represent marks of the demon with which he marked his sheep, and those who even today practice this are suspected of practicing idolatry if these marks are made after baptism, but of old, children were thus marked every year.

Festivals and Sacrifices Performed Under the Signs of the Sixth Month Called Etzalqüaliztli

In the sixth month, Etzalqüaliztli, they held a festival in honor of the gods of rain, whom they call Tlaloques. For four days previous to this festival the priests of the idols fasted and before beginning this fast they went to gather cyperus at a (certain) spring close to the village of Citlaltepec where they grew very tall and very thick. This kind of cyperus they called astapillin, or tolmomilli; the reeds grow very long and the part under water is very white. They gathered them from a spring called Temilco, or by another name Tepexit, also Ostoc. After having pulled them out they did them up in bundles, wrapping them in their blankets in order to carry them on the back after having bound them in the "mecapal" (leather band with ropes for carrying loads). They then started back, carrying the load lengthwise on the back, not horizontally. These priests of the idols, whenever they went for the cyperus and when they returned with their loads, were in the habit of robbing whomsoever they met on the way but, as everyone knew about this practice, nobody went out at such times, not even for a walk. If perchance they met anyone, even if it were the collector of tributes, they took everything he carried, and if he defended himself they ill-treated him dreadfully with kicks and blows, even dragging him across the road. No penalty was inflicted on these priests for such misdemeanor, because they were held in high esteem and reverence.

As soon as they reached the temple where the festival was to be celebrated, with their loads of cyperus, they sewed them at once, arranging the reeds, white against green, so they looked like painted blankets; they also made seats out of these reeds with and without backs to them. In order to make the blankets they first spread them on the floor, arranging the design as they wanted it to look, and then sewed them with cords made of maguey roots (agaveroots). When the time for their fasting, which they called netlalocacaoaliztli had come, all the priests and ministers of the idols retired within the calmecac into confinement. All those who called themselves Tlamacaztequioaque, which means priests who had done some brave deed in war and had secured three or four captives, confined themselves in this place. These priests, although they did not live exclusively nor continually in the Cú, went there whenever called upon to do their duty there. Still others, called Tlamacazcayaque, which means those who have captured one enemy in war, retired there; those did not live continually in the temple either but were ready to serve whenever called upon. Another group of priests retired who were called Tlamacazquecuicanime, or priest-singers; these resided permanently in the temple, for they had not yet distinguished themselves in war. After these came all the other ministers of the idols who were of lower rank (or younger) and were known as the Tlamacazteicahoan, meaning minor ministers; they also went into confinement; still other boys who served as little sacristans, the Tlamacatoton, or tiny ministers, joined in the fasting within the temple. After all these priests were gathered they placed around the fires the reed blankets they thus had made, calling them aztapilpetlatl, which name means blankets of variegated reeds in green and white. When these blankets were all spread, the priests of the idols donned their ceremonial robes for the services. They wore a jacket they call Xicolli of painted cloth, and on the left arm they wore a maniple similar to what Catholic priests wear to say mass, and which these people called matacaxtli; then they took a bag of copal-incense in their left hand, while in the right they held the incensory, temaitl, which is made of baked clay shaped like a low pot or frying pan. Thus attired, they came out into the court of the temple and, stationed in the middle, they all took live coal from the hearth into their incensories, threw copal onto it, and incensed in the four cardinal directions of the world: east, north, west and south. After this ceremony they emptied the tall braziers which always burnt all night in the court and which were one yard, 85/100 high, more or less, and so wide that two men could barely span them, taking out all the fire. The priest who had offered the incense entered the Calmecac, which was like a sacristy (vestry), as soon as his service was ended, and right there he divested himself of the vestments. Then the priests began to offer before the hearth little balls of dough, each one offering four of them, placing them on the cyperus mats. They placed them there with great care to prevent their rolling off or even their moving. If one of these pellets rolled away from the rest, and if one or the other moved, they all denounced the one who had done it, and he was to be punished. Therefore, they all took great care and watched one another about the way the offering was placed. These pellets were called ventelolotli; some offered four tomatoes; others four green "chiles" (peppers). They also watched the one who placed his offering whether his blankets were clean and if he had a thread, a straw, a hair or a feather or animal hair on any of them, he was to be punished for it. Neither was anyone to stumble or fall as this, too, was a cause for punishment. During those four days and nights of fasting they all were exceedingly careful not to commit any fault for fear of punishment. After the offering each day there came certain old men called Quaquaviltin, whose faces were painted black, their hair shorn with the exception of the top of the head where the hair was long (just the opposite of the tonsure of Catholic priests). These Quaquaviltin each day divided the offerings among themselves. This was the custom among all the priests and in all the temples, and while they fasted those four days, they awoke at midnight and for an hour they blew horns, shells and other musical instruments, similar to the singing of matins in the Catholic church. After a certain number of them (probably those who were the musicians among them), had thus played, they all rose and went naked, without any covering, to the place where they kept the points of agave which they had cut on the previous day and brought home for that purpose, together with pieces of the same plant (which they put over the sharp points), and then cut their ears with small flint (stone) knives, and with the blood they tinted the maguey points; they also besmeared their faces with blood. Each one tinted as many agave points with his blood as his devotion called for, some only five, others more, and still others even less than five. After this, all the priests went to bathe irrespective of the cold, playing tunes on sea-shells and whistles made of baked clay. They all carried small bags on their backs, tied with strings made of iztli with tassels at the end. From others (other such bags) hung painted strips of paper sewed together with the bag which they call yiequachtli. In these small bags they carried a sort of flour made into little crumbs like mouse-dirt, called yyaqualli. This flour was mixed with ink and the powder of a herb called yietl, which looks like the henbane of Castile. At the head of all marched a priest with an incensory filled with live coal and a bag of copal (incense). Each one carried a short agave-leaf into which were stuck the thorns each one was to use. Ahead of all went one of the Quaquaviltin, who carried on his shoulder a board about two yards long and one span wide, perhaps a little more. Onto this board jingles were fastened, and he who carried it was jingling with every step. This board was called aiochicaoaliztli, or nacatlquoavitl. With the exception of four of their number who remained at the Calmecac, all the priests went in this procession to carry out their devotions. These four who remained in the Calmecac, that is, their convent, to guard it, were meanwhile singing and playing on a kettle drum and shaking some rattles while seated, and these were the characteristics of a service to their gods. It is done even today at times.

There were four houses near the water's edge where the priests were to bathe, and these houses they called aiauhcalli, which means houses of fog. They faced the four cardinal directions of the world. On the first day they all went into one, the second day into another, the third into the third, and the fourth into the fourth. As they were naked they trembled, some of them chattering their teeth from the cold. One of them, whom they called Chalchiuhquacuilli, spoke and said: coatl icomocaian, amoiotl, icaoacayan; atapalcatlyne-chiccana oaianaztapilquecuetlacaian, which means: this is a place of snakes, of mosquitoes, of ducks and cyperus!" As soon as he had uttered these words, all the others threw themselves into the water and began to paddle in the water with their feet and hands, making much noise, shouting and screaming and imitating the water-fowl, some squawking like ducks or geese, others imitating the aquatic bird known to them as pipitzti; others the sea-raven and still others the white or the gray heron. The words spoken by the priest appear to have been invocations to the demon to enable them to speak those tongues of birds. The place where they bathed was staked off by long poles. This ceremony of bathing was repeated daily for four days. After the bath they came out of the water, picked up their jewels they had brought with them and returned naked to the monastery, always playing on the shells and whistles. Upon arriving at the Calmecac they threw themselves onto the cyperus mats and, covering themselves with their blankets, went to sleep. Some were deathly cold, some slept, others kept awake; a few slept profoundly, some lightly; some were dreaming, a few even speaking in their sleep; others got up in their sleep; some snored, others snorted (breathed hard), while still others groaned (moaned in their sleep); all were upset and resting uncomfortably, and none arose till after mid-day. When finally they got up they clothed themselves immediately in their ceremonial vestments. The (high) priest of the idols in his customary robes took up his incensory and went with it through all the chapels, incensing all the altars and statues of idols. In front of him marched the old priests called Quaquacuilti. After this ceremony they all went to eat, squatting on the floor in small circles (clusters), each one receiving his meal such as it was sent to him from his home, and if anyone took the food of one of his companions or tried to exchange it, he was punished. Their manners were very modest, and they were exceedingly careful not to spill a drop nor crumb of the food. If anyone spilled a drop of the left-over mush or of the "chilmolle" (chilli sauce) in which he dipped his food, such a fault (breach of etiquette) was at once noted for punishment unless he redeemed himself by paying a fine. After this meal they at once went out to cut twigs from a bush called acxoiatl, and if these could not be had, they took green canes (reeds?) and, making small bundles of them, they carried them to the temple and sat down all together, awaiting the signal of the propitious hour when they might go to decorate the chapels assigned to them. As soon as this signal was given they all jumped up, each one with his boughs and canes, and with great haste went straight to the place he was to adorn. If anyone failed to find the place assigned to him or if he lagged behind or did not reach the spot together with his companions, he was fined and had to pay this fine with a chicken (fowl), a maxtle, or a blanket; the poor ones released themselves with a ball of dough in a jicara (bowl made of wood or gourd). These fines were paid to the accuser (informer), and this had to be done within the four days; on the fifth day no one could redeem himself; he had to suffer the punishment.

On the day of the festival everybody prepared the dish called etzalli, and there was no one who did not make it in his home. This etzalli consisted of corn boiled like rice, and its color was a deep yellow. Everybody ate it and gave to others, and after this meal those who wished to do so danced and made merry, many distinguished themselves in different ways and carried earthenware pots with two handles which are called xacuicolli; with these they would go from house to house begging etzal, singing and dancing at the doors. They would recite their canticles and then say: "If thou dost not give me corn, I shall pierce thy house!" and the owner would give them at once a little saucer of that food. These disguised merrymakers would go around in pairs or in threes, and they started this rejoicing at midnight and ceased at daybreak. At sunrise the priests dressed themselves in their usual ceremonial robes, a jacket, over which they wore a thin, transparent blanket, aiauhquemitl, painted with parrot-feathers laid cross-wise. On their back they carried a large, round, paper flower like a shield, and on the back part of the head they wore flowers of shirred paper which stuck out from the head on either side like ears, in the shape of semi-circles. The front part of the head, that is, the face, was painted blue, and over this they powdered pulverized white pyrite. Hanging from the right hand of the priest hung a bag or pouch made of tiger-skin embroidered with small, white shells in the shape of bells which clanged against one another; from one corner of the bag hung the tail of the tiger and from the other the two feet; from a third hung the two front paws. This pouch was meant to carry incense for the offerings. This incense was made of a dried and ground herb called ytauhtli. In front of this priest walked one of the ministers called quaqualli, who carried a board, 1 span (8 inches) wide and 2 fathoms long, on his shoulder. On this board little jingles and small, round pieces of wood were fastened at equal distances, so that as the man walked they would clang together and produce a jingling sound; this board was called ayauhchicaoaztli. Other priests marched in front of the Sátrapa (high priest), carrying in their arms certain images made of that black gum, called ulli, which shines. These images were known as Ulteteu, i. e., gods made of ulli. Still other ministers carried in their arms pieces of copal (crystals of the resin of copal) shaped like pyramidal loaves of sugar; on the top of each of these copal pyramids was fastened a rich quetzal (trogon) plume. In this order, blowing their trumpets and shells, they started in procession to lead all those (priests) who had committed a mistake or fault during the ceremonials of the fast as mentioned above, to the place where punishment was to be meted out to them. To prevent their escape they were conducted like prisoners, held by the hair of the neck or by the girdles about their waist, and the boy-sacristans (sextons) who had sinned were carried on some man's shoulders seated on small seats (stools) made of green rush; still other boys, a little older, were held by the hand. Thus they took them to the water (lake) where they were to be punished. All along the way, whenever they found some pool, they would throw them in, ill-treating them with cuffs, kicks and blows; they would roll them in the mud or slime of any water-hole until they reached the banks of the lake they called Totcco, where they gave them a ducking. Upon reaching the shore of that lake the (high) priest and his ministers first burnt paper, the incense in the shape of sugar cones, and the images made of ulli (the Uleteteu) as sacrificial offerings; they threw a part of the incense into the fire, another part they sprinkled onto the reed mats which adorned the place. At the same time the men who had conducted the prisoners thrust them into the water, and the blows produced a great noise, and the water rose high in the commotion. If any of them scampered out of the water they ducked them again. Those who could swim were wont to remain under water, swimming with all their might thus submerged, to some far away shore, and in this manner they escaped. But all those who could not swim fared very badly, for they were ducked time and again, and they so tired them that they left them for dead on the edge of the bank, where their relatives picked them up and hung them on high by their feet, thus causing them to throw off all the water they had swallowed through mouth and nostrils. Then the procession wended its way back to the Cú (temple) over the same road, playing their shells, with the exception that now the chastised children and youths went home with their relatives to recuperate, for they were all bruised and trembled with cold, and their teeth chattered. The priests, upon entering their monastery, spread again their mottled cyperus mats as well as some rush, and then began a four days' fasting, which they called netlacacaoaliztli. During this fast they did not eat at noon nor did they watch and accuse (denounce) one another. During these four days the boy sacristans (sextons) prepared and made all the paper ornaments needed by all the priests and by themselves. One of these ornaments was called tiaquechpaniotl, which means ornament for the neck; another one was called amacuexpalli, an ornament they wore below the crown of the head, and which was like a paper flower; still another one was called yiataztli, which was a bag or pouch in which they carried incense. This pouch, made of paper, was bought at the tianquiztli (market); there they also bought strings of wooden beads (he says "sartales de palo," which would be wooden strings, but it is obvious that this means "wooden beads").

As soon as the four days of fasting were over, the priests dressed themselves in the above-mentioned ornaments; so did all the ministers. Early in the morning of the day of the festival they (the priests) put on their heads . . . . [1] of a blue color; they anointed (besmeared) their faces with honey mixed with ink (paint) and all carried their incense bags (or pouches), embroidered with small white shells. The bags of the high (principal) priests were made of tiger skin, those of the minor (or sub-

[1]A couple of words were omitted. Must have meant hoods or headdresses.

ordinate) priests were of paper painted to represent tiger skin. Some of the smaller bags (for the same purpose) were fashioned like the bird they called atzitzicuilotl; others looked like ducks, and in all of them incense was carried. When all were ready they started the festival by going in procession to the Cú, at the head the priest of the god Tlaloc; he wore on the head a crown shaped like a casket, adjusted about the temples and widening towards the top; from the center of this crown rose many plumes. His face was smeared with liquid ulli (gum) which in this state is black like ink; he wore a jacket of cloth called aiatl; he also wore a very ugly mask with a big nose, and a mane of hair down to the waist; this hair wig was inserted in the mask (fastened to). All the other priests and ministers followed him, all murmuring as if they were praying, until they reached the Cú of Tlaloc. As soon as the high priest of Tlaloc reached the Cú, they all stopped and at once spread rush-mats and cyperus-leaves, powdered with incense. Upon the mats they placed four round chalchivites shaped like little balls. Then they gave the priest a small hook, dyed blue. With this hook he touched each one of the little balls, making each time a motion as if to withdraw his hand, then turned around and then again touched one of the four pellets, and so on till he had touched all four of them, always making these little turns. After this he sprinkled incense on the mats, of the kind they call yiauhtli. This done, they handed him the board with the jingles, and he started at once shaking it to make the small pieces of wood tied or fastened in the center jingle. This done, they began to go home to their houses or monasteries, while those who had been punished (as above mentioned) went home with their relatives. The priests divested themselves of their festive garb and sat down and at night began their festival, playing their instruments at the Cú of Tlaloc. In the monasteries they sang and sounded the rattles they used for the dances. The music caused by all these diverse instruments was very festive and prevented the captives who were to be sacrificed on the following day and who were called images of the Tlalocs, from sleeping. At midnight, which they called ioaxcliui, the priests began killing them (sacrificing them). The first ones they killed and who were clothed like the images with all their ornaments they called the origin of the Tlalocs, while all such they called their images were sacrificed afterwards, and these had to go and sit on the ones killed first and were victimized there.[1] After this sacrifice the priests took all the offerings of paper, plumes, precious stones and chalchivites, and carried them to a certain place in the lagune called Pantitlan, which lies opposite the arsenal. Along with these objects they also took the hearts of the sacri-

[1]This sentence is involved and poorly edited.

ficed captives in a big earthenware jar painted blue and dyed with ulli (gum) on four sides; the papers above mentioned were also all spotted with that gum. All those present at this sacrifice and offertory held in their hands a herb called iztauhiatl, which is very similar to the incense of Spain, and with those they were frisking or flicking very swiftly as one who flicks a fly off his own or off his children's faces. They said they did this to startle the worms and thus prevent their entering their eyes, and avoid the disease called ixocuillooaliztli; some put this herb in the ears. Still others carried it clasped tight in one hand for some superstitious reason.

Upon reaching Pantitlan with the hearts of the sacrificed men in the jar and all the other offerings, they entered a large canoe[1] which belonged to the king, and began to row with great speed. The oars of this canoe were all painted blue spreckled with ulli (gum). Arriving at Pantitlan they entered the canoe within an enclosure of poles rammed in the bottom of the lagune around this enclosure or sewer, which was called aohtoc. Within this enclosure the priests began to play their trumpets and shells standing upright at the bow (prow) of the canoe, and handed to the high priest the bowl with the hearts, which he threw at once into the center of that space between the (circle of) stacks surrounding the submarine cave which served as sewer. They say that as soon as these hearts touched the water it became agitated and made waves and foam. After the hearts they also threw in the precious stones and the sacrificial paper which they called tetevitl; they tied this latter onto the tops of the stacks and also fastened a few of the chalchivitl and precious stones on these papers. When all this had been attended to they rowed out of the enclosure, and one of the priests took an incense burner and, acting like a poltroon (or even fool), placed on it four of those papers they call tetchuitl, set fire to them and made the motion of offertory, while they were burning, towards the sewer, and then threw the incensory away. After this the canoe was headed landwards, and they began to row with all their might towards Tetamacalco, which is the landing place (stage) for the canoes. There they all bathed and then put the canoe away where it was their custom to keep it.

All this was done from midnight until dawn. At daybreak and after everything was finished, the priests went to wash themselves at their customary places, and they did it with water to get the blue paint off, only leaving the front of the head (forehead) untouched. In the case that one of the priests or ministers of the idols, having been accused of some fault, had to be punished, they did so with the blue water in the manner

[1]He calls it "la madera," should be el madero—ship, skiff or boat.

above stated.[1] Then they all went to their monastery pulled out all the rush mats and threw them out, behind the house. Such were the ceremonies of the festival called Etzalqualiztli.

About the Festival and Ceremonies Connected with the Signs of the Seventh Month, Called Tecuilhuitontli.

In the seventh month, Tecuilhuitontli, a festival and sacrifices were celebrated in honor of the goddess of the salt, whom they called Vixtocioatl. She was the goddess of all those who make salt[2] (or cut it from the salines). They said that she was a sister of the gods of rain, and that on account of a certain misfortune (disgrace) which occurred among them she was pursued and (finally) banished by her brothers to the salt-waters and there she invented salt, obtaining it in the same manner it is done today, by means of large earthen jars and by heaping up the salty earth. Due to this invention she was worshipped and honoured by salt-dealers. The vestments of this goddess were yellow and she wore a mitre with many green plumes which topped it in high tufts shimmering in iridescent hues. Her ears were of very fine gold and shone like the flowers of the pumpkin. Her vipil was shaped like waves and embroidered with mottled chalchivites, her "nasas" (the round fish-net which formed the skirt) were embroidered in the same manner as the vipil (bodice). Around the ankles she wore small gold jingles or else small white sea-shells, which were fastened to a strip of tiger-skin, in such a way that when she walked they made much noise. Her sandals were woven of cotton; the buttons as well as the strings to tie them were of the same soft material. On her shield the wide leaves of a plant (aquatic weed) called atlacuecona were painted, around the edges hung parrot feathers with flowers on the ends which were made of eagle feathers. It had a fringe made of (a band of) glued-on quetzalli-feathers; it was also decorated with the feathers of a bird they call teuxolotl. When she danced with all these ornaments she frisked the shield about her. In one hand she carried a round stick (cane) on the top of which were three paper flowers, a span or two in height and about as wide as a ball. They were arranged in the shape of a trefoil enhanced by ulli-(gum) spreckled papers; these flowers were filled with incense, and on either side of the flower quetzalli-feathers were stuck crosswise. When she danced she would draw the stick closer to her and, raising it high, would beat time with it.

For ten continuous days she took part in these dances with women who danced and sang with her in order to gladden her. These women were all those who made salt, old women, young ones and girls, and they danced in

[1]This is involved. See Clavigere about it. Vol. I, p. 279.

[2]See note C on p. 124. Vol. I. C. It seems that even in Bustamante's time salt was obtained by evaporation in State of Oaxaca.

pairs holding on to small cords, each one holding an end. On their heads they wore garlands made of iztauhiatl,[1] the fragrant herb which is so much like Spanish incense. They sang in very high pitched soprano, and their singing was led by a few old men who directed them at the same time. The one dressed in the vestments of the goddess and who was to be sacrificed, danced in the midst of the others and in front of her marched an old man holding a very beautiful plumage in his hands. It was made in the shape of the stem of a cross, and they called it vixtopetlacotl.

The singing commenced towards evening and lasted until midnight, and the woman destined to die danced and sang with the others during these ten days, and after that still a whole night without rest or sleep. She was held by the arms by two old women, who danced with her that entire night. The slaves who were to die in front of her and over whose bodies she was to walk in the morning (to her death), danced and kept vigil the same length of time.

On the day of the festival when the priests were to kill this woman whom they called after the goddess Vixtocioatl, and the captives called Vixtoti, they dressed themselves in their ceremonial robes and wore the ornaments proper of the festival. These consisted of papers around the neck and a headdress of plumes falling backwards in the shape of an eagle's foot, leg and feathers, all in featherwork over a cacaxtli, perforated in various places. Plumes were inserted in these perforations and it was adjusted by bands of red cloth, about two hands wide. The foot of the eagle was so arranged the claws went upwards while the muscle was pressed down between the claws. The center of the foot was perforated with a very beautiful plumage fastened in the orifice.

The people who watched this dance carried either yellow flowers called cempoatlxuchitl, or the fragrant iztauchiatl in their hands. The woman said to represent the image of the goddess Vixtocioatl who had to die was then taken up the steps to the top of the Cú, and behind her ascended the captives who were to be sacrificed before her. When all were assembled at the top, they began killing the captives, and after them they killed the woman. She was thrown on her back onto the sacrificial stone; five young men now held her by the feet, the hands and the head, holding her very well stretched out. Across her throat they placed a round stick which was pressed down very firmly by two men to prevent her from screaming when they cut her breast open. Some say that this was not a stick but the mouth of a sword-fish, which has a sword-like bone in its mouth and long fangs on both sides, and that this was the object they pressed down across her throat. According to others, the

[1]Clavijero calls it "ajenjo"—wormwood.

one whose duty it was to kill her was pressing it down, where it should be.[1] They then stabbed her in the chest, holding the flint-knife with both hands, and as she lay stretched so flat and the breast was exceedingly taut, as soon as the cut was made the blood gushed out with great force and the priest who had killed her reached into the wound and tore out the heart, offering it at once to the sun, and then putting it into a xicara (bowl) that was in readiness for that purpose, and which they call chalchiuhxicalli.

While all this was going on during the sacrifice of this woman a great many trumpets and shells were played. Then the body of the poor creature was brought down from the Cú, the heart in its bowl being covered with a blanket. All this took place in the morning, and as soon as it all was over the people who had assembled to witness the sacrifices returned to their homes, and they all ate and made merry and invited one another; that is, the people who traded with salt only. The drank pulque freely, but not to the point of intoxication. As the day passed, however, and night came, some would get drunk and start fistic or merely word-fights, abusing one another. When tired they went to sleep wherever sleep overtook them, on the floor or earth, where they are accustomed to rest. On the following day they drank the left-over pulque which they called cochiutli, and those who had quarreled the previous night and had cuffed others, now being sober, felt sorry and invited those they had insulted, begging them to forgive. The offended ones forgot at once their anger after drinking that cochiutli, and readily forgave their aggressors.

Thus ends the account of the festival called Tecuilhuitontli.

About the Festival and Sacrifices Celebrated Under the Signs of the Eighth Month, Called Veytecuilhuitl

Four or five days before the festival of Veytecuilhuitl, the king and all the people prepared a festivity for the poor, not only of the town proper but of the entire province, in order to feed them. They prepared a certain beverage which they called chiampinolli, in great quantities. The beverage, mixed with chian-flour, was then placed in a canoe. Everybody drank that beverage in bowls (or large cups) called tizaapanqui. Each one of those present drank one or two such cups of chiampinolli, children, men and women, no one being left out; if they couldn't finish it all, they saved what was left over. Many brought separate bowls or pots to put the leavings in, and in case they had no container of any kind they simply poured it into their laps. No one went to drink twice, but everybody got as much as he could or cared to drink; if he came back for more they slapped him with a green cane (cornstalk).

[1]This sentence is not at all clear.

After all had partaken of the chiampinolli they sat down and rested; they gathered in small groups and talked with one another, and there was much merry-making; it was then that they would drink the left overs or give them to their small children.

At dinnertime, which was the noon hour, they would again sit in their proper order, the children, boys and girls with their fathers and mothers. Once everybody was seated, those who were to distribute the food fastened their blankets to the waist, as the etiquette of that service demanded, and likewise tied their hair with reed-mace in the shape of a garland or wreath to prevent it from falling over their eyes; then they began to serve. This they did by taking up large quantities of tamales to distribute them to all their guests from beginning to end of the long rows. They gave each one as many as he could hold in one hand, and there were many varieties of tamales, such as the tetacxmalli, the xocotomalli, miaoatamalli, the iacacoltamalli and the necutamalli, the iacacolaoio and the exococolotlaoio. All those who served took special care of the children, boys or girls, and some of the officials and hosts gave extra large quantities to their friends or relatives. No one took twice, for if anybody dared to do so he received a whipping with a twisted twig of reed-mace and, furthermore, he lost all he had taken the first time and whatever had been given to him. It happened that those who were at the very end of the line did not get anything; therefore, everybody tried to reach the most advantageous place possible in order to receive his allotted portion. Those who were left without any cried and were irritated, saying, "In vain have we come here, since they don't give us anything." And they went from group to group that were eating to see whether they might obtain something. They did not even desist when slapped or ill-treated, but kept on tarrying among the others and making comments.

This feast which the rich lord made for the poor lasted eight days, because this same time each year there is a great lack of all food staple and famine is widespread; many died of hunger during this period. As soon as this festivity was over the festival (of the month) began, and when the sun had left the court of the Cús (temples) the singing and dancing started. In the court there were a great many braziers, almost one estado (1.85 yards) tall, and so large in circumference that two men could barely span them. They stood in a row and at nightfall they lighted fires in them, and by that light the people (assembled there) danced and sang.

The dancing was started by the singers (really professional minstrels, I think) who came forth from the houses of their order, singing and dancing in couples and between each two of them was a woman. The people who danced this (particular dance) were all specially chosen men, such as captains and other valiant men well versed in matters of warfare; the men who danced with the woman between them held her by the hands. None of the nobles who were warriors took part in this dance.

The women were very richly dressed in vipilis (a sort of blouse or shawl arranged like it) and skirts elaborately embroidered in different manners and of very costly material. Some wore skirts which they call iollo, others were called totolitipetlaio, still others cacamoliuhqui; or ilacatziuhqui, also tixtzcalotl, and some of these skirts were called petztic. All of these different kinds of skirts had very elaborate borders. The vipilli also had different names, some wore a kind called quapachpipilcac; others, pocuipilli, still others the iapalpipilcac, or the cacallo, also the mimichcho, while some women wore the simple white vipilli without ornament. The necks of these blouses or waists were elaborated (either in open lace work or embroidery—lace work more likely) in wide pattern, so as to cover the breast and the lower edge had a very wide fringe. These women danced with hair flowing, the braids into which they usually bind the hair were tied from the forehead to the occiput; they had no paint of any kind on their faces, which were clean and clear.

The men also were very elaborately dressed; they wore a blanket of cotton very thin like a net. Those among them noted for their bravery and who were entitled to wear a ring in the lower lip wore these mantles or blankets embroidered with small white shells; these blankets thus adorned were called nochpalcucchintli; the others were not given this name. Other men wore black blankets with their fringe trimming. All men wore earrings made of some common material, but those who were at the head (of the group) wore copper earrings with gold pieces hanging from them, and the lip-rings were of the same material and style. Some wore them in the shape of lizards, others shaped like little dogs; some were square or of four corners. All young men who had distinguished themselves in war wore round lip-rings shaped like a circle with four small circles crossed within the circumference of the large one, which was wide. The rest of the youths wore simple circles as lip-rings without any other design on them. All these lip-rings were made of sea-oyster shells. All the courageous warriors wore necklaces made of leather, from which pended large flower-like tassels to the chest; a large number of small white shells were attached to and hanging from these flowers. Others wore marine conches around the neck, and these necklaces were called quaquachicti, others otomin. They also wore beavers or lip-rings[1] made in the shape of eagles, of the same shell. Others who considered

[1]While until now "barbote" appeared alone to mean beaver of helmet or neckpiece, now he says "barbote bezote"—the latter is—lip-ring!

themselves more valiant would buy white beads made of shells called teuchipoli. The common people adorned themselves with yellow beads which, although they were also made of marine shells, were of little value. Men who had made captives in some war wore a tuft of plumes on their heads in order to distinguish them, for this demonstrated that they had captured enemies. Captains wore plumes on their back, which showed their valour; these plumes were called quauhtzontli, because they looked like trees, the branches of which were made of thread and feathers with flowers at the points (ends); these flowers were fastened in tiny cups of tiger skin. Others wore plumes made in various ways; some were called xiloxoquiquetzalli, others aztagelli; some quatototl. Other men wore plumes of various colors on their feet; these plumes were made by hand. There were some who tied to the left foot the hoofs of deer,[1] tied to the foot (or leg) by thin deer-skin cords. They painted their faces in many different ways; some painted rings (wheels) on the cheeks with black ink and across the forehead, from temple to temple, a line also of black ink, and over the ink they sprinkled white pyrite-powder. Others drew a black ink line from the earlap to the mouth. All wore the hair in the same way cut towards the temple, closely shaved; across the forehead a little longer; on the front part of the head the hair stood on end, but around the neck they allowed it to grow long, falling over the shoulders and the back. They painted their temples yellow. While dancing, lighted torches were carried in front of them by young experienced warriors, whom they called Telpuchtequioaque. These torches were very heavy and made those who carried them bend; resin was constantly dripping from them, sometimes even burning tar (resin) often the entire burning torch would fall from the hands of the bearers. However, there were the tall candelabra, tlemaitl, with burning torches in them to shed light, and these were carried by young men who had made a solemn promise to do penance for twenty days in the Cú. On one side walked the Tenuchcas (men from Tenochtitlan), on the other the Tlaltelucas. These two groups did not dance, they simply provided the illumination. However, they also watched carefully in case anyone should commit any indecency, be it by looking at or touching any woman. If they noticed anyone doing one or the other of these things, on the following day or after two days he was severely punished, being either smutted or else they hit him by blows with firebrands, so much so that they left him for dead.

The king at times was present at this dance; at other times he did not come out, just as he chose. The dancers either danced holding hands or

[1]Doc. says: pescunes which mean: wedges of ploughs which seems incongruous for they were of deer. To my mind it should be pesuñas—deer-hoofs.

else with their arms about their partner's waist; all of them keeping good time in lifting their feet, taking a step forward or backward, and in making the turns. They danced between the (two rows of) candelabra or braziers, making the contrepas (steps in dancing) within these limits. They danced till night, stopping at nine. As soon as the one who beat the drum and the teponaztli stopped, they all stopped and started to go home. The principals (chieftains) among them were accompanied home with torches carried before them. The women dancers assembled after the dance, and those who were in charge of them took them to the houses where they were wont to gather. They were not allowed to disband nor go with any man except the chieftains. If one of these women were called by some in order to give her something to eat, they were obliged to call also one of the matrons who were in charge of them. In such cases they gave them food and blankets to take home with them; the food that was left after they had eaten they also were allowed to carry home with them.

If anyone of the principal soldiers desired to take one of these girls home with him, he spoke secretly to the matron in charge to bring her to him. They did not dare to call them publicly. The matron would take the girl to his house or wherever else he might order to have her taken, but she would bring her at night and take her back also in the dark. If anyone should dare to do this overtly it was considered wrong, and he was punished publicly by cutting off the hair he had allowed to grow to a certain length as a token of his valor, and which they call tzotzocolli. They also took away his weapons and the finery he wore. The punishment consisted in a thrashing and scorching his head and entire body so that it became blistered from the fire. Then, after the beating, they kicked him out of the way, saying: "go on, scoundrel, you may be courageous and strong, but we do not think anything of you, and even if our enemies should come and wage war on us, we shall not count with you." Such and other injurious words were said to him as he was cuffed and thrown out, and he left in silence, doubled up (from pain) and moaning over the ill-treatment he had received. He never again came there to dance and sing. The woman with whom he had slept was also separated from her companions, and never again was she allowed to dance nor sing nor see the other girls and the matron in charge of them did not mention her nor look at her again. The young man punished for his misdemeanor made the girl, who had thus been ostracized on his account, his wife.

On the tenth day of this month the festival called Veytecuilhuitl was held, and in honor of the goddess Xilonen (or Centeatl) they killed a woman, whom they dressed in the vestments and ornaments of that goddess. They said that the woman whom they adorned in this manner was her image. They painted her face in two colors; from the nose down in yellow, the forehead in red. Her head was adorned by a paper crown with four corners, from the center of which rose many plumes, like tufts. Around her neck they hung many strings of wide (square-cut) precious stones which also adorned her breast. Over the stones she wore a round gold medal. Her vipil (blouse) had images of demons woven (or in open work) in it, and the skirts bore a similar design, and the ensemble was curious and rich looking. Her sandals were painted with red stripes. On her left arm they placed a shield, and in the other hand she held a stick painted in a bright reddish color. After she had been dressed in all that finery, a great many women surrounded her, and in their midst she was taken to offer incense in four different places. She made this offering in the evening before her death. They called her Xaloquia, because she was to die on the next day. The four places where the offering was made bore the following names: one was Tetamacolco, the second Necocixecan, the third Atenchicalcan, and the fourth Xoloco. These four places where offerings were made were held sacred in honor of the four signs of the counting of the year. The first sign is called acatl, which means cane; the second one is tecpatl, which means flint (it also means extreme hardness, and I think in this case it is this latter, for he says: *like the iron point of the lance*); the third one is called calli, meaning house; and the fourth tochtli, that is, rabbit. With these signs recurring thirteen times each, they counted the years up to fifty-two (that is, four units of a cycle of thirteen seasons).

After having made the offering at the above-mentioned four stations, the women who accompanied Xaloquia (the victim) sang and danced without rest all that night in front of the temple of the goddess, Xilonen and the woman who was to die the following day was in their midst. When morning came all the prominent men began to dance, carrying in their hands cornstalks in such a way that it looked as if they were bending over them (coming close to them). These cornstalks were called totopanitl. The women also danced with the one who was going to be sacrificed. They had legs and arms covered with red feathers; the face painted yellow from the chin to the nose, as well as the jaws, and the forehead red. They all wore garlands of yellow flowers which are called cempoalxuchitl, and strings of the same (around the neck). Those who went at the head leading the dance were called Cioatlamacazqui, and they were women who served in the temples and who lived in their convents. The men also were dancing, but not among the women, because these were all closely surrounding the one who had to die and who represented the goddess Xilonen, singing and dancing with her. The dancing and singing of the women was accompanied by a teponaztli which had only one clapper on top and one underneath. To the bottom was fastened a jicara (small bowl or cup) used for drinking, for in this way the teponaztli has a much stronger sound than if the two clappers are on the top of it and none underneath. This teponaztli was called tecomopiloa, and the man who played (beat) it carried it in the armpit because it was fashioned in this manner.

The noblemen who took part in this dance marched at the head but they did not follow that measure of the dances, their dancing was like the one of Castilla la Vieja, namely, holding each others' hands and proceeding with snakelike motions. The ministers of the idols also were dancing to the sound of the above-mentioned teponaztli, at the same time blowing their own trumpets and shells. When in their turning about the priests arrived in front of the goddess Xilonen, they threw incense on the path, and the high priest whose duty it was to kill that woman was dressed in his ornate, and wore on the back a tuft of plumes fastened between the claws of a fictitious eagle, while another priest carried before him the board with the jingles which has been described elsewhere.

Upon reaching the temple of the god called Cinteutl, where the woman was to be sacrificed, the priest who carried the jingle-board, which was called chicaoaztl, stood in front of her placing the board upright before her, and began to make noise with the jingles by shifting the board from one side to the other. They strew incense before her, and while doing this they took her up to the top (where the temple stood). Once up there, one of the priests lifted her on his back, her back to his and at once another priest approached and cut her head off; after having done this, they cut open the breast and tore out the heart, which they put in a bowl (jicara).

After the ceremonies of this sacrifice in honor of the goddess Xilonen were over, everybody was allowed to eat xilotes and bread made of these and of corn stalks (?). Prior to this sacrifice no one dared eat any of these things. From then on they also ate green wild amaranth, cooked; they were allowed—from that date on—to smell (the perfume of) the flower called cemxalsuchite, and the others which they call iresuchitl. At this festival a (special) dance was executed by old and young women and girls, but no men at all danced with them. All these women were in festive garb, their legs and arms covered with red parrot-feathers; their faces painted yellow and powdered over with pulverized white pyrite. At this feast (dance) they all ate a certain kind of tamales called xocotamalli, and they made offerings to their gods in the homes. The old men and women drank wine (pulque), not so the young men and girls. If anyone did it without having the necessary permission, they were imprisoned and punished by the men of the council. Some were sentenced and sent off to prison, some were sentenced to death just for drinking pulque (when they were not allowed to do so). And there was no appeal possible. They were killed in sight of all the people so that others should take warning. In order to scare the people thoroughly their judges took them, with hands tied (shackled?) to the tianquiztli (market), and there warned the people, saying that no one except the old men and women should drink pulque. After this speech they at once hit the condemned youths with a stick in the neck to knock them down (or against the wall to break their necks?). These executioners were called Quauhnochtli Czoacacatl, Ticocaoacatl, Tezcacooacatl, Macatecatl, Atempanecatl. These men did not belong to council nor were they of the common people whom they called achcacauhti; neither were they elected for this office, but rather commanded. All that was required of them was that they should be courageous, strong, and of good speech. Whosoever witnessed this execution would be frightened (scared) and take warning if he was wise, but the stupid and flighty ones laughed at it and made fun of what was told them publicly; they disregarded the punishment and the talk, threw them to the winds, and did not fear death.

As soon as this judgment was over, those who had seen it done began to turn away, scattering or going home, raising a great deal of dust with their feet and shaking their blankets, and soon no one was left in the tianquiztli. With this account ends the report of the festival called Veytecuihuitl.

The Festival and Sacrifices Which Took Place Under the Signs of the Ninth Month, Called Tlaxochimaco

The ninth month was called Tlaxochimaco. Two days before the festival began all the people went out into the country and the cornfields to gather all sorts of flowers, wild ones from the virgin lands and forests and whatever flowers bloomed among the cornstalks, of many known names such as: acocoxuchitl, vitzitzilocoxuchitl, tepe, cempoalxuchitl, nextamalxuchitl, tlacoxuchitl, others by other names, as for instance: oceluxuchitl, cacaloxuchitl, ocoxuchitl, or aiocoxuchitl, quauheloxuchitl (mentioned already), xiloxuchitl, tlaccacaloxuchitl, cempoalxuchitl, and atlacucconan; still others like the tlapalatlccueco, nan, atzatza mulsuchitl. After having gathered a great quantity of all these kinds of flowers, they put them all together and took them to the house (either the monastery or an annex) of the Cú where this festival was to take place, and kept them there over night. The following morning, at daybreak, they at once began to string them on thread or thin cord; once strung, they made thick ropes (garlands) well twisted and of great length, and then hung them in the court of the Cú, thus presenting them to the god whose feast they celebrated. In the evening of that same day, which was the eve of the festival, all the people prepared tamales; they killed chickens and little dogs, dressing the chickens and scorching or singeing the little dogs, together with all else they needed for the preparation of tamales, etc., for the next day. They spent all that night without rest, preparing everything.

Very early on the morning of the feast-day of Vitzilopuchtli, the priests offered flowers, incense and food to this idol, adorning it at the same time with strings and garlands of roses. Then, after having thus adorned the statue of Vitzilopuchtli with flowers and having placed before him a great many more, most artistically grouped and very fragrant, they did the same with all the other statues of their gods in all the temples, then with those in the houses of the chiefs and prominent personages which they adorned with other flowers, placing them before the images. The common people did the same with the idols that protected their homes. When all this was done, they began to eat and drink everywhere in the houses of the humble, of the great, and of the middle classes.

At noon a very pompous (magnificent) dance began in the court of the very temple of Vitzilopuchtli, which was led by the most valiant warriors. Some of these were called Otomin, others Quaquachicti, these two groups leading the dance. Immediately following came others called Tequioaque, and after these came the Telpuchiaque, then the Tiachcaoan, and finally the young men known as the Telpupuchti. There were also women taking part in this dance, but they were prostitutes and danced either one woman between two men or one man between two women, all three holding hands. The dance was like the popular dances of Castilla la Vieja among the country people. While they danced, winding in and out in snake fashion, they sang, and those who provided the music and led the singing were close by, leaning against a round altar called momuztli.

In this dance they did not take any fancy steps nor make gestures with head or hands, they did not make turns of any kind, but marched with even steps, very slowly to the measure of the music and the singing. No one dared to make any noise, nor to cross the space where they danced. All the dancers proceeded with great care, especially the ones in the lead, in order to avoid mistakes, because they were the greatest warriors; they had their arm about the waist of their woman partner as if they were embracing her, while those following were not allowed to do so. At sunset the dance ended and they all went home.

The same sort of celebration was held in every house, each family celebrating in front of the images of their gods, hence there was an enormous noise throughout the town with the singing and the music indulged in by each household. The old men and women drank wine (pulque) until they were drunk, and then quarreled with one another in loud voices. One or the other of these drunkards would begin to brag about the courageous feats he had accomplished in his youth.

Here ends the report on the festival called Tlaxochimaco.[1]

Festival and Sacrifices Celebrated under the Signs of the Tenth Month Called Xocotlvetzi.[2]

The tenth month was called Xocotlvetzi. As soon the festival of Tlaxochimaco was over, they cut a big tree in the forest, twenty-five fathoms in height (150 feet); they cut off all the twigs and branches, only leaving the tender shoot at the top. Then they cut down other (smaller) trees, hollowed them so as to form a sort of litter, placed the felled tree on these, tied it with ropes, and as they dragged it (from the forest) it never touched the soil, nor was its bark scratched because it rested on these bent or hollowed-out trunks. As they approached the town, the ladies and prominent women came to meet them. They carried bowls (jicaras) of cocoa, that the bearers of the tree might drink, and also flowers, with which they decorated the men who brought the tree. As soon as they reached the court of the temple the "Tlayacanques" or leaders began to shout with all the power of their lungs to have all the people assemble in order to help lift that tree (rather trunk), which they called Xocotl. As soon as all the people had arrived they tied ropes around the tree and, after having dug a hole in the place where it was to stand, all tugged at the ropes amid great shouting until the tree stood erect. They then closed the hole with rocks and earth and thus the tree stood for twenty days. On the eve of the festival called Xocotlvetzi, they felled it again, lowering it little by little to prevent its breaking or cracking. They rested it on some logs tied two and two together, which they call quahtomacatl, and thus they laid it down without injury. There they left it and went away. The ropes were left tied to the tree. Thus it remained all that night. At dawn of the feast day, all the carpenters came together, bringing their tools, and tooled the tree until it was very straight and, taking off any curb or knot, they succeeded in getting it very even. They then prepared another pole of five fathoms (30 feet) in length and curbed it, to put it against the top of the tall tree where the shoots of the crown began. These shoots or branches were gathered in

[1]It seems that Clavijero claims that this dance (festival) ended in the sacrifice of several prisoners.

[2]Clavijero called it Xocohuetzi; it began August 25 of our calendar.

the curb of the other pole where they were tied with a rope, which was wound from there closely around the crown and down again to the juncture.

Now that this was done, the priests, dressed in their vestments and ornaments, adorned the tree with papers and were assisted in this by the so-called Qüaqüaciviltin and the Tetlepantlaz, who were three very tall men. One of these was called Coicoa, the second Cacancatl, and the third one Veicamecatl. They put these papers on amid great noise and with much solicitude. A statue resembling a man and made of a dough of wild amaranth-seeds was also adorned with papers. The paper used was pure white without paint or dye. On the head of this statue they fastened cut papers which looked like hair; on both sides they fastened paper-stoles reaching from the right shoulder to the left armpit. On the arms they put paper fashioned like waves, on which were figures of the sparrow-hawk. He also received a belt of paper. Above this other papers placed back and front simulated the vipil (blouse or shirt). On the sides of the statue and on the tree, from the feet of the former down to about the middle of the tree long papers were hung, which waved in the air. These latter were about one-half fathom (3 feet) wide by a length of 10 fathoms (60 feet), more or less. They also placed three large tamales made of wild amaranth-seed, on the head of the statue, fastened on three sticks. When the tree was adorned with all this, they tied ten ropes about its middle, and then pulled, with big shouts encouraging one another to heave simultaneously. As it was being lifted they shoved logs, always two and two tied together, under it, as well as props to rest on as it rose slowly. A great shout was given and much shuffling of feet as the tree stood erect, and at once large stones (rocks) were put against it with earth on top, so that it could not fall. Then everybody went home, no one remaining in the court.

Then came those who had war-captives who were to be burnt alive at this festival, bringing them to the place where this sacrifice was to be enacted. They were dressed for the dance. Their entire bodies were dyed yellow, and their faces a bright reddish color. They wore plumes in the shape of butterflies made of red parrot-feathers on the head. In the left hand they carried a shield adorned in white plumes with a fringe hanging down from the lower edge. The center field of this shield bore tiger or eagle feet, drawn for that purpose. This sort of shield was called chimaltetepontli. Every one of those dancers, dressed in this manner, entered with his captive as partner (of the dance), and the two danced as a pair together. The bodies of the captives were painted white, the belt (sash) which girded their loins was of paper, and they wore also stoles of white paper which reached from the shoulder to the armpit. They also wore hair (a sort of wig) made of small strips of paper. On the head they wore a coif[1] of white plumes; also a lip-ring made of feathers. Their faces were painted a bright reddish color (hue) and the cheeks black. They carried on this dance until nightfall. At sunset they stopped and put the captives in the houses they called calpullis, where their owners watched over them, all of them without sleep, including the captives. Near midnight the old inhabitants of that district (of the town) went home (went to their own houses). At midnight each owner cut the hair off the crown of his slave's head close to the skull, in front of the fire. This hair they kept as relics and, in remembrance of their valor, they tied these hairlocks with red thread to the aigret of night herons, two or three together. The small knife with which they cut the hair they called claw of the sparrow-hawk. These hairlocks they kept in small chests (or trunks) made of reeds and called them "chest or casket of the hairlocks," a rather diminutive chest. The owner of the captive took this little chest home with him and hung it among the rafters of his house in a prominent place, so that it would be known that he had made a capture in war. The chest remained in that place all the time of his life. After the top of the head of their captives had been shorn, their masters slept for a short while, but the captives were closely guarded to prevent their escape.

At dawn all the captives were at once lined up (or put in line) in front of the place called tzompantli, which was where they impaled the heads of those they sacrificed. After they were thus lined up, one of the priests at once began to take from them the paper flags they carried in their hands and which were the signs of their being condemned to death. They also took off the other papers they were adorned with and one or the other blanket, if they had covered themselves with one. All this was thrown into the fire (which was built) in a stone trough which they called quauhxicalli. In this order they were divested of all their clothes, which were thrown into the fire, since they would not have any more need of clothing nor anything else, like anyone who is to die forthwith. When they were all naked awaiting death, a priest in full vestments (ornaments) came forth; he carried in his arms a statue of the god they called Paynal, also dressed in his finery. As soon as that priest with the statue which he carried in his arms had arrived, he ascended to the Cú where the captives were to die, to the place called tlacacouhcan; then he descended again and again passed in front of the captives, then ascended a second time in the same manner as at first. The owners of the captives stood also in line, each one close to his captive, and as Paynal ascended a second time to his temple, each one of the men took his slave (captive)

[1]"Vilma," which I cannot find in dictionary, but no doubt it means a sort of headdress or coif.

by the hair and led him to a place called apetlac, and there all of them were left. Then those who were to thrust them into the fire came down (the steps) and powdered their faces with incense which they carried, pulverized (ground) in bags, and throwing it onto them by handfuls. They then held them and tied their hands behind (on the back), and also tied their feet. After that they carried them on their backs up the steps to the (platform of) the Cú, where a big fire with a great deal of embers (live coal) was burning. As soon as they reached the top they threw them into that fire. As they were thrust in, a great cloud of ashes arose (from the fire) and wherever anyone of them fell, a deep hole (hollow) was made (by the body) in the fire because it was ablaze with embers and live coal. The poor captives at once began to twist and turn in that fire and to suffer from nausea (have vomiting spells), his body beginning to squeak (I think sizzle would be better), as does the body or part of an animal when roasting, and big blisters would rise all over the body. While in this (infernal) agony, the priests called Quaquacuiltin pulled him (or them) out with gambrels (grappling irons) and placed, one after the other on the block they called techcatl, and at once cut the breast from nipple to nipple or a little below, and tore the heart out and threw (the body) at the feet of the statue of Xiuhtecutli, god of the fire. In this manner they killed all the captives they offered for sacrifice at that festival, and after all of them had been sacrificed, all the people went home and the same priest who had brought the statue of Paynal now carried it back to the place where it was wont to be. In this he was accompanied by all the old men who were in the service of that god. Once restored to his place, they descended from the temple and went home to eat.

After that (dinner) all the young men, youths and boys would gather; all those who wore long locks of hair in the neck (who wore their hair in long locks in the neck?), which they called cuexpaleque, and all the rest of the people, met in the court of Xiuhtecutli, in whose honor this festival was held, and at noon they began to dance and to sing, women dancing in orderly manner among the men. The court became so filled with people that there was no way to get out, and they were all greatly crowded (packed). When they got tired of singing and dancing they gave a great shout and left the court and went to the place where the tree (pole) had been erected, and the roads were so very full of people that they jostled against one another (knocked one another down). The captains of the young men were (stationed) around the tree so that nobody should go up until it was time; they defended the ascent with blows of their clubs, and the youths, determined to climb the tree, shoved those who defended the ascent out of the way with fist-blows and, taking hold of the ropes, began to climb. Along each one of the ropes a great many youths climbed up in competition; on every one of these ropes hung a cluster of young men, determined to get to the top. Yet, though many attempted the climb, only very few succeeded. The first one to reach the top took hold of the idol (statue) made of dough of wild amaranth-seed, which had been fastened there, took from it the shield and the darts and spears with which it was armed as well as the instruments with which to shoot off the shafts (spears) and which is called statl. He also grabbed the tamales on the sides and broke them into pieces over the heads of the people (gathered below). And all these people looked upwards as the pieces fell for them to catch; some quarreled and cuffed one another in order to get a few morsels. There was great shouting before they obtained all that was thrown to them. Others (of the youths who had climbed to the top) took the tufts which were on the head of the statue, and he who had taken them threw these down too. This done, he who had climbed up first came down with the weapons he had taken; as he reached the bottom they received him with great applause and carried him, and took him to the top of the Cú called tlacacouhcan. There many (of the) old men gave him jewels or devices for the valor he had shown. Then they all pulled at the ropes with great force and threw the tree down on the soil. It caused a great clash and broke to pieces. After this they all went home and no one remained there. They accompanied the one who had been the first one in climbing up to the top to his home, and put a lion-colored (tawny) blanket on him, tied over one shoulder and under the other arm in the same way the deacon wears the stole. This blanket had a fringe around the edge, (made of) tochomitl and feathers. This kind of blanket was licit to be worn only by those who had accomplished that act of bravery, not for any one else. They could take them home and sell them if they wished to do so, but the buyers could not wear them. The one who had won the victory was carried (braced?) by the arms of two old priests whom they called Quaquacuiltin, and many of the priests of the idols went behind them blowing trumpets and shells; he (the victor) carried the shield he had taken from the (top of the) tree on his back. After leaving him at his home they (the priests) returned to the Cú whence they had come from. Here ends the report on the festival called Xocotlvitzi.

Festivities and Ceremonies Held under the Signs of the Eleventh Month, Called Ochpaniztli.

The eleventh month was called Ochpaniztli. During the first five days they did not do anything regarding the feast, but as soon as these five days were passed and fifteen days (two weeks) before the date of the festival, they began to dance a dance they called nematlaxo, which lasted eight days. For this dance they were ranged in four rows to dance; they did not sing at this dance; they moved in silence, carrying flowers in both hands, which they called cempoatl xuchitl, not arranged in any way, but just cut with stems and all. A few mischievous youths, although the others danced in silence, imitated with their mouths the sound of the kettle-drum, to the music of which they danced. They did not stir (wiggle) their feet, nor the body, only their hands were lowered and raised to the measure beaten on the kettle-drum. They kept the rule with great care so that no one should differ (in his motions) from the rest. This dance was started toward afternoon and ended at sunset; it lasted eight (consecutive) days, and when they were over, the women doctors (healers), old and young, began to enact a skirmish or fight, in equal numbers, divided into two squadrons. They did this in front of the one who was to die during the festival, in order to amuse her and thus prevent her being sad or crying, because they considered it a bad sign if the woman who was to be killed became sad or cried. They said (believed) that this meant that many soldiers were to die in war, or that many women were to die in child-birth or from its effects.

When they commenced this skirmish or sham-fight, the woman who was destined to die, and whom they called the image of the mother of the gods (and in whose honor the festival was celebrated) made the first attack upon the rival (opposite) squadron; she was accompanied by three old women who acted like her mother and who never left her side. One of these was called Aba, the second Tlavitecqui, and the third Xoquauchtli; the sham-battle consisted in stoning one another with pellets made of the fibres or strings[1] of (in Mexico) hay, which grows on and hangs from trees, or else made of leaves of reed-mace or prickly pear leaves and yellow flowers which they call cempoalxochitl. All the women were girded and around their waist hung several small gourds filled with powder of the herb called yietl. One squadron pelted the other from behind, and then the other did the same, pelting the first one; in this manner they fought certain turns (a certain number of turns) which, when done, ended the skirmish. They thereupon took the woman who was to die to the house where they kept her. This unfortunate creature

[1]Commonly called old man's beard.

they called Toci, which means "our grandmother," for thus they called the mother of the gods, in whose honor she had to die.[1]

This skirmish was repeated on four continuous days, after which time they took the said woman for a walk to the tianquiztli, or market, and with her went all the women doctors (healers) through the market-place. This outing (walk) they called the leave-taking (bidding good-bye) of the tianquiztli (market), for never again would she visit it. Upon leaving the market-place she was met by the priests of the goddess Chicomecoatl, who at once surrounded her, and she strew corn-meal wherever she stepped (walked) as a sign that she was taking leave of the market-place. Then the priests took her to the house where she was kept (lodged), which house was near the temple where they were going to kill her. There the women doctors (medicine-women) and the midwives consoled her, saying, "Do not be sad, daughter, for tonight the king is going to sleep with you, therefore be content." They did not give her to understand that they were going to kill her, because her death was to be sudden, without her suspecting it. They then adorned her with the vestments (ornaments) of the goddess Toci. At midnight they took her to the temple where she was to die, and nobody spoke nor coughed when they led her there; they all went amid great silence, although the entire town accompanied her. As soon as they reached the place where she was to be killed one man lifted her on his back and at once they beheaded her and, while she (her body) was still warm they flayed her and one of the priests, whom they called Teccizqüacuilli, dressed himself in her skin; for this office they chose the tallest and strongest man. They first flayed the skin off the thigh, which they sent to the temple of her (the goddess') son, called Tzinteutl, who was in another temple (than Chicomecoatl), and dressed him in it; that is to say, after the priest above mentioned had dressed himself in the skin of the said woman, he carried the piece for the goddess' son Cinteutl. He at once went to the edge of the temple-platform and descended speedily. He was accompanied by four persons who had made a solemn vow to render him that service; they took him in their midst, two on one side and two on the other; several priests walked behind the one dressed in the skin, and chiefs and soldiers who were awaiting him placed themselves in front to have him follow, as if pursuing them, while they at once fled before him hurriedly. They ran, turning their heads and tapping on their shields as if demanding battle, then again ran at top speed. All those who witnessed that were frightened and trembled, seeing that game which was called cacacalli, because all those who fled before him carried in their hands blood-

[1] Clavijero says: Teteoinan was the mother of the gods. vol. I.

stained straw-brooms. The one dressed in the woman's skin and his accompaniment pursued those who fled before them, who in turn tried to escape from their pursuers, as if they were greatly afraid of them. As they reached the foot of the temple of Vitzilopuchtli, the one who wore the human skin raised his arms and then crossed them before the image of Vitzilopochtli, and he repeated this four times. Then he returned to where the statue of Cinteutl, son of the goddess Toci was, whom he represented. This Cinteutl was a young man who wore as identification mark the skin of the thigh of the woman they had killed; he then joined his mother. His vestments consisted, in the first place of the skin above mentioned, slipped over his head (face, like a mask), a small cap of feathers also on the head. This cap or hood was attached to a feather-garment which had sleeves and bodice; the point of the hood was long and made into a twist towards the back. There was a ridge on the twist (rosette) shaped like a rooster's crest; this hood was called liztlacoliuliqui, which means god of frost. He walked close by his mother's side very slowly, and they went to the temple of Toci, the mother, where the above-mentioned woman had been killed. The one who represented Toci, but who was the man who wore the rest of the skin of the woman, entered the temple. All this happened in the night.

At daybreak the next morning he who represented the goddess Toci placed himself on the edge of the platform at the top of the temple, while down below were assembled all the chieftains awaiting that demonstration. They at once began to try to climb up the steps of the temple at top speed, carrying their offerings, which they presented to him (her?). Some of them adorned her head and feet with eagle feathers, those white ones close to the bird's body (the down); others painted her face with red paint; others dressed her in a not very long blouse (vipil) which bore across the breast an eagle embroidered or woven in the vipil itself; still others dressed her in painted petticoats. Some of them beheaded quails in her presence, others offered her incense (copal). All this was done with great speed, and nobody remained there.

Later on they took off her rich garments and a very gorgeous crown which was called amacalli and which had five tiny flags, the one in the center higher than the others. This crown was very wide at the top and not round but square, little flags rising from the middle, four at the four corners, the largest one in the center. This crown was called miotli.

Then they arranged all the captives who were doomed to die in a row, and she (Toci) grabbed one, threw him on the stone block, called techcatl, cut open his breast and tore the heart out; then she took another one, still another, and so up to four, and after she had killed these four, she left the rest of the victims to be killed by the priests, while she left with her son to go back to the temple, where she was wont to stay, and the name of which was called Cinteutlitztlacoliuhqui. Before them marched their devotees, whom they call icuexoan. They marched a little ahead (of the two) adorned with their papers, a belt of twisted paper around the waist, on their backs a shirred paper, round like a shield. They carried over the shoulder (or on the back?) a plumage made of cotton, and from it hung threads made of the same, not twisted, but loose. On one side and the other, the medicine-women and the women who sell lime at the tianquiztli accompanied the goddess and her son, and were singing. The priests, called Quaquacuiltin, were also singing and directing the singing of the women, and beating time on the teponaztli of one clapper which had a tecomatl, little gourd bowl, underneath. When they reached the Cú of her son Cinteutl they found the heads (chiefs) awaiting them, and there was a kettle-drum on which the one who was dressed in the skin of the sacrificed woman and represented the image of the goddess Toci, raised one foot as if he (she) were kicking it. Many old soldiers were there awaiting Cinteutl, son of that goddess, who was a vigorous, strong youth. They took him in their midst and departed with him, all running, because they had to take the skin of the thigh of the dead woman which the one they called her son wore on his head and over the face like a mask, to a hill which was called popotltemi, on the border of their enemies' country. They were accompanied by many soldiers and men of war, running at top speed.

When they reached the place where he (Cinteutl) had to deposit the skin, and which place was called mexaiacatl, it often happened that their enemies sallied forth against them and there they fought with each other, killing one another. They hung the skin in a sentry-hut which was erected on the border line where the fight took place. From there they returned, and their enemies also went back to their own country. When all these games and ceremonies were over, they took the one who represented the image of the goddess Toci to the house called atempan. The king took his seat on the throne in the royal houses; he had as dais the skin of an eagle with its feathers, and as back of his chair a tiger-skin. All the warriors were assembled there; in the front the war captains and the valiant men, in the center the old warriors, and at the end the recruits. In this order they appeared before the lord (king, ruler), passing in front of him as if in a parade, with great reverence and obeissance. Close by, the king had numerous (many) shields, swords and plumes, which are war ornaments, blankets and belts. As they paraded before him, he ordered these weapons and plumes given to them; to the most prominent and distinguished ones the best and richest weapons as well as blankets and belts. Each one, after accepting what had been given him, went to one side to clothe himself in it and gird the weapons. These in the center received the less elaborate and those at the end (of the line) were given what remained. After all of them had donned their garments and girt their weapons, they formed again and once more passed in front of the lord, dressed and armed, each making a deep obeissance.

While this ceremony was drawing to a close, they were already dancing in the court of the goddess Toci, and at once all those who had been given the various gifts went to the dance. All those who had been given weapons understood that they were expected to die in war. They did not sing during this dance, nor did they take dance steps, but merely lifting and lowering their arms to the tune beaten on the drum and carrying flowers in both hands. All the dancers looked like flowers, and all those who looked on marveled at their finery. They went around the goddess Toci.

The women who looked on, cried and said, "These, our sons, who are so gaily dressed, will be forced to go to war if from now in a short time war is declared. Do you think they will ever come back? Perhaps we shall never see them again!" In this way these poor women condoled with one another and worried about their sons.

The man who represented the image of the goddess Toci, her devotees, and the medicine-women danced apart, behind the others, and they sang at a very high pitch, starting at noon. The next day they repeated the same dance, and they all participated in it, because on the previous one many had not taken part. On account of the manifestation which was made on that day, all the chieftains and the "piles" (pilli-son?) participated, magnificently (very richly) clothed. The king marched at the head, clothed in precious ornaments, and the amount of gold was such that it shone in the sun with great splendor over the entire court. In the afternoon, as the dancing ended, the priests of the goddess Chicomecatl appeared, dressed in the skins of the captives they had killed on the previous day; these priests were called Tototecti. They ascended to the top of a small temple called the table of Vitzilopuchtli, and from up there they threw down or sowed all the different kinds of corn, white and yellow, red and blackish, over the people who were assembled below; also squash (calabash)-seeds, and everybody gathered that corn and the calabash-seeds, and the maidens who served the goddess Chicomecoatl and who were called Cioatlamacazque, fought with their fists over it. All of these maidens carried each seven ears of corn, which were streaked with molten ulli (gum) and wrapped in paper and in a rich blanket, on their backs. These Cioatlamacazque had their legs and arms covered with feathers, their faces painted and powdered with white pyrite-powder. They sang together with the priests of the goddess Chicomecoatl who directed their singing. After this the priests retired to their sacristies and later one of them descended from the top of the temple of Vitzilopuchtli, carrying in his hands a large wooden basket filled with white marl (also chalk or clay) ground like flour, and with white feathers which looked like cotton. At the foot of the temple he placed this basket in a place called Coazalpan, which was a certain space between the steps to the temple and the bottom court. To this place (Coaxalpan) they mounted over four, five or six steps. At the moment he placed the basket there, many armed warriors were near-by waiting, and they commenced to run to see who arrived first, to grab what came in that basket, and here it became apparent who were the best and fleetest runners, to get hold of the basket, taking by handfuls what was in it, marl as well as feathers. Having taken all they could, they returned, running back to the place whence they had started. The one who wore the skin of the dead woman and who was the image of the goddess Toci, was present when they took that feather and marl, and after they had taken them, he started to run after them as if pursuing them, and they all yelled. As he, the fleetest runner, passed through the multitude of people in full flight, they all spat at him and threw whatever they had in their hands at him, and even the king made an attempt running a short stretch after him. In this manner the latter entered his house, running, and all the others did the same, thus leaving the one who was the image of the goddess Toci alone, with the exception of a few who followed him (her), together with the priests who then led him (her) to the place where he was to divest himself of the (human) skin, which place was called Toeititlan, where they hung it up in a sentry-hut which stood there. They stretched the skin very carefully so that the arms were stretched out and the head (towards the street or highway). With this the festival and ceremonies of Ochpaniztli were at an end. This is the end of the report on this festival.[1]

About the Festival and Ceremonials Celebrated under the Signs of the Twelfth Month, Which Was Called Teutleco.

The twelfth month was called Teutleco, which means the arrival or coming of the gods. After the first fifteen days (two weeks) of this month were passed, they embowered certain altars which they called Momoztli, with canes tied three and three together (in three's); this was the task of the young men and boys who were educated in the houses

[1] See report by Clavijero (p. 156 of Sahagun).

called telpuchcalli. Only the altars of the houses (temples or oratories) of the goddesses were embowered. The altars where the statues of personal idols stood in the houses of the town were also embowered, and these young men and boys were given in each house either a basket of corn or four ears of the same for this service, and·to the poorest they gave two or three ears of corn (each). This (gift) they called cacalatl, i.e., like "aquinaldo" (in Spain) or New Year's gift; they were to eat them toasted, but not all of them would eat (have) them, only those who were already known as diligent (active) and good workers. After three days they had thus been embowering altars, the god they called Telpuchtli or Tlamatzincatl arrived. He came first because, being a young man, he walked faster and was stronger and swifter, and thus they made offertories to him on the third day. These offerings consisted of wild amaranth-seeds, toasted and ground, some of which they mixed with water, others with honey. They made four balls (pellets) with this dough and put them on a plate. This was the offering of each one of those whose duty it was to make this offering. They took them at once to the god upon his arrival in his Cú and placed them in front of him. That night they commenced to drink pulque; the old men and women said by so doing they washed the feet of the god Telpuchtli, who had arrived from the road. On the fourth day they removed the boughs from the altars where they had put them, and on the fifth day the festival of Teutlaco took place, which is the last day of this festival of the arrival of the gods and also the last day of this month. At midnight of this day they ground a small quantity of corn flour and of it they made a small, quite compact heap; and they made it also of flour, round like a cheese, on a mat. By this (or from this cake or heap) they were able to tell when all the gods had arrived, because there appeared the imprint of a small foot on the flour, and then they knew that the gods had come. A priest called Tevoa was waiting all night to see when this sign of the arrival of the gods would show, and he came and went every hour, many times, to look at the little heap. When he saw the imprint on it, at once he would say, "His majesty has come." The other priests and ministers of the idols, as soon as they heard this voice, rose at once and played on their shells and trumpets in all the Cús of all the districts of the town and the villages. By this all the people understood that the gods had arrived, and they all started to go to the temples with their gifts they were to offer to the newcomers. Their offerings consisted in those (well-known) tamales of wild amaranth-seeds, and which they had made the day before. After the offering they at once returned to their homes, no one remaining in the temples, and at midnight they drank pulque. The old men and women said that they washed the feet of the gods. On the following dav the god of the merchants, called Yacapitzaoatl or Yiacatecutli, arrived, as well as another god called Yxcocauhqui or Xiuhtecutli, who is the god of the fire, and for whom the merchants have great devotion; these two gods arrived last, one day after the others. When this was over they at once burned alive a great many slaves, throwing them into the fire on a large altar which was called tecalco, and which had steps on four sides. On top of the altar a young man was dancing, adorned with a switch of long hair with a tuft of rich plumes and a crown. His face was painted black with white lines, one from the point of the ear towards the top of the forehead, and the other one from under the eye towards the cheek, thus forming a half circle. He carried on his back a plumage which was called vocalli, with a dried (dissected) rabbit on it. When they threw one of the slaves into the fire, he (the dancer) whistled by sticking one finger into his mouth, as is their custom (when whistling). Another youth was dressed like a bat, with wings and all the rest to look like that animal. He carried rattles, one in each hand; these rattles were made like the heads of the large poppies, and with them he produced sounds.

After having thrown the captives into the fire, the priests formed in procession, arrayed in paper-stoles from the left shoulder to the right arm-pit, and from the right shoulder to the left arm-pit. They came forth to the fire holding hands, and made one turn around it, very slowly; then, running down the steps, they let go of each other's hands almost forcibly; some of them fell, a few headlong; others on one side, and this game was called mamatlavicoa.

The following day they (the people) assembled in the districts and on the streets, and they performed dances in which they crossed or held hands. They covered their arms and bodies with feathers of different colors, glueing them to the skin by means of resin. This was done by young and old, and even babies in the crib were covered with these feathers, although only the male babies. This kind of dance began at noon and they sang songs (whichever they liked), and danced till night, and those who so wished also during the night. These last two days belonged already to the following month.

This is the report of the festival called Teutleco.

Festival and Sacrifices Celebrated under the Signs of the Thirteenth Month, Called Tepeilhuitl

The thirteenth month was called Tepeilhuitl. For this festival celebrated in this month they covered certain sticks, which they had previously shaped like snakes, with dough of wild amaranth-flour; they also made images of hills (mountains) over a foundation made of sticks, and shaped them like young girls or children, and they called them Ehecatontin. The image of the mountain (hill) was made of wild amaranth-dough, in front of it they put round, longish pieces of dough of the same wild amaranth, like baker's kisses (a special kind of pastry), and these were called yonio. These images were made in honor of the high mountains where the clouds gather, and in memory of those who had died in the water, or were hurt by lightning, and also of those whose bodies were not cremated, but buried in the soil. They placed these mountains on twists made of hay tied with grass, which they kept from one year to the next. On the eve of the festival they carried these twists of hay to wash them in the river or in a fountain (spring), and as they took them there, they played (for them) on baked clay whistles or on marine shells. They washed them in certain houses or oratories which were erected on the edge of the water, called aiauhcalli, and the washing they did with the leaves of green cane. Some washed them in the water which flowed close by their houses. After having them washed they returned them to their homes with the same music, and then built on them the images of the mountains, as stated above. Some made these images at night, before dawn, but near daybreak. The head of each one of these mountains had two faces, one of a person, the other of a snake. They rubbed melted (liquid) ulli on the person's face (of this mountain), and made very tiny "tortillas" of yellow, wild amaranth-dough, and put them on the cheeks of that face. One side and the other they covered with certain papers called teteuitl, and on the (two) heads they put crowns with their tufts. They also made images of the dead and placed them on these twists of hay, and at dawn carried them to the oratories on stretchers of reed-mace, or cyperus, or rush. Once placed there, they offered them food, tamales and mush (mazamorra) or "cachuela" (a stew made of heart and liver, or else these latter just fried) made of chicken and dog-meat, and then incensed them by putting incense into a "mano" (hand) made of baked clay, the size of a large spoon, filled with burning coal or embers. This ceremony was called calonoac. The wealthy people sang and drank pulque in honor of these gods and of their departed; the poor people did not do more than offer food, as stated.

During this festival they killed a few women and one man, in honor of the gods of the mountains. One of the women was called Tepoxoch, the second Matlalhuac; the third Xochetecatl, and the fourth Mayabel, this latter represented the image of the maguey. The first one killed was a man, whom they called Milnaoatl, and this man was the image of the snakes. They were dressed up in paper crowns; all the papers which adorned them were spotted with melted ulli (gum); the man called Milnaoatl, who as is stated was the image of the snakes, also wore such a crown. These women and the man were carried in litters; the women very elegantly dressed in embroidered (elaborate) skirts and blouses, their faces painted.

When the hour of the sacrifice had come, they placed the women and the man who had to die in their respective litters, and carried them to the top of the temple. Once up there they took them out of the litters, and one by one threw them onto the sacrificial block; they opened their breasts with the flint knife and tore out their hearts, which they offered to the god Tlaloc. Then brought down the bodies, sliding them down the steps, little by little, however, holding them with their hands. Once down on the ground, they carried them to the place where they kept the heads impaled, and there they beheaded them and, piercing their heads through the temples, stuck them on poles, which were laid horizontal like the fence. The bodies were taken to the districts whence they came from. The following day, called texinilo, they cut them in pieces and ate them. It was then, also, that they broke the images of the mountains into pieces in all the houses where they had been made. They carried the pieces up to the tlapancos (flat roofs?) to let them dry in the sun, and then began eating them, little by little, every day. With the papers with which these images of the mountains had been decorated they covered the hay-twists on which they had been placed and hung them on the rafters, everyone in the oratory of his home. A whole year they hung there, until this festival was due again. They then took the pieces (that were left?) together with the twist and carried them to the oratories called aiauh-calli. The paper they left there (at the oratories), but the twist they carried home, in order to prepare again the offering to the images. Here ends the report on the month and festival called Tepeilhuitl.

The Feast and Sacrifices Celebrated under the Signs of the Fourteenth Month Called Quecholli (which began November 15th)

The fourteenth month they called Quecholli. For five days after the end of the preceding month no ceremony of any kind nor festival were celebrated in the Cús (temples). There was perfect quiet as far as the service of the gods was concerned. On the sixth day those who were in charge of the districts gathered to make darts (shafts). Each one of the warriors brought a load of reeds, and all together those of Tlaltelulco with those of Mexico offered these reeds to Vitzilopuchtli, carrying them to the court in front of the temple of this god. From there they were distributed to the other people, and everyone took home all he could carry. On the following day all those who had carried home reeds came to the court of Vitzilopuchtli to straighten them in the fire; this day nothing else except the straightening of reeds was done; so after doing it, they returned home. The next day they returned with them to the courtyard of Vitzilopuchtli, and (this time) everybody came, small and grown-up (young and old), no one staying away. All the children were taken up to the temple of Vitzilopuchtli; there they made them play on the shells and bugles (cornets), and they had their ears pierced to extract blood and anoint their temples and faces with it. This sacrifice was called momacaico, because this was done in memory (honor?) of the deer they were going to hunt.

When all were assembled in the court of Vitzilopuchtli, the Tenuchcas and the Tlaltelulcas, the former gathered in one place (part of it), the latter in another, and they began to make darts. This day was called Tlacatintlacochtli, and on this day they all did penance; all drew blood from the ears, and if anyone failed to bleed himself, certain men who were appointed to catch (get) such people, whom they called tepanmani (these laggards), took his blanket away from him and never returned it. During the days set apart (destined) to make these darts (arrow-shafts), none of them slept with a woman nor drank pulque. All the darts or arrows were made after the same measure, and the tips, which were points as long as a "geme"[1] (the distance from the point of the thumb to point of fore-finger, both extended) made of oak-wood, were also all alike. They all cut the reeds (canes) after one measure; once cut, they handed them to those who attached the points to them, which they did by tying them very well (solidly) with ixtli, threads of henequen (hemp), very well twisted. In order to prevent the canes (reeds) from splitting, they put paste in the split part of the reed and adjusted the (oak) point in the paste. After inserting the point as it was to be, they covered the fastening of the cane with resin as well as the other end where it was to rest on the string of the bow. When they had finished with the preparation of the darts, they divided them into little bundles of twenty, then formed as in procession, taking them all to present and deposit them before Vitzilopuchtli; once all of them placed there, they went home.

The fourth day they called Calpannemitilo, which means the day on which personal darts are made, and on that day they played with them in order to become efficient in shooting. To this effect they put as target a maguey leaf and shot at it; here shone those who were the best (most accurate) shots.

On the fifth day they made a number of small darts in honor of the dead; they were as long as a span, or the space between the point of an extended thumb and fore-finger. They put resin on points and on the end; the cap was of wood, and they tied to this tip four arrows (darts) and four torches by means of loose cotton thread, and then placed them on

[1]In modern Spanish "jeme."

the graves of the dead. Together with these they put a pair of sweet tamales. This remained on the grave all day. At sunset the torches and the darts (arrows) were burnt; the coal and ashes of this they buried on the grave in honor of those who had died in war. They took a cornstalk which had nine knots and placed on top of it a piece of paper like a flag or banner, and another long one which hung down to the foot of the cane; against it they leaned the shield of that dead man and one arrow (dart), and tied to the cane also his blanket and belt. On the banner or flag they marked or embroidered with red thread a reel on both sides; they also embroidered the long (strip of) paper from top to bottom with well twisted red and white thread, and from the white thread hung a dead little bird which is called vitzitzilin (a humming bird).[1] They also made small bundles of white feathers of the bird called aztatl (Garza-heron), tying two and two together. They gathered all the threads of these bundles and fastened them to the cane (cornstalk). The threads were lined with white chicken feathers glued to them with resin. All this was carried to a stone-pile, which was called quauhxicalco, and burnt there.

The sixth day they called cacapanquixoa, and they called it thus because (on that day) they spread in the court (yard) of the temple of the god they call Mixcoatl, a lot of hay brought from the mountains, and on it (this hay) sat the old women who served in the temple, and who were called Cioatlamacazque. In front of them they spread a mat, and then came all the women who had sons or daughters and brought them along. Each one of these women brought five sweet tamales and laid them on the mat in front of the old women. Then each one gave a tamal to her child, first showing it to the children and they would jump into their arms in order to take it. After that they went home. This (ceremony) began in the morning and ended at the dinner hour; the tamales placed on the mat were eaten by the old women.

On the eleventh day of that month they went hunting on the mountains which rose above Atlacuioayan (today Tacubaya), and this was a separate festival, so that in this month they celebrated two feasts, the one mentioned before and this one which begins now. The above mentioned mountain or mountainside where they went to hunt was called Cacatepec, and they also called it Yxillantonan. The day they arrived on that mountainside they spent the night in their straw huts and built fires in order to spend the night there. (On the tenth day of the month above mentioned they celebrated the feast of the god of the Otomies,

[1]Clavijero says that the Chupaminto or Huitzitzilin sleeps like the swallow, from October to April—(page 164 of Sahagun copy).

called Mixcoatl, in the manner explained hereafter).[1] On the following morning they all took their breakfast and then got ready for the hunt; they fastened their blankets to their loins and went hunting. Not only the Mexicans participated inthis festival, but also the men of Cuauhtitlan, of Cuauhnavac, those of Coioacan, and other neighboring villages. They all carried bows and arrows (darts or spears?) and they proceeded, scattering over the territory and then gathering, little by little, surrounding (corraling) the game, which consisted of stags, rabbits, hares, and coyotes. When the game had collected, all of them (the huntsmen) attacked it, and each took what he could; very few or hardly any of the animals thus corraled escaped. Having obtained the animals, each one returned to his village, and those who killed any (larger) game, killed it and carried the head home. Men who had succeeded in killing a number of animals received blankets for being swift and daring, and they were also given food. Once the hunting was over, they returned to their homes; the heads of game they had killed, and which they took with them, they hung up in their homes.

On the sixth day, which they called cacapinquixoa, they adorned the slaves who were to be killed in honor of the god, Tlamatzincatl, and also in honor of another god called Ixquitecatl, with papers. Those who brewed pulque and those who made it especially for Mochtecuzoma bought the slaves who were to die in honor of the above mentioned gods. Two other slaves who were to be killed in honor of the god Mixcoatl and of his wife, who was called Coatlicue, were bought by the Calpixques. Besides other men whom they killed in honor of Tlamatzincatl, they also killed a number of women, called Eoatlnicue, and these were (considered) the wives of Tlamatzincatl and Ixquitecatl, and these hapless creatures also were adorned with their papers.

On the day of the festival, which was the last day of the month, they rounded up all those who were to die and brought them in procession around the temple. After mid-day they took them to the place where they were to be killed, leading them in procession around the stone-block of the place of sacrifice, and then made them go down again. Then they took them to the house of the Calpulco, and there had them wake all night. At that hour (probably as soon as they arrived at the Calpulco), they cut the hair off the crown of the head in front of the fire, and after that the slaves burnt all their wearing apparel, which consisted of a paper banneret, their blanket, and their belt; some even burnt the rest of their "cañas de humo" as well as the cups they used for drinking. All this they reduced to ashes, there in the Calpulco. The women (who were to be

[1]These brackets appear in the book and should evidently precede the description of the hunt.

sacrificed) also burnt all their clothing, jewels, their small trunks (chests), and their spindles and other implements used by them for weaving; all these trifles were burned by the person who owned them. They said that all these jewels would be given back to them in the other world after their death. All this was done on the eve of the festival. On the day proper, at daybreak, they dressed them at once in the papers in which they were to die; they were then taken to the place of death, each one being helped by two young men, one at each arm, to prevent their fainting or falling; after death two different youths took the body down the steps. Before each one of these slaves a paper banner was carried, and amid this accompaniment every one was conducted to the temple. As they ascended the temple steps, four slaves with hands and feet tied were carried in front of them. These had thus been tied in the vestibule of the temple, which was called Apetlac, and which is situated at the foot of the stairway. Each one was carried by four men, two held them by the feet and two by the arms, holding them face upward; as soon as they reached the top, these four slaves were successively laid on the stone-block, their breast cut open, and the hearts torn out. They carried them up to the temple in this fashion because they were to symbolize deer which, after having been slaughtered, is brought home with its feet tied together; the rest of the slaves walked. After all (these victims) had been killed, the (one who represented the) image of the god Mixcoatl was also slain, because all these slaves were sacrificed in his temple. Those who belonged to (were of) the god Tlamatzincatl were killed in the temple dedicated to him; they ascended to his temple and were slain on the stone block. The women were killed first (before the men) in another temple called Coatlan, and some of them, upon climbing the steps, were singing, others screamed, and still others cried; they were led by the arm by men so that they should not become faint-hearted. After they had been killed they did not throw their bodies down the steps, but lowered them, sliding little by little. At the bottom near the place where they impaled the heads, two old women called Teixamique were waiting; they kept close by a few bowls with tamales and molli-sauce in a bowl or cup, and when the bodies of those who had been killed were brought down to where these old women were, the latter put into the mouth of each corpse four little morsels of bread moistened in the sauce, and sprinkled their faces with corn leaves dipped in clear water. Then those who were in charge of this (office) beheaded the bodies and impaled the heads on poles which were stuck in boards like lance-racks.

Thus the festival ended and everybody went home.

Festival and Sacrifices Celebrated under the Signs of the Fifteenth Month, Called Panqüetzaliztli

The fifteenth month was called Panqüetzaliztli. Previous to the beginning of this month, and in reverence to the festival celebrated in its course, the priests and ministers of the idol did penance for eighty days. They placed boughs in all the oratories and shrines of the mountains (or woods?). This festival started one day after the end of the month called Ochpantztli (Ochpaniztli). At midnight they went to embower altars, oratories and shrines of the mountains, even if they were far away, and this they did at night and naked, and repeated it day and night until the beginning of this month of Panqüetzaliztli. For boughs they took green cane and maguey-thorns and went along the road playing their shells, or horns (trumpets), and the whistles. For a little while they would play the cornet, another while the whistle, thus alternating the music. At the end of the month of Quecholli, which is this past one, they at once began to dance and to sing, singing a song called tlaxotecuiotl, which is a song in praise of Vitzilopuchtli. It commenced at night-fall and ended at midnight, when they called to matins (morning prayer). At this festival the women sang and danced, also intermingling with the men.

Nine days before they killed those destined to be sacrificed, they bathed them with water from a spring called Vitzilatl, which is near the town of Vitzilopuchco. The old men of the different city wards (districts) went to get that water, and brought it in new jars covered with cedar-leaves, which they call abebetl. When they reached the place where the slaves were assembled, namely, in front of the temple of Vitzilopuchtli, they poured a jug of water over their head and over all the clothes they had on, men as well as women; then they took off their wet clothes and adorned them with the papers in which they were to sleep, and also dyed their arms and legs pale blue; then by means of tiles they drew lines on these limbs and arms. They painted their faces in yellow and blue bands across the whole face, one yellow, one blue; through the nose they put a small arrow, and a half circle, which hung low down. On the head they wore a crown made of small reeds, tied together with a bunch of white feathers on top. The women had yellow feathers instead of white ones in their crowns.

Clothed in this manner in front of the temple of Vitzilopuchtli, they were taken past the Calpulli, and each owner took his (respective) slave home. Upon reaching the home they divested them (the slaves) of the papers with which they were adorned, putting these latter in the trunks, and from then on they began to dance and sing, men and women forming couples. Thus they reached the fifth day previous to the one on which they were to be killed, and the owners of slaves began to fast, and fasted the entire five days. The old men of the city wards (districts) were also fasting. During this period of fasting they ate at mid-day and bathed, as a sign of penance, in the oratories called Aiauhcalco, which were situated on the bank of the river. The wives of the slaves and the ladies (wives of their owners) bathed in the water which flowed by their houses (homes). Each one of those who thus bathed took four points (thorns) of maguey with him, and before the bath pierced (cut) his ears with them. With the blood that flowed they stained the aforementioned points; one of them they threw into the water; another one they stuck in the bank on the edge of the water, and the other they offered to the idol that stood in the oratory of Aianhcalco. The women who bathed in their homes stained (only) one maguey-point with blood and stuck it in the bank on the water's edge.

After these four days of penance the male and female slaves, their owners, men and women, also those who were to assist them up (the steps) to the temple, as well as those who were to take the bodies down after death, and also those who were to wash their faces, and the ones who were to carry the banners in front of them (the victims). All of these held hands and danced, sang, and were winding in and out in snake-fashion, holding on to one another. They made a sort of twists like garlands or ropes of reed-mace, and held these between them instead of seizing each other's hand, and the slaves who were to die danced interspersed among the others who participated in this dance, and (all) danced with great speed, jumping, running, dancing, galloping and panting. The old men of the city-wards played the tunes and sang, and a great many people watched the dancing. Those who had done penance had not slept with their wives during those days of mortification, nor had they indulged in any other luxury out of respect for their fasting; men, as well as women ended their dancing at midnight and then went home, all of them, and at dawn began the festival, because this was the last day of the month. Then the slaves who were to die went to the homes of their masters to bid them good-bye. Before them was carried a small bowl of ink (paint or dye) or of red ochre(Indian red)or blue paint. They were singing in a very loud voice, so loud that it seemed to split their breast, and upon reaching the house of their masters they dipped both hands in the bowls of paint or of ink and put them (the hands) on the lintels of the doors and the posts of the house, leaving their imprint in colors; the same they did in the houses of their relatives. Some of them who were lion-hearted would eat as usual, others could not eat thinking of the death they soon would have to suffer. After this, the owners (masters) of slaves had in readiness blankets and belts they were to distribute at the festival, done up in separate loads, which they put on the shoulders of those who had to carry them. The slaves who were to be killed dressed themselves in their papers, took up their banners to carry them on the shoulder; the women also picked up their small jewelry-boxes to be carried on their backs. Then they all formed in procession at the door, the slaves mounted the sedan-chairs of the house (of their respective masters probably), and circled around the homesteads, making several turns around each house. After that they started towards the Calpulco, and the slaves were walking in the rear (last of all); upon arriving at the Calpulco they danced through the court, and those who carried the bundles placed them there and then separated each thing by itself; the blankets all on one heap, as well as the belts, the vipils (blouses) and the skirts. After a while the guests arrived, and those who gave the festival presented them with belts and blankets (the men), or whatever else they wished; the women entered in orderly fashion from another side and received vipils (blouses) and skirts, if they wanted them.

These celebrations (festivals) were arranged by the merchants only who bought the slaves. After having given the blankets and the rest to their guests, they took the slaves to the temple and, after the procession had made the entire turn of its base, they took them up the steps. Arrived at the top, the procession made one turn around the stone-block, and then went down the steps again, and as soon as they reached the bottom, they ran to the Capulco. Others didn't run, but walked slowly. Upon reaching the Capulco they made them (the slaves) sit on mats, then brought them food and also pulque, so that those who wished to do so might eat and drink. Then they kept them awake there all night, and at midnight they made them stand in a row in front of the fire and cut their hair off the top of the head which (hair) they kept as relics, as stated before. This done, they commenced to eat wild amaranth-dough (made into tamales), which they had in readiness, and none omitted eating it. They did not break these round tamales with their fingers, but with a thread of ixtli. After eating these tamales they picked up the mats, rolled them up, and put them all away in one place. This was done in all the houses of the town. They lay down on the bare floor or on some old, shabby blankets which they spread under them. At dawn, before daybreak, the god Paynal was brought down from the top of the temple of Vitzilopuchtli and was taken at once to the ball game which took place in the center of the court they called teutlachco. There they killed four captives, two of them in honor of the god Amapan, and the other two in honor of the god Oappatzan, whose statues stood near the tlachco. After the victims had been sacrificed they dragged the bodies through the tlachco, and the entire floor became tinted red with the blood they shed from being thus dragged. Then the god (Paynal) departed at once on a run towards Tlaltelulco, and he was accompanied by four necromancers (magicians or conjurors), and a great many other people. From there he went forthwith on the road they call Nonoalco where now stands the church of San Miguel, and there he was met and received by the priest of that temple carrying the image (effigy) of the god Quavitlicac, who is a companion of the god Paynal; they both wore certain ornaments or finery. Then the two together went toward Tlacuba, to the place which is called Tlaxotlan; from there they went to the suburb called Popatlan where (now) stands the church of San Estevan. Opposite or in front of a temple which stood there they killed other captives, and they then parted at once, running towards Chapultepec, passing at the foot of the hill of that name, and crossed a river which flows by there, and which they call Izquitlan. In front of the temple which stands there they killed again a number of captives, whom they call Izquiteca. From there they went straight towards Coyoacan, and there reached a place called Tepetocan, close to the houses of Coyoacan. From there they went straight to Mazatlan, which is close to the church of San Matias Iztacalco, and from that point they returned to a place called Acachinanco, which is near the houses of Alvarado.

While this procession was going on, the slaves who were to die enacted a skirmish. One band belonged to Vitznaoa, the other one was (made up) of other slaves. Those on the part of Vitznaoa were assisted by some of his soldiers, and the chieftain gave those soldiers yellow doublets (jackets?) to wear and shields with white and black circles or spheres painted on them, linked into one another. For swords these soldiers carried pine-wood clubs and darts with which they fought, and which they threw; the slaves shot with arrows with flint points. They killed one another in this skirmish (sham-battle), and those who captured the slaves of the soldiers also killed them. They threw their captives onto a teponaztli[1], and there tore their hearts out.

When the god Paynal was coming back, and as soon as he approached the temple where the sham-battle took place, the watchman on the top of the Cú called out saying: "Oh, Mexicans, do not fight any more, stop struggling, the lord Paynal is coming!" Upon hearing this voice, the soldiers who were fighting took flight, the slaves followed them, and thus the strife was over. In front of the god Paynal two plumages, round like shields, were carried, their center being hollow; these plumes resembled maces carried before the god, and were fastened on staffs like lance-shafts. They were carried by boys who ran ahead (of the god),

[1]This no doubt should be "texcatl," which is sacrificial block—for a teponaztli is a musical instrument!

and as soon as these maces were seen approaching from afar, the lookout shouted the warning to stop their battle. As the procession approached the temple of Vitzilopuchtli, two soldiers from among those who accompanied it took the two maces from the boys and carried them, running swiftly, as far as the temple, where two others came forth to take them and carry them another stretch, and thus they alternated until the very door of the temple of Vitzilopuchtli, which was called Quahquinaoac. Once there, no one could take the maces from the hands of those who carried them, and they were the ones who took them up to the temple of Vitzilopuchtli and, arrived at the top, placed them onto the statue of the god which was made of dough of wild amaranth-seeds; there they collapsed and were panting from fatigue. A priest came at once to cut (pierce) the ears of the two (men) who had thus arrived so fatigued, with a flint (knife), and they at once recovered and were able to descend from the temple, taking with them the statue of Vitzilopuchtli, made of wild amaranth-dough, as their prey. They carried it to their homes and made a celebration for it, inviting all their relatives and all the people of their district.

After this they gathered all the captives and the other slaves who were doomed to die and brought them in procession for only one turn around the temple. All the captives walked at the head, and when they were ranged in their (due) order, a priest came down from the top of the temple, and in his hands he carried a large amount of white papers which they call teteppoalli or, by another name, tetevitl. As he reached the bottom (of the stairway) he raised them, as in offering, towards the four parts of the world; then he put them down on a trough (or fountain basin?), which is called quauhxicalco. Afterwards another priest came down (from the temple), who brought with him a very long torch of firebrands, which they call xiuhcoatl. Head and tail of this torch were made to resemble a snake; in its mouth they stuck red feathers so that it looked as if fire were emanating from it; its tail was made of paper two or three fathoms in length. As it came down it looked exactly like a large serpent crawling down and wiggling like a snake, and moving its tongue. Upon reaching the bottom he (the priest bearing this torch) went straight to the trough or basin where the paper was deposited and offered it to the four parts of the world, then piled it in again and threw the burning snake onto it, and it all burnt up together, while the priest remounted the steps to the temple, and as he reached the top they at once began to blow their horns (cornets) and shells.

Then descended a priest in great haste, carrying in his arms the statue of Paynal, the deputy (representative) of Vitzilopuchtli. Upon reaching the bottom with the statue, he passed by the trough or basin, and by the captives and slaves who were to die, as if guiding them. Then he ascended to the temple once more and, upon reaching the top, they first killed the captives so that these should precede the slaves in death, and then sacrificed the latter. After killing one they at once blew horns and shells, and threw the body rolling down over the staircase, spilling blood over the steps. This they did with all the slaves they killed in honor of Vitznaoatl; they were the only ones to die, no captive was killed with them, and they killed them in the temple of Vitznaoatl.[1] After having killed the slaves and captives, everybody went home, and on the following day the old men and women, married people and chieftains, drank pulque. The pulque they drank here (on this occasion, it probably means), was called mataluhtli, which means "blue pulque," because they coloured it with a (certain) blue colouring; all the others drank uctli, which had to be prepared secretly, because if it was known they punished them (meaning those who made it); they hit them with bludgeons and had their hair shorn; they were dragged, pummeled, and then thrown down on the floor in a heap in very bad shape. In the homes of the owners of the slaves they sang and played musical instruments and the jingles. They did not dance but remained seated; they presented blankets to those who served at the festival and who were in charge of providing food, drink, smoke-sticks and flowers, etc. They also gave skirts and waists (vipiles) to the women who made tortillas, cooked the food, and prepared beverages; and to all the neighbors of the district they gave blankets.

On the third day, which they called chonchaiocacalioa, which means skirmish (sham-battle) of "caharrones"[2] (grotesque masks); that is, they dressed one such caharron in cassocks and frightful masks, and then formed two parties (bands), on one side the ministers of the idols, and with them the said caharron (mask), and on the other side the young men of the Telpuchcalli, and these two bands began to fight with one another at noon. They fought with branches (boughs) of oiametl or pine, with canes or also with these latter made massive and heavier by tying them together in two's, three's or four's, and when they hit each other with them they made a great noise. They injured one another with them, and they rubbed the backs of those they captured with ground maguey thorns, which produces a pungent pain (itching?). If the ministers of the temple made any captives on their part, they pierced their ears with maguey-thorns, as well as the fleshy parts of the arms, the chest, and thighs, which made them scream. If the young men of the Calmecac defeated their opponents they locked them up in the royal house

[1]There is contradiction in this, as above he states that captives were killed before they killed the slaves!

[2]Caharrones or Matachines—dance of grotesque masks or figures dressed in fantastic costumes.

or palace, and those who went after them stole whatever there was to steal, such as mats, icpales teponaztli, pevetes (petete-aromatic burning stick). And if the young men of the Calpulco defeated the ones of the Calmecac, they locked them all up in this latter place and stole whatever they could find. They separated, and the sham-battle was at an end at sunset.

The fourth day they called Nexpixolo; the old men said that the slaves who had been killed were still about this world, that they had not yet gone to hell (hades), and that until the fourth day they did not enter it. Thus on that same day they placed the papers with which the slaves and captives had died, on their mats. Also on that same day the other people bathed, soaped themselves, and washed their heads, and after that everybody went home, because now the festivities were at an end.

The Feast and Sacrifices Celebrated under the Signs of the Sixteenth Month, Which Was Called Atemuztli[1]

They called the sixteenth month Atemuztli, which means the falling of rain (rainfall or, literally, the coming down of rain), and it was so called because in this month usually it begins to thunder and the first rain falls up in the mountains; the common people in general used to say: "The gods Tlaloques (Tlalocs) are coming!" At this time (of the year) the priests of the Tlalocs went about very devout and penitent, praying to their gods for water and awaiting the rains. As soon as it began to thunder and there were indications of rain, these priests at once took up their incensories, which consisted of a sort of large spoons with holes in them, filled with live coal; the handles of these incensories were long, thin, round and hollow, with jingles inside, the end having the shape of a snake's head. On the live coal they strew incense called yiauhtli and started at once to make noise with the jingles which were in the handle, shaking them from side to side. In this manner they began at once to incense all the statues of the temples of the Tlaxilacales. By means of these services they solicited and hoped for rain. The rest of the people, for their love of rain, made vows to make the images of the mountains.

Five days previous to this feast, they bought paper, ulli (gum), henequen and knives and, with great devotion, prepared themselves by means of fasts and penances, to make the images of the mountains and cover them with paper. During this period, although they bathed, they did not wash their heads, but merely the neck; men abstained from intercourse with women, and these latter from that with men. On the eve

[1]According to Clavijero it is Homomoztli—descent of (fall) of the water (rain). Atemuztl seems more appropriate, as it is derived from atl—water.

of the festival of Atemuztli, which came on the twentieth day of that month, they spent the entire night cutting papers in diverse shapes and these, when cut, were called tetevitl. They stuck (glued) them on long sticks or poles, from the bottom up, in the fashion of flags. All these papers were spotted (spreckled) with ulli (gum). Then they stuck this pole in the courtyard of their homes, each one his own, and there it stood for the entire day of the feast. All those who had vowed to make the image (of the mountains) invited the ministers of the idols to come to their homes and make (shape) the papers with which they were to cover (adorn) them. They made the images in the Calmecac, and from there they took them to the houses of the people who had made vows, and at the same time they took their teponaztli, their jingles, and the tortoise-shell to play on. As soon as they reached the house they began at once to adorn the images made of dough of wild amaranth; some had prepared five of them, others ten, and still others even fifteen images which represented the mountains over which the clouds formed, such as the volcano, the Sierra Nevada, the Sierra de Tlaxcala, etc., and others of their kind. They placed them in their proper order in the oratory of the home, and then offered food to each one separately, then sat down in front of them. The tamales were made exceedingly small to fit the size of the images, which also were very small, and they put these tamales into very little plates; in very tiny boxes, they put a little bit of mazamorra (a sweet mush or porridge), and in likewise exceedingly small tecomates (cups) they poured a very small quantity of cacaoatl (cocoa). In the course of one night they presented food in this manner four times; they also put two tecomates of green squash, which is called tzilacaitli (today chilacayotes—bottle-gourd), and filled them with pulque. All night long they were singing before them and playing the flute. This, however, was not done by the regular flutist, but by certain young boys whom they selected for this occasion, giving them food in return.

At dawn the ministers of the idols asked the owners of the house for an implement used for weaving and called tzotzopaztli, which they thrust in the breast of the images of the mountains, as if they were killing them; they cut their throat, tore out the heart and presented it to the owner of the house placed in a green bowl (jicara). All these images or statues as stated, being now dead, they removed the papers with which they had been bedecked and burnt them all in the court of the same house, and together with them they also burned the little boxes of food. All the mats of green reeds which had adorned these images, as well as all the small vessels in which they had offered them food or drink were carried to the oratories, called tiauhcalco, which are built on the water's edge. After this, all the guests assembled and ate and drank in honor of these dead statues, which were called tepieme. They placed food before everyone (of the guests), and after they had eaten they gave them pulque to drink. The women included in this invitation, all brought either corn in grain or ears of corn in their "almantos," and none went without bringing something, anything they chose, or else fifteen to twenty ears of corn. Upon entering the house they kept apart from the men and food was given them there, to every one of them separately, also pulque to drink. This latter was kept in dark coloured earthen jars and to drink it it was taken out by means of black cups. After the meal they (all) went out to tear the paper called tetevitl off the poles in the court and took it to certain places on the water which were marked by sticks rammed in the bottom (of the lake), or else they carried it up to the mountains. This ends the report of this festival.

The Festival and Sacrifices Celebrated under the Signs of the Seventeenth Month, Called Tititl

The seventeenth month was called Tititl, and during this month they killed a woman slave, who was bought by the Calpixques. She was sacrificed in honor of the goddess Illamatecutli. It was said that she was (represented) her image, and they dressed her in white skirts and a white vipil. Over the white skirts they put others made of leather, which were cut so as to form straps (like heavy fringe) around the hem, and on each one of these straps or strings they hung a little shell. These (leather) skirts were called citlallxicue, and the little shells which were hanging on the ends were called cuechtli; when this woman walked the little shells touched one another and made much noise, which could be heard far away. The sandals they wore were white, and the heels[1] were woven of cotton. They (she) also carried a white shield which had been whitened with chalk; in the center of the shield there was a circle (or ring) made of eagle-feathers and sewed on to this shield. The border at the lower end was white, made of plumes of the night heron, and into the ends of these eagle feathers were inserted. She carried this shield in one hand while in the other she held the tzotzopaztli (implement of weaving), with which they weave. Her face was painted in two colors, black from the nose down, and from the nose upwards yellow; she also wore a wig which hung down over the back. For a crown she had eagle-feathers glued to the wig, and the latter (with the crown) was called tzompilinalli.

Previous to being killed, this woman had to dance, and the old men played the tune for this dance, and the (official) singers sang the songs; and while she danced she cried, sighed and worried, knowing that her

[1]Calcaños—heel, but it might mean calectin—short sock).

death was so close at hand. This lasted until noon or a little longer. As soon as the sun declined towards evening she was taken up to the temple of Vitzilopuchtli, followed by all the priests, clothed in finery (ornaments) of all the different gods, and wearing masks. There also was one who wore the vestments and mask of the goddess Illamatecutli. As soon as she reached the top they killed her, tore her heart out, beheaded her, and handed her head to the one (priest) who wore the ornaments and vestments of the aforementioned goddess; he went at the head of all the rest, bearing the head by the hair in his right hand, dangling from it, and as he danced with the others he raised and lowered the head of the dead woman to suit the motions of the dance, leading all the other gods or personages who were impersonators of the deities. Thus he danced around the top of the temple. After having made several rounds they turned to descend in their (proper) order like a procession, and as soon as they reached the bottom of the stairway they dispersed at once, each going home, that is, to the respective Calpules where the vestments were kept.

While the one (priest) wearing the vestments of the goddess Illamatecutli danced, he made graceful bows, walking backwards, as if he were checking himself at the same time swinging his feet backwards. As staff he carried in one hand a solid cane which he straddled; this cane had three roots and its stalk, the former pointing upwards and the point downwards. This kind of dance was called vecula. The goddess Illamatecutli also wore a mask with two faces, one in the back and one in front; the mouths (of both) were very large and the eyes protruding; on the head she wore an embattled paper crown.

As the gods (i.e., priests dressed as such) went towards the Calpules, a Sátrapa descended at once from the temple, dressed as a young man; he was covered by a blanket made like a net which they called quechintli; his head was adorned with white tufts of plumes; on his feet were tied rattles or jingles made of deer-hoofs, and he carried the pulpy leaf of a maguey which was topped by a small paper banner, in one hand. As soon as he reached the bottom (of the stairway) he went straight to the trough or basin called quauhxicalco, where there was a small box like a cage, made of torches, the top of which was papered like a tlapanco; this was called the trough of the goddess Illamatecutli. This priest placed the maguey leaf (or point) close to the trough and then set fire to it. Other priests who were near there at the very moment fled up the stairs of the temple in competition (on a wager). This ceremony was called xochipayana; at the top a flower called teuxochitl was placed, and he who arrived first took that flower and threw it into the quauhxicalco, where the trough was burning. After this they all left.

On the following day they started the game called nechichiquavilo. For this game all the men and boys who wished to participate made small bags or nets filled with the blossoms of reed mace (or great cattail) or paper torn to bits. They tied these bags or nets with strings or ribbon, half a fathom (3 feet) long, in such a way that they could hit with them (swing them to hit a person). Others fashioned these little bags like gloves and also filled them with the above flowers or with green corn-leaves. Anyone who should try to or fill them with stones or anything that might hurt, was punished. The boys at once started to play the game in the manner of a skirmish or sham-battle, and hit each other with the little bags over the heads or wherever else the blow might fall. Little by little their numbers increased, and the most mischievous ones also hit the girls who passed on the street. Calling to each other, three or four would gather to hit one girl until they tired her in such a way that they even made her cry. Girls who were more audacious would carry a stick or anything else that might make the boys fear her defense, and so she continued her way unmolested. There were frolicsome fellows who would hide their bags, which they called chichiquatli, and then, if a careless woman or girl passed by, they would suddenly hit her, saying at the same time: "chichiquatzintonantze," which means, "Our mother, this is the bag of this game," and she at once fled. This game lasted all the days of the festival, and the women, if they had to go out, went along very carefully.

This is the report of the festival called Tititl.

Festival and Ceremonies Celebrated under the Signs of the Eighteenth Month, Which Was Called Izcalli

The eighteenth month was called Izcalli. On the tenth day of this month they made tamales of the leaves of wild amaranth, very well ground; they called this festival Motlaxquiantota, which means, "Our father, the fire toasts in order to eat." They made the statue of the god of the fire of small arches and sticks tied together, which they call caloliotli, which means cradling or model of a statue. They put on this a mask made of a mosaic all made of turquoise with bands of the stones they call chalchivites across the face. This mask was very beautiful and resplendent (glittering). They put a crown on it which they called quetzalcomitl and which was made of rich plumes, and it was narrow to fit the roundness of the head on its lower border, but became wider towards the upper part. The top plumes stood very erect like carnations which are trained on sticks and have all their flowers at the top overlapping the staves. This crown had two more plumes, one on the left and one on the right directly above the temples, like horns leaning forward. To the ends of these were fastened a number of rich quetzalli-(trogon-plumes) feathers, which came out of cups made like very small jicaras (bowls). These two plumes or horns were called quammavitli. Around the lower edge of this crown, in the back, a blond wig was sewn, which hung down the back. The lower ends of the hair of this wig were clipped very evenly, and it looked as though the hair flowed down from under the crown and was natural. This statue also had an ornament of very rich feathers glued around the neck as wide as the chest (from shoulder to shoulder), and which hung down to the feet in the same width, and even if it was some two spans longer than the foot of the statue, they spread it over the feet of it. This ornament was made in such a way that the least little breeze moved and lifted it, and all the feathers glittered and shone in many hues (colours). This statue was seated on a throne of tiger skin with its four feet and its natural head, although dissected. This statue (or image) thus adorned was nor far from this place which stretched in front of it.

At midnight they produced new fire so that it should burn in that place, and they made it with logs (sticks?); one they placed at the bottom, one over it, and then they drilled with another one, twisting it between their hands with great speed, by which movement and the heat (produced by it), the fire started. From there they took it with tinder and carried it to their homes.

On the following day at daybreak, all the young men and boys came, bringing all the game they had killed on the previous day. They all formed in line and presented themselves before the old men who were close to the calpulli where the statue was erected, and they offered the birds they had killed, all kinds of them as well as fish, snakes, and other reptiles of the water. The old men received (took) these offerings, throwing them into the fire, which was big, burning in front of the statue.

The women and all the people (in general) busied themselves in preparing certain tamales which they call chalchiuhtamalli and, also at daybreak, they went to offer them before this statue, and so there was a large quantity of them in front of the statue.

When the boys offered the game they brought, they entered as they were ranged and made one turn around the fire as they were approaching it; then other old men gave each one of the boys a tamal, and they went out again in their proper order. These tamales were also called chalchiutamalli. This food was prepared in all the homes, and they worked in competition one against the other to see who was first to finish them. The one who finished first went at once to invite her neighbors to show thus her greater industry, and also her greater civility (politeness). The viands eaten with these tamales consisted of crawfish (common prawn), which they called aeocilte, made in broth they called chalmulmulli, and everybody ate this kind of food at home, very hot and close to the fire (hearth). The corn husks which covered the tamales were not thrown into the (home) fire after taking them off to eat the tamales, but were all gathered together to be thrown into the water.

After eating that meal the old men of the district (city ward) at once drank pulque in the house of the Calpulco where the statue stood, and this sort of drink (pulque) was called texcalcevia; there they drank and sang in front of the statue of Xiuhtecutli until nightfall. This is the account of the festival they called Vauhquiltamalqualiztli. The above mentioned (ceremonials) took place on the tenth day of this month.

On the twentieth day of the same month they again made the statue of the god of fire with little sticks and rings (circles) all tied together as explained above, and after this was done they put on the statue a mask made of mosaic of little pieces of shells called tapachtli. The lower part of this mask from the chin up to the mouth was made of black stones which they called teutetl, and it also had a black band which ran across the nose, while the cheeks were of stones called tezcapuctli. On its head they put a crown made of rich plumage which went all around the head, and from the center rose many sumptuous and high (tall) quetzales (trogons), while down to the shoulders and back drooped very beautiful green plumes. The top of the crown was made of very black feathers such as hens and roosters have on their necks, and between those they interspersed little ribs of plucked feathers which looked like taffeta ribs. Around the neck they folded a piece of parrot feather-work which was so wide that it reached from one shoulder to the other and hung down to the feet and even longer, and it was equally wide from top to bottom. After this statue, which they called Milintoc, was thus arrayed and seated on its throne, they offered it corn-meal which, stirred in hot water, was made into a dough of which they made very tiny cakes (loaves). These tiny loaves were stuffed with beans which had not been ground (but made like pie), and then they were offered before the statue. Everyone carried five of these tiny cakes, which were put at the feet of the said statue. The young men and boys, ranged in due order, also brought the game they had killed and gave it to the old men, who then threw it into the fire, which burned in front of the statue. This game consisted of birds, snakes and other small reptiles; the smaller birds and snakes were completely consumed by the fire, while the large snakes and big fowl, as soon as they were roasted, were taken out and placed on the outer edge of the fire, and after they had somewhat cooled off the old men ate them. They called this morsel (delicacy) Calpuleque. After the boys had filed in, presenting their offerings, they made an entire turn (circuit) around the fire, and as they filed out again each one was given some of the little breads (cakes) that had been offered (to the god), and which were called macuextlaxcalli. After eating the little breads and the rest of the food, the old men at once began drinking pulque; they called this special kind of beverage (pulque) texcalcevilo, and they drank it in the oratory proper where the statue of Milintoc stood, that is, the Calpulco. All those who made maguey-wine, which they called tlachique or tecutlachique, were commissioned to bring the pulque for drinking in the quantities they chose. It was brought in its jugs or jicaras (in which it was made), and they poured it into a glazed earthenware tub which stood in front of the statue. Those who drank this (kind of) pulque did not get drunk. These two above-mentioned ceremonies were not celebrated everywhere, but only around here in Tlaltelulco.

At the end of this month there remained five days over the 360 already mentioned, each twenty of which were dedicated to some deity. As these five left over days were not devoted to any god's services they called them nemontemi, which means "left overs," and (as such) they considered them exceedingly unfortunate. Nothing was done in those five days; children born in their course were held to be unlucky, and they were given no special sign (distinctive).[1]

For three consecutive years the above mentioned celebrations were held during this month, but in the fourth year they did a great many other things as mentioned below.

In this fourth year they killed (sacrificed) many slaves as images of the god of fire, every one of them with his wife, who also had to die. At dawn of the last day of the month of this fourth year they took all those who were to die to the temple where the sacrifice was to take place. The women who were to be killed carried their little bundles and their jewelry on their back; likewise the men. They did not wear the papers in which they were to die; these were carried by a man in front of them, on a tripod, its top (shaped) like a globe resting on tripod—feet, and altogether one-half estado high (1 estado—1.15 yards). Over the globe (or knob) the papers were hung in their order, and this tripod was then carried by one man before the (individual) slave who was to wear them (so that each slave was preceded by his own tripod-bearer).

Upon reaching the Cú where they were to be sacrificed, the slaves were dressed in the papers in the manner of the god Ixcocauhqui, the men as well as the women, and then they were taken up the steps to the temple proper, in their due order. Once at the top they passed in front of the stone-block where they were to be sacrificed, and then were taken

[1]According to Clavijero, boys born in those days were called Nemoquichtli, i.e., "useless men"; girls were called Nemihuatl, or "useless women."

down the stairway again in the same order. They were conducted to the Calpulco and divested of the papers and then lodged in a house, where they were very carefully guarded. The men were tied with cords around the waist, and when they went out to urinate those who guarded them held the cord to prevent their running away. At midnight they cut their hair off the crown of the head in front of the fire and covered their heads with a vilma (sort of scull-cap or wig?) glued with resin, and adorned with white chicken feathers; this was done to men and women. During that night nobody slept; after a while they burned (incinerated) their little bundles and their jewels right there in the Calpulco, and then were locked up again. Some of them did not burn their bundles, but gave them as a free gift to their relatives.

At dawn those who had to die were again adorned with their (respective) papers, and then were taken at once in procession to the place where they were to be sacrificed. Dancing and singing, they went as far as the temple, and (all the way) they uttered very loud shouts (shouted very loudly). This dancing and singing lasted until after midday. Then a priest descended the staircase from the temple, clothed in the ornaments (vestments) of the god Paynal, and passed in front of those who were to be immolated, and after that he mounted the steps of the temple again. The captives ascended after him, because they were to die first.[1] As soon as the captives were sacrificed they were followed by the slaves who were the images of the god Ixcocauhqui. After all of them had been immolated, the principal lords (chiefs) were ready to begin a very solemn dance, which was led by the king. All wore on their heads paper crowns resembling half mitres, that is to say, they had only a point in front and none in the back; a very tiny mitre of blue paper embellished the nose and hung down as far as the mouth; it was almost the shape of a crown. From the mouth to both sides it had ears made of turquoise-mosaic. Others who could not afford these elaborate ears had them made of wood carved in flower-design. They wore a jacket painted in blue with quaint flowers; hanging from the neck as a jewel (trinket) they wore the figure of a dog made of paper with flowers painted on it. They wore belts with black bands at the ends which hung down and carried in their hands (the right hand) sticks resembling cutlasses (cane-knives), one-half of them painted red, the other white, i.e., the upper half red, the lower one white. From the left hand (or wrist?) a small paper bag with copal (incense) was hanging. This dance began at the top of the temple where the stone-block stands, and after having danced there a little while, they came down (the staircase) to the temple-court, and there they made four turns around this court; after completing them, the dance was dissolved

[1]This is the first time he mentions any captives being killed during this festival.

and they (the dancers) entered the royal palace, accompanying the king. This dance was called netecuitotoli, because no one else but the king and the chieftains was allowed to dance it. It took place every four years only.

On this same day the ears of all the children, boys and girls who were born in the three preceding years, were perforated. This operation was performed by means of a bone-bodkin (awl), and after the perforation they cured them (rubbed them) with parrot-feathers, that is to say, with the very soft ones which are like cotton and are called tlachaiotl, and with a little ocotzotl (oil?). When this was done, the fathers and mothers of the boys and girls looked for godfathers and godmothers, whom in their language they call uncles and aunts, tetlacavtz. These were to hold the children during the operation on their ears, and on that occasion they offered flour made of a seed they call chian. The godfathers received a tawny or bright red blanket, the godmothers were given a vipil. After the ears had been perforated, the godparents took them to be surrounded by the flames of a fire which had been built for that purpose and which (ceremony) is called lustrare in Latin and is disapproved of by the Holy Writ. There was much screaming on account of the perforation of their ears on the part of the boys and girls. When all this was over they all went home, and the godparents ate with them, and all danced and sang. At noon the godparents went again to the temple, taking their godchildren with them. At the same time they took along jugs of pulque, and at once began to dance. While dancing they carried their godchildren on the back and gave them pulque to drink in very small cups. This was the reason why they called this festivity the intoxication of boys and girls. The dance lasted until evening, when they went home and there continued the same dance, and the whole household and the neighbors drank pulque.

Still another ceremony took place, namely, they lifted the children, boys and girls, way up in the air by pressing their temples between the palms of both hands. It was said that this made them grow, and for this reason they called this festival izcalli, which means growth.

This is the report of this festival, although there is a more detailed (a fuller one) which follows later.

The Festival Called Oauhquiltamalqualiztli, Which Was Celebrated on the Tenth Day of the Above-Mentioned Month, and Which Was in Honor of the God Ixcocauhqui

Here follows a fuller account of this same month, namely, that it always began on the eighth of January, and with it the year ended. In this month, as mentioned above, in all the towns (villages) tamales were eaten in all the homes, and the people invited one another to share them.

Also, as aforementioned, everyone offered five cauhquiltamales in a dish to the fire in his own home, and they likewise offered a tamal each on the graves of their dead. This they did before they ate themselves, and then ate all the rest without leaving one for the morrow; this was in the way of a ceremony.

When the festival during which they killed slaves in honor of Yococauhqui, god of the fire, approached, all those who had bought several such slaves and had fattened them like pigs, after having shown them publicly a day or two previously, now dressed them up in the papers and ornaments of that said god. This demonstration was carried out in order to be honored and considered wealthy and devout by the others (the rest of the people), as well as to have their wealth increased on the strength of that devotion. The owners who killed such slaves were called tealtiani, that is to say, bathers, because they bathed those destined to be sacrificed, every day in hot water. This and many other luxuries were offered to them so they might grow fat for the day of their sacrifice. For the same reason they gave them very dainty and luxurious food, and every owner of a slave gave this latter a concubine, who was to entertain him, play with him; she should cheer (caress) him, not allowing him to grow sad, because the principal aim was to fatten him (as much as possible). When the time had come for the slave to die, he gave all his clothes to the girl who had been with him and had gladdened the days preceding his immolation.

This festival was called Izcalli on account of the aforementioned ceremony of piercing the children's ears so that they might grow better. Toward the end of the feast they also clipped (trimmed) the maguey plants as well as the tunales (prickly-pear cactus), to increase their growth. They also called this festival Pillaoano, which means drunkenness or intoxication of children. Everybody drank pulque during this festival: men and women, boys, old men and youths, and they all got publicly drunk and invited everyone else who happened along. Pulque flowed abundantly like water, and they all carried their own cups or tumblers, which had three feet and four corners, and were called tzicuiltecomatl. These they used for drinking themselves and for inviting others to drink. They all were very glad, gay and red in the face from the abundance of pulque they imbibed. Once drunk, (of course) they would quarrel among themselves, they cuffed one another and fell on the floor on top of each other, or else they would go home hugging one another (embracing each other); this they considered as being a good omen because the (character of the) festival demanded it. Immediately after this festival came the five days called nemontemi, which were considered unfortunate, so that they did not dare to do a thing in those days, not even sweep their house, much less attend to judiciary matters. Children born within those five days, if males, were called nemon or mentlacatl or nenquizquiquiz, which means "is not worth anything, will never amount to anything, nor will there ever result any advantage (profit) from it." If it was a female child, they called her nencioatl, that is, "good for nothing woman." In those fatal days they were careful not to sleep in the day time, nor to quarrel with one another; neither to stumble or fall, for they said that if any one of the above-mentioned things occurred, it would forever recur; if anyone fell ill, he was not supposed to recover. No one entertained hopes for his recovery or his escape; they did not even make efforts towards curing the sick, nor pay the slightest attention to them. If by chance anyone got well again, they said that god had been merciful to him, for only he knew how to heal or cure him.[1]

[1]Let us remember that even today in Spain, principally in Andalusia, the common people hold certain days of the year as unfortunate when husbands abstain from sleeping with their wives, to prevent their bearing monsters. Filangieri said very justly that the Spaniards needed the Inquisition rather to correct their superstitions than their heresies. Note by Sahagun.

Appendix to Book II.

Account of the Festivals to the God Vitzilopuchtli, Celebrated by the Mexicans

Among the Mexicans or Aztecs three festivals were celebrated every year in honor of Vitzilopuchtli, the first one taking place in the month called Panquetzaliztli. At this festival they carried him (Vitzilopuchtli) and others (other divinities) whom they called Tlacavepancuexcoltzin, to the top of the temple (the highest level); they made their images of Tzoalli of the size of a person (human being), and when finished, all the young men of the Telpuchcali carried them in the palms of their hands to the highest platform of their (respective) temples. The statue or image of Vitzilopuchtli was made in the (city) district called Itepeioc, the one of Tlacavepancuexcoltzin in the one called Vitxnaoao.[1] The dough (of which they made these statues) was cooked first, then it took them a whole night to shape the images. After they were made of the above-mentioned dough, at dawn they at once adorned them and for the greater part of that day they offered (placed offerings) before them. Towards evening they started solemn dances and rhythmic motions with which they conducted them (the images) to the temple, and at sunset they mounted them to the top. Once these statues were put in their places, everybody came down again, with the exception of the guards, who were to keep watch over night. These guards were called yiopuch.

At dawn the god called Paynal, who was the vicar of Vitzilopuchtli, descended from the temple, carrying the latter in his hands, as in a procession; one of the priests was clothed in the ornaments (insignia) of Quetzalcoatl, which insignias were precious; so was the image of Paynal, carved in wood and richly decorated as already stated. At this latter festival a mace-bearer (harold) walked before him (Paynal), and carried on one shoulder a sceptre in the shape of a snake covered entirely with turquoises made into mosaic and quite monstrous. As soon as the priest with the image (who carried the image) arrived at a place called Teutlachco, which is the ball game within the enclosure of the court, right there before him they killed two slaves who were the images of two gods

[1]Today there is no trace nor memory left of this ward, as Mexico has changed its form of ancient times entirely.

whom they called Amapantzitzin, as well as many captives. From there the procession started and went directly to Tlaltelulco. A great crowd of people and priests came out (on the road) to receive them and to incense them, and they beheaded a great many quails before the god. From there they went straight to a place called Popotlan,[1] which is near Tlacuba where now stands the church of San Esteban, and there again the procession was received in the same manner as in Tlalteluco. Along this whole road a flag, made of paper in the shape of a fly-trap and perforated throughout, was carried at the head of the procession. The perforations were filled in with feather-balls, and this procession looked very much like one of the Christian faith, with the cross carried before it. From there (Popotlan) they came back to the temple of Vitzilopuchtli, and with the banner they performed the ceremony mentioned elsewhere in connection with this festival. All the rest of the ceremonies held upon this occasion are mentioned in the report on the month of Panquetzaliztli.

Account of the Festival Celebrated Every Eight Years

Every eighth year these natives celebrated a feast which they called Atamalqualiztli, which means "fast of bread and water." For eight days preceding this festival they ate nothing but tamales prepared without salt, nor did they drink anything else but clear water. In some years this feast fell in the month called Quecholli, at other times in the one called Tepeilhuitl.

The tamales they ate in these days of fasting were called atamalli, for the reason that they did not mix anything else into the dough of which they made them, not even salt; they did not eat the maize (corn) with lime, but merely with water. They all ate at noon, and if anyone failed to fast they punished him for it. They held this fast in great reverence and in great awe at the same time, because it was said that those who did not keep it, even if they broke it eating very secretly without anyone seeing them, god punished them by inflicting them with leprosy. This celebration was called Ixneztioa, which means "to search for good luck (fortune)." It was their belief that on this festival all the gods were dancing, and therefore all the natives who danced were dressed in diverse fancy costumes, some impersonated birds, others different animals; some represented the bird called "tzinitzcan," others butterflies, some dressed like drones, others like flies, still others like beetles; some carried on their backs a sleeping man who, they said, represented sleep; some carried on their backs strings of tamales they call xocotamalli, and some had strings of another kind (of tamales) called catamalli; some brought

[1]Popotlan today is called Popotla, between Mexico and Tacuba, and is a most miserable little hamlet.

food made with tamales and other things, and gave it to the poor. There were also such who impersonated poor people, as, for instance, those who bring wood for sale, or vegetables, or they represented people with diseases, such as lepers, or those afflicted with buboes. Some represented birds.

The image of Tlaloc, in whose honor the dance took place, stood in the center of the dance-floor, and at its feet was a pool of water, with snakes and frogs. Certain men called maxatecaz were (stationed) on the border of the pool, swallowing the snakes and frogs alive; they caught them with the mouth, not with their hands, and as soon as they had taken them in their mouths (one at a time, I suppose?), they went to dance, swallowing them as they danced. The one who succeeded first in swallowing a snake or frog at once called out: "papa, papa." They danced around the temple of this god (Tlaloc), and as they advanced and passed by certain baskets called tonacacuaxcomatl, they were given some of the tamales these contained. The old women who watched the dance were weeping, for they thought by themselves that when the next one of these festivals would be celebrated, they would probably be dead.

It was said that this fasting took place to save their provisions (give their provisions a rest, ms. says), because, as a matter of fact, nothing was eaten with the bread (tamali) during the fast. They also said that at all other times they tired their food-staple or bread by mixing it with salt, lime and salpetre (nitrate or nitre), and thus dressed and divested it in different ways and dress which it (this food-staple, which was corn) resented, and which made it get old, so that by this fasting they thought —it would rejuvenate.

The day after the fast was called Molpololo, which means that: "they ate other things with the bread," since penance for food was now ended.

Account of the Various Buildings of the Great Temple of Mexico (I)

The court of this temple was very large; it might have measured as much as twenty fathoms (1 braza—6 feet) square (120 feet); it was all flagged, and within its area stood many edifices (buildings) and towers. Of these, some were taller than others, and each one of them was dedicated to a god (deity). The main one of all these towers stood in the center and was dedicated to the god Vitzilopuchtli, Tlacavepancuexeotzin. This tower was divided at its top part so that it looked like two;[1] it had two chapels or altars at the top, each one topped by its spire; each of these in turn bore its distinct insignia or device. In one of those chapels,

[1]The temple was called Theucalli, which means "House of God" from Teutl—God and Calli-house; the Spaniards called the temples cues (cu)—See Chimalpain, vol. I. Chap. 104.

the principal one, stood the statue of Vitzilopuchtli, which they also called Ilhuicatlxoxouhqui; in the other one the image of the god Tlaloc. In front of each one of these statues was a round stone like an executioner's block, called texcatl, where they killed all those whom they sacrificed in honor of that god. From the block to the ground there was a puddle (rivulet) of the blood of those immolated on it, and the same was repeated in all the other towers. They all faced the west, and very narrow and straight (steep) steps led up to all these towers.

The second temple, which was also considered as being one of the foremost, was dedicated to the gods of the water called Tlaloques; this temple was called Epcoatl. In this temple they (the priests) fasted and did penance for forty days prior to the festival to honor this god or gods, and after the fast they punished the ministers of the idols who had committed a mistake or error in the service during the year. The punishment consisted of ducking (dipping) them into marshes of mud (mire) and water; after having received their punishment, these penitents washed themselves, and then started to dance, carrying in their hands cornstalks as staffs. Likewise, all the people danced in the streets. This festival was called the festival of "mazamorra" (a sort of mush or porridge), which is called etzalli. At its close they killed captives in honor of these gods.

The third temple was called Mocuilcalli or Macuilquiavitl, and in this temple the spies of their enemies whom they captured when at war either with those of Vexotzineo, or of Tlaxcala, etc., were killed. All these who came to the city of Mexico to spy, as soon as they were found out and recognized, were taken into custody, conducted to that temple, and there they dismembered them, tearing limb from limb.

The fourth building was called Tecuxcalli. In this house were many statues of the gods, and to that building or house the chief of the village or town retired at the time of the great (solemn) feasts to fast and do penance for four days. He incensed all the statues in the place, and there also they killed captives to honor the gods.

The fifth was called Poiauhtla, and there the high priests, two in number, fasted. One was called Totectlamacazqui, the other Tlalocantlenamacac. For four days they did penance in that building, incensing the statues (of the gods) in that house. They did this for four days every year during the festival of Etzalqualiztli, and they also sacrificed captives in that house in honor of the statues.

The sixth edifice was Mixcoapantezonpantli, and here they skewered (impaled) the heads of those they killed in honor of the god Mixcoatl; these poles or beams on which the heads were stuck were rammed in the ground about two estados (one estado—1.85 yds.), and were perforated at intervals (at certain distances), and through these perforations shafts or canes of the thickness of a lance-shaft were stuck about seven or eight to one pole, and onto these shafts they speared the heads of those killed in honor of Mixcoatl. Their faces were turned towards the south.[1]

The seventh building or temple was called Tlalxico. In this temple they killed every year one captive in honor of the god of hell. This sacrifice was performed in the month called Tititl. After the priest called Tlillantleuamacac had sacrificed him (the captive) he built the fire and burned incense before the statue; this was done at night.

The eighth edifice was named Quaxicalco, and was an oratory where the king or chief retired to do penance and to fast when a certain fasting called netonatiuhcaoatl was held. They fasted for four days in honor of the sun, and this fast took place every two hundred, and then every two hundred and three days. Here (in this house) they killed four captives who were called chachanme, and two more whom they named the images of the sun and of the moon respectively, also a great many more after these.

The ninth edifice was called Tochinco; it was a low temple, square, with stairs on all four sides. In this temple they killed every year the image of Umetochtli[2] when this sign was ruling. The image was represented by a captive who was dressed in the ornaments (regalia) of the god of the wine, whose name was the above-mentioned as is stated elsewhere.

The tenth edifice was Teutlalpan, which name means "craggy land;" it consisted of a little grove enclosed by four walls like a corral (yard) in which there were cliffs (crags) made by hand (artificial), with such shrubbery planted in each as grows on craggy land, as, for instance, small agaves and other shrubs called tzioactli. Every year in the month called Quecholli they made a procession about this little grove, and at its conclusion left immediately for the slope of the mountain chain called Cacatepec, where they hunted and did whatever else was required, as told in the report on that month.

The eleventh building was called Tlilapan, which means "black water;" it consisted of a fountain or pond (tank?) and as it was very deep, the water looked black. In this pond or tank the priests bathed at night during their fast-days, which were four every month, previous to the feasts; they were like the eve of a festival. After bathing, they incensed the temple of Mizcoatl, and after this burning of incense they retired to their monastery.

The twelfth building was Tlilancalmecac, which was an oratory built

[1]Bustamante. Andres Tapia and Gonzalo de Umbria, captains in the army of Herman Cortes, out of curiosity, counted once 136,000 heads thus impaled on the poles and on the steps of this building, while those which formed the two towers, they were unable to count.

[2]P. 77. Vol. I. It is called Ometochtli!

in honor of the goddess Civacoatl, who appeared to them visibly, resided there (among them), and also visibly left to go wherever she pleased. It seems certain that this was Demon in the shape of a woman.

The thirteenth house was called Mexicocalmecac, and was a monastery where the priests (Sátrapas) and ministers who served daily in the temple of Tlaloc, lived.

The fourteenth building was Couhealco, or Quaucalli; this was a hall fenced (in) with grating like a prison, and they kept in it all the gods of the towns (villages) they had conquered in war, and preserved them therein like prisoners, or captives.

The fifteenth edifice was called Quauchxicalco, and was a small, round temple about, or almost, three fathoms (18 ft.) wide, and in height one and a half fathoms (9 feet). It had no covering (roof) whatever. In this temple the priest of Titlacaoan incensed daily the four parts of the world, and up here came also that youth who was maintained (fed and feasted) for a whole year to be sacrificed, on the day of the festival of the god Titlacaoan. Up there he would play the flute at night or in the daytime, whichever time he wished to do it. After playing the flute, he, too, would burn incense towards the four parts of the world, and then return home, to his room.

The sixteenth edifice was called Quauchxicalco the second. It was built like the first one (fifteenth), and in front of this one they raised the tree which they called xocotl, adorned with a great many papers. On top of this temple or mumuztli, a buffoon (clown) dressed like the little animal they call tehzalotl, or squirrel, danced.

The seventeenth edifice was called Teccalco, and this was the temple where, every year, they threw a great number of captives alive into a big fire on the occasion of the festival called Teutleco, and where the priests performed the ceremony called Amatlavitzoa, as it is described in the report of the feast of Teutleco.

The eighteenth house (building) was Tzompantli. This consisted of a few wooden poles or beams, three or four of which were pierced by shafts similar to lance-shafts; into these they stuck the heads of the ones they killed (sacrificed); (this appears to refer to women, as in the Spanish transcript the feminine article "las" is used!)

The nineteenth building was called Vitznaoacteucalli. In this temple they sacrificed the images of the gods called Centzonvitznaoa, in homage to (honor of) Vitzilopuchtli. There they also killed many captives, and this was done every year on the festival of Panquetzaliztli.

The twentieth building was Tezcacalco; it was an oratory containing the statues called omacamo. In this place they also killed a few captives, although not every year.

The twenty-first house or edifice was called Tlacochcalco, Acatlyiacapan, and in this building they kept a large amount of darts (arrows) of war, so that it was like an armory or arsenal. Here, too, they were wont to sacrifice captives, and they did it at night; they had no determined (special) day on which to do it, but rather did it whenever they pleased.

The twenty-second edifice was called Teccizcalco; this was an oratory containing the statues (images) of the god called Tmacatl and other deities. For devotional motives they killed a few captives in this oratory, but they had no fixed days for it.

The twenty-third building, called Vitztepecalco, was a corral or enclosure within four walls, where the ministers of the idols threw the points of maguey leaves after having pricked themselves with them, as well as certain green (unripe) canes, after having steeped them in blood and offered them to the gods.

The twenty-fourth building, called Vitznaoac, Calmecac, was a monastery inhabited by the ministers of the idols who served in the temple of the god Vitznaoac, incensing and performing all the other services they were accustomed to perform every day.

The twenty-fifth building bore the same name of Quauchxicalco (sixteenth), and was built like the other one above-mentioned. In front of this temple stood a Tzompantli, that is, the rammed-in poles and shafts on which they impaled the heads of the dead. In the temple above (at the top) stood a statue of the god they called Umactl, made of wood, and there they killed a few (several) captives, whose blood they made that statue taste by smearing it over its mouth.

The twenty-sixth edifice, called Macuileipactli and Teupan, was a large temple, built in honor of the said Macuilcipactli, and here they sacrificed captives at night under his (the god's sign,) called Cipactli.

The twenty-seventh building was called Tetlanmancalmecac. It was a monastery by the name of Tetlanman, inhabited by the priests (Sátrapas) and ministers of the temple dedicated to the goddess Chantico, and they served there day and night.

The twenty-eighth building was Iztaccinteutliteupan, a temple dedicated to the goddess Cinteutl. In this temple they sacrificed their leprous captives, whose flesh they did not eat; they killed them during the fast of the sun, as above-mentioned.

The twenty-ninth building was called Tetlanma, and consisted of a temple dedicated to a goddess whom they called Quoxototlcantico. Here they killed slaves by devotion under the sign of Cexuchitl.

The thirtieth building they called Chicomecatl and Teupan. This was a temple dedicated to the god Chicomecatl. In this temple they sacrificed captives in the night when the sign of Cexuchitl commenced.

The thirty-first edifice was Tezcaapan, a fountain or pond where those who had vowed to do penance, bathed. Many of the people were accustomed to do penance for certain (several) months or a (whole) year, serving in the temples or to the gods of their devotion, and these (people) bathed in that pond.

The thirty-second building was called Tezcatalchco; this was a ball game (park) which was situated between the temples. Here they sacrificed several captives by devotion during the sign of the Omacatl.

The thirty-third edifice was called Tezompantli, where they speared the heads of the dead, for there they (also) killed captives in honor of the gods called Omacama. This sacrifice was performed every two hundred and two days.

The thirty-fourth building, called Tlamatzinco, was a temple dedicated to the god Tlamatzincatl, in whose honor they sacrificed slaves every year at the end of the festival called Quecholli.

The thirty-fifth edifice was called Tlamatzinco Calmecac. This was a monastery where the priests and ministers who served in the above mentioned temple, lived.

The thirty-sixth edifice, Quauaxicalco, was a small, wide temple, somewhat concave and deep, where they burned the papers they offered by virtue of some promise they had made. It was also there where they burned the snake mentioned elsewhere, on the occasion of the feast of Panquetzaliztli.

The thirty-seventh building was called Mizcoateupan, a temple dedicated to Mizcoatl, where the ceremonies described on the occasion of the festival called Quechollitlami, were celebrated.

The thirty-eighth edifice, Netlatiloia, was a temple at the foot of which was a cave, where they hid the skins of the flayed, as told in the report on the festival of Tlacaxipecaliztli.

The thirty-ninth building was called Teutlachco, and was a ball game (court) situated in the temple itself; here they sacrificed certain captives whom they called Amapanme, at the festival of Panquetzaliztli. A description of these Amapanme is given when that festival was mentioned.

The fortieth edifice was called Hilhuicatitlan, and consisted of a thick (massive) and tall (high) column, on which the morning-star was painted; on the capital of this column another capital of straw was erected. In front of this column and this star, captives were sacrificed yearly when the star appeared again in the heavens.

The forty-first building, called Veitzompantli, was the one standing in front of the temple of Vitzilopuchtli, where they impaled the heads of the captives they killed there each year in honor of that building, during the feast of Panquetzaliztli.

The forty-second edifice was Mecatlan. It was the house where the ministers of the idols learned to play the horn.

The forty-third building was called Cinteupan and was a temple dedicated to the goddess Chicomecoatl. Here they sacrificed a woman who, they said, was the image of the said goddess; they flayed her as is related in the account of the feast of Ochpaniztli.

The forty-fourth building was called Centzontotochtininteupan, and was a temple dedicated to the gods of wine. In this temple they sacrificed three captives in honor of these gods of intoxication; one of them they called Tepuztecatl, the other one Totoltecatl, and the third one Papaztac, and they killed them in daytime, not at night, and did so every year on the festival of Tepeilhuitl.

The forty-fifth edifice, called Cinteupan, was a temple where the statue of the god of the corn-fields stood, and there they killed every year his image (the captive who represented the image), together with other captives, as has been told in the description of his festival.

The forty-sixth building was Netotiloian; it was a (limited) place or part of the court where the captives and slaves danced a short while before they were killed, and with them danced also the image of the sign of Chicunavecatl. They all were sacrificed at midnight on the festival of Xilomaniztli, or on that of Atlcaoalo, and it was done every year.

The forty-seventh edifice was called Chililico. This was a temple where they killed slaves under the sign of Chunavecatl. They killed them at midnight, and the slaves sacrificed in this temple were given by the lords (or chieftains) only. It was done during the festival of Atlcaoalo.

The forty-eighth building was called Cocoaapan, and consisted of a pond (or tank) where the priest who officiated in the temple called Coatlan bathed, and no one else but he bathed there.

The forty-ninth building was Puchtlan, a monastery where the priests and ministers lived who officiated in the temple where the statue of Yiacatecutli, "god of the merchants," stood. They served day and night in that temple.

The fiftieth edifice was called Yopioco, and was a temple where every year many slaves and captives were slain. These were sacrificed in the daytime during the festival of Tlacaxipecaliztli.

The fifty-first building was the Atlauhco, a monastery where the priests and ministers lived who officiated in honor of a goddess in the temple of Vitzilinquatec, day and night.

The fifty-second building was called Xiacatecutli, and Teupan. It was a temple of the god of the merchants (traders), and in this temple they killed each year the image (he who represented it, rather) of that god at the festival of Tititl.

The fifty-third building was called Vitzilinquatec and Teupan. It was a temple, and every year they killed there the image of that goddess on the feast of Tititl. It was a woman whom they sacrificed.

The fifty-fourth building was Yopico Calmecac. In this monastery or oratory they killed many captives every year during the festival of Tlacaxipeoaliztli.

The fifty-fifth building was called Yopico Tezompantli; in this building (or structure) they impaled (onto poles) the heads of those they killed at the festival of Tlacaxipeoalizitli.

The fifty-sixth building, called Tzompantli, was (also) used for the skewering of the heads of those they sacrificed during the festival of Yiacatecutli, god of merchants, on the first day of Xocotlvetzi.

The fifty-seventh building was called Macuilmalinaliteupan. This was a temple containing two statues, one of Macuilmalinatl, and the other of Topantlacaqui, and under the same sign they celebrated a festival in said temple every two hundred and three days. They also celebrated a festival there in honor of the sign called Xuchitlhuitl.

The fifty-eighth edifice, Atiepac, was an oratory where they made a festival and offerings to the goddesses whom they called Civapipilti; they celebrated this festival under the sign of Chicumecoatonalli.

The fifty-ninth structure they called Notlatiloian. This was a cave where they hid the skins of those (the dead) whom they flayed every year during the festival of Ochpaniztli.

The sixtieth edifice was called Atlaulico. This was an oratory where they venerated the goddess who was called Civateutl, in whose honor they killed every year a woman who, they said, was her (the goddess's) image. They sacrificed her in the temple called Coatlan, which was near the oratory. This was done yearly on the festival of Ochpaniztli.

The sixty-first building was the Tzonmolcocalmecac, a monastery inhabited by the priests of the god Xiuchtecutli; here they built (and distributed) the new fire every year, during the festival of Oauhquiltamas.

The sixty-second monument was called Temalacatl, and consisted of a stone like a large upper mill-stone, which had a hole in the centre. On (top of) this stone they put (placed) the slaves and fought with them with knives; they (the slaves) were tied to the stone by means of a rope fastened around the waist in such a manner that they could walk around the whole circumference of the stone; they were given weapons with which to fight. This was a very frequent spectacle, attended by people from all the districts. A priest, dressed in the pelt of a bear or cuetlachtli, was the sponsor of the captives to be killed there, and he conducted them to the stone and tied them to it, handed them their weapons, and bewailed them while they fought. If one of these fell, he would turn him over to the man who had to tear out his heart, and who was another priest dressed in another skin called tooallaoan. The description of this spectacle is given at length on occasion of the festival of Tlacaxipeoaliztli.[1]

The sixty-third building they called Nappatecutliyteupan. It was a temple dedicated to the god Nappatecutli, where they sacrificed the image of that god, namely, a captive dressed in his vestments. They killed him at midnight during the festival of Tepeilhuitl every year.

The sixty-fourth edifice was called Tezonmolco; it was a temple dedicated to the god of fire, Xiutecutli, and in this temple they sacrificed four slaves as images of the god, dressed in his finery (ornaments), although in different colors. The first one was called Xoxouhquixiuhtecutli, the second Cocauhquixiuhtecutli, the third Iztacxiuhtecutli, (the fourth seems to have been omitted). In that same place and on the same day they sacrificed many more captives who were called Ihuipanecatemimilolca. At the foot of the steps of this temple there was a small platform which was also reached by a stairway. On this platform they sacrificed two women, one of whom they called Nancotlaceuhqui, while the other one had no given name. After all those who were destined to die had been sacrificed, they at once began a very solemn dance, as is told at great length in the description of the festival of Xiuchtecutli (Xiutecutli).

The sixty-fifth edifice (house), called Coatlan, was a temple where captives were killed in honor of certain gods whom they called Centzonvitznaoa, a thing they also repeated every time when they built the fires anew (when they made up new fires?), and also on the festival of Quecholli.

The sixty-sixth building was called Xuchicalco, and was a temple erected in honor of the gods called Tlatlauhquicinteutl, and of the goddess Atlatonan. After they had sacrificed, in this temple, a woman who represented the image of the goddess (Atlatonan), they flayed her, and one of the priests dressed himself in her skin. This having been done at night, on the following morning he danced with the skin of that woman drawn over his body. This was repeated every year on the festival of Ochpaniztli.

The sixty-seventh building was Xopicalco, also Eoacalco, and was a house or inn (lodging-house), where the lords and chiefs lodged who

[1]Bustamante thinks that the stone in the lower corridor of the U. of Mexico is one of these "millstones."

came from afar (a great distance) to visit the temple, especially those from the province of Tenaoac.

The sixty-eighth monument was called Tozpalatl, and was a greatly valued spring which issued on that spot and from which the priests of the idols obtained the drinking water, and on the occasion of the festival of Vitzilopuchtli and other feasts the common people drank at this spring with great devotion.

The sixty-ninth structure, called Tlacochcalco, Quahquiaxaoac, was a house in which stood a statue of the god Macuiltotec, and here they sacrificed captives to honor this god on the occasion of the festival of Panquetzaliztli.

The seventieth edifice, Tulnaoac, was a house where captives were killed in honor of Tezeatlipuca as soon as the Mexican calendar entered the period of the sign called Cemiquiztli.

The seventy-first building was Xilocan, the house where the dough was cooked of which they made the image of Vitzilopuchtli when they were about to celebrate his festival.

The seventy-second structure was Itepeioc, the house where the priests made the image of Vitzilopuchtli, of the (above-mentioned) dough.

The seventy-third structure was called Vitznaoaccalpulli, and was the house where they made the image of another god, companion of Vitzilopuchtli, who was called Tlacavepancuexcotzin.

The seventy-fourth building was called Atempan, and this was a house where they gathered the children who were to die (sacrificed), as well as the lepers called zizioti, and whom they also killed (on that occasion). After having gathered them in the above house they took them out in litters, forming procession, and then took them to the various places where they were to be sacrificed.

The seventy-fifth building was called Tezcacoactlacochcalco, and was a house where they kept many (a great number of) darts and arrows for times of war, and in certain years they killed slaves here by devotion.

The seventy-sixth building was Acatlayiacapan Veicalpulli, a house where they assembled the slaves they were going to sacrifice in honor of the Tlaloques, and whom they cut up as soon as they were dead and cooked the flesh in that same house. Into the cooking vessels they threw (together with the human flesh) flowers of calabash (gourd), and when all was well done the lords and chieftains ate it; the common people did not partake of it.

The seventy-seventh edifice was called Techielli. It consisted of a small temple, and in it they made offerings of a kind of cane which they called Acxolate.

The seventy-eighth monument was the Calpulli, or cluster of small houses which surrounded the entire court on the inside. All these little houses were called Calpulli, and here came all the chiefs and officers of the republic to do four days' penance on the eve of festivals which occurred every twenty days, and here also they fasted for four days. During this fast some ate at midnight only, others at noon.

An Account of the Objects Presented as Offerings in the Mexican Temple

They offered many (a great variety of) objects in the houses they called Calpulli, which were like churches (or chapels, oratories) of the city wards where all those of the same district (ward) gathered, be it to present their offerings or to perform the many different ceremonies held there. They offered food, blankets, fowl (wild birds), ears of corn, "chian," beans and flowers; all this was offered by the women or by marriageable maidens in the Calpulli, while in the oratories of their own homes they merely offered food to the images of the gods they had there. This they did every day, in the early morning, and the mother of the house was careful (took great care) to awaken all the members of her household each morning, and make them go to place their offerings before the gods of their oratory.

In the temples the priests offered incense day and night, at certain determined hours. They incensed with incensories (thuribles) made of baked clay in the shape of a bowl of medium size, with its handle of the thickness of a yard-stick, more or less, and about one cubit long. This handle was hollow and held a few little pebbles for rattles. The cup or bowl itself was fashioned like an incensory in an open-work design which perforated the cup from the centre to the bottom. In this thurible they gathered live coal from the hearth and threw copal (incense) onto them, then went before the statue of the "demon" and raised their incensories towards the four (cardinal) parts of the world, and also incensed the statue. After this they returned the live coal to the fire in the hearth. The same ceremony was performed by the common people in their homes, once every morning and once in the evening, to honor the images they had in their oratories or in the yards of the house (wherever the images were kept), and parents compelled their children to do the same, morning and night.

The Mexicans and all the inhabitants of New Spain used incense or copal for their offerings and this copal is a white resin called copalli (which is even now used a great deal), to incense before the altars of their gods. They used copal only, not incense, although it also exists in

Mexico. This incense or copal was used by the priests in the temple and by all the other people in their homes as stated above, as well as by the judges when they had to perform any judiciary duty. Before they began to officiate they threw copal onto the fire to honor their gods and to ask for their guidance. The same was done by the singers for the (ceremonial) dances. They, too, before starting their singing, threw copal on live coals as an act of reverence to their gods while praying for help.

One ceremony was customary in general throughout the land, and among men, women and children, namely, whenever they entered any place where there were images of idols, either many or only one, they at once touched the earth with one finger (tip) and then raised this finger to their lips or the (point of the) tongue and called this "to eat earth in homage of their gods." Anyone, after having left the house, upon his return, even though he had not gone beyond the city or town limits, performed this same ceremony; and if on the road he passed by a temple or oratory, he did the same. It was also done in place of an oath and in order to affirm that they spoke the truth, and if anyone wished to be certain that another spoke the truth, he demanded that he should perform this ceremony, after which he was believed as firmly as if he had said it under solemn oath.

Another general ceremony was what they called Tlatlacalizte, which means "the spilling," that is to say, that nobody should eat without first throwing a small portion of what he was going to eat into the fire. Still another very general (customary) habit was the one of not drinking any pulque unless a small quantity had been spilled at the entrance (doorstep?) of the house, and whenever they first opened a new jug of pulque they would pour a quantity in a glazed earthenware tub and place this near the fire; from there they would take it out with a tumbler; then pour a cup at the entrance of the house in the four directions, and only after this was done could the guests drink; before that, no one dared to do so. This ceremony they called Tlatoiaoaliztli, which means libation or gustation (tasting).

Account of the Blood Which Was Spilled in Honor of the "Devil," Within and Outside of the Temple.

Blood was spilled in the temples by day and by night, killing (sacrificing) men and women in front of the statues of the "demons" (gods) as has been stated in many places. They also did it for devotional purposes on specially assigned (determined) days, in the following manner. If they wished to bleed (from) the tongue, they pierced the latter by means of the point of a knife, and through this orifice (hole) they passed a great number of thick straws, according to the devotion of each individual; some tied these straws end to end and then pulled them through the hole of the tongue like pulling a string; still others passed them through one by one in great quantity and then left them all bloody in front of "demon" (the god), or on the roads (highways), or in the calpulcos. The same they did when bleeding arms or limbs. The priests also bled themselves away from the temples, in the mountains or in caves. Moved by devotion, they did this at night in the following manner: they took green (unripe) canes and maguey-thorns (points) and, after having tinted them with blood which they drew from their legs, they gathered all those thorns (or pricks) and then went at night, naked, into the forest, wherever their devotion led them, and left them, seeped in blood, on a little bed (litter) made of corn-leaves which they fashioned especially for that purpose. There were four or five different places where they deposited them, according to the devotion of each individual.

As devotion prompted them, men would also bleed themselves five days before the main festival (of the month), which recurred every twenty days. They would cut their ears to draw blood, with which they bedaubed their faces, drawing lines of blood; the women made circles (or rings), while the men drew a straight line from the brow to the chin. As a testimonial of their devotion, the women also were wont to bleed themselves in the same manner as the men over a period of eighty days, cutting themselves (making incisions) in their ears every three or four days during that time. For the same purpose they offered the blood of birds (fowl) to their "demons" (gods), especially to Vitzilopuchtli, and for his feasts they would buy live quails, whose heads they tore off in front of the idol, the blood being spilled right there. The beheaded bodies of the birds were thrown on the soil (or floor), where they fluttered about until life was extinct. Some would thus sacrifice or behead one bird, others two, still others three, according to the intensity of their devotion.

When they sacrificed a slave or a captive, his owner or master gathered the blood (of the victim) in a bowl (jicara), threw a white paper into it, then visited all the statues of the "demons" (gods), and smeared this blood-soaked paper over their mouths; others dipped a stick in the blood and painted the mouth of the idol (statue) with that.

Account of Other Services Held Within the Temple and Outside in Honor of the "Demons" (gods).

Those who, through the advice of their astrologers, were able to ward off a disease, chose a very lucky day, and on that day burned, in the hearth of their homes, a great many papers on which the astrologer had painted with ulli (gum) the images of all those gods who, they guessed (conjectured), had helped them to ward off that illness. The astrologer (after thus painting them) handed them to the man who made the offering, telling him (the name of) the god painted thereon; the man then burned all the papers; they gathered the ashes and buried them in the courtyard of the home; this they called Neztlaoaliztli.

Impelled by their (personal) devotion, some of them offered their blood in the temples on the eve of a festival, and in order that their votive offering might be more acceptable, they went first to gather wild laurel (mountain-laurel), which they call axoiatl, which is plentiful in those woods. They then drew blood from their limbs by means of two maguey-points (thorns), in the calpulco, and when these points or thorns were well steeped in blood, they made a small bed of tender twigs of the laurel, placed the maguey thorns on it, and offered this to the god of their devotion. This ceremony they called Acxoiatemaliztli.

When they were ready to go to war, all the soldiers went first to the mountains for firewood, which they used in the temples. In the monasteries where the priests lived, they made piles of this firewood, and from there they took it to be used because a great deal of it was burned between night and day (during the night) in the courts of the temples in tall hearths which had been built for that purpose in these courts. At other epochs (i.e., times of peace), the ministers or priests of the temples and those who lived in the Calmecac, had charge of the gathering (and bringing in) of the firewood. This service was called Teuquauhquetzaliztli.

To honor the gods they had in their homes, they took great care in sweeping these houses, the court and the entrance daily, or rather early every morning, and the master or the mistress of the house had the duty to compel every one who lived there to do this daily. After the sweeping they incensed the images they had in the house and placed offerings before them. This (service) they called Tlachpanaliztli.

At night the priests and ministers of the temples held careful watch to keep the fire burning in the hearths of the court, and also to wake up all those who had to play the instruments during the hours they (the priests) were incensing the idols and placing offerings before them. This (sort of service or vigil) was called Tocoaliztli.

The common people had the custom to (were accustomed to) do penance for many days in the course of the year, and this penance consisted in not using soap on their heads, not to bathe, or to sleep with a woman, or the woman with a man in the days of said penance, but they did neither abstain from eating, nor did they fast. This (sort of penance) was called Necaoaliztli.

Account of Certain Ceremonies They Performed in Honor of the "Demon."

When they celebrated a festival they called Atamalcualiztli, which occurred every eighth year, certain Indians called mazatecac, as a proof of valor, would swallow live snakes; while dancing about they were swallowing them little by little, and after they had swallowed them entirely they were given blankets as a reward for their courage. These same men also ate live frogs in the course of the same festival. Another ceremony which took place at the same festival of Etzalcualiztli consisted of the catching of little birds by youths, who then tied them with strings to boughs which they carried when walking in the procession of this festival, the birds fluttering around the boughs.

They were wont to form processions in the course of many of their festivals, carrying the images of their idols in litters, sometimes only making the rounds of the temples, but often they went to places farther away, and the entire population participated in these processions. There was also a custom, on the occasion of great (solemn) festivals that the women danced together with the men.

In honor of the goddess Toci the young men (youths) played a game after the image of the goddess (the women who represented it) had been sacrificed, that is to say, they put a glazed earthenware tub, containing feathers and clay (marl) in a certain (determined) place, and all the youths assailed it, each one taking a handful of its contents, then speedily running away after one another. As soon as they all had taken off the feathers and clay, the youth dressed in the skin (of the slain women representing the goddess) of the goddess Toci, followed by his own party of young men, pursued the others who had taken feathers and clay, throwing stones at them and the onlooking populace threw stones at both parties, and there were always some that were hit and fell.

During the festival called Izcalli, which was celebrated in honor of the fire they were in the habit of performing a certain ceremony on their children, boys and girls, namely, they placed a hand over each ear of the child and so lifted it up high. They did this to make children grow.

Account of Other Ceremonies Also Held in Honor of "Satan."

They performed a superstitious rite to cure sick or sickly children, which consisted of tying around their necks strings of loose (soft or loosely spun) cotton hanging on it a small ball of copal; or else they tied similar strings around their wrists or ankles. These strings were tied (around neck, wrists, or ankles) by an astrologer under a determined sign, and they had to wear them the exact number of days this astrologer ordained, when he himself would take them off and burn them in the

Calpulco. This they repeated four times, to benefit (or insure) the health of the child.

Another superstition of theirs was to feather (paste feathers on) their breasts and their backs, opposite the chest, with feathers of different colors; around the wrists and ankles they wore (moorish) bracelets and anklets, also made of feathers, one white, one yellow, and one red. The feathers were pasted on by means of a pine-resin called ocozotl. This they wore on the festival of Teuhtleco to prevent the god Acolmiztli from harming them. This ceremony or superstition, as it is called here, was performed every four years, on the festival of Izcalli.

The following ceremony was performed in homage of the sun and the fire, when someone finished a new house or when the sun was in its own sign; they drew blood from their ears and received it (let it drip) on the nail of the finger next to the thumb, or the middle finger, and from there flicked it into the fire, like one flicking a fillip; in the same way they flung it towards the sun; this was called Tlazcaltiliztli, as has been stated before, as it is the same as Acxiatemaliztli.

Upon passing in front of an idol, they would pull a wisp (or handful) of grass and scatter it before the image of the idol with reverential bows and homage. This same ceremony was performed at times in fulfillment of a special vow or ceremonial.

Every night a little before midnight the ministers of the idols who were in charge of this ceremony blew their shells and horns and trumpets, and at once everybody arose and offered blood and incense to the idols in the temples and in private houses.

When midnight, which they called quaquaaciltin, approached, they beat (kettle-) drums to waken everybody, and whoever did not wake up at that hour was at once punished by throwing water at him, or cinders from the fire.

They pierced their ears to wear ear-rings and also the lips for the lip ornaments, and this was done in honor of "satan;" they called it Nenacazxapotlalitliz and Netenxapotlaliztli.

Differences (in grade) of the Ministers Who Officiated and Served to the Different Gods.[1]

There was one minister or priest who was called Mexicatlteuoatzin, and he was like a patriarch, being elected by the two pontifs; he had charge of other, somewhat minor priests, who were like (our) bishops, and their duty was to watch and see that everything connected with the divine cult in all the towns and provinces should be accomplished with

[1]That is, an account of the hierarchical order and the obligations of the priests of the idolatrous cult.

due care and perfection in accordance with the laws, customs (precepts) of the ancient pontifs (high-priests) and priests, especially concerning the education of the youths who were brought up in the monasteries, called Calmecac. He (this patriarch) ordered all the houses to be built in the provinces subject to Mexico, where the çult of their gods was to be held, and it was also given into his power to punish all such priests under his orders who sinned in any way. The distinctives of this priest were a cloth jacket, an incensory (thurible) such as they used, and a bag in which they carried copal for incensing. He had a coadjutor called Vitznaoc-teuhoalzin, who had the same duties.

There was still another coadjutor like the preceding one, called Tepan-teuhoatzin, whose special duty it was to watch over the good behavior of and the fair ruling over those who were educated in the monasteries (Calmecac) in all the provinces subject to Mexico.

The Umetochtzin was the teacher of all the singers, whose duty it was to come to sing in the temples; he had to see to it that they all appeared to do their duty there. They performed a certain ceremony with the wine they called Teuvetli at the time they were attending to their duties, and the leader of this ceremony was Pachsecatl. This latter was in charge of the cups from which the singers drank; he had to bring them out, distribute them, and take them off again; his duty it was to fill them with the wine, also called Macuiluctli. He placed (before them) two hundred and three canes, of which only one was hollow, and as they (the singers) took them up, only he who secured that one (the hollow one) drank (of the wine); this was done after they had sung (or after they had complied with their duty of singing).

The Epcoaquacuiltzin was in charge of the festivals of the calendar and of all the ceremonies which were to be held, and that nothing should go wrong; he was like a master of ceremonies.

The Moloncoteuhoa had the duty to get ready all the necessary things, such as paper, copal, etc., for the moment of the sacrifice or the offerings before the gods on the festival of Chicunavecatl.

The Cinteutzin had the same duties, preparing everything necessary for the festival of Xilonen.

The Atempanteuhoatzin held the charge of providing the white, fluffy, cotton-like feathers which birds have close to their skin (down) as well as other things needed at the time they celebrated the feast of the mother of gods. It was also his duty to assemble the youths called Cuecuexteca, who were to fast in the suburb of Atempan.

The Tlapizcatzin was a sort of preceptor, whose duty it was to teach, direct, and improve (correct) the songs which were to be sung in honor of the gods at all the festivals.

The Tzaputlateuhoatzin had charge of preparing all the things necessary for the feast of the goddess Tezapotlatona, such as paper, copal, ulli (gum), and an odoriferous herb with which they incensed the idols.

The Tecammateuhoa had, as his duty, to prepare the candlewood to make large torches, as well as red ochre, ink, sandals, jackets and small marine shells (sea-shells), all of which were needed for this festival of the goddess of the fire.

The Tezcatzoncatl had charge of preparing all the above-mentioned material for the time when they celebrated the festival of the god of wine, which was due in the month called Tepeilhuitl.

The Umetochtli had to prepare all the above-mentioned for the time of the feast of the god of wine, called by the same name of Umetochtli, in the month of Tepeilhuitl.

The Umetochtlitomixauh's main duty consisted of getting all the above-mentioned things ready for the time of the festival of the god of the wine, Tomixauh, in the above-mentioned month.

The Acaloaomezochtli had charge of preparing all the above-mentioned articles which were needed for the festival of the god Acaloavmetochtli.

The Quatlapanquivmetochtli's obligation was to prepare all the above-mentioned effects for the festival of the god of the wine called Cautlapanqui.

The Tlilhoavmetochtli had to prepare all the above-mentioned effects for the time of the feast of the god of the wine Tlilhoavmetochtli, in the month of Tepeilhuitl.[1]

The Umetochtlipantecatl had the obligation of obtaining the wine which they called cuilxtei or tevctli, which was used on the festival of Panquetzaliztli.

The Umetochtlinapatecutli had to prepare all the necessaries for the feast of Tepeilhuitl.

The Umetochtlipapaztac had to procure (prepare or get ready) the wine, which was called ticavctli, which was to be used in the house of the king and at the festival of Tozoztli, and where men, women and children (boys as well as girls) drank wine.

The Umetochtli's duty was to do the same as the above-mentioned at the festival of Atlcaoalo.

The woman called Cioaqualli had to provide everything necessary to be offered on the festival of the goddess Toci, such as flowers and smoke-canes and everything else that women presented at this festival.

The woman called Cioaquacuilliztaccihaztl had charge of all those

[1]There were several gods of the wine, therefore do not wonder at their different names. We have stated elsewhere that the drunkards had a number of tutelar spirits.

who had to sweep the temple called Atenchicalcan, also of the ones who were to light the fire there and those who had made a solemn vow to perform any kind of service at the temple, applied to her.

The Ixcocahuquitzonmolcoteuhoa had charge of the bringing in of the firewood which was used in the monastery called Tzommolcocalmecac. This wood was brought by young men, and they delivered it at said monastery.

The Tlalcolquaquilli guarded the temple called Mecatlan. He was dressed in the vestments of the priests, as has been stated elsewhere, and which consisted of an unxicolli or jacket, and of a gourd filled with tobacco, picietl. He took great care that no one should approach this temple unless he came with great reverence, and that no filth whatever existed in it, and if anyone dirtied (soiled) himself near this temple, he was at once caught and punished.

The Tecpantzincotenhoa guarded the temple called Tecpantzinco, so that no irreverence should be committed there; he also obtained (or procured) the offerings that were to be made in this temple.

Epceacuacuillitecpictoton had charge of making up and composing the songs that were needed anew in the temples as in private houses.

The Ixtlilcoteuhoa was in charge of the temple of Ixtlilton, and had to obtain the offerings which were promised when the children, boys and girls, first began to talk, on which occasion they were brought to the temple, where certain ceremonies were performed for this reason.

The Aticpacteuhoatzinxochipilli was in charge of the temple called Atiepac, and he obtained all that was necessary on the occasion of sacrificing a woman there, whom they flayed in honor of a goddess called Aticpaccalquihioatl. He also dressed himself in the skin of that woman and when, thus attired, he went through the streets, he held a live quail gripped between his teeth.

The Atlixeliuhquiteuhoaopuchtli had to provide everything needed for the time when they sacrificed the image of Opuchtli at the festival of Tepeilhuitl.

The Xipecopicoteuhoa had to provide everything necessary for the killing (sacrifice) of the image of Tequitzin in the temple Yopico.

The Pochtlanteuhoayiacatecutli had to provide all the necessary things for the sacrifice of the image of Yacatecutli in the temple called Pochtlan.

The Chiconquiavitlpoctlan was coadjutor of the above-mentioned, and had the same duties as expressed above.

The Izquitlanteuhoatzin had to provide the jackets called xicolli which belonged to the vestments of the priests, as well as little seashells, sandals and other ornaments. He also gathered the honey from the maguey, which was the first extracted from these plants, to make the wine for the priests.

The Tzapotlateuhoatzin had to provide the paper, copal, incensories and everything else needed for those who died or whom they killed during the festival of Tepeilhuitl.

The Chalchiuhtliycucacatonalquacuilli had to provide the offerings that were needed for those whom they killed on (or during) the festival of Chalchiuhtliycue, such as copal, ulli (gum), etc.

The Acovlaoacatlacolmiztli had to provide everything that was needed for the time when the chieftain or king was to fast on the festival of Tlaloc, during the fast of the sun and of Quecholli, all of which are very solemn fasts. He provided the vestments, sandals, etc., which the chief was to wear during these fasts.

The Tullanteuhoa was to provide paper, copal and ulli when they sacrificed the image of Tultecatl, whom they killed at the end of the month of Quecholli, or at the beginning of the month called Tepeihuitl.

Account on the Art of Playing Musical Instruments and How Often They Were Played in the Temple between Night and Day, Which Was Like Sounding the Hours.

Every day of the world (time) they offered blood and incense to the sun; at sunrise they at once offered blood from their ears, and the blood of quails whose heads they tore off and, snatching them up while their blood still flowed, they raised them towards the sun like offertories, saying as they did so, "The sun, called tonametl xiuhpitontliquauhtleoamitl, has risen, we do not know how it will end its course this day, nor do we know whether some misfortune will befall the people;" then, addressing the sun directly, they exclaimed, "Our lord fulfill your duty (ministry) prosperously (luckily)." This was done daily at sunrise; then they offered incense three times during the day and five during the night, as follows: first, at sunrise; then at the third hour (in the forenoon); at high noon, and a third time at sunset; at night they offered incense first when night had come, the second time when everyone was ready to retire, the third time as they began to strum their instruments to rise for matins, the fourth time a little after midnight, and the fifth a little before dawn. When they made the first offering of the night they greeted the night saying, "The lord of night has come, who is called Ioatltecutli; we do not know how he will perform his ministry or finish his course."

The festival of this Ioatltecutli came and was celebrated under the sign called naviollin, on the two-hundred and third day of the counting of the tonalamatl (sun). They fasted for four days previous to this festival and (each day) at noon played (sounded) their shells, whistles and horns (or trumpets), etc., and, passing reeds or straws through their tongues, they offered him (Ioatltecutli) that blood. They even bled small babies in their cradles, piercing their ears, to offer that blood, and everybody, old or young, offered blood from the ears at that hour (noon). They performed this (act) without saying anything (without utterance of any kind), and it was done in front of the image of the sun which stood in a temple called Quauhxicalco, it (the image) being painted and sculptured in the same manner the sun is depicted today, namely, as a human face with rays emanating from it like a wheel. At the yearly festival of the sun they sacrificed many slaves in its honor, and in all of its temples, and they said that all those who died in war went to the house of the sun to rest.

Account of the Exercises or Work Performed in the Temple

One of the priests of the temple was in charge of teaching and instructing all those who worked and officiated there whom, after they had been taught, he turned over to the ministers (priests) so that they might exercise the offices they had learned. The same teacher also trained them to live decently and not to be mischievous. It was this man's duty, furthermore, to make this great number of pupils he taught sweep every place in the temple and, furthermore, he had to watch over the fire in the hearths of the temple, not to let it go out.

Certain youths who by vow or devotion did penance in the temple, had to watch through the night to prevent misdeeds in it; younger boys who were educated in the Calmecac had the obligation to go to the woods (forests) and bring the firewood needed in the temple, and the novices of the monastery went to get the points (thorns) of maguey that were used in the temple as well as the laurel branches. The youths or young men (in the temple's service) were called Tlamacozque; they lived in the temple, and it was their duty to play (strum and blow) the shells, whistles and trumpets (horns), like the bellman (bell-ringer) of today. The small boys who served in the Calmecac and who were like sacristans (in the Christian church), had to prepare the ink with which the priests daily, at dawn, painted their bodies black. They did this at night, in a canoe which was kept for that purpose, and in the morning all the priests painted themselves with that ink.

Account of Vows and Oaths

If anyone of their children or another member of the household became ill or lost their footing (fell) and hurt themselves, they were in the habit of offering vows to the idols consisting either of sacrifices or offerings, and they did this not only to one but to two or three of their idols simultaneously, in order to obtain their help in their trouble.

It was also their custom to make a (solemn) oath to fulfill a certain promise, and anyone who made such a promise was exacted a solemn oath, to be certain of his word. This oath was administered as follows: "For the life of the sun, for the life of our lady (matron) the earth, I shall not forget what I promised, and for greater guaranty I herewith eat this earth,"—and he forthwith touched the soil with his fingers and then raised them to his lips and licked them, thus eating earth (soil or dirt), and making a solemn promise. If, in some need or other, anyone asked his god for help, he made a vow or an oath to do a certain thing in that god's service, and he always kept his oath or promise.

Account of the Songs Which Were Chanted in Honor of the Gods within the Temples and Outside.

It is a very ancient custom of our adversary, satan, to look for hiding places in which to perform his evil doings as, according to the Holy Writ: "He who does evil shuns light." In accordance with this saying our enemy in this country (Mexico) planted a forest or craggy place full of very dense brambles (underbrush) to enact his evil doings from there, and hide within that place, never to be found, as do wild beasts and very poisonous snakes. This forest or craggy spot represents the songs which in this land he enticed the people to compose for him and to use in his service as his divine cult, and psalms in his honor within the temples as well as on the outside (which are so full of cunning—guile), that they may say whatever they wish, they declare what he ordains, and they can only be understood by those who dedicated, or invented (composed) them. It is a well established fact that these songs and psalms he (satan) had them compose for him are all (hidden) in those caves, forests and crags where this accursed enemy hides, and that they sing them to him, but their meaning cannot possibly be understood except perhaps by natives who, born right there, are accustomed to that kind of language. So that while no doubt they sing about everything he wants them to sing, be it war or peace, be it his praise or abuse against Christ, no one aside from them can understand it or knows what it is all about.[1]

Account of the Women Who Served in the Temple.

There were also women who served in the temples since they were very young, for the reason that the mother, perhaps, offered them while

[1]Note by Bustamente, which might prove interesting. p. 227, Vol. I. Bustamante is of the opinion that the Indians who furnished information on their ancient history to Fray Bernardino did not give him the texts of their songs, although they were well known by all Mexican Indians, high or low.

very small, to the service of the temple as an act of (special) devotion. As soon as they (the babies) were between twenty to forty days old, they were presented to the one who was in charge, called Tequacuilli, and who was something like a curate. They (the mothers) brought brooms for sweeping, a clay incensory, and incense called white copalli. All this they gave to the Tequacuilli or curate. Then this latter returned the baby to the mother and recommended very earnestly that she take great care in the bringing up of her daughter and he also reminded her to go every twenty days to the Calpulco or parish of her district and make an offering of brooms, copal and firewood for the hearths of the temple.

As soon as that child attained the age of understanding (discretion), being informed by her mother about her votive offering, she went of her own free will to the temple where the other maidens were and took her offering with her, which consisted of an incensory and copal. From that time on until she was of marriageable age she lived in the temple under the tutelage of the matrons who educated the maidens.

When she was of the age to have a suitor and such a one asked her in marriage, the parents and chiefs of the district having approved of the marriage, they prepared the offering, which was to be made and which consisted of quails, incense, flowers, smoke sticks, and a clay incensory, as well as prepared food. They then took the girl and led her in front of the priests of that same (her) temple; there they spread a large blanket of white cotton, placed on it all the offerings they had brought, as well as another blanket, which was called tzazaquachtli, into which many human heads (faces or images of people) were woven and, after the reasons were given on one part and the other, the parents of the girl took their daughter home with them.

BOOK III.

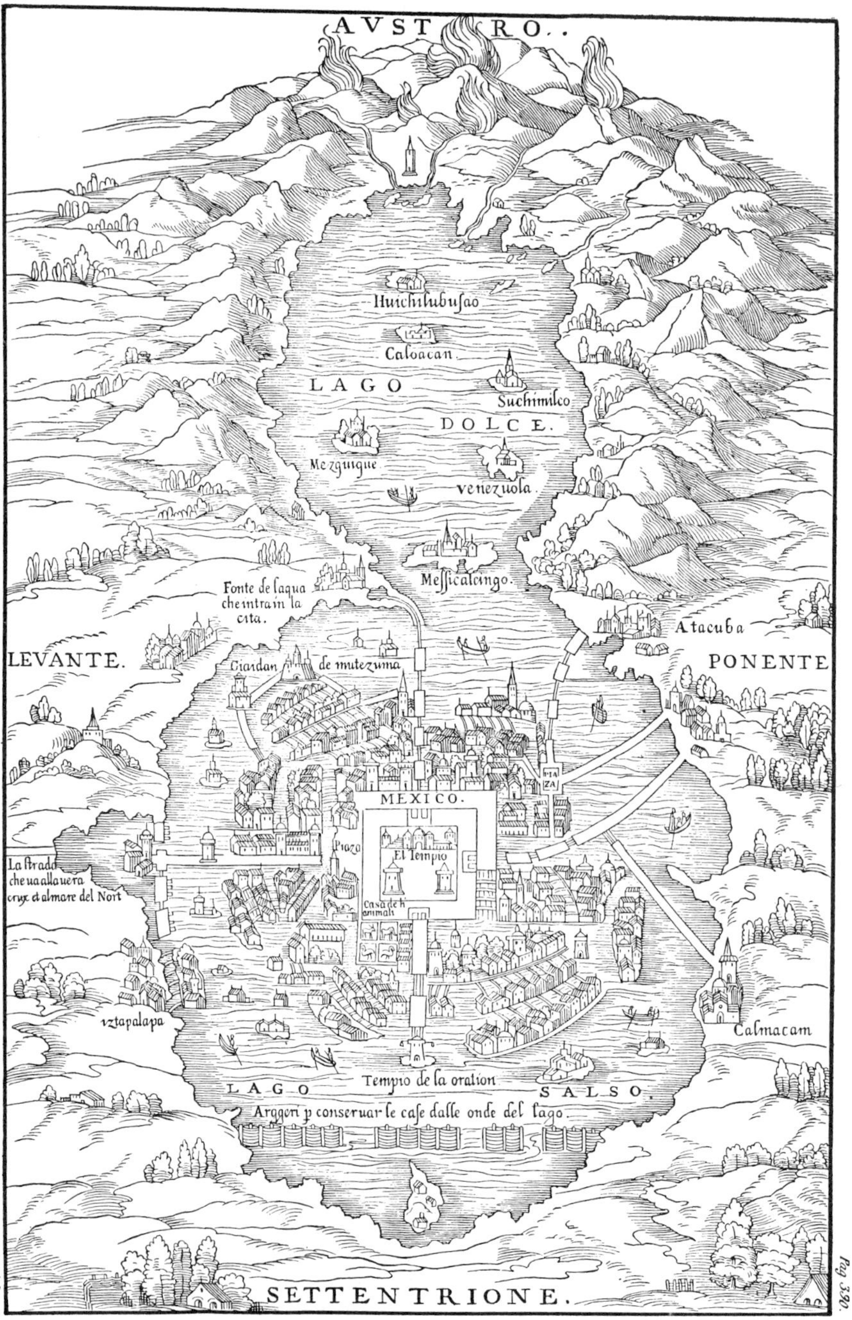

Pag 390.

Map of Mexico and Lagune from "Conquistador Anónimo"

Chapter I.

Of the Beginning of the Gods (Origin).

There exists no clear nor genuine (truthful) account about the origin of the gods, in truth, nothing is known about them. What they say (about it) is, that there is a place called Teutióacan, and there, since time immemorial, all the gods gathered and conversed, saying, "Who is going to govern and rule the world? Who is going to be the sun?" (This was told elsewhere.) And that when the sun was born and came forth, all the gods died and not one of them remained, as will be seen further on in Book VII, Chapter 2.

Paragraph I.

About the Birth of Vitzilopuchtli.

According to what the old natives told about the birth and beginning of satan, whom they called Vitzilopuchtli, and to whom the Mexicans paid great honor and homage, it happened as follows: There is a mountain range which is called Coatepec close to the village of Tulla, where a woman by the name of Coatlycue lived. She was the mother of certain Indians who called themselves Centzonvitznaoa, and they had a sister called Coyolxauhqui. This woman, Coatlycue, did penance by sweeping every day in the mountains of Coatepec.

One day it happened that while she was sweeping a little feather pellet, like a ball of spun wool, floated down over her, and she took (caught) it and put it in her bosom, near her abdomen, under the skirts. After having finished sweeping she wanted to take the little ball (or pellet) out, but did not find it, and they say she became pregnant of it; and when the said Centzonvitznaoa Indians saw their mother, who was already pregnant, they became furiously angry, asking who had begotten (impregnated) her? "Who has dishonoured and shamed us?" Their sister, the said Coyolxauhqui, said to them, "Brothers, let us kill our mother, because she has dishonoured (disgraced) us, allowing herself to become pregnant by stealth." When the said Coatlycue became aware of this deal, she pondered it greatly and became frightened, but her unborn baby (child) spoke to her and, consoling her, said, "Do not fear, because I know what I have got to do!" When the said Coatlycue heard these words, her heart was appeased and the grief (sorrow) she had felt left her. After the said Centzonvitznaoa Indians had held and concluded their council about killing the mother for that infamy and dishonor she had brought upon them, they were very angry, together with their sister called Coyolxauhqui, who importuned them (pestered them) to kill their mother, Coatlycue. The said Centzonvitznaoa Indians had taken their weapons and, arming themselves with them ready to fight, they twisted and tied their hair, as courageous (brave) men do. One of them, called Quavitlycac, who acted like a traitor, because whatever the Centzonvitznaoa Indians said he at once went to tell Vitzilopuchtli, who was still in his mother's womb (was carrying the news to him of what they said), and Vitzilopuchtli answered him, saying, "Oh, my uncle, see (watch) what they do and listen very well to what they say, because I know what I have got to do!" After they had adopted the resolution to kill Coatlycue, these said Centzonvitznaoa Indians went to (the place) where their mother, Coatlycue, was and, at the head of them went their sister Coyolxauhqui, and they were all armed with all their weapons and papers, rattles and darts in their proper order, and the said Quavitlycac climbed the mountain range to tell Vitzilopuchtli how those said Centzonvitznaoa Indians were coming against him to kill him. Vitzilopuchtli said to him, "Watch well where they arrive (reach)." And Quavitlycac replied that they were already arriving at (reaching) a place called Tezompantitlan; later Vitzilopuchtli asked Quavitlycac, saying, "Where are the Tzontvitznaoa Indians now?" Quavitlycac said they were now approaching another place called Coaxalco. And again Vitzilopuchtli asked, "Where to are they getting now?" and Quavitlycac replied that they were reaching another place which was called Apetlac. Again Vitzilopuchtli asked Quavitlycac, "And now, where are they?" and the the latter replied that they were reaching the centre of the mountain range. Thereupon, again Vitzilopuchtli asked, "Where are they now?" and Quavitlycac said they were very close by and that at their head came the said Coyolxauhqui.

At the instant the said Centzonvitznaoa Indians arrived, Vitzilopuchtli was born, carrying a shield which was called teucueli, with one dart (arrow); both were blue (shield and dart), and his (Vitzilopuchtli's) face was as if it were painted, and he wore on his head a plumage of pasted feathers; his left leg was thin and also feathered, and both thighs were painted alike in blue, as well as his arms. Now Vitzilopuchtli ordered one who was called Tochaucalqui to light a snake made of torches and which was called Xiuchcoatl. He lighted it and with it the said Coyolxauhqui was injured (wounded), and she died, torn to pieces, and her head remained in that mountain range of Coatepec.

Vitzilopuchtli rose, armed himself, and went forth against the said Centzonvitznaoas, pursuing them and throwing them out of that mountain range to its very bottom, fighting against them and four times encircling the said mountain-range. The Centzonvitznaoa Indians could not defend nor help themselves against Vitzilopuchtli nor could they harm (wound) him, thus they were defeated and many of them died. These Centzoncitznaoa Indians begged and entreated Vitzilopuchtli not to pursue them, to withdraw from the battle, but Vitzilopuchtli did not wish to do so, nor did he tolerate them there until he had killed almost all of them. Only a few of them escaped, who fled from his power and went to a place called Vitztlampa. He (Vitzilopuchtli) took from them and won many spoils and also the weapons they carried, which were called anecuhiotl.

Vitzilopuchtli was also called Tetzavitl for the reason that they said that the said Coatlycue became pregnant of a little feather ball, and no one knew who his father was. The Mexicans held him in great reverence and served him in many ways. They considered him as the god of war, because they said that he favored them greatly in battle. The order and customs the Mexicans had to serve and honour the said Vitzilopuchtli were adopted by them from what was the use and habit in the said mountain-range called Coatepec.

Paragraph II.

How They Honored Vitzilopuchtli as a God.

Likewise, they say that the day they venerated him by celebrating the festival of Panquetzaliztli, they took wild amaranth-seeds and cleaned them very well, picking out the straws and separating other seeds from them, which are called petzicatl and tezcaoauhtli; then they ground them very carefully. When the flour was very light, they mixed a dough, and with this formed the body of Vitzilopuchtli. On the following day a man, called Quetzalcoatl, shot a dart with a stone point (arrow-head) at the body of this said Vitzilopuchtli, and this (stone arrow-point) stuck in his heart, the king or chieftain being present (at this ceremony), and also a favorite (or intimate) of Vitzilopuchtli, who was called Teuoa. There were also present four high priests, furthermore four teachers of young men who were in charge of the instruction of youth, its school being called Telpuchtlotoque. All these (personages) were present when the body of Vitzilopuchtli was killed; after having killed it, they broke it into pieces, since it had been made of dough of wild amaranth-seeds. The heart of Vitzilopuchtli was taken for (to give to) the chief or king, and the whole body and some pieces that were like the (mouth and) lips of Vitzilopuchtli they divided in equal parts among the natives of Mexico and Tlaltelulco. Those of Mexico who were the priests of the said Vitzilopuchtli and were called Calpules, took four pieces of the body and an equal amount was taken by those of Tlaltelulco for the men of the same calling (order, i.e., priests). In this manner they divided among them the four pieces of the body of Vitzilopuchtli; they belonged to the Indians of two city districts (wards) and to the priests of the idols who were called Calpules, all of whom, every year, ate the body of Vitzilopuchtli in the order and custom they had. Every one ate a piece of the body of this god, and those who ate it were unmarried men (bachelors), and they said that it was the body of god called Teuqüalo, and those who received and ate the body of Vitzilopuchtli were called the ministers (priests) of god.

Paragraph III.

About the Penance to Which Those Who Received the Body of Vitzilopuchtli Obligated Themselves.

The unmarried men (bachelors) who received the body of Vitzilopuchtli obligated themselves to serve one year in the temple and (so) each night they lighted (the fires), using a large amount of firewood amounting to over two thousand sticks and candlewood, which cost them ten large blankets called quachtli, causing them heavy loss (expense) and inconvenience. Each one was obligated to pay one large blanket, five small ones, called tequachtli, a basket of corn and 100 ears of corn of the same seed, and those who were unable to pay and considered themselves seriously aggravated by the said tribute, ran away. Some decided to die in war at the hands of their enemies, since these said bachelors knew that as soon as they would have finished and complied with the service and penance to which they had agreed among themselves, another tribute would be collected.

Each one paid six small blankets, with which they bought candle- and fire-wood and everything that was necessary to wash the said Vitzilopuchtli at the end of the year, the hour when this idol was washed being midnight. Before they washed him, they formed a procession which was called necololo, and one of them dressed himself in the vestment of the idol, and this one (person) was called Liopuch. He advanced dancing, representing the person of Vitzilopuchtli (impersonating V.). Ahead of him went another one who was called Vitznaoactiacheauh, and after him came all the most prominent young men (bachelors) who were called Tiacheauhtlatoque and the valorous (courageous or brave) men, and behind them other people who carried torches (made) of candlewood, to the place where the said Vitzilopuchtli was to be washed, and which (place) was called Ayauhcalco. There they played on their flutes for him, and at once seated him and the favourite of the idol who was called Tevoa took water in a gourd bowl, painted blue, four times, and placed it before him with four green canes (reeds); and he washed his (the idol's) face and the whole body of the idol, and after it (the idol) was washed, he who wore the vestment of the said idol took this statue up again and, amid the playing of flutes, it was again carried back and placed (in its place) in the temple. As soon as the statue was replaced (reinstated), everybody went out and returned home, and in this way the service and penance of those who had eaten the body of Vitzilopuchtli that year, and who were called teuquaque, was at an end.

Paragraph IV.

About Another Exasperating Tribute Those Who Ate of the Body of Vitzilopuchtli Had to Pay.

As soon as the said year was ended, other young men (bachelors) started obligating themselves to serve and do penance, as was their order and usage when they received and ate the body of the idol Vitzilopuchtli. All of them and the priests called Calpules, of the other gods, began a great service and penance which caused them very great expense and fatigue which was hard to stand, namely, every night during the whole year they spent and consumed a large, even an excessive amount of firewood, candlewood, axi (chilli-pepper), tomatoes, salt and seeds, cocoa beans and food, and if they were short of the wherewith to purchase the necessary things, they would buy them with the blanket they dressed in, or they borrowed something, or they sold their arable land or a piece of woodland of these that were adjudicated to the idols whom they served, and whosoever was unable to pay the tribute at once left the land. As soon as the time approached when they would be through with their service and penance which they had promised the said Vitzilopuchtli, they cleansed and washed themselves and prepared a feast-day-meal with tamales and well prepared stews; or they killed one of the little dogs. They ate and they drank to excess on account of having complied with and finished the service and penance to which they had obligated themselves. It was, perhaps, that the tribute they had paid appeared hard to bear and so, once over, they were greatly pleased and relieved; now they were rid of the great work and worry; they now could sleep quietly and peacefully, and look freely for a living either by fishing, tilling the maguey fields, or by doing some trading (become merchants to some extent).

Chapter II.

About the Esteem (regard) in Which the God Titlacaoan or Tezeatlipuca Was Held.

The god called Titlacaoan was, they said, the creator of heaven and earth, and was all powerful; he gave to the living everything they needed, such as food, drink and wealth. This said Titlacaoan was invisible, like darkness or air, and if he appeared and spoke to a man, he was like a shadow. He knew the secrets they held (hid) in their hearts, and for this reason they clamored and entreated him, saying, "Oh, god all powerful who gives life to men and whose name is Titlacaoan, do me the favor (mercy) to grant me what I need to eat and drink and to enjoy your tranquility and delight, because I live in dire affliction and need in this world. Have mercy because I am so poor and sparsely clad, and I work to serve you, and in this your service I sweep, clean and light the fire in the hearth of this poor home, where I am awaiting what might be your pleasure to ordain me. Oh, let me die at once and thus end this troublesome and miserable life, so that I may rest and my body may be at ease."

Furthermore, they said that this god sent to the living (creatures) poverty, misery, and incurable and contagious diseases such as leprosy, buboes, gout, mange and dropsy, all of which diseases he sent when he was angry with those who broke their vows and penance to which they had obligated themselves; if they had promised to fast and broke their fast, or if in time of fasting the men slept with their wives and the wives with their husbands or friends.

Those who were afflicted with the said diseases, being in great pain and anguish, would entreat him, saying, "Oh, god, who calls himself Titlacaoan, do me the charity (grace) to take away this disease which kills me; I shall do nothing else but mend my ways. If I were cured of this disease, I vow to serve you and earn my living, and if I earn anything by my labor I shall not spend it for eating nor for anything else, but to honor you. I shall give a feast and banquet and shall dance in this poor (miserable) house!" If the sick man, in utter distress, saw that he could not get well, he would scold and in anger, say, "Oh, Titlacaoan, you are making fun of me, why (then) do you not kill me?" Some of them thus afflicted, died; others got well.

Titlacaoan was also called Tezcatlipuca, Moiocoiatzin, Iaotzin, Necociautl, and Necaoalpilli. They called him Moiocoiatzin because he did whatever he wanted to do, and thought about doing, and that no one could interfere with what he did or contradict him, either in heaven or on earth; he could give wealth to whom he pleased, and they said, moreover, that the day it should please him to destroy the heavens and make it fall he would do it, and mankind would disappear.

Titlacaoan was adored and prayed to by everybody and on all the roads and street crossings they put a stone seat in his honor, which was called Momuztli, and on this seat they put cèrtain bunches of flowers in his honor and service, renewing them every five days, besides the twenty days' festival they celebrated for him. It was their custom and rule to always do this.

Chapter III.

Account of Who Quetzalcoatl Was, Another Hercules, a Great Necromancer (conjuror or magician), Where He Ruled and What He Did When He Left.[1]

Quetzalcoatl was revered and considered a god, and in ancient times they worshipped him in Tulla; he had a very high temple with many steps, which were so narrow that there was not room enough for one foot. His statue was always stretched out and covered with blankets; the face was very homely, the head long, and he wore a very long beard. His vassals (subjects) were all workmen in the mechanic arts and skillful in cutting the green stones called chalchivites, also in the art of smelting silver and making other objects. All these arts had their origin and commencement with Quetzalcoatl, who had houses made with those precious green stones called chalchivites and others made of silver, still others made of red and white shells, others all made of boards, and again others of turquoises, and some all made of rich plumes. The vassals he had were very light-footed, to go wherever they wished, and they were called Tlanquacemilhitime. There is a mountain range called Tzatzifepetl (until this day it is thus called), from the top of which a public crier cried out to call the distant towns and people which are at more than one hundred leagues and are called Anaoac, and they heard and understood the crier there and at once, without loss of time, they arrived to know and listen to what, they said, Quetzalcoatl wanted (wished) of them. Furthermore, they say he was very wealthy, that he had whatever he needed for eating and drinking, that the corn was exceedingly abundant, and the squash or gourds were very large, a fathom (six feet) in circumference; the ears of corn were so big that they had to be carried in the arms, and also the reeds (or canes) of the wild amaranth were very tall and thick, and that they climbed them like trees. They sowed and gathered cotton of all colors as, for instance, red, bright red, yellow, purple, whitish, green, blue, dark brown, gray, (dark) orange and tawny; these colors

[1]See account of Father Dr. Servando Mier, *Historia de la Revolucion de Nueva España*, London, 1813.

of the cotton were natural, as thus the cotton grew. They say, moreover, that in the said village (town) of Tulla they reared many and different kinds of birds of rich plumage in many colors as those called xiuhtototl, quetzaltototl, caquan and tlauhquechol, as well as song birds who sang very sweet and softly.

Quetzalcoatl also owned all the wealth of the world in gold, silver, and the green stones called chalchivites, and other precious things; he had a great abundance of cocoa-trees of different colors, which are called xochicacatlao. The said vassals of Quetzalcoatl were also very wealthy, and did not lack anything at all; they never suffered famine nor lack of corn; they never ate even the small ears of corn, but rather heated their baths with them, using them instead of fire-wood. They also say that the said Quetzalcoatl did penance by pricking his limbs and drawing blood, with which he stained the maguey points; that he bathed at midnight in a spring called Xicapaya. This custom was adopted by the priests and ministers of the Mexican idols; they do exactly what Quetzalcoatl used to do in the town of Tulla.

Chapter IV.

How the Good Fortune of Quetzalcoatl Came to an End and Three Other Necromancers Came Against Him and (about) the Things They Did.

The time came when the good fortune of Quetzalcoatl and the Tultecas came to an end, because there appeared against them three necromancers by the names of Vitzilopuchtli, Titlacaoan and Tlacabepan, who played many tricks in Tulla. Titlacaoan was the one to invent the first fraud, because he turned himself into an old man with very gray hair, and in this disguise he went to the house of Quetzalcoatl, saying to his pages: "I want to see and speak to the king." They replied: "Clear out, go away, old man, you cannot see him because he is ill, and you would annoy him and leave him sorrowful." The old man thereupon said: "I must see him!" The pages replied: "Wait," and they went to tell Quetzalcoatl how an old man had come to speak to him, saying, "Sir, we have thrown him out to make him go away, but he refuses (to leave), saying that he is going to see you by force." Quetzalcoatl said, "Let him come in here and appear before me, because I have awaited him for many days." Thus they went to call the old man, and he entered where Quetzalcoatl was and said to him: "My son, how are you? Here I have (bring you) a medicine which you must drink." Quetzalcoatl answered, saying, "Well and good that you came, old fellow; it is for many days that I have been expecting you!" The old man asked Quetzalcoatl, "How are you in body and health?" To this Quetzalcoatl replied: "I am very ill; my whole body aches; I cannot move my hands and feet." The old man said to the king: "Sir, you see here the medicine I brought you; it is very good and wholesome, and whosoever drinks (takes) it becomes intoxicated (drunk); if you should wish to drink it you will become intoxicated, but you are to get well, and it will soften your heart; it is going to remind you of the sufferings and anguish of death or of your (past) life."

Quetzalcoatl replied, "Oh, old man, where must I go?" The old man answered, "By force (forcibly or necessarily) you have to go to Tullantlapalan, where there is another old man awaiting you; he and you will talk together, and after your return you will once more be like a young man; nay, you will even become a boy again."

As Quetzalcoatl heard these words his heart softened, and the old man repeated: "Sir, drink this medicine," but Quetzalcoatl replied, "I do not wish to drink." The old man insisted, saying, "Drink it, sir, because if you do not drink now, later you will want to do so; at least put it on your forehead and drink a little bit." Quetzalcoatl agreed and tasted it and afterwards he drank (more), saying: What is this? It appears to be something very good and tasty, and it has already cured me and taken away the illness; I am well now." Again the old man said, "Drink of it again, sir, because it is very good and you will be healthier." Quetzalcoatl drank again and became drunk (intoxicated), and he commenced to cry very sadly and had a turn of heart which softened so that he wanted to leave; but he could not help thinking about what he considered the deceit and mockery (hoax) the said old conjuror had played on him.

The medicine they said Quetzalcoatl took was white wine of the country (land) made of maguey (agave), the kind (of agave) they call teumetl.

Chapter V.

About Another Fraud (trick) Which the Conjuror Called Titlacaoan Played (conceived).

Titlacaoan played another trick, disguising himself as a strange Indian and calling himself Tobeyo. He presented himself, his entire body naked as was the custom among those of his generation, and was selling green "chile" (peppers). He settled down (seated himself in a stand) in the market place opposite the palace of Vemac, who was the secular (worldly or civic) chief of the Tultecas, because Quetzalcoatl was like a priest and had no children. Vemac had a very beautiful daughter, and as such she was greatly coveted (desired) by the Tultecas who wanted to marry her, but he (Vemac) did not wish to let anyone of them have her. She looked towards the market-place and she saw the Tobeyo, completely naked, liked him, and wanted to have him, and on account of the love she felt for him her whole body began to swell. Her father, Vemac, learned about her condition, and he asked the maidens who took care of her: "What ails my daughter?" They replied, "Sir, the cause of this disease was Tobeyo who walked about naked. Your daughter saw him and . . . she is love sick." When Vemac heard these words, he said, "Here, ye Tultecs! Look for this Tobeyo who is around here selling green chile (peppers)." They searched for him everywhere, but he was nowhere to be found. A public crier went up into the mountain-range called Tzatzitepac and proclaimed, saying, "Tultecs, if you should meet (find) a Tobeyo who wanders about here selling green peppers, bring him before the lord (chief) Vemac!" They looked for him everywhere and could not find him, and so they came to tell the king. Later Tobeyo appeared again seated in the market where he had been before, selling green peppers, and as soon as they found him there, they at once went to tell Vemac, who said, "Bring him here to me at once!" Brought into his presence, he asked him, "Where are you from?" Tobeyo replied: "I am a stranger and have come here to sell green peppers." Vemac said to him: "And why do you not wear a girdle and cover yourself with a blanket?" To which Tobeyo replied, "We have this custom in my country." Vemac said to him: "By force (forcibly you are to cure my daughter; do not be afraid (fear not)." They at once took him to wash him and cut his hair, and they dyed his entire body with ink and girt him with a girdle (maxtli) and covered him with a blanket. Then Vemac said to him, "Go and enter to see my daughter in there where they keep her (guard) her," and he did so. Tobeyo slept with her, by which she at once was cured and got well, and thus Tobeyo became the son-in-law of the chief Vemac.[1]

Chapter VI.

How Those of (the people of) Tulla Resented the Wedding and about Another Deceit (trick) Titlacaoan Played.

After the marriage of the Tobeyo with the daughter of the chief, Vemac, had been accomplished, the Tultecs began to get angry and utter injurious and ignominious words against the latter, saying among themselves, "Why has our lord Vemac married his daughter to a Tobeyo?" As Vemac heard and understood all the injurious things the Tultecas said against him he called them to appear before him, saying: "Come

[1]This chapter, according to Bustamante, is not a true translation, but has been modified by him, for he says Sahagun wrote it true to Indian-lore, which is not possible in Spanish translation on account of obscenity.

here; I have understood all the injurious words you have said against me on account of my love for my son-in-law, who is a Tobeyo, hence I ordain that you take him with you, dissemblingly (under pretext) to fight in the war against Cacatepec and Coatepec, so that our enemies may kill him." Upon hearing these words on the part of Vemac, the Tultecs armed themselves, assembled, and went to war with many (a great number of) foot-men (foot-soldiers), and with the son-in-law of Vemac. When they reached the battle-field, they hid the said Tobeyo among the pages, dwarfs, and the lame, to await the enemy. After having done this (which is a strategem they used to adopt in war), the said Tultecs went to fight against the enemies from Coatepec. Tobeyo said to the pages, dwarfs and lame, "Do not be afraid; be valiant, for we shall kill our enemies. Most of the enemies from Coatepec succeeded in defeating and pursuing the Tultecs, who fled before them and, escaping out of their reach very astutely and deceitfully they left Tobeyo alone, interned with the pages among the enemy, while they fled. They thought that these would surely kill Tobeyo and the pages, for he was left alone with them. They (the Tultecs) returned at once and said to Vemac, "Sir, we left your son-in-law Tobeyo and the pages alone in the war, in the hands of the enemy." As soon as he heard what the Tultecs had done with his son-in-law, Vemac was greatly pleased, thinking that by now he would be dead, for he was deeply ashamed to have such a son-in-law, a foreigner and a Tobeyo.[1]

The latter, finding himself hidden away (among enemies) looked at the enemies and said to the pages, "Have no fear; the enemy is coming upon us, but I know that I shall kill them all." He arose and sallied forth against those of Coatepec and Cacatepec and, pursuing them, he slew a great number of them.

News of this feat reached the lord Vemac, and it frightened him and caused him deep regret, so he called together the Tultecs and said to them, "Let us go and receive my son-in-law." So they all went with the chief Vemac to meet him, carrying with them certain weapons or emblems called quetzalapanocayutl, and shields, which are called xiuhchimalli. They put them on him (the Tobeyo) as a sign of victory and reward, and received him, dancing and playing their flutes, and singing, together with the said pages, in great rejoicing and gaiety. When the Tultecs reached the palace of Vemac they adorned (crowned) his (the Tobeyo's) head with plumes; they painted his whole body yellow, and the same they did to the pages. This was the present they used to make to those who returned victorious from war. After that, chief Vemac said to his son-in-

[1]Bustamante states that the word "Tobeyo" cannot be found in any dictionary, but seems to infer it to mean a "plebeyan," or person of low birth.

law, "Now I am happy over what you accomplished, so are the Tultecs. You have behaved very well against the enemy, now repose and rest yourself."

Chapter VII.

About Another Trick This Same Necromancer Played by Means of Which He Killed Many Tullanos (people of Tulla) Moving in a Formal Dance Measure or Just Dancing.

The said necromancer (conjuror) called Titlacaoan, after having thus fought and conquered the said enemies, played another trick, for after having his whole body embellished with the rich plumes called Tocivitl, he ordained that all the Tultecs should move about in rhythmic dancing steps and dance (common dances), and he caused a crier to proclaim it in the mountains of Tzatzitepec, saying that all the Indians, outsiders, or visitors should come to a festival to dance, so that subsequently Indians without number came to Tulla. As soon as they had all gathered, the said Titlacaoan went to a place called Texcalapa with a countless number of people, young men as well as young women, and (there) this said conjuror Titlacaoan began to move about and dance and sing, beating a drum, and all the people did the same, beginning to dance and make merry, singing the verse which the said magician sang to them. He would sing every verse to those who danced, and thereupon they all would repeat the same verse, although they did not know that song by heart.

They kept up this rejoicing until almost midnight, which was called tlatlapitzalizpa, and because the number of those who danced was so great, the people pushed one another, and many of them fell over the cleft (or gorge) of the river, called Texcaltlauhco, and were turned into rocks. In (across) the said river there was a stone bridge, but the necromancer broke it up, and all those who wanted to cross it fell and tumbled into the river and were turned into stones. Nothing of all that which the necromancer did was seen or felt by the Tultecs, for they were like drunkards without brains, and whenever they turned about and danced, they kept pushing one another, so they fell over the cleft into the water.

Chapter VIII.

About Another Trick Played by the Same Necromancer, by Means of Which He Killed Another Large Number of the People of Tulla.

The said necromancer played another trick by presenting himself as a courageous man whose name was Tequioa. This man sent off a public crier who was to call (together) all the neighbors of Tulla to come for certain work in a flower-garden called xuchitia, fertilizing and cultivating it. (It is said that this garden belonged to Quetzalcoatl.) They all obeyed the call and came for this work, and once all the Tultecs were gathered, the said necromancer set to work and began to kill them by hitting them with a hoe. In this manner he killed a very large (a countless) number of them. Some tried to flee to escape from his hands, but by stumbling and falling down they soon died, others pushed and shoved one another, and killed themselves in this way.

Chapter IX.

Still Another Trick Played by This Same Necromancer Which Killed Many More of the Tultecs.

In this other above-mentioned trick the conjuror took up a seat in the midst of the market of the Tianquiztli, saying his name was Tlacavepan, or by another name Acoxcoch, and he made a tiny boy dance in the palms of his hands (they say this boy was Vitzilopuchtli), whom he thus placed in his hands to dance. As the Tultecs saw it they all rose and went to look and, jostling one another, many perished, smothered or were torn to pieces. This happened a great many times that the Tultecs killed each other jostling and pushing (in a crowd). The said necromancer then asked them (the Tultecs): "What is this? What fraud is this, and how is it that you do not understand (that it is such?). This man who makes that little boy dance is a trickster (impostor); kill him, throw stones at him!" So they killed the necromancer and the little boy with stones (throwing rocks at them). After having killed him, the body of the conjuror began to (stink) smell bad, and the stench corrupted the air, which carried this terrible smell to the Tultecs so that a great many died. Then the necromancer said to them, "Throw the corpse far away, because too many Tultecs are dying from the bad smell of the body of this said trickster." This the Tultecs did; they tied the corpse with ropes and threw the ill-smelling body out, but it was so heavy that the Tultecs could not lift it, although they thought that very quickly would they be rid of it. So a public crier was sent from Tulla and he proclaimed and called loudly, "Oh, Tultecs, come, all of you and bring your ropes to tie this body to throw it out!" When they had all gathered, they at once tied the body with ropes and began to drag it, saying, "Ready, let us drag this corpse." But it weighed so much that they could not even move it, the ropes broke, and whenever one of these ropes parted (tore) those who held on to it fell down and died suddenly, falling over one another. Since they were unable to drag away the body of the dead, the necromancer said to the

Tultecs: "Tultecs, this corpse wants a verse from a song; and he himself sang it for them and then said, "Now drag Tlacavepan, the conjuror." And while singing a verse they began to pull at the ropes and drag the body, which was stretched out, at the same time shouting and calling. Yet, whenever a rope split in two, all those who were holding on to it perished, as well as those who pushed forward, falling over one another. In this fashion they carried the corpse into the woods (forest), and those who returned home did not know a thing of all that had happened to them, because they were like intoxicated men.

Chapter X.

Of Other Tricks of the Same Necromancer.

The conjuror played still another trick in the town (village) of Tulla, for they say he let fly a white bird of the kind they call Iztaccvixtli, pierced by an arrow, somewhat high over the earth, but the Tultecs could see it clearly if they raised their eyes heavenward.

Another one of his tricks was that the Tultecs would see, by night, a mountain range called Cacatepec in flames, which could be seen from a great distance. Whenever the Tultecs saw this conflagration they got excited and shouted and screamed and were (generally) anxious; they would say to one another, "Oh, Tultecs, our good luck is coming to an end; we shall perish; Tultecaiutl is doomed! Ill luck has descended upon us! Alas! Where shall we go? Oh, unlucky people that we are, let us exert ourselves—and mend our ways!"

Still another trick played the necromancer, by causing stones to rain down upon them (instead of rain), and when that was over, a large stone fell from heaven of those called techcatl, and from then on an old Indian woman was wandering about a place called Chapultepecuitlapico, or by another name Veizinco, selling small paper banners and shouting, "To the flags!" Whoever was willing to die at once would say, "Buy me a banner; and this having been purchased for him, he at once went to the place where the said stone techatl lay, and there they killed him, and there was no one who would say, "What is this; what is happening to us?" For they all were like people gone crazy (mad).

Chapter XI.

About Another Trick by the Same Necromancer, by Means of Which He Killed Many More Tullanos.

They say that all the provisions (food) became sour so that nobody could eat food, when suddenly an old Indian woman appeared (they say it was the necromancer, presenting himself in the disguise of an old Indian woman). She settled down in a place called Xochitla and began to toast corn, and the odor of this toasted corn spread over the towns (villages) of the whole district (province rather), and as the Tultecs smelled that corn they all came running. They reached this said place of Xochitla where the old woman was in a very short time (because it is said that the Tultecs were very spry (fleet of foot), and although they lived very far away, they reached the place they wished to go to very quickly. All these Tultecs that came and gathered there were then killed by the old woman and not one of them returned home, and by means of this great deceit he killed a great many.

Chapter XII.

About the Escape of Quetzalcoatl to Tlapallan, and the Things He Did on the Way.

A great many more tricks were thus played on the Tultecs, because their good luck had left them, and Quetzalcoatl, feeling great sorrow for them, agreed to leave Tulla and go to Tlapallan. Therefore he ordered that all the houses of silver and shells which he had caused to be built be burned, and he had all his other very precious things buried in the mountains or clefts; he changed the cocoa-trees into others called mizquitl, and he, moreover, commanded all kinds of birds of rich plumage, such as the Quetzaltolotl and the Tlauchquechol, to go farther on, and they went to Anaoac, which is at a distance of more than a hundred leagues.

Quetzalcoatl prepared to take the road leaving Tulla, which he did. He arrived at a place called Quauchtitlan, where there grew a large tree, big and tall. He went close to it and asked his pages for a mirror, and they gave it to him; looking at his face (in the mirror), he said, "I am old now," and he thereupon called the place Vevequauhtitlan. Then he took (picked up) stones with which he hit the tree, and every stone Quetzalcoatl thus threw entered the bark of the tree and stayed there. For a long time afterwards the stones remained and showed in the bark, and anyone could see them from the soil up to the top. Thus Quetzalcoatl went on wandering, with flute-players, playing flutes before him (ahead of him). He reached another place on the road where he rested; he sat down on a stone (rock), putting his hands on it, and he left the marking of his hands on that same rock or stone. Looking back towards Tulla, he commenced to cry bitterly, and the tears he shed hollowed and perforated the stone on which he thus sat resting and weeping.

Chapter XIII.

About the Traces He (Quetzalcoatl) Left on the Stones Made by the Palms of His Hands and by His Body Where He Sat Down.

Quetzalcoatl put his hands on the big stone when he sat down, touching it, and thus left the impression of the palms of his hands on that stone, just as if he had placed them in mud, where they would make a slight impression. He also left traces of his rump as he sat down on that same stone (rock), and all these traces (or impressions) show on the rock and can be clearly seen. He (Quetzalcoatl) on that occasion called the said place Temacpalco as he rose from his seat. Continuing his way, he reached another place called Tepanoalla, through which a large and wide river flows. Quetzalcoatl ordered a stone bridge to be made across that river, and over it he passed, and the place was called Tepanoaya. Continuing on his way, he came to another place called Coahpa, where the necromancers met him in order to prevent him from going any farther, saying to Quetzalcoatl, "Where are you going? Why did you leave your village? To whom did you commend it? Who is going to do penance?" Quetzalcoatl, responding to the conjurors, told them: "In no way can you prevent my departure, for I have to leave forcibly." The said necromancers again asked Quetzalcoatl, saying, "Where are you going?" and he replied, "I am going as far as Tlapallan." "What for are you going there?" asked the necromancers. Whereupon he replied, "They came to call me and the Sun is also calling me." To this they answered, "Well and good; go then, but you are to leave here all the mechanical arts, such as the smelting of silver, stone- and wood-carving, painting, making feather-work, and other trades." The necromancers took everything away from Quetzalcoatl and he (himself) commenced to throw all the valuable (rich) jewels he had taken with him into a spring (fountain), for which reason that spring was called Coscoapa, while now they call it Coahapa.

Continuing on his way, Quetzalcoatl reached another site called Cochtoca, where another necromancer came to meet him and said to him, "Where are you going?" Quetzalcoatl replied, "I am going to Tlapallan," to which the conjuror answered, "Well and good that you are going (there), but first drink this wine I brought you." "I cannot drink it, not even taste a little of it," replied Quetzalcoatl. The necromancer said, "You are to drink it by force then, or at least taste a little of it, because I dare not give it to any one of the mortals; they all get intoxicated; therefore, here now, drink it." Quetzalcoatl took the wine and drank it through a hollow cane, and having taken it, he got drunk and fell asleep, and he began to snore. When he awoke, he looked from side to side, he shook out his hair with the hand, and after that the said place was called Cochtoca.

Chapter XIV.

How from the Great Cold All of the Pages of Quetzalcoatl Died in the Pass Between the Two Mountain Ranges, the Volcano and the "Sierra Nevada," and about Other Adventures (feats).

Quetzalcoatl continued on his way, and as he got farther on between the two mountain ranges, that of the Volcano and the Sierra Nevada, all the pages who accompanied him, and who were dwarfs and hunchbacks, died from the cold. He mourned deeply the death of his pages and, crying very bitterly, singing his song of sorrow and sighing, he saw the other mountain range, which is called Poyauhtecatl, situated near Tecamachalco. In this manner he passed through sites and towns, and left many traces in the mountains and on the roads of his transit.

It is said that Quetzalcoatl was amusing himself and playing on a (certain) mountain, sat down on top of it, and thus descended (mounted on it) to the bottom; there he dismounted and repeated a similar trick many times (at other places). They tell how at another place he ordered a ball game to be erected made of square stones, where they used to play (ball); the game was called tlachtli; that in the midst of the game he himself drew a mark or line, called tlecotl, and that where this line is the mountain appears very deeply rent (gashed). At still another place he shot at a large tree, called pochutl, with an arrow which also was a tree, likewise called pochutl, and he pierced the tree with this arrow, and in this manner a cross was formed. It is moreover said that Quetzalcoatl created and built houses under the earth (under ground) which are called mientlancalco, and he also ordered a large stone to be so placed (erected) that it can be moved with the little finger. They say that even if there were many men who meant to move the stone, it wouldn't move, even though there be a great many.

There are other notable (noteworthy) things Quetzalcoatl did in many towns, and he gave names to all the mountain ranges, forests and sites. When he reached the sea-shore he ordained a raft to be made of snakes of the kind which is called coatlapechtli; he entered it and sat down as in a canoe, and thus he left, navigating on the sea, no one knows how and in what manner he arrived at Tlapallan.

Appendix to Book III.

CHAPTER I.

About Those Who Went to Hell and About Their Obsequies (Funeral Rites).

What the ancient natives and chieftains of this country (land) knew and told about those who died was as follows:

The souls of the departed went to one of three different places: one was hell, where a devil (demon) lived whose name was Mictlantecutli or, by another name, Tzontemoc, and also a goddess called Mictecacioatl, who was the wife of Mictlantecutli. The souls of the dead who went to hell were the souls of people who had died of some disease, be they lords, or chiefs, or common people, and on the day of the death (of anyone of those), be it man, woman or boy (child), they said to the body, lying on the bed before it was buried: "Oh, son, you have suffered and passed the woes of this life, now our lord has deigned to take you because we have no permanent life in this world and our life is as short as if we were just warming ourselves in the sun, and he did us the favor to let us know one another and talk to each other in this life. Now, at this time the god called Mictlantecutli, or by another name Aculnaoacatl or Tzontemoc, and the goddess who calls herself Mictecacioatl, have put you on their seat, for we all shall go there and yonder site is for all (of us). It is very large and there will be no memory left of you. Thus you departed for the most somber place which has neither light nor windows, and you never will return nor get out of there; you will have neither anxiety nor solicitude (temptation) about your return after you have gone away forever. You left your children poor orphans and grandchildren, not even knowing how they are going to end, nor how they will withstand the sorrows (troubles) of their present life, and we, too, shall journey to where you are now, before long!"

After that they would talk to the relative of the deceased, saying, "Oh, son, be brave and take courage, do not neglect food and drink, let your heart be quiet (calm), for how could we oppose what god ordains? By chance did this death occur because someone hates us or makes fun of us? It certainly is so because our lord ordained that this should be his end. Who can bring it about that an hour or a day should prolong our present life in this world? Therefore, since this is a fact, be patient in the endurance of the hardships of this life, in seeing the house where the departed lived deserted (unoccupied) and dark from now on; do not harbor any more the hope of seeing again your dead. It is not wise to worry much over your orphanage and your poverty left to you. Take courage, my son, and let not sadness kill you, for we came here to visit and console you with these few words which are fit for us to say, since we are fathers and we are old, our lord having already taken from us those who were older and those of ancient times; they who knew far better than we do to say consoling words to the mourners, so we shall end our discourse; god be with you (rest with god)."

Thereupon the very old men and the official paper cutters cut, adorned and tied the papers, as was their duty, for the dead; they contracted (doubled) his legs and dressed him with those papers, then tied him and took a little water, which they poured over his head, saying to the deceased, "This is the water you enjoyed while living in the world (on earth)." Then they took a tiny jar of that water and gave it to him, saying, "See here with what you are going to wander." They then put him in the shroud, this being the way they buried their dead, with his blankets and papers, tying him very strongly. They gave the deceased all the papers that had been prepared (for the occasion), placing them in orderly fashion before him, saying, "See here with what you are to pass (travel) between two mountain ranges which are joining one with the other." Moreover, they gave him other papers, saying to the dead man, "See here with what you are to pass the road which is guarded by a snake." Still other papers they gave him, saying, "See here with what you are to pass the road over which the green lizard (newt) roams, which is called xochitonal." Then they said to the dead, "Here you see with what you are to pass eight "paramos" (moors), and then gave him other papers and said, "See here with what you are to pass eight hillocks (fells)." After this they said to the deceased, "See here with what you are to pass the wind of knives (knife-sharp?), itzchecaya, because that wind was so strong that it carried stones with it and pieces of (stone-) knives. On account of these winds and the (severe) cold the dead were supposed to have to withstand, they burned all the chests and weapons and all the remains of the captives they had captured in war, as well as all the clothes these had worn, saying that all these things were to go with the deceased (in question) in order to keep him warm in that passage, and thus protect him and prevent his too great suffering. They did a similar thing when women died, for they burned all the tools with which they wove and span, as well as all their clothes, so that these might keep them warm in that passage and protect them from the cold and strong wind which blew there and which they called itzchecaya; he who had no wearing apparel suffered greatly from the wind through that pass. They also had the dead take with him a little dog of bright reddish hair, and they put around its neck a loose cotton thread (string), because they believed that the deceased swam astride on a little dog when they crossed a river of hell which was called Chicunaoapa. When the dead arrived and stood before the devil who is called Mictlantecutli, they offered and presented to him the papers they carried, and bunches of candle-wood (torches) and cones of perfume and loose cotton thread, as well as red yarn, a blanket, a belt if they were men, and the skirts and the entire bundle of clothes of a dead woman who departed from the earth, all of which they wrapped together the moment she died. After eighty days they burned it (such a bundle), and the same they did again after a year, and then again the third and fourth year, when the excequies for the dead came to an end, according to their custom. They believed that all the offerings they made for the dead on this earth went straight before (the seat of) the devil (satan) called Mictlantecutli. After these four years the deceased left Mictlanticutli's domain and went to the nine hells, where he had to pass a very wide stream, and there in that (particular) place, on the shores of the river, dogs live and roam, close to the place where those who have just died swim across on the backs of little dogs. It is said that as soon as the dead person reached the bank of the above-mentioned stream, the dog would look across to see whether he recognized his master, then at once swim across the stream to where his (said) master was, and carry him over on his back. It was for this reason that the natives used to keep and raise little dogs. It is said, however, that dogs of white and black fur (hair) could not swim and pass the river, because the black dog, it is said, would say, "I have washed myself," and the dog with white fur (pelt) would say, "I have become spotted with dark colour and therefore I cannot pass you across.[1] Only the reddish colored dog would carry the dead on its back, swimming well across.

Thus, at this place of hell, called Chicunamictla, the deceased finished and brought their wanderings to an end. It is said, moreover, that after having shrouded the corpse with the said ornaments of papers and other things, they at once killed his dog and then carried both to the place where he was to be incinerated (burnt) together with the dog, and that there were two old men whose special duty it was to take charge of the burning of the dead. Other old men sang, and while the body was burning the aforesaid old men were piercing it with poles, to insure total incineration. When the body was completely incinerated they gathered the ashes, coal and bones (which had not burned), took water, saying,

[1]This should certainly be reversed.

"let the body be washed," and poured the water over the coal and bones. Then they dug a round hole and buried these remains. This was done at the burial (rites) of the nobles as well as of the common people. They put the bones within a jar or pot together with a green stone of those they call chalchivitl, and then buried it in a room (chamber) of his (the deceased's) house and daily they placed (and offered) offerings on the place where the bones had been buried. They also say that when a chief or noble died they placed a green stone (chalchivitl) into his mouth as he was dying. In the mouth of a dying person of the lower classes they did not insert such a precious stone, but one of little value which is called texoxoctli or knife-stone (flint or obsidian?) which, they said, represented the heart of the deceased. When a chief or lord died they made many and diverse ornaments of paper, consisting of a banner or pennon of four fathoms (1 braza—6 feet) in length adorned with different plumes, and they also killed twenty slaves, because they said that since in this world they had served (attended) him, so they had to serve him in hell. On the day they burned the body of the master they forthwith killed the male and female slaves with arrows, shooting them in the throat (front part). They did not incinerate them together with their master, but buried them somehwere else.

CHAPTER II.

About Those Who Went to the Terrestrial (earthly) Paradise.

The other place where, according to them, the souls of the departed went, was the terrestrial paradise which is called Tlalocan where, they say, there is much rejoicing and coolness (comfort also), without any suffering. There they never lack green corn (ears of corn), calabash, wild amaranth seeds, green pepper, tomatoes, green beans and flowers. There certain gods called Tlaloques reside, who look like the ministers (priests) of the idols and who wear long hair (wear their hair long). Those who go to this place (Tlalocan) are all those who are killed by lightning, those who are drowned, the lepers, those afflicted with pustules, the mangy, and gout-stricken, and those with dropsy. The day (or whenever) they died of these contagious and incurable diseases, they were not burned, but the bodies of all such people were buried, and they put wild amaranth seeds on their jaws over the face. They also put blue paint on their foreheads, with cut-up papers; other papers they put on the occiput (hind part of the head). They dressed them in papers and placed a cane in one hand, and thus they said that in the terrestrial paradise, which was called Tlalolocan (Tlalocan?), it was always summer and everything was green, i.e., there were flowers and trees.

CHAPTER III.

About Those Who Went to Heaven.

The other (third part) where the souls of the departed went was heaven, where the Sun lives. Those who went to heaven were those killed in war and the captives who had died (in the power) at the hands of their enemies, some of whom died by knife-thrusts, others burned alive or wounded by sharp-pointed canes or clubbed with pine-wood clubs, or those who died fighting with them; also those who died from having had torches tied all over their bodies which, being lighted, burned them to death. All these, they say, were gathered on a plain, and at the hour of sunrise they lifted their voices to shout, beating on their shields at the same time; he whose shield was pierced by the enemy's arrows could not look at the sun. It is likewise said that in heaven there are trees and forests of different kinds of trees and that the offerings which were made to them by those living in this world (on earth) came into their presence and were received by them there. After four years, when the souls of these dead went on, they changed into different kinds of birds of rich plumage, of fine hues, and they flew off to drink honey from all flowers as well in heaven as on the earth, as do the tzinzones (humming-birds).

CHAPTER IV.

How the Common People Offered Their Children to the House Which Is Called Telpuchcalli, and of the Customs They Were Taught There.

When a child was born, the parents at once made vows over it, offering it to the house of the idols, which is called Calmecac, that it might become a minister of them (the idols) when of age. By thus offering it, they intended to have it educated there with the other young men (bachelors) for the service of the town and for matters of war. However, before he (the boy child) was taken away to the house of the Telpuchcalli, his parents prepared and cooked a very good meal and invited the teachers of the children (boys) they were commissioned to educate and teach the manners customary in that house. When the feast in the home of the boy's parents was over (drawing to a close), these latter made a speech to the teachers who were to educate their son, saying, "Our lord the creator of heaven and earth has brought you here to let you know that it had pleased him to grant us the favor of allowing a child, like a jewel or a precious plume, to be born to us, perhaps it (the child) may be reared and will live; it is a boy, and it is not right that we should show him the task of woman, keeping him in our home, therefore we give him to you as your son and place you in charge of him, because you hold the office (position) of raising the young men (youths) and teaching them our customs so that they may become courageous men and serve the gods Tlalteculi and Tonantiuh (who are the earth and the sun) in war. For this reason we offer him to the almighty lord god Iaotl, or by another name Titlacaoan or Tezcatlipuca. Perhaps he is going to grow and live, pleasing to god; he will enter the house of penance and of weeping, which is called Telpuchcalli, and we turn him over to you from this moment (from now on), that he may live in the said house where courageous men are reared, and come forth as such, because in that place they strive to deserve the treasures of god, by praying, doing penance, and asking to be granted the mercy and grace of giving them victories, so that they may become chiefs (leaders), possessing ability to govern and rule the common people. And we, the unworthy parents, may we by chance deserve it that our weeping and our penance should cause this boy to be reared and live? Certainly not, for we are unworthy, decrepit, old people. Therefore we most humbly entreat you to receive and accept him as a son, that he may enter and live with the sons of chiefs and others who are being educated in this Telpuchcalli."

The teachers of the boys and young men answered in the following manner: "We consider it a high favor to have heard (listened to) your reasoning (argument); it is not to us you are addressing this discourse or petition; you are making it to the lord god Iaotl, in whose representation we have listened to it. It is he to whom you speak, to whom you offer and give your son, your precious stone and rich plume, and we receive him in his name. He knows what it will be his pleasure to do with him. We, the unworthy, decrepit (frail) servants, await with uncertain (dubious) hope what this may be, and what he will be pleased to do with your son in accordance with what he had already granted as favours to suit his disposition and determination, which the unknown one had decided to grant before the beginning of the world. In truth (forsooth), we do not know the natural abilities which at that time were granted him, as his property and condition (standing); we also ignore what the favours might have been that he granted this boy when he was baptized. We also ignore the sign, good or bad, under which he was born and was baptized, for we, the humble servants cannot divine these things; not one of all those that are born receives his good luck in this world, because, in truth, we bring our good fortune with us into the world when we are born, for it was allotted to us since before the beginning of the world. In conclusion, we receive your boy, and he is to start by sweeping and doing other humble work in the house of our lord. We wish and pray that he may be given all the wealth (riches) of the same lord god. We also wish that the natural gifts (abilities) and favors with which our lord adorned and endowed him before the beginning of this world may manifest themselves and shine (while he lives) in this house. We do not know whether by chance god may claim him for himself by taking his life in childhood, and whether, perhaps, we do not deserve it that he should live a long time in this world. We know nothing for certain, except to say to you in order to be able to console you, that we cannot tell you with certainty this he will be, or that he will do, nor this will happen or he will be esteemed, he will be extolled (praised or aggrandized), or he will live on earth. Perhaps on account of our unworthiness he will be despicable, poor and despised on earth, or perhaps he will become a thief or adulterer, or else live a hard and wearisome life. We, however, shall do our full duty, which is to rear and educate him like parents, but we shall be unable to enter within him and put our (own) heart into him; you could not do that either, notwithstanding the fact that you are his parents. There only remains to say to you not to fail to commend him to god in prayers and tears, that he (the god) may tell us his will."

CHAPTER V.

About the Mode of Life and the Exercises Those Who Lived in the Telpuchcalli Had to Follow.

After having entered (enrolled in) the house of the Telpuchcalli, the boy was put to sweep, clean house, light the fire, and perform the exercises (services) of penance he obligated himself to do. It was customary that at sunset all the youths went to dance and do rhythmic exercises in the house called Cuicacalco nightly (every night), and the boy (novice) also went to dance with the other youths.[1] As soon as he reached his fifteenth year and having become thus a little man, the older youths took him into the woods to gather fire-wood which was needed for the houses of the Telpuchcalli and the Cuicacalco, and they made him carry one or two big logs to try and see whether he already might have the strength (ability) to be taken to war, and, if he was found strong enough for it, they took him along, making him carry the shields, which they made him pile on his back. If he was well-trained and had good manners and knew all the exercises he was obliged to know, he was elected teacher of the youths and called Tiacucauh, and when he had become a courageous (valiant) and able man, he was elected to rule over all the young men and to mete out punishment to them, and then they called him Telpuchtlato. If he had become a brave (courageous) man in war, had captured four enemies, he was elected and appointed as Tlacatecatl, or Tlacochcalcatl,

[1]Rhythmic dancing belonged to the principles of education among the ancient Mexicans.

or Quauhtlato, who ruled and governed the town, or else they elected him for Achcauhtli, which is what today we would call constable (or bumbailiff), and he carried a big stick (cane), and he arrested evildoers and put them in prison. In this manner the young men who were educated in the houses of the Telpuchcalli ascended by degrees, and there were a great many youths thus educated; each district (or city ward) had ten or fifteen such Telpuchcallis. The life they led there was very hard; they did not sleep all together, but rather apart from one another. In every Telpuchcalli the boy or youth who did not return to sleep there was punished; they ate their meals in their own homes. They all went out together for work wherever this work was, either to make clay, or to build an edifice, to work in the fields, dig ditches or canals. For this kind of work they went all together or split into groups (gangs); or they went in a body to carry fire-wood on their backs from the forests, for this was needed for the Cuicacalco and the Telpuchcalli. If they did any kind of menial work, they stopped a little before sunset, then went to their own homes to bathe and to paint their entire body with the exception of the face, with ink; after that they dressed themselves in their blankets and strings of beads; the courageous (valiant) men put on strings of sea-shells which are called chipolli, and also strings of gold (beads). Instead of combing their hair they made it stand on end in a wild fashion, to make themselves look ferocious, and painted certain lines on their faces with ink or white pyrite; in (the perforations of) the ears they wore turquoises, which are called xiuhnacochtli. On the head they wore white plumes in the shape of tufts; they dressed in maguey-blankets, which are called chalcaayatl, which were woven of twisted maguey-cord (thread), and were not closely knit, but loose and thin, like net, and they strew over them and fastened to the tissue (a certain number of) sea-shells. The superiors (principal teachers) wore the same kind of blankets, but the shells were of gold. The courageous (brave, gallant) men, who were called Quaquachicti, tied large balls of cotton-yarn to their hands. Every day at sunset it was the custom that the youths lighted the fire in the house of Cuicacalco, and then they all commenced to dance and move about in rhythmic evolutions until after midnight; for this they wore no other blankets but only the said chalcaayatl, so that they were almost naked. After the dancing all went to sleep in their respective Telpuchcalli of the different districts, and this was repeated nightly. Those who lived in concubinage went to sleep with their lady-friends.

CHAPTER VI.

About the Punishment They Gave to Those Who Were Intoxicated.

The youths who were brought up in the house of Telpuchcalli and had charge of the sweeping and cleaning of that house (as already stated), were not allowed to drink wine, with the sole exception of those who were old, and this very secretly, and even they drank little and did not become intoxicated in public. If a youth was found drunk in public or if he was found with the wine, or else they saw him fallen on the street (in that condition), or he was met singing and accompanied by other drunkards, such a youth, if he was a mazevalli (that is, of plebeian birth) was punished by beating him to death, or else they killed him with a bludgeon (garrote) before all of them (all the young men) in order to set an example and frighten them about getting intoxicated; if the culprit was of noble birth they killed him with a garrote in secret. These young men had their lady-friends, each one having two or three; one they kept in their own home, the others remained with their own families, and whoever of these youths wished to leave his respective Telpuchcalli and abandon the conversation among (or association with) the young men, paid their teachers ten or twelve large blankets called quachtli, if he had wealth (was wealthy). If the teachers consented, the young man could at once leave that house and get married, and he was then called Tlapaliuhcati, which means: he is not any longer a bachelor but is married. The one who was well bred and liked the customs of the bachelors would never leave the Telpuchcalli of his own free will, even if he was of the correct age; he would only leave it upon orders from the king or chief. The former youths (the married ones) were not elected to become senators to rule a town or village, they only could become subaltern officials such as Tlatlucateca, Tlatlacuihcalco and Achcacauhti, because they did not lead a good life, living, as they did, in concubinage, and because they dared to use frivolous words and vulgarisms and talked with haughtiness and daring.

CHAPTER VII.

About the Lords and Prominent and Mighty People Who Offered Their Sons to the House Called Calmecac, and About Customs Taught There.

Lords, chieftains or old men[1] offered their sons to the house which was called Calmecac; it was their intention that they should be educated there in order to become ministers (priests) of the idols. They said that

[1]This expression of "old men" possibly refers rather to "wise and learned men" among the Aztecs.

in the house of the Calmecac they learned good customs (habits), received instruction and exercises to fit them for a hard and chaste life; that there was no shamelessness nor reprehension (blame) or affront of any kind in the customs of the ministers of the idols who were reared in the said house. Any lord or principal leader or wealthy man owning large property, whenever he offered his son to the house of the Calmecac, ordered and disposed a very good repast to be prepared, to which he invited the priests and ministers of the idols who were called Tlamacazque and Quaquacuilti, and old practicians who were in charge of the district. After the feast in the house of the father of the boy, the old men made a speech to the priests and ministers of the idols who educated the boys, as follows:

"Gentlemen, priests and ministers of our gods, you have taken the trouble to come here to our home, and our lord almighty brought you. We make it known unto you that it pleased the lord to favour us by giving us a child, like a jewel or a precious plume. We hope to deserve that this boy may be reared and live, and as it is a male child, it is not suitable for us to assign to him woman's duties, and thus keep him in the home. Therefore we give him to you as your son, and we recommend him to you now at this moment. We offer him to the lord Quetzalcoatl, or by another name Tilpotonqui, that he may enter the house of the Calmecac, which is a house of penance and tears, where the nobles are reared. For it is the place where the treasures of god are deserved (attained) through prayer and by doing penance with tears and sighs, and entreating god to be merciful and favor them with his treasures. Thus from now on we offer him to you so that when he reaches the required age he may enter and live in the house of our lord, where the nobles are brought up and educated, and that this our son be in charge of the sweeping and cleaning of the house of our lord. We therefore humbly entreat you to receive and take him as your (own) son, that he may enter and live with the other ministers of our gods in that house, where by day and by night all the exercises of penance are held, such as crawling on knees and elbows, praying, entreating, weeping and sighing before our lord!"

The priests and ministers of the idols replied to the parents of the boy in the following way (manner):

"We have heard (listened to) your address, although we are unworthy to hear it, stating that you wish that your beloved son, your precious stone or rich plume, enter and live in the house of the Calmecac. It is not to us that this entreaty should be made; you must make it to the lord Quetzalcoatl, or by another name (called) Tilpotonqui, in whose name we heard it. To him it is that you must speak; he knows what it will be his pleasure to do with your precious stone and rich plume and with you, his parents. We, the unworthy servants, await with uncertain (dubious wavering), hope what it may be. For certain, we do not know anything positive, that is to say, this or that will be done with your son. We hope in our almighty lord to dispose as to what it will be his pleasure to do with this youth."

They then took the boy and carried him to the house of the Calmecac, and the boy's parents took papers, incense and belts with them, as well as a few gold bead-strings and rich plumes and precious stones, to place before the statue of Quetzalcoatl, which stood in the Calmecac. Upon reaching it, they all at once played their musical instruments and painted the boy's body and face with ink and put certain wooden beads, called tlacopatli on him (around his neck); if he was the son of poor people they used loose cotton strings; they pierced his ears to extract blood, which they offered before the statue of Quetzalcoatl. If he (the boy) was still small, his parents took him back home, and if he was the son of the chief or a principal, they at once took off the beads made of tlacopatli and left them in the house or Calmecac, because they said they did this for the reason that the spirit of the boy had entered the beads of tlacopatli, and this same spirit would perform the humble services of penance for the little boy. When he had reached the necessary age to go and live and remain in the Calmecac, they went to leave him in the care of the priests and ministers of the idols, who were to bring him up and teach him all the customs practiced (observed) in that house.

CHAPTER VIII.

About the Customs Observed in the House Called Calmecac, Where the Priests and Ministers Were Educated Since Childhood.

The first custom (or rule) was that all those ministers of the idols who were called Tlamacazque were to sleep in the house of the Calmecac. The second rule was that they all swept and cleaned that house at four o'clock in the morning. The third one was that the already bigger boys had to go out to look for and gather maguey-points (thorns); the fourth rule was for still older boys to bring in fire-wood on their backs from the forest; this wood was needed for the fires which were lighted every night; and when any construction work in clay was to be done, be it building walls, ditches, watering canals, or field work, they all went to work together at daybreak, only those who had to watch the house and those who had to carry the food to the workers, remaining; no one ever lagged behind, and they all worked with great discipline and good order. The fifth rule was to stop work somewhat early; they then went at once to their monastery to be in charge of the services of their gods and to perform penance exercises and, first of all, to bathe. At sunset they began to get all the necessary things ready, then, at eleven o'clock at night, they went on their way, each one alone by himself, carrying the points of maguey, a shell on which to play a tune on the road, an incensory of clay, a pouch or bag in which to carry the incense, torches (or candle-wood) and the points of maguey. Thus each one went out naked to deposit the maguey thorns at his particular place of devotion, and those who wanted to do very severe penance went far towards the forests, mountains and rivers. The older boys would go as far as half a league (from the monastery) to a determined place; there they would deposit the points of maguey, inserting them in a ball made of hay, and then would return, each one alone, playing on his shell. The sixth rule was that the ministers of the idols never slept two together covered with one blanket, but apart, everyone by himself. The seventh rule was that the meals that were consumed there had to be prepared in the house of the Calmecac, because they had a communal income which they spent in food, and if to anyone food was brought from his home, they all shared it. The eighth rule was that every midnight all had to get up to pray, and he who did not awake and rise was punished by pricking him with points of maguey leaves in the ears, the chest, thighs and legs, in short, sticking maguey thorns into his whole body in presence of all the ministers of the idols, so that he might take warning. The ninth rule was that no one should be overbearing, or offend one another, nor should anyone be disobedient to the order and customs they observed, and if at one time or another one of them appeared intoxicated, or should live in concubinage or commit some criminal act, they killed him outright, executed him with garrote, roasted him alive, or shot arrows at him. If anyone committed a venial sin they pierced his ears and sides with maguey thorns or awl. The tenth rule was that the boys were to be punished by piercing their ears or by whipping them with nettles. The eleventh rule demanded that all the ministers of the idols were to bathe in a fountain (tank) at midnight. The twelfth rule ordained that when there was a fasting day they all fasted, the youngest as well as the oldest ones, and were not allowed to eat until noon; and when it was one of the fasts called atamalqualo, they fasted with bread and water; others fasted by not eating all day until midnight, and again the following day fasted until the subsequent midnight. Still others ate only once at noon and at night, never tasted a thing, not even water, because they believed that they broke their fast by tasting anything, even by drinking water. The thirteenth rule was to teach the boys to speak well, to bow and courtesy, and anyone (of the boys) who did not speak correctly or did not bow to whomever he met, or remained seated, they pricked with the points of maguey leaves. The fourteenth rule was to teach (the boys) all the verses of the songs to sing, which they called divine songs; these verses were written in their books by signs; furthermore, they taught them Indian astrology, and the interpretations of dreams and the counting of years. The fifteenth rule was that the ministers of the idols had to make their vow to live chastely without ever knowing a woman carnally (sensually); to eat abstemiously; not to tell lies, and to live devoutly in fear of god. Herewith we finish with the rules and customs observed by the ministers of the idols and we leave out other customs (observances) which will be told elsewhere.

CHAPTER IX.

About the Election of the High-Priests, Who Were Always Two in Number, One Called Teoteztlamacazqui, and the Other Tlalocatlamazqui, and That They Always Elected the Most Perfect Ones from Among Those Who Lived in the Temple.

The one who was perfect in the performance of all the customs, exercises and learning (wisdom) observed by the ministers of the idols, was elected highest pontiff; he was elected by the king or chief and all the principals (foremost men), and they called him Quetzalcoatl. There were two high priests, one being called Teoteztlamacazqui, the other Tlaloctlamacazqui. The one called Quetzalcoatl, Teotectlamacazqui, served the god Vitzilopuchtli; the other, Tlaloctlamacazqui, served the god Tlalocantecutli, who was the god of rain. These two pontiffs were equal in standing and honor, even if they should be of very low birth and of very lowly and poor parents; the only reason why they were elected to be the high pontiffs was their having faithfully complied with and followed all the customs, rules, exercises and teachings (doctrines) observed by the ministers of the idols in the convent (monastery) of the Calmecac. And for this reason, by the election which was held, one of them was called Quetzalcoatl, or the other name of Teoteztlamacazqui, while the other one was Tlaloctlamacazqui, and in the election no attention was paid to lineage, but rather to the customs, exercises, learning and good (clean) living; (meaning) whether they led this life unalterably (steadfastly); kept all the rules, observed by the priests of the idols. He who was virtuous, humble and peace-loving, considerate and discreet (judicious), not light, but serious and rigorous, zealous in observing the rules; loving and compassionate, tender-hearted (merciful), and a friend of all, devout and in fear of god, was the one elected to this highest honor. The degrees he had to pass in order to attain this highest position were as follows: First, he became a Tlamacazto, which corresponds to accolyte; then he became Tlamacazqui, which is deacon. The third degree was Tlanamacac, that is to say, priest. From among these priests the best were elected as high pontiffs, who were called Quequetzalcoa, which means successors of Quetzalcoatl. The life led by the ministers of the idols was hard; the education of the boys was divided into two distinct classes, the one in the house of Calmecac, and the other in that of Telpuchcalli.

BOOK IV.

About Judicial Astrology or Art of Divining Which These Mexicans Used in Order to Know Which Days Were Lucky and Which Were Unlucky; About the Fate of Those Who Were Born on Days Attributed to the Marks or Signs Given Below. It Appears Rather a Matter of Necromancy Than of Astrology.

Chapter I.

About the First Sign, Called Cecipactli, and of the Good Luck of Those Who Were Born Under It, Men as Well as Women, Provided They Did Not Lose It Through Their Own Negligence or Laziness.

Here begins the description of the signs for each day, or rather the cycle of thirteen days they counted for each sign. Their week had thirteen days; their year formed a circle of two hundred and sixty days, after which they began at the first sign, or beginning. The first sign is called Cipactli, which means the sword-fish, a large fish which lives in the sea, and this (sign) is the beginning of the cycle of signs they had. They counted every day until they had a round of the two hundred and sixty; now begins the count of the days, allowing thirteen days to each sign, and this is called the year of the signs. The first day of the thirteen is the day of the first sign, which is called Cipactli. The second is of another character, called Acatl, which means cane; the third is another sign called Calli, which means house; the fourth is the sign called Cuetzpalin, which means small lizard. The fifth day is another sign called Coatl, meaning snake; the sixth day is the sign of Miquiztli, which means death; the seventh is Mazatl, which means deer; the eighth day is another sign called Tochtli, which is rabbit. The ninth is another sign called Atl, which means water; the tenth day is under the sign of Uzomatli, which is female monkey; the eleventh day is another sign called Itzcuintli, which means dog; the twelfth day is under the sign of Malinali, which means hay (or twisting or wreathing). The thirteenth day is another sign called Acatl, meaning cane.[1]

These thirteen days they believed were the lucky ones, and those born on any one of these days, if he was the son of a prominent man (principal or chieftain) would become a chief (lord) or a senator, and would be wealthy; and if he was son of common people or of poor parents, he would become courageous and honorable (honest) and esteemed by all, and would (always) have enough to eat. If the newly born on any one of these thirteen days was a girl, she would become or be wealthy and would have everything that was necessary in her house to spend on food and drink, to celebrate feasts (invite guests) to dance and celebrate in her home, and to give food and drink to the poor, the old, to orphans

[1]This is the same as the sign for the second day.

who have nothing to live on; that everything she did, the work to earn her living, would prosper, and she would not lose a thing of her own labor; she would be clever to sell all kinds of merchandise and earn as much as she could.

They believed, however, that notwithstanding the child's birth under a lucky sign, if it did not do penance, did not chastise itself, did not accept the penalties imposed, nor the zealous advice given him, or was ill-bred, did not go on the straight path, such a child or youth would lose whatever he had (originally) deserved on account of the lucky sign under which he was born. He would lower himself and become obfuscated, and if he lived in concubinage he would lose the good luck he used to have, and thus become poor, without food or drink. He would have nothing but hard labor all his life because he had brought ill luck upon himself through his roguery, being disobedient, overbearing and careless, and not finding contentment anywhere, hence he would always be poor and unlucky, everybody despising him and belittling him; no one would want him for friend, he always would have to walk (be left) alone, nobody would like him, everywhere he would be hated; all would curse him, and he would be detestable to all. They would look at him askance for being a public sinner, cursed by all for being disobedient and having gone astray and not obeying to what had been ordered or advised him, and for not using good breeding (manners).

The parents of a child born under a lucky sign would say, "our child is very lucky and has a good sign called Cipactli." They at once baptized it and gave it the name of the sign, calling (naming) it Cipac, or some other name of the lucky signs. Or, if they thought it best, they would wait with the baptism till another day of luckier omen within the period (of thirteen days) of the same sign.

If the child was a boy they made for its baptism a small shield with four tiny arrows and tied to the latter the navel (or umbilical cord?) and gave all this to the soldiers to carry it to a battlefield where they (the soldiers) buried it. If the newly born was a girl, when they baptized her they put into the glazed tub all the implements of woman, with which they spin and weave, because the life of a woman is to be reared in the home and live and remain in it. In this case they buried the navel close to the hearth (or home).

This astrology or necromancy was obtained and originated from a woman whose name was Oxomoco, and from a man called Alpactonal,[1] and the teachers of this astrology or necromancy who counted these signs, which were called Tonalpouhque, painted the woman Oxomoco and the man Cipactonal and placed them in the middle (center) of the

[1]Both these names are given in original; Alpactonal and Cipactonal.

books where all the signs of every day were written down (depicted), because they said that these two were the lords of this astrology or necromancy, as the principal astrologers, for they had invented it and made (had made) the count of all the signs.

Chapter II.

About the Second Sign (the second cycle of thirteen days) Called Ocelotl, and About the Bad Luck of All Those Who Were Born under This Sign, Men as Well as Women, if They Did Not Improve Their Fate by Their Own Intelligence. The Greater Part of These Born Under This Sign Were Slaves

The second sign is called Ocelotl, which means tiger, and it also ruled over a cycle of thirteen days. They believed it to be an unlucky sign throughout the thirteen days it ruled. Ocotl led the first house or day. The second day (of this cycle of Ocelotl) was Cuauhtli, which means eagle; the third was Cozquacauhque, which is another large bird by this name; the fourth was Olin, which means movement (motion). The fifth day was the sign called Tecpatl, which is flint; the sixth Quiavitl, which means rain; the seventh was Xuchitl, or flower; the eighth Cipactli or sword-fish; the ninth had the sign of Checatl, which means wind; the tenth, Calli, meaning house. The eleventh day had the sign of Cuetzpalli, which is lizard; the twelfth Coatl, that is, snake, and the thirteenth day had the sign of Miquiztli, which means death.

Anyone born under these signs, beit a noble or a plebeian, was believed to be made captive of war (sooner or later), and he was supposed to be unlucky or vicious in everything and very fond of women; that even if he should be a brave man, in the end he would sell himself as slave, and that he did this just because he was born under such an unlucky sign. He could improve his fate by the adroitness and cunning he displayed in not sleeping much, also by fasting, doing penance, stabbing himself to draw blood from the body; furthermore, by sweeping the house where he was reared and lighting the fire or, upon awakening, to go at once to earn a living, thinking of what he would have to spend later on if he should fall ill, or with which to support his children. His ill luck would also vanish if he was wary (cautious) in his barter of merchandise, and if he was intelligent and docile (obedient), suffering the punishments (chastisements) or injustice without taking vengeance.

The same they said of the girl born under this sign; she would be unlucky; if she was the daughter of a chieftain (or prominent man) she would become an adulteress and would die with her head crushed between two stones or she would live in extreme poverty and suffering, needy and hard; she would not be well married because they said she was born under an unlucky sign, which was called Ocelotl.

The fourth house of this sign was called Olin. This was said to be a sign of the sun and was greatly esteemed by the lords because they considered it as their (own) sign, and in its honor they killed quail and lighted fires and burned incense before the statue of the sun and dressed it in a feather ornament (plumage) called cuetzaltonamelutl; at noon they killed captives in its honor. The child born on this day had indifferent luck, it might be good or bad; if it was a boy it would grow to be a courageous man who was to capture enemies or would die in war because he was born under this sign, so they said. All born on this day did penance, children, men and women, and pierced their ears to draw blood in honor of the sun; they said (believed) that this pleased that heavenly body. The seventh house of this sign was called Xuchitl, which they also said was an indifferent sign which might be lucky or unlucky. It was especially honored by the painters, who made a statue of it and placed offerings before it. It was also honored (venerated) by the women embroiderers (or lace-workers); they all fasted eighty, forty or (only) twenty days previous to the festival of the sign of Xuchitl, for the reason that they begged of it to grant them and favor them with success, the men in their painting, the women in their handicraft such as embroidering well, or weaving nicely. They lighted fires and burnt incense and killed quail before the statue, and as soon as their fasting was over they bathed in order to celebrate the festival of the said sign of Chicomaxuchitl. They believed, however, that this sign was also unlucky; that if any woman embroiderer (or lace-maker) broke her fast, it would happen, and she deserved it, that she would become a bad public woman. They said, moreover, that these needle women (today embroiderers) were almost all sick of the body for the reason that they inherited (derived) the origin of their handiwork from the goddess Xuchiquezatl, who cheated them, and this same goddess inflicted them with mange (itch), buboes, and other contagious diseases. The woman who did her penance, which she was obliged to do and thus deserved to be called a woman of good reputation and honesty, would get well married.

It was furthermore believed that anyone born under the said sign of Xuchitl would be skillful (expert) in all the mechanic arts if he was diligent and well brought up, for if he was not that, nor intelligent, he neither deserved good luck (fortune) or success, but rather hard luck (misfortunes) and shame.

The ninth house of this sign, Acatl, was unfortunate; anyone born on that day would be unlucky; his life would be like wind, which carries everything before it; he wishes to become something worthwhile, and instead always becomes less so; he wants to prosper and gets more deteriorated (decayed) all the time; he tries to take up some trade, but never gains anything. Even if he is a brave man or a soldier, no one thinks of him, everyone despises him, and nothing that he attempts to do is successful, and he is unable to carry out successfully whatever he tackles.

Chapter III.

About the Third Sign Called Cemacatl, and About the Good Luck Those Born under It Had, Men as Well as Women, if They Did Not Lose It by Thier Own Carelessness (negligence).

The third sign is called Cemacatl, which ruled another thirteen days (the third cycle). This sign (Cemacatl) ruled the first day of the thirteen; the second day was under the sign of Tochtli; the third, under Atl; the fourth had Itzcuintli; the fifth, Ozomatli; the sixth, Malinali; the seventh, Acatl; the eighth, Ocelotl; the ninth, Quauhtli; the tenth, Cozcaquachtli; the eleventh, Olin; the twelfth, Tecpatl, and the thirteenth day was under the sign of Quiyahuitl. Of all these thirteen days they believed some were of good fortune and others quite the contrary, as appears by their description. They said that if the one born under the above-mentioned sign was the son of a chief (leader or prominent man), he would also be noble or become a leader; he would have plenty to eat and to drink, and to give clothes to other men, jewels and wearing apparel to women; if the one born under this sign was the son of a man of low standing at that time, he would, so they believed, be very lucky and would deserve to become a warrior and would excel all the others by his manners; he would become (or be) a man of great seriousness (or sobriety of behavior), never a coward nor pusillanimous (faint-hearted).

If a girl was born under this sign, no matter whether she was the daughter of nobles or plebeians, her fate was the same; that is, she would be very lucky, vigorous and brave, and she would not cause sorrow to her parents. They, moreover, said that anyone born under this sign of Cemacatl was timorous, of little courage and pusillanimous, for whenever they (any one of these) heard thunder, or saw flashes of lightning, they could not watch them without great fear and got easily frightened, and it might at one time or another happen that one of these was killed by lightning, even though it did not rain, nor was it cloudy; or else when bathing he might get drowned, and aquatic animals would tear out his eyes and nails. They believed that to be born under the sign of Cemacatl, which is deer, meant that they were as timorous as deer and even more so; and as parents knew the sign under which a child (of theirs) was born, if it was this one, they did not even take great care of the child, for they knew it would anyway come to harm.

They also said that under this same sign the goddesses who were called Cioateten descended to earth, so they prepared a festival for them, offered gifts and sacrifices, and adorned their statues with papers.

Chapter IV.

About the Second House of This Sign Called Umetochtli, under Which the Drunkards Were Born.

The second house or day of this sign (Cemacatl) was called Umetochtli. They said (believed) that anyone born under this sign would become a drunkard, be inclined to drink wine, and he would not look for anything else in life but wine, even upon waking in the morning he would drink it, and only crave it in order to get intoxicated; thus he would be drunk daily; he would even drink it before breakfast; and at dawn at once he would go to the homes of the tavern-keepers, begging them to give him a drink, for gracious' sake. All these cannot rest (calm down) without drinking, and drink does not harm them and it does not even nauseate them to drink the dregs with dead flies and straw and what not in them, even this they drink, and if they do not have the wherewith to buy wine they try to trade it for their blanket, or the belt they wear. It is for this that later in life they become poor, because they cannot stop drinking nor can they forget it; not even a day can they pass without being intoxicated; they totter along, falling down and getting full of dust, and reddish (in the face), all disheveled, unkempt and very filthy; they will not wash their face, although by falling they hurt themselves, injuring the face or the nose or else legs and knees, even breaking hands or feet, etc. They do not care, although they may be covered with bruises and wounds from falls, provided they can get drunk; nothing else matters. Their hands tremble and when they speak they do not even know what they say, for they speak like drunkards and utter ignominious and injurious words, scolding and defaming (libeling) others, giving howls and shouts, praising themselves as courageous men. They will dance and sing aloud, despising everybody, whereas they are the ones who have nothing; they are apt to throw stones and whatever else they find within reach, disturbing and hindering everyone on the street from passing. They impoverish their children, frighten and scare them; they cannot go to sleep quickly, but walk around incessantly until they are exhausted. A drunkard will not think (or remember) of what is needed in his house, to light the fire with or all the other necessities, he only thinks of getting drunk, therefore his house is very dirty, filled with filth, dust or mire;

there is no one to sweep it and light the fire; his house remains dark with poverty (is poverty-stricken); he does not sleep there but rather in the houses of others, and he has no thought of anything else but the tavern. And, if he cannot obtain wine and cannot drink, he is afflicted and sad (morose), and wanders from one place to another looking for wine; upon finding it and entering a house where a few are drinking wine, he is overjoyed and his heart is at peace. He sits down with the other drunkards, restful now and gay, and forgets to leave the place. If he is invited to go and drink wine at someone's house he at once gets up and readily runs there, for by now he has lost all shame; he is shameless and fears no one. That is the reason why everybody despises him for being a publicly dishonoured man; people have nothing but loathing and hatred for him, no one desires his conversation because he bewilders his friends and drives away those who had gathered, and they leave him alone because he is the enemy of his friends.

It is their belief that because a drunkard is born under the (abovementioned) sign, he cannot be cured, and they are all hopeless about it, saying that he will either get drowned in some brook or lagune, fall off a cliff or else some highwaymen will steal from him everything he owns, and leave him naked. Furthermore, a drunkard is apt to commit many shamelsss acts, such as to sleep with married women, abscond another's property, jump walls, abuse and force young women to make merry with him. All this he does because he is drunk and not in his right mind. In the morning early when he gets up, his face is swollen and deformed and he does not look like a human being; he is always shouting. And if one is not very fond of drinking wine or not accustomed to do so, he becomes ill if he gets drunk, his eyes hurt and also his head, and he does not get up (from bed), but rather sleeps all day; he doesn't want to eat, to see food makes him nauseated, and he recovers with difficulty.

Chapter V.

About Different Kinds of Drunkards.

Moreover, they said that the wine was called Centzontotochtli, which means four hundred rabbits, because there are many and diverse ways of intoxication. On account of the sign under which they were born, wine is not detrimental or contrary to some drunkards; when they are drunk they at once fall asleep or else become crestfallen (morose), remain seated and secluded; they never commit nor say any nonsense. Others begin to weep bitterly, to sob, and tears begin to roll down their cheeks like threads of water. Still others begin to sing but do not want to speak nor listen to jests, and only find consolation in song. Other drunkards do not sing, but begin to chatter and to speak to themselves or to defame others or say shameless things about a few people they know, or they begin to praise themselves, saying they are the most honoured leaders while they despise all the rest; they are apt to utter injurious things about them, lifting and shaking their heads, claiming to be wealthy and chiding others for being poor; they hold themselves in high esteem, proud and rebellious in speech. They speak strongly and harshly, moving their legs and kicking. Yet when they are in their senses they are mute, afraid of everybody; they are timorous, always excusing themselves, saying, "I was drunk, I do not know what I may have said." They (always) suspect evil and make themselves suspicious and of an evil disposition; they understand everything to the contrary and raise false testimony of their wives, saying they are bad, etc. If someone talks they (or rather he) thinks they whisper about him, if someone laughs, he fears they make fun of him, and thus he quarrels with everybody, without reason, without knowing why. The cause of all this is that the wine has befuddled him.

If it is a woman who is drunk, she falls seated on the floor, her legs drawn up (knees under chin), or sometimes stretched out on the ground, and if she is very drunk she may dishevel her hair and appear all unkempt, and she goes to sleep this way, with the hair all untidy, etc.

All these various kinds of drunkards above mentioned would say that that drunkenness (probably should be drink) was his rabbit[1] or the cause of his intoxication, or the demon that possessed him. If a drunken man fell off a cliff, or killed himself in some other way, they said he became rabbit-like or was possessed by a rabbit, and because they have so many kinds of wine they call it Centzontotochtli, or four-hundred rabbits, as much as to say that such wine causes an infinite variety of drunkards and intoxication.

Moreover, they said that when the sign of Umetochtli began (appeared), they prepared a festival to the principal one of the gods of wine, who is called Izquitecatl. They also celebrated a festival in honor of all the other gods of wine; they erected a statue in the temple and made offerings there, danced and played their flutes and before this statue they placed a stone tub or trough, called umetochtecomatl, which they filled with wine. Into this tub canes were inserted through which those who came to attend the festival could drink. Those who drank wine from that stone trough were old men and old women, courageous warriors and men of war, for they thought that they might some day be made captives by their enemies, or, being on the battlefield, make captives themselves among their adversaries and so they now were enjoying themselves (while they could), drinking wine; this wine was never exhausted, because the

[1]Not at all clear.

tavern-keepers every little while refilled the trough. Those who arrived at the tianquiztli where the statue of the god Izquitecatl stood, as well as all those who bored (tapped) the maguey plants again, to make new wine which was called vitztli, brought the wine in jugs which were emptied into a trough of stone.[1] The tavern-keepers did this not only during the festival but daily, for such was their custom.

Chapter VI.

About the Other Houses (days) of This Sign, Some of Them Lucky, Some Unlucky, and Some Indifferent.

The third house (day) of this sign is called Cistl; they said it was indifferent, of good or bad luck, because whoever was born under it (on that day) would be wealthy and prosperous; he would have great wealth which he would earn by his work, but he would lose it quickly; it would melt like water or disappear like things the river carries off, and he would never retain anything, neither would he have rest nor contentment, for everything would crumble in his hands and all his work would be in vain.

The fourth house of this sign is Navictzcuintli; they believed that anyone born on this day would be wealthy and fortunate, and would have enough to eat and to drink, even if he did not work a single day. He would not even know wherefrom that which he ate, came. In any kind of home he would be happy all day and would even earn a little to support his children. And thus, being even careless, he obtains what he needs for eating, although he does not know wherefrom it comes and how it happens this way. Even if he works little he earns something for his support. Moreover, they said, if one born under this sign dedicated himself to raise little dogs, any amount he wished to raise would multiply and give him pleasure, and he would become wealthy through them because they were in great demand, hence, clear profit; it was said that he, the man, and they, the dogs, were of the same sign, and as fast as he sold some, others were born to him, and with their sale he obtained clothes, called quachtli (bartering dogs for clothes?). He got rich from the price of the dogs, because in ancient times it was customary to eat dogs and to sell them (for that purpose) in the market-place. Those who raised them brought many dogs to market, and the customers at their own pleasure and satisfaction would select the one they liked best, be it one of either short or long hair. Some of these dogs as they were being sold in the market would bark, while others panted; they muzzled them to prevent them from biting. To kill them they made a hole in the earth (soil)

[1]This probably means that there was another similar feast celebrated at the "Tianquiztli"—which means the market-place.

and put the dog's head into it, thus choking him; the owner of the dog, that is, the one who had it for sale, tied a loose cotton string around its neck and petted it, stroking its back, saying: "Wait for me over there, because you have to pass me (carry me) across the nine rivers of hell." Sometimes thieves killed these dogs after stealing them, by tying them with lazoes.[1]

The fifth house (day) of this sign is called Macuilocomatli. They said that anyone born on this day (under this sign) was inclined to pleasure, enjoyment and buffoonery (vulgarism), and that with his witticism and rascality he would give contentment and gaiety to those who heard him, and that he would make jokes and jests without thinking (much) about them. They said this was a natural gift with them on account of the sign under which they were born.

The sixth house (day) of this sign is called Chicucenmalinalli. This, they said, was an unlucky house (day) because those born on it would always live in poverty and suffering, their children would invariably die in infancy, and it was impossible to raise even one of them; in fact, these unfortunates would finally sink so low that they would sell themselves as slaves.

The seventh house (day) of this sign is called Chicomeacatl, which they said was very lucky because anyone born under this sign would be wealthy; that anything they undertook would have a prosperous outlook.

The eighth house (day) is called Chicueyocelutl, the ninth, Echiconaviquiavil; the tenth, Matlactli-olin; the eleventh, Matlactli ocecozcacuauhtli; and the twelfth, Matlactli-omometecpatl. All these houses (days) were said to be unlucky, and those born on them would never have good luck.

The thirteenth house (day) of this sign they called Matlactliomayquavitl; this day they said was lucky, for it was the last house (day) of all of the same sign, and they believed that those born on this day, men as well as women, would be rich and well provided with all necessaries; they would enjoy a long life and reach old age on account of being born on the last day (in the last house) of the sign.

[1]Clavigero asserts that these dogs were small, castrated dogs, and their meat was very tasty and replaced lamb. It seems that the Spaniards from the very first liked this dog meat so well that they soon exhausted the supply.

Chapter VII.

About the Fourth Sign Called Cexuchitl. Men Born Under This Sign Were Gay, They Said, Ingenious, Inclined to Music, to Pleasure and Great Wits; the Women, Great Fancy Workers (Embroidery and Lace or Drawnwork), Liberal with Their Body if They Were Not Careful. They Said This Sign Was Indifferent, for Good or Evil.

The fourth sign is called Cexuchitl and had thirteen houses (days) of which Cexuchitl was the first; the second was Umecipactli; the third, Yexecatl; the fourth, Navicalli; the fifth, Manuilli-cuezpalli; the sixth, Chicucencoatl; the seventh, Chicomemiquiztli; the eighth, Chicuimacatl; the ninth, Chiconauitochtli; the tenth, Matlactliatl; the eleventh, Matlactli oceitzcuintli; the twelfth, Matlactli omoneazomatli; the thirteenth, Matlactliomey-malinali. All these houses (days) were considered unlucky. They also considered them as indifferent, and believed that anyone born in them or in anyone of them, be it a noble or a common man, would be a joker, a buffoon and a wit. His good luck (humor rather) would be his consolation, and he would derive great satisfaction from these things, provided he was devoted to his sign; but if he did not value (esteem) it (his sign), no matter whether he was a singer (or one who composed their songs) or an official of any kind; or, even in case he had enough to eat but would be overbearing, disdainful, of a bad disposition and presumptuous, or if he did not look up to his elders nor his equals, nor old people or young men, but would speak to all of them with pride or contempt, such a one was considered as crazy by all the people, for they would say that god had forsaken him and through his own fault he had lost his good luck and therefore he was despised by everyone. And he, upon seeing himself despised by all, would contract some disease through sorrow and anguish (dismay); he would become impoverished, lonely, forgotten by everybody, and would long for death in order to leave this life, since no one looked at him, or came to visit him, not even remembered him. Thus everything he owned vanished like salt in water and he finally would die in misery with hardly enough to bury him; all this happened to him for not being devout, for not being grateful to his sign, and for following his evil inclinations, rending and destroying himself through his vices. This, they said, occurred to anyone who had lost the good luck of his sign.

If a woman was born under the sign called Cexuchitl, they said she would be a good fancy-worker (either embroidery or lace or drawnwork), but in order to enjoy this talent it was necessary to be a devotee to her sign and to do penance during all the days it ruled. If she failed to do this, her sign would be against her; she would live in poverty, forsaken by all. Also she would be vicious with her body, selling herself publicly and this, they said, she would do by virtue of the sign under which she was born, and which was equally for good or evil.

It was also said that under this sign the lords danced to show their devotion, as many days as they wished. Whenever they were to begin this solemn act they put two sticks with flowers in the door of the palace, which was the signal that they were to dance, in honor of the sign, for several days. The songs that were to be sung on this occasion the king (or chief) ordained that they be done by one called Ceuxtecoiutl or Tlaoancamextecaiutl, or (also) Vexotzincaiutl, or else by one called Anaoacaiutl or any one of the others, here mentioned. Those who had charge of the (safe)- keeping of the plumages that were used for dancing took out all they had so that the king might choose the one he wanted and, according to that one, devices and plumes were given to the principal leaders, men of valour and soldiers, and all the other warriors. They also gave the singers their blankets and belts, and to all such who played the teponaztli and beat the drum, to those who whistled, and to all other dancers and singers. They also gave food to everyone present, consisting of diverse kinds of tamales and moles as explained here.[1] When they were tired of dancing, the flowered staves which had been placed in the door were taken off to signify that the dance was over, and they burned them after which everybody stopped dancing in the palace. However, the principal leaders (prominent people) could continue the dance in their own homes.

Chapter VIII.

About the Fifth Sign Called Ceacatl (which was) Unlucky. They Believed That All Those Born under This Sign, Especially If Their Birth Happened in the Ninth House (on the Ninth Day) Called Chiconavicipactli, They Would Become Great Murmurers (Backbiters), Gossips, Tale-bearers, Hypocrites, Etc. It Was Said to be the Sign of Quetzalcoatl, and the Nobles Made Many Offerings and Sacrifices in Honor of This God.

The fifth sign is called Ceacatl. This is said to be entirely unlucky. The second house (day) is called Umeocelotl; the third, Eyaquauhtli; the fourth, Navicozcacuauhtli; the fifth, Nacuilliolin; the sixth, Chicuacentecpatl. All these houses (days) were said to be unlucky because they belonged to Quetzalcoatl, god of the winds. As soon as this sign began to rule, the lords and principal leaders (prominent men) made offerings

[1]This may be so in the original; here no further explanation is given.

in the house of this god, that is to say, the Calmecac where his statue stood, which they adorned in (during) those days with rich ornaments, placing flowers, smoke-sticks, incense, food and drink before it. They said that this was the sign of Quetzalcoatl, and that all those who were born under it, whether they were nobles or common people, would always live in misfortune, because everything they owned would be carried off by the wind.

The same was said of the women born under this sign. In order to remedy the evil in store for those born on such days, the wizards who were learned (versed) in this art ordered that they be baptized in the seventh house (on the seventh day) of this sign, which was called Chiconquiavitl, for in this manner (way) the evil of the day of their birth was avoided and they recovered good luck, for it was believed that this house (day) of Chiconquiavitl was a house (day) of mercy. This was the reason why they at once baptized all those who were born on that day. Of the same kind, they said, was the following house (day), called Chicuyxuchitl. Chicuyxuchitl was the eighth house or day, and those born at that time were well fixed, they said, hence they baptized them on the same day. The ninth house or day was called Chiconavicipactli, and was supposed to be unlucky, so that all those born then were going to be of a bad disposition and mischievous (prankish), fond of quarrels, of sowing discord, and of being liars; that they were unable of keeping any secret, and remained poor and unfortunate for all the days of their lives, etc.

The tenth house (day) of this sign is Matlactliecatl, which was said to be lucky, together with the other three following, namely, Matlactliocecalli, Matlactliomomecuetzpali, and Matlactliomeicoatl. It was said that all those born in these four days would be honest and wealthy, respected by everyone, no matter whether they were women or men.

Chapter IX.

About the Sixth Sign of Cemiquiztli and Its Good Fortune. They Said This Sign Belonged to (was of) Tezcatlipuca, in Whose Homage, Particularly, They Made Many Offerings and Sacrifices. They Also Celebrated a Festival with Presents to Their Slaves, Each Slave-owner to His Own and in His Own Home.

The sixth sign is called Cemiquiztli. It is said that this sign was in part good and in part bad; they said this was the sign of Tezcatlipuca. The lords (chiefs) and principal leaders (prominent men) were greatly devoted to this sign and made offerings in its honor, sprinkling blood of quails and celebrating other ceremonies, each one in his private oratory, as well as in the oratories of the Calpules. They did all this because it was the sign of Tezcatlipuca, whom they considered as the creator of the universe. All prayed with devotion on this day, asking that he concede them some special grace; not only the lords (chiefs or rulers), but also the warriors, wealthy merchants, and all those who knew that at that time the sign of Tezcatlipuca reigned. They believed that he was severe because this god was wont to take away the wealth he had given to anyone, as a punishment for ingratitude or haughtiness (presumption), which this particular person might have indulged in on account of his wealth. He, Tezcatlipuca, would then grant these riches to those who had humbly begged him for them, and had sighed and wept for their possession. For this reason they entreated him everywhere, saying that his gifts did not remain with one person, but that he shifted them from one to the other.

Others said that those born under this sign were lucky and honorable, if they were devoted to his sign and if they did penance in its honor; if they gave (the newly born child) its name at once and invited the children, fed them and let them know the name of the one who had been born, and divulged (shouted) it through the streets in a loud voice. If the newly-born was a male-child they gave it the name of miquiz, or yautl, also ceyautl, or necociautl, chicoyautl, or yaumavitl. One of the above names was given; all of them were names of Tezcatlipuca. They believed that no one could hate such a child nor wish death upon it, and if anyone should do so, this one would meet death during this sign.

Nobody dared scold or ill-treat his slaves. On the eve of the ruling of this sign they took off their shackles or collars by which they were tied (fastened) and soaped their heads, bathed them, and treated them as if they were very beloved sons of Titlacaoan. All owners of slaves gave very strict (peremptory) orders to all (the members) of their household not to quarrel with or distress any of their slaves. It was their belief that if in those days anyone should scold a slave, he would bring upon himself poverty, sickness and misfortune, and would deserve to become a slave himself, because he had ill-treated "the very beloved son of Tezcatlipuca." It was said that Tezcatlipuca was not a faithful friend to anyone because he looked for opportunities to take away what he had given them, and for this reason some, after losing their wealth, in their despair would scold Tezcatlipuca, exclaiming, "You are a fiend, Tezcatlipuca, for you have deceived and cheated me!" The same thing was said if one of their slaves or a captive escaped, or if it so happened that a slave became free and prosperous while he who had been an owner of slaves, became enslaved. They blamed it all on Tezcatlipuca because, so they said, he had favored the slave who had entreated him, and had punished the master for being hard (cruel) towards his slaves. He who from servitude rose to prosperity made (prepared) banquets and presented his guests with blankets and this, they said, was his due for being born under this sign.

Chapter X.

About the Other Attributes of This Sign, Some of Which Were Unlucky While Others Brought Good Fortune.

The second house (day) of this sign was called Umemacatl, which, they said, was unlucky and calamitous. The one born in this house (on this day) had no luck at all; he was timorous, cowardly and scary, anything would scare him and make him tremble.

The third house of this sign was called Eytochtli. This house or day was very lucky, and anyone born on this day had (always) enough to eat, with very little work (effort) on his part. They said it was like the rabbits who feed on the things the fields produce, and do not have to work to gain their food and drink, but find it ready for them anywhere, so all those born under this sign become rich without great effort.

The fourth house (day) of this sign was called Naviatl, which, they said, was unfortunate, and those born under it would forever live in poverty, affliction and sadness (sorrow); they never had either contentment or joy, and if they succeeded in earning anything, it all went through their fingers like water.

The fifth day was called Macuilli, which they believed to be unlucky, because it was the house (day) of the god of hell, who was called Mictlantecutli. The sixth house or day was called Chicuacen or Comatli, and it was also considered to be unlucky. Those born on the above-mentioned days were not baptized until the seventh day (house), called Chicomemalinali. They said that the seventh house or day of all the different signs was lucky on account of its being the number seven. On this day they baptized them and gave them their names.

The eighth house was called Chicuiacatl, and the ninth Chiconaviocelutl. Both these houses (days) were said to be unlucky, and those born on them would be wretched (unlucky or miserable), and they therefore were not baptized until the following day (house), which was called Matlatliquauhtli. This house or day (the tenth) was said to remedy (mend) the misfortune of the past days, provided one did a great deal of penance to improve (one's condition). They said the tenth house or day was very lucky, and all born on that day would be lucky in matters of war and bravery, for they were daring and gallant. The eleventh house (day) was called Matlactlcocecozcaquauhtli which, it was said, was lucky, and those born on that day would live long and die of old age. The twelfth day or house was called Matlactliumoneolin and the thirteenth Matlactliomeytecpatl; all these were said to be of good fortune in all of the signs, and those born in such days were quite lucky. From the tenth day on, all born then would be very lucky and fortunate.

Chapter XI.

About the Seventh Sign, Called Cequiavitl, and Its Wretched Luck (misfortune); It Was Said That Those Born under This Sign Became Necromancers, Wizards and Swindlers. It Is to be Noted That the Word (expression) Tlacateculotl Means Really Necromancer or Wizard, and Is Improperly Used for Devil. Almost All the Attributes of This Sign Were of Evil Augury; the Tenth and Thirteenth Houses (days), However, Were, as Generally in All the Signs, of Good Luck.

The seventh sign, called Cequiavitl, was said to be of ill luck, for under this sign the goddesses, called Cioateten, came down to earth and inflicted many diseases on boys and girls, so that the parents ordered their children with great severity not to leave the house, saying to them: "Do not go out, for if you do you will meet the goddesses Cioateten, who are at present coming down to earth." The parents, fathers as well as mothers, feared that their children might contract paralysis (palsy) if they went out anywhere. During the rule of this sign offerings were made to the goddesses in the oratories, and there were many such oratories in many parts (of the city); at each one they covered the statues of these goddesses with papers.

Under the rule of this sign they also killed all those who had been imprisoned for some criminal act which deserved death. They likewise killed slaves to insure longevity for their master. Children born under this sign were not baptized at once, baptism being deferred till the third house (day) called Eyecpactli; this day, they believed, would improve their fortune, and all those born on this day would become necromancers, swindlers, or wizards; they could transmute themselves into animals; they knew words by means of which they bewitched women or turned hearts (to do) what they wished, and other acts of witchcraft. For such purposes they were hired by those who wished to do evil to their enemies or desired their death.

These enchantments (or incantations) were performed at night, and for four consecutive nights, these being chosen under some unlucky sign. They went, at night, to the home of those they intended to harm, caught them right there as quickly as possible, for if they whom the wizards intended to harm were at all brave (courageous) they waylaid them and (if catching them) tore the hair off the top of their heads so that they died from it upon reaching home. Some said that this would be prevented by borrowing something from the house they had gone to (to exercise their witchcraft), like water, fire, or a cup. The one who had torn off the hair, if he was told, would watch all that (following) day to prevent anyone from taking things out of his home, either borrowed or in any other way, so that the necromancer was bound to die.

All these (necromancers or wizards) never had any pleasure nor contentment; they were always poorly clad and of ill humour; they had no friends, nor did they ever visit anybody or were loved by anyone.

If the child born under this sign happened to be a girl, this latter even being the daughter of prominent people, would never marry, nor ever become prosperous; she would always wander from house to house, and everyone said that the sign under which she was born was to blame for her wretched condition.

Chapter XII.

About the Rest of the Houses (days) of This Sign, Some of Which Were Indifferent and Others Absolutely Bad.

The fourth house (day) of this sign was called Nauhecatl, which was said to be indifferent, for good luck or bad. During this sign they killed the adulterers at night and threw them into the water at dawn; they also killed the captives for the life of the king, that he might live many years, as has been told under the other sign of Cequiavitl. During this sign, Nauhecatl, the necromancers performed their witchcraft and incantations, thus this sign was greatly dreaded, and they put or inserted thistles in their windows for the reason that it was supposed that this would put the sorcerers to flight. The wealthy merchants who are called acxoteca, honored this sign and in its homage took out all the precious things they had in their houses, such as precious stones, rich jewels, all the plumes of varied colours, wrought animal hides, cocoa products, (fresh-water)-tortoise-shells for tecomates (bowls), and all the jewelry they had; all this was placed in proper order in the court of their calpules (church of their district) on a rich blanket. At the same time they burned incense and offered blood of quails.

They said that they did all this in honour of the said sign, the act seeming to mean that they were heating all the above-mentioned articles in the sun. After they had attended to their devotions, all the merchants and their guests commenced to eat and drink, each one receiving his smoke-stick (cane) and flowers, and there was so much smoke that it was like fog. That night the merchants and the old men and women gathered in order to drink until they were intoxicated, and then each one bragged about the amount of money he had earned; about the countries he had visited, and the remote places he had reached. He would tell where he had roamed, the perils he had experienced in the lands of enemies. With such tales they would confront others who had not gone to such remote lands, and they would tell them that they (these others) had always remained close to the home-fires and therefore only knew the market place close to their home. Thus they would spend the whole night, chatting with one another and boasting, depreciating one another, while each one praised himself (his own prowess).

Chapter XIII.

About the Evil Omen (augury) They Predicted If Anyone Stumbled or Hurt His Feet or Fell Down in Those Days; Also About the Ill Luck (bad fortune) of All Those Born on the Eighth Day (in the eighth house) Called Chicuymiquiztli, Where Much Is Said about the Unlucky Ones, Men and Women.

Moreover, it was said that the fourth house (day) of this sign was of evil (omen), and everybody was careful not to quarrel or to stumble. They were afraid if anyone stumbled, or fell, or quarreled, because they said such would from then on continuously happen to him, that sign prognosticating it. They believed, however, that those born under this sign would be prosperous, lucky and brave, although they did not baptize them at once, but deferred this ceremony to the seventh house of another sign called Chicomecoatl. Then, so the masters of this art (of prognostication) said, the good fortune of the one born under the previous sign (of the fourth day) would improve; he would become more prosperous even, because Chicomecoatl was the sign of every livelihood (all sustenance), very lucky, and, moreover, the seventh (in number), this number always being considered very lucky.

The fifth house (day) of this sign, called Macuillicalli, and the sixth, Chiquacencuetzpalim, were believed to be unlucky because these two days (or signs) were of the gods Macualxuchitl and Mictlantecutli. Anyone born in these two houses (days), be it a man or woman, would be unfortunate, of bad disposition, unlucky, seditious (mischievous), quarrelsome, and an agitator (rioter), and of whom they said upon reproving him: "He is a rascal and of evil disposition, because he was born under such a sign." The masters of the art (of prognostication) said that the bad luck of the one born on these days could be improved if he was not baptized under this sign but rather in the seventh house, called

Chicomecoatl. It would also improve if he did proper penance, because the number seven, of all signs, was lucky and prosperous, as they always attributed it to Chicomecoatl. The eighth house (day) was called Chicuymiquiztli, which was of bad luck; so was the ninth, Chiconavimacatl, for they believed that all the ninth days (houses) were unlucky, and whoever was born on that date was disliked and detested by everybody, and they had all the evil inclinations and vices there are. In order to improve such misfortune, the wizards ordained that they should be baptized under the subsequent sign (house or day) called Matlactlitochtli, because from that sign he would derive some good luck, since all the tenth houses (days) brought some good at least.

Chapter XIV.

About the Four Lucky Houses (days) of This Sign, Which Were Considered as Bearers of Happiness, Also about the Good Disposition of Those Who Were Born on These Days.

The tenth house (day) of this sign is called Matlactlitochtli; they believed it to be very lucky and happy. All those born under this sign or on this day, men or women, would be prosperous and wealthy, because as stated above, the tenth day of all the signs was fortunate. However, they did not baptize them at once but deferred till the last day of this sign, which they called Matlactle omeiozomatli, for the reason that the good luck of the one born on the said tenth day would then even improve. They believed that all the last houses (days) of all the signs were fortunate. The eleventh day of this sign was called Matlactliocoatl; the twelfth Matlactliomomeitzcuintli, and the thirteenth Matlactliomeyocomatli. All these four houses (days) were fortunate and lucky. Those born on any one of these days would be very prosperous, honest, and well liked by all; they would be wealthy, liberal, brave, capable, intelligent and forcible to persuade others and incite them even to tears. If the child born in any one of these houses (on these days) was a girl, they believed likewise that she would be prosperous, wealthy, etc. If anyone born under these signs or days was unfortunate, they said it was his own fault because he had no devotion for his sign, nor did he do the necessary penance in its homage. The reason for the belief that the four last days (houses) of every sign were very fortunate was because these four houses (days) were attributed to four (latter) gods, the first of whom was Tlavizcalpantecutli, the second Citlallicue, the third Tonatiuh, and the fourth Tonacatecutli. That is why the astrologers said that all those born on the above days would be lucky or prosperous, and live long if they all were baptized on the last one of these days.

Chapter XV.

About the Eighth Sign Called Cemalinalli and Its Adverse Luck. The Second House (day) of This Sign Was Generally Considered Lucky, and from the Ninth On, That Is to Say, Ten, Eleven, Twelve and Thirteen Were Thought to be Fortunate.

The eighth sign is called Cemalinalli, which was considered unlucky and was as awe-inspiring as a wild beast. Those born under it had bad luck; they would be prosperous for a while, but soon would lose all their wealth. Many children would be born to them, but they would lose them just as quickly; after the first one's death the others would follow, so that the anxiety and sorrow over the demise of their children would be far greater than the joy they experienced in having them, and that was the reason for their saying that this sign was like a wild beast. Those born in this first house (on this first day) were not baptized until the third, which was called Yeyocelutl, for, according to the astrologers, the third houses (days) of all the signs were fortunate.

The second house or day of this sign was Umacatl, which was said to be very lucky, since it belonged to Tezcatlipuca, because it had the face painted in the same manner as the god's image; some people took the image of Umacatl to their homes and kept it there for two hundred days, to show their devotion, taking it home with them on the day of Umacatl.

The fourth house was called Naviquauhtli, and the fifth Maculli-cozcaquatli, the sixth Chicuacenolin; all these houses (days) were said to be unhappy and those born on these days were to be unlucky, of bad disposition, seditious and detested by everybody. The astrologers in such cases also believed that it was best not to baptize them until the following day, which was Chicometecpate, so that from that they might derive a somewhat improved fate, because all the seventh days were good, since they were ascribed to the goddess Chicomecoatl, who is the goddess of sustenance.

The eighth house of this sign is called Chicuzquituitl and the ninth Chicanavixuchitl, both of which are, as all the eighth and ninth days, always unfortunate, and those born on such days would become thieves, highway robbers, and adulterers.

About the tenth house (day), Matlactlicipactli, they said it was very lucky, and that those born on this day were, as a rule, prosperous and light-hearted in this world, men or women alike. The same was true of the following houses (days): Matlactliceccatl, Matlactliomomecalli and Matlactliomeycuetzpali, of which they said that the tenth house (day) exercised its good influence over them, and that, as a matter of fact, under all the signs the tenth day improves or makes the remaining three lucky.

Chapter XVI.

About the Ninth Sign Called Cecoatl. Its Good Luck, Provided Those Born Under It Do Not Lose It Through Negligence. Merchants Held This Sign as Very Favorable for Their Trade.

The ninth sign was called Cecoatl. They said it was quite lucky and prosperous, and those born in its first house (on its first day) were to be happy and prosperous. They considered it to be lucky, or propitious to attain wealth, also that it would bring good luck in warfare. In the case of women (born that day) they would be honest and become wealthy, but, as already stated, if they were careless about doing penance, and if they did not accept the advice of their elders, they would lose their good fortune, would be lazy and sleepy, unfortunate, miserable, and altogether unhappy. To merchants this sign was very favorable, and they were great devotees of it. They always awaited this sign to come around again before leaving home to go on their long journeys to remote provinces to make their barters and purchase their merchandise. Before departing, and with their packs already made, they would invite old merchants and their relatives to a feast, telling them to which provinces they intended to go and what they meant to do there, and this was done principally to gain fame among merchants, and to let them know that while they were absent from home they were earning their livelihood in different provinces.

Chapter XVII.

About the Speech or Allocution Which One of the Old Merchants Addressed to the One Who Was About to Leave in Order to Go Bartering in Strange and Far-away Provinces (especially) When It Was His First Journey.

After the meal was over and when the one who had offered the feast was ready to leave for the journey, more particularly when this was his first trip, every one of the old merchants made a speech, encouraging him to face all the hardships he would meet. The first (to speak) would address him as follows: "My son, you have assembled here all of us who are your fathers (elders) and merchants like yourself, and it is therefore well that we should advise you and play the part of elders that must encourage and advise you now. I, the first one to speak, wish to give you my opinion as I would to a son. You are about to depart for far-away lands and to leave your village, relatives and friends, your comfort and rest, to travel over long roads, mountains, valleys and deserts. Exert yourself, my son, for there is no reason why you should end your life here (at home), nor that you should die without having accomplished something worthwhile to gain honor as we, your elders, wish you to gain and, therefore, though with tears, we pray that thus it may be, and that your efforts may crown our good wishes. Your forebears in these hardships have toiled on the road and have attained the honors accorded them as valiant men attain them in war. Through these toils they obtained from our lord the wealth they left. You must be courageous to stand the hardships that await you, such as hunger, thirst, fatigue and lack of provisions; you will have to eat your bread hard, your tamales mouldy, and drink turbid and bad-tasting water; you will reach swollen rivers with freshets that make a frightful noise and cannot be waded, and which therefore will detain you for several days, suffering from hunger and thirst. Beware, my son, not to lose heart on account of all this, nor forsake the work already started, for by so doing you would offend us who are your elders. Over the same road went our forebears, risking their lives a good many times, but being courageous, they became honored and wealthy. Finally, my poor young man, if our lord grants you some luck, it is best for you to first suffer hardships and poverty, almost intolerable fatigues such as are experienced by all who wander from town to town, from village to village. These fatigues are excessive with copious sweats, great colds or extreme heat. You will travel covered with dust, the mecapal[1] will press hard around your head, you will wipe perspiration from your brow with both hands; your hardships may increase when you are compelled to sleep in a corner or behind the door of strange houses, where you will stand with bowed head and ashamed; there will be times when from hunger your stomach will feel as if glued to your ribs, when you will travel from village to village reasoning in your mind, worried and doubtful about the sale of your ware which perchance may not sell at all, so that it will cause you sadness and tears. Ere you amass any wealth or good luck, you will have to suffer to the utmost, you will be distraught and down-hearted and, moreover, you will many times find yourself forced to spend the night in some deep ravine, a cave, or under a protruding rock or close to a large boulder. We know not whether, perchance, our lord might kill you at any one of these places, and thus, perhaps, you may never again come back to your country; who knows? It is wisest that you should travel along these roads, devoutly invoking god and doing penance, and at the same time meekly attending your elders by humble service, such as carrying water for them, sweeping, etc. Beware not to get discouraged; beware not to turn your back to what you commenced

[1]Mecapal is the leather band with ropes attached and worn across the forehead by porters to carry loads. It is still used throughout Mexico.

to do; and beware not to think of all the (good) things you left behind; continue and persevere on your way and accept its hardships. Perchance it may please our lord to let you return wealthy so that we, your elders, and your relatives may see you again; mind and accept the advice we, who are your parents, give you herewith as a good support that will encourage and inspire you to go on. Very beloved son, be of good cheer and go with god; we your elders give you godspeed that you may carry your deal through, leaving behind your relatives, etc."

In this manner the old merchants encouraged and harangued the young men who departed for the first time in the company of other dealers; they told them of the suffering and difficulties they would face, in villages as well as in deserts, while they were engaged in their trade.

Chapter XVIII.

About the Speech the Same Older Merchants Addressed to Those Who Had on Other Occasions Gone on Trading Expeditions to Far-away Lands.

Even to young men who were about to leave on trading expeditions having had experience on roads and their hardships from previous trips, those old merchants gave a short allocution at the time of departure, speaking about as follows: "Young man here before me, you are not a child any more, for you have already had experience on the road and know its hardships and the dangers this trade presents when traveling from village to village, bartering. You have been over the roads and have visited the towns you now intend to see again. We do not know what may happen nor do we know whether we shall see you again. Perchance your life may come to an end in one of those towns or on one of those trips, but always remember, wheresoever this might happen to you, the counsels and the tears of your elders are with you, since we love you like a son and we hope to deserve the pleasure of your safe return, of seeing you here once more in good health and prosperity. Thus, my son, take heart and go with god, for well we know that on your journey you will find hardships, because the road in itself is rough and troublesome. Beware not to leave behind those who accompany you, do not forsake them nor stray away from them, but rather consider them and treat them like younger brothers; teach them what to do upon reaching the stopping places, make them gather grass and make seats that the older ones of your company might rest. We have already admonished all such of your companions who have not yet gone to trade and hence do not know the roads; you all are now to travel together, and it is therefore not necessary to talk any longer. We have told you in few words, my son, what your duty will be; go therefore, in peace, exert yourself in attending to your business."

After the old men had thus spoken, the youth answered briefly as follows: "I consider it a great favor, honoured sirs, that you should have granted me this consolation, for I am not worthy of it. You have acted like parents, as if I had been engendered by you, in thus giving me your advice. You have uttered golden words from the treasure in your hearts more precious than gold, precious stones or rich plumes, and as such I receive and honour them. Never shall I forget such beautiful expressions; in my heart and soul shall I enclose them forever. What I now entreat you is that in my absence you will see to it that there is always someone in my house to sweep and "light the fire," for there remains my father, or mother, or sister, or my aunt (as the case might be), and I entreat you to so favour and protect them that no one may injure them. And if it should please our lord to end my life on this journey, I beg the same favour of you, and with this (assurance) I depart comforted."

After this speech all those present began to weep, men as well as women, taking leave from the one who departed, and after his departure they all commenced to eat and drink.

Chapter XIX.

About the Ceremonies Celebrated by Those Who Stayed Behind (at home) for the Absent One, If He Lived, and Those They Held upon Being Informed That He Had Died.

After the trader had taken leave of his relatives or those of his own household, father, mother, wife, or children, all these left behind only washed their heads or faces every eighty days, which meant that they did penance for their son, husband or father who was absent. And, although they washed their bodies during this period, they never washed their heads until the return of the absent one. If by chance he died over there (on the road), it was the old merchants who were informed first, and they went to announce his death at his house, that they might mourn him and celebrate his exequies, as was their custom. In such a case all the relatives of the deceased went to visit and to console his widow or parents and, four days after the funeral rites, they washed their faces and soaped their heads (hair), saying that this took away the sadness (sorrow). If, perchance, that merchant was killed by his enemies, as soon as those of his household were informed of this, they made his statue (effigy) of torches (candlewood) tied together and adorned it with the apparel they would have put on the body had he died at home. This consisted mostly of different kinds of paper with which they were wont to adorn the bodies of their dead. They offered other papers before this statue and carried it to the Calpulco (community house), that is, the church of his district, and there it remained one day, and they mourned him there. At midnight they carried the statue into the court of the temple and burned it in a certain place of that court which they called Quauhcicalco or Tezompantitlan. If the trader had died on the road from some disease or other, they made a similar statue, but they burnt it in the court of his own house at sunset.

(NOTE: Here follows the second part of the description of the sign Cecoatl in Chapter 16, page 309 of the original, which appears to have been interrupted merely to tell about these two episodes of godspeed and leave-taking of a young merchant. Thus we continue the narrative of the above mentioned sign:)

They also said that this sign, Cecoatl, was favourable to soldiers leaving for war. They said that those born under that sign would have good luck; they would become wealthy, provided they did penance in reverence of their sign. Should they neglect this duty, however, they would lose their good fortune. They did not christen the child born under this sign, forthwith, but waited till the third day which was called the house of Cimacatl, when they gave the newly born its name, for, as we have stated before, all the third houses (days) of the various signs are considered lucky. The second day of this sign is called Umemiquiztl, which they said was unlucky; the third is called Cimacatl and, for reasons above mentioned, was considered very lucky. The fourth house (day) was Navitoctli and meant hard luck, since, as a matter of fact, the fourth days of all the signs bore that reputation. The fifth day was Macuilliailli, also unlucky, as were all the fifth days, and it was believed that those born on the fourth and fifth days were of an evil (or bad) disposition. However, it was believed that if children born on these fifth days were carefully brought up, they would become even tempered and prosperous, due to the fact that they listened to the advice of their elders.

CHAPTER XX.

ABOUT THE REST OF THE DAYS OF THIS SIGN.

The sixth day, called Chicuacemitzacuintli, was said to be unlucky, as are the sixth days of all the signs. People born on those days become murmurers, tale-bearers, wary, deceitful and hypocrites altogether, and the astrologers said, moreover, that such people would be always sickly and would either die early in life or else if they survived would be affiicted with various diseases. To avoid that all those who were born on these days were christened on the next day, called Chicomecocomatli, for they believed that this would somewhat improve the evil omen of their birthday. And, moreover, if they did penance for love of the sign (Chicomeocomatli), ill luck would turn into good fortune. Thus the seventh day, Chicomeocomatl, is a good luck day, and those born then would be mirthful, witty, rather vulgar in their jokes, playing the buffoon, friends with everybody. In the case of a woman, she would be wealthy, thrifty, and a good trader who never lost her wealth.

The eighth day was Chicueymalinalli, which was said to be of evil boding, being unlucky. The ninth day, Chiconoviacatl, was likewise unfortunate because on that day the goddess "Venus" ruled, whom they called Tlaculteoutl. All those born on this day were forever unlucky, and leading a miserable life. The tenth day was Matlactliocelutl and was, as already stated, a very lucky day, for it was always ruled by Tezcatlipuca, their principal god, and people born on this day would, if they lived, always be wealthy. They either christened them on the same day or else waited till the thirteenth day, which improved their good fortune. The eleventh day was Matlactliocequauhtli, and the twelfth Matlactli omome cozcaquauhtli, both of which were said to be partly good and partly evil, so that children born on these two days were christened on the thirteenth day, Matlactliomeiolin, to improve their fate, as above stated.

Chapter XXI.

About the Tenth Sign, Called Cetecpatl, and Its Happiness (luck). They Said That This Was the Sign of Vitzilopuchtli, God of War, and Also of Camaxtle. On the Day This Sign Began (set in) They Celebrated a Great Festival in Honor of Vitzilopuchtli Which Lasted All the Thirteen Days, Which Were All Lucky, So They Said.

The tenth sign was called Cetecpatl, and they attributed its first day to Vitzilopuchtli, god of war, and to Camaxtle, who was the god of the provinces of Vexotzinco and Tlaxcala. On this day they prepared in his (the god's) temple, called Tlacateco, a great, solemn ceremony before his statue. They took out all the ornaments and spread them in front of the said statue and incensed it (the statue). These ornaments were made of rich plumes, one being called Quetzalquemitl, which means cape made of green quetzal (trogon), very resplendent, another one they called Xiuhtotoquemitl, that is, cape of resplendent blue feathers; another was the Tozquemitl, cape of shining yellow feathers, still another was the Vitzitzilquemitl or cape made of the shining feathers of Cintzones, or humming birds. There were many other capes not quite as precious and beautiful as those just mentioned. All of them were spread on rich (fine) blankets in the sun, before the image, for an entire day, and they called this sunning or warming it (the image), offering at the same time rich food of many kinds. This was done by the prominent people and by the masses. After a short while these food offerings were removed, and the priests of the temple divided them among themselves, and all such who were priests of Vitzilopuchtli ate them while gathered there. The king or chief offered a great many and different kinds of flowers, arranged (grouped) in many ways and in varied designs before the statue of Vitzilopuchtli; all these flowers had delicate perfume (scent) and filled that temple with it, and with the beauty of their varied colors. They also offered smoke sticks (aromatic canes) tied in bundles of twenty, and they were lighted and smoked there in front of the image, and the fumes formed a sort of fog or smoke screen. The owners of maguey plantations and the innkeepers who sold pulque, cut and hollowed (the heart) of the maguey plants to obtain the honey under this sign.[1] They believed that by cutting it at this time it would not ooze out, and thus be partly lost; the first of this liquid was offered to Vitzilopuchtli as first-fruit offering, and this new pulque was called Vitztli. They poured it into certain cups called acatecomatl, over which were laid hollow canes used for drinking by the old men who had obtained (through age) permission to drink uctli (pulque).

They said that all those born under this sign, if men, would be valiant, honest and wealthy; if women, would always have plenty to eat, would be very vigorous (mannish), very well spoken, discreet, etc. The second day of this sign was Yincquiavitl; the third, Cixuchitl; the fourth, Navicipactli; the fifth, Macuilliecatl; the sixth, Chiquacencalli; the seventh, Chicomecuezpalin; the eighth, Chicueicoatl; the ninth, Chiconavimiquiztli; the tenth, Matlactlimacatl; the eleventh, Matlactliocetocatli; the twelfth, Matlactliomomcatl; the thirteenth, Matlactliomeitzquiztli. All these days are said to be as lucky as the first one.

Chapter XXII.

About the Eleventh Sign, Called Ceocumatli, and Its Luck.

The eleventh sign, Ceocumatli, was said to be quite lucky. They also said that during this period the goddesses called Cioateteu, who injure children, came down upon the earth, and to prevent this they locked

[1]Today this operation is called gilding (copar el maguey) to obtain what is called the "agua miel" or honey, and they cut the beautiful stalk with its flowers, which rises in the center of the plant.

their children into the house, to prevent these goddesses from poisoning them or afflicting them with some disease or other. Whosoever suffered from some ache while this sign ruled was at once declared as beyond recovery by the doctors, male or female, saying that the patient could not possibly escape, because the goddesses had injured him. If any good-looking person fell ill during this period they said it was because the goddesses envied his beauty and had therefore taken it away from him. Male children born under this sign were said to be of good disposition, joyful and friends with everyone; moreover, they were said to be singers, dancers, or painters, or else they would learn some useful trade on account of being born under the above sign.

The second house (day) of this sign was called Umemalinalli and was considered to be unlucky. Those born on this day would have many children, but none of these would live; all would die early in life (childhood). The third day was Eyacatl; the fourth, Naviocelutl; the fifth, Macuilliquahtli; the sixth, Chicuacen cozcaquautli; the seventh, Chicomeollin; the eighth, Chicueyticpatl; the ninth, Chiconaviquiavitl; the tenth, Matlactlixuchitl; the eleventh, Matlactliocecipactli; the twelfth, Matlactliomomeccatl; the thirteenth, Matlactliomeycalli. All the days of this sign bear the characteristics of their numeral, as is generally the case, to wit: the third days are good; the fourth, fifth and sixth, bad; the seventh, good; the eighth and ninth, bad; and the eleventh, twelfth and thirteenth, again good. (The tenth day appears to have been overlooked, but to judge from previous reports, it is always a lucky day.)

Chapter XXIII.

About the Twelfth Sign, Called Cuetzpalin, and Its Fortune.

Cuetzpalin, the twelfth sign, signifies lizard, and it is said that those born under this sign are very strong, vigorous and healthy; that even falls do not injure them as they do not hurt the lizard, their birth-sign, even though it falls from great height, it does not resent it but scurries off. All such people (born under this sign) are said to be great workers and attain wealth easily. The days of this sign are, as far as their effect on man's fate is concerned, in accordance with their numerals as previously stated, and their nomenclature is as follows: the second day is Umecoatl; the third, Cimiquiztli; the fourth, Navimacatl; the fifth, Macuillitochtli; the sixth, Chiquacenate; the seventh, Chicomeitzcuintli; the eighth, Chicuiocumatli; the ninth, Chiconavimalinalli; the tenth, Matlactliacatl; the eleventh, Matlactlioceocelutl; the twelfth, Matlactliomomequauhtli; the thirteenth, Matlactliomicozcaquauhtli.

Chapter XXIV.

About the Thirteenth Sign, Called Ceollin.

The thirteenth sign, called Ceollin, was said to be indifferent, partly good and partly bad, and those born under this sign would be careful in doing penance. If their parents took pains in their education and brought them up endowed with good habits they would be very fortunate, but if they were not well educated they would always be unlucky, poor and miserable.

The second house (day) of this sign is Umetecpatl; the third, Cequiavitl; the fourth, Navixuchitl; the fifth, Macuillicipactli; the sixth, Chiquacenzecatl; the seventh, Chicomicalli; the eighth, Chicuyauzpalin; the ninth, Chiconavicoatl; the tenth, Matlactlimiquiztli; the eleventh, Matlactliocemacatl; the twelfth, Matlactliomometochtli; the thirteenth, Matlactliomeyatl.

Chapter XXV.

About the Fourteenth Sign, Called Ceitzcuintli, and Its Good Fortune.

They called the fourteenth sign Ceitzcuintli, and it was said to be very fortunate, because it was ruled by the god of the fire, Xiuhtecutli, and for this reason they exposed his image publicly in the temple, and they offered quail and other objects before it. The image itself was embellished with paper ornaments cut out by masters of this art who were (besides) the official paper cutters for this purpose. These papers were, moreover, enhanced by rich plumage and chalchivites. They also offered all manner of food to the image by throwing it (the food) into the fire. All the wealthy people and the merchants made these offerings to the fire in their homes and offered food and drink to their guests and neighbors, and then towards morning they burnt the offerings of paper and copal (incense). They said by doing all this they were feeding the fire. They beheaded quail, which were then left fluttering near the hearth, and after that they sprinkled pulque in the four corners. The poor people offered an incense called copalzalli on their own hearth, while the extremely poor offered a ground (pulverized) herb called yauhtli on the fireplaces of their huts.

They also said that chieftains who happened to be elected under this sign would be lucky in office. They at once offered a great festivity to the chiefs of the district, and this festival began on the fourth day of this sign, Naviacatl. All the invited guests came on this day to congratulate the lord or king, bringing him a present and making a very elegant and decorous speech in his honor. He (the lord or king) was seated on his throne, and all the principals (chiefs) were seated in their proper order (near him). As soon as the orator, speaking at the time, finished his speech (or address), another one arose at once and in behalf of the chief or king, made the response to the allocution of the first speaker. Whenever the newly elected chieftain prepared such a festival he gave a great number of blankets and richly ornamented belts to the chiefs who gathered around him, so much so that the latter left more loaded with what they received on such occasions than they had been upon arrival with their own gifts to the chieftain. The blankets presented by the latter were all made in his house, very beautifully woven or embroidered in many patterns, according to the status of the person to whom they were to be given. The guests also received so much food that they were loaded down with the remnants they took home with them.

Chapter XXVI.

How, While the Above Sign Ruled, the Lords (chieftains) Prepared Themselves for War against Their Enemies; Also, How at This Time They Sentenced All Such That Were in Prison for Some Big Crime, to Death.

As the festivities of installation of the newly elected chieftains in their new offices came to a close, the latter at once caused war to be proclaimed against their enemies, and this was the second (public) act by means of which they were to demonstrate the greatness of their dominion in war. To this end they at once chose the most valiant men and strongest warriors, and all those who considered themselves as such approached the chief in competition, for each one wished to be the one selected for such activity. This would not only afford them an opportunity to show themselves worthy of the honour and to give them a means of livelihood, but it also credited them with the desire to die in battle.

They also said that under this sign all those who had been imprisoned for some serious crime were sentenced to death, and that the innocent were at once liberated. They also would free all slaves unjustly held in servitude, and these latter would at once go to bathe in the spring of Chapultepec as a sign that they now were free men.

They held all those born under this sign as being very lucky; they would become wealthy, would own a large number of slaves, etc. Children born at this time were christened and given names on the fourth day, called Naviacatl, and they offered banquets on this day and invited the boys to witness the christening and the imposing of a name on the child. There was also a special ceremony held, under this sign, by all those who raised small dogs for a livelihood. It consisted in their dyeing the heads of these dogs with red ochre (Indian red).

The second day of this sign was called Umeocumatl; third, Eymalinalli; the fourth, Naviacotl; the fifth, Macuilliocelutl; the sixth, Chicuacenquauhtli; the seventh, Chicomecozcaquauhtli; the eighth, Chicuiolin; the ninth, Chiconavitecpatl; the tenth, Matlactliquiavitl; the eleventh, Matlactliocexuchitl; the twelfth, Matlactliomomecipactli; the thirteenth, Matlactliomeyecatl. All these days follow the usual rule of their numeral, as previously stated with regard to their good or bad luck.

Chapter XXVII.

About the Fifteenth Sign Called Cecalli and Its Highly Adverse Fortune.

Cecalli, the fifteenth sign, they said was unlucky and engendered nastiness and obscenity. During its rule the goddesses called Cioateteu descended upon earth and inflicted the ailments they were said to dispense, as stated elsewhere. All physicians and midwives were great devotees of this sign, and made sacrifices and offerings in its honour in their own homes.

People born under this sign were said to die an unnatural death, and all such people expected a tragic end; they were convinced that they would either die in war or would be taken prisoners, be knifed to death on the round challenging (duelling) stone or be burned alive, or else they might be strangled in the net, be thrown against a stone wall, have their entrails torn out by the navel, get killed by lance-thrusts in war, or be roasted in their bath. And if they were not destined to die in any one of the above-mentioned ways, perhaps they would commit adultery and thus get killed, together with the adulteress, by crushing the heads of both of them. And if this did not happen either, they would become slaves, that is, they themselves would sell their bodies and would consume their price in food and drink. Even if nothing of all this happened to them they would always lead a sad and discontented life; they would become thieves, highwaymen, robbers, violent snatchers or great gamblers, cheating and deceiving at games or lose all their possessions; they would even steal whatever their own parents owned, to gamble with. They never had clothes to cover themselves nor ornaments of any kind in their homes. Even if they should happen to make several war prisoners and thus would be appointed (or called) Tequioa, it all would take an evil turn in the end. They were unable to escape their adverse luck, even though they did penance from childhood on through their whole life.

Chapter XXVIII.

About the Bad Condition of Women Born under This Sign.

A woman born under this sign was likewise unfortunate; she was good for nothing; she could not spin nor weave; she was stupid, a smiling rustic, overbearing, vociferous and (they say) always eating Tzictli (called chicle today, i.e., the sap of the zapote chico, and even to this day chewed and cracked between the teeth by lewd women). She would be talkative, a tale-bearer, a defamer, and using bad language in torrents. She would be a jeerer (scoffer), an idler, lazy and a sleepy head. All these bad habits contributed to her infallible bad end; she was apt to sell herself as slave, but as she did not know a thing, neither grind corn nor bake bread or anything else, her master would be forced to sell her to the traders who buy slaves for food, and thus she would end on the sacrificial block of the idols.

In order to mend somewhat the evil influence of this sign upon those born under it, they baptized them on the third day, called Cicoatl, or on the seventh, Chicomeatl, both of which were good or lucky days. The second day was called Umecuezpali; the third, Cicoatl; the fourth, Navimiquiztli; the fifth, Macuillimacatl; the sixth, Chicuacentochtli; the seventh, Chicomeatl; the eighth, Chicuciitzcuintli; the ninth, Chicunaviocumatli; the tenth, Matlactlimalinali; the eleventh, Matlactliocea-catl; the twelfth, Matlactliomomeocelotl, and the thirteenth, Matlact-liomeyquauhtli.

Chapter XXIX.

About the Sixteenth Sign, Cozcaquauhtli,[1] and Its Fortune.

The sixteenth sign was called Cocozquauhtli (?), and was considered unlucky and (they said) that it was the sign of the aged. Those born under it were said to live long, were prosperous and lived joyously. Not all of them, however; only if the parents of those born under this sign could afford to invite their friends to a feast. They at once baptized the newly born under the sign of Cecozcaquauhtli (?) on its first day, but all such who could not spend money on a baptismal ceremony deferred it till the seventh day.

The second day was called Umecalli; the third, Citecpatl; the fourth, Naviquiavitl; the fifth, Macuillixuchitl; the sixth, Chicuacencipactli; the seventh, Chicomeacatl; the eighth, Chicuicali; the ninth, Chiconavi-cuezpali; the tenth, Matlactlicoatl; the eleventh, Matlactliocomiquiztli;

[1]There is no explanation as to the reason why there are three different names given to this sign, namely: Cozcaquauhtli, Cocozquauhtli, and Cecozcaquauhtli. Evidently they were all used.

the twelfth, Matlactlionememacatl; and the thirteenth, Matlactliomaytochtli, and they all represented the virtues (good or bad luck) of their respective number.

Chapter XXX.

About the Seventeenth Sign, Called Ceatl, and Its Wretched Luck (Fortune).

The seventeenth sign is Ceatl, and they said that this sign was indifferent (neutral), as it was ruled by the goddess Chalchiuhtliyicue. All those whose business or livelihood was derived from or connected with water made offerings and sacrificed in honour of this goddess in the temple, before her image. The reason for saying that this sign was neutral was that one or the other born under it had good luck, but most of them were unlucky and died an unnatural death. If they had some of this world's comforts they enjoyed them for only a short while, for, when least expected, they lost it all; their good luck had come to an end, and for this reason the refrain originated which says: "that in this world one day good and the other bad," and that those who are prosperous at one time will end in poverty, while those who have been poor during most of their life, before the end may attain some comfort. Children born under this sign were not christened at once, but either on the third, the seventh, the tenth, or one of the later days. The second day was called Umeitzcuintli; the third, Eyocumatli; the fourth, Navimalinalli; the fifth, Macuilliacatl; the sixth, Chicuacenocelutl; the seventh, Chicomequauhtli; the eighth, Chiqueicazquanhtli; the ninth, Chicunaviolin; the tenth, Matlactlitecpatl; the eleventh, Matlactliocequiavitl; the twelfth, Matlactliomonicxuchitl; the thirteenth, Matlactliomeicipactli.

Chapter XXXI.

About the Eighteenth Sign, Called Ceacatl, and Its Hopeless Fortune.

Of the eighteenth sign, Ceacatl, it was said that it was unlucky because it was ruled by Quetzalcoatl, who is the god of the winds and of the whirlwinds; that whoever was born under this sign, if of noble birth he would become a swindler and would (be able to) change into many shapes; he would be a necromancer, bewitching and malignant. He would know all sorts of witchcraft and enchantments, transmuting himself into different animal forms. If he was a commoner, a "macevalli" (today it is "mazehual"), he would also become a wizard and enchanter and a swindler of those they call Temacpalitotique, and in the case of a female she would be a witch they call Mometzpopinque. All these wizards (male and female) awaited a propitious sign to exercise their witchcraft, one of which was Chicunavitzcuintli, the other Chicunavimalinalli; moreover, the ninth days of all the signs were favorable to do their tricks, which are against all good luck. All those who belonged to this guild (of wizards) always were abject (morose or depressed) and poor, they had never enough to eat nor a house to live in, and supported themselves on what was given them by those who ordered some act of witchcraft (or spell on someone). When they lost their power of enchanters, and the time approached to end their evil life, someone would get hold of them (grasp them) and cut the hair off the crown of the head, and by so doing they lost the power of conjuring and they died.

The wizards, called Temacpalitotique, or by another name Tepupuxaquavique, when anxious to commit a robbery, first made the image of Cecoatl or of Quetzalcoatl; then, being about fifteen or twenty of them, they went together to the place they intended to rob, dancing, led by one who carried the image of Quetzalcoatl while another one carried the arm, from elbow to hand, of a woman who had died in her first childbirth. It was always the left arm, and they (these thieves) cut it off stealthily, and whenever they intended to commit an evil act, one of them carried it before them over one shoulder. Upon reaching the house they intended to rob and before entering it, in the courtyard, they first hit the soil with the arm of the dead woman, then, at the door itself, they hit the threshold with it. After doing this they said the owners and all those within the house would become drowsy or would faint, no one was able to speak or even move, they were all like dead bodies (or in a hypnotic trance?), although they could hear and see what was going on. Still others would be fast asleep and snoring, while the robbers lighted candles (this must mean firebrands, since they had no candles), and searched the house first for food, which they ate with great deliberation and ease, since no one prevented them nor spoke, all being stupefied and in a trance. After having eaten their fill, they went into the storeroom and gathered all the blankets, gold, silver, precious stones, plumes, and whatever else they could find, carried it all outside, made bundles of it, which they lifted on their backs, and left. Yet, before they left that place, it is said they committed many misdeeds in the house and outraged the women. Upon leaving they ran all the way to their own homes with what they had stolen and, moreover, they said that if any of them sat down by the roadside to rest, he could not rise again, and had to stay till morning, and then he was arrested with his loot, whereupon he denounced the others (his companions).

Chapter XXXII.

About the Tears and Lamentations of Those Whom the Necromancers Had Robbed; Also About Other Incidents of This Sign, Ceacatl.

After the thieves left, those in the house they had entered began to revive and to rise from where they had tumbled, and began to look through the house from living quarters to store-rooms, to examine trunks, boxes and cases, and when they found none of their possessions, they started to cry and to shout and to clap their hands in anguish. The women then began to shout aloud: "Quecannelocnenquenolocnen," which means, "Oh, how wretched (unlucky) we are!" They threw themselves on the ground and hit themselves with their own fists, pummeled their faces, saying: "All we had they have stolen!" They said many other things, too! These thieves are also called Tetzotzomme, because if they were caught they were at once stoned, and whatever they had stolen and carried to their houses was taken away from them.

The rest of the days of this sign can be said to be like those of other signs, as stated elsewhere. The second day was called Mavaumecalli; the third, Eycuetzpalli; the fourth, Navicoatl; the fifth, Macuillimiquiztli; the sixth, Chicuacenmacatl; the seventh, Chicometochtli; the eighth, Chicuiatl; the ninth, Chiconavitzcuintli; the tenth, Matlactliocumatli; the eleventh, Matlactliocemalinalli; the twelfth, Matlactliomomeacatl; the thirteenth, Matlactliomeyocelutl.

Chapter XXXIII.

About the Nineteenth Sign, Called Cequauhtli, and Its Adverse Luck.

Of the sign, Cequauhtli, they said that it was unlucky, and that while it ruled the goddesses Cioateteu came down upon earth, although not all of them, only the younger ones who were, however, the most terrible, because they did greater harm to children and young girls, whom they attacked, and they also made wry faces at them. It is for this reason that during this sign they adorned the oratories of these goddesses with reed-mace and flowers, and all those who had made a special vow to honour them covered their images with (cut) papers. On the day they kept this vow or promise they first offered the papers, spotted with ulli (gum), before the images; others who did not cover their images offered them food, drink, white, finely ground copal (incense). The food thus offered was (afterwards) taken and eaten by the priests of those oratories and after having eaten, each one drank the pulque (also offered) in his own home, and all by himself. They also gave it to the old men and women, and they paid visits to one another in their homes.

They said that if those born under this sign were males they would be valiant, audacious, bold, shameless, presumptuous, haughty, speaking in an arrogant and conceited manner, boasting of their elegant and courteous language; they would be vainglorious and idle flatterers, and in the end they would die in battle (war). If the child born at that time was a female, she would be impudent and wicked; her pastime would be to speak evil and shame everybody, and at the same time she would be bold, ready to strike with her fist and scratch other women's faces, imitate or mock everyone, and tear the blouses off their bodies.

Chapter XXXIV.

About the Superstition Practiced by the Women Who Went to Visit a Woman Recently Delivered and Other Rites Observed in Her Home.

We relate here the ceremonies observed by women when visiting a woman lately delivered. As soon as the news spread that some relative had given birth to a child, all her relations, neighbors and women friends went at once to visit her and to see the new-born baby. Before entering the house they rubbed their knees hard with ashes, and the same they did to their children if they brought them along; also all the joints of their bodies, for they said that by so doing they strengthened the joints and prevented their becoming loosened. Another superstition was to keep the fire burning continuously for four days in the house of the lately delivered woman. They took great care of this practice, and no one was allowed to take any of this fire out, for they believed that by so doing good luck was being carried away from the newly born baby.

Chapter XXXV.

About the Ceremonies Celebrated When the Child Was Christened and the Invitation Extended to the Children When Giving the Baby Its Name, as Well as About the Speech the Old Men Made upon This Occasion to the Child and Its Mother.

The christening was performed at sunrise, and they invited all the children for that time and gave them something to eat. If the baby was born under a propitious sign it was christened at once,[1] (according to Fray Agustin de Vetancurt, Teatro Mexicans, vol. 1, p. 462, the midwife performed the baptismal ceremony in the center of the courtyard) and if there was no opportunity for immediate christening they deferred it to the third, seventh or tenth day. This was usually done in order to provide the necessary things for the christening festivities. On that day the old men and women were eating and drinking, and then greeted the newly born and its mother with the following speech: "My grandchild! you came into the world where you will have to suffer many hardships and anxieties, for such are common down here upon earth. Perchance, you may live a long time and we shall (be allowed to) bring you up and enjoy you, because you are the image of your parents, you are the tender shoot and renewal of your grandparents and forebears, whom we knew when they lived in this world." After saying this and other similar words, they caressed the child, stroking its head as a sign of love, and then they turned to greet the mother by saying: "My daughter (or my lady), you have suffered travail in giving birth to your son (or daughter), who is lovely like a rich plumage or a precious stone. Up to now you were only one, you and your (unborn) son, but now you are two, distinct from one another; he will have to live his own life, and each one of you will have to face death. Perchance, we shall enjoy and raise your son for some time and we shall treasure him like a string of precious stones. Be courageous, my daughter, and take care of your health; beware not to fall ill of your own fault and take care of your little son; remember that ill-advised mothers kill their babies while sleeping or when nursing them if they do not remove them from the breast with care, for by taking them off brusquely, it has happened that the baby's palate becomes pierced and it dies. Beware that, since our lord had given it to us, we may not lose it through any fault of yours. But basta, it is unnecessary to mortify you with a longer speech."

[1]Fray Agustin de Vetancurt, Teatro Mexicans, Vol. 1, Chapter 8, p. 459g et seq. says as follows: ". . . the most usual way after the child was born was to give it two washings, the first one immediately after birth. The midwife, after she had cut and buried the umbilical cord, washed the newly born, recommending it to the goddess of the water, called Chalchihuitlcyene (alias Chalchihuitlatomac). After having washed the newly born she took water in the hollow of her right hand and blew it into the mouth, breast and head, with a prayer to their false gods, whom they believed to be sheer creators, namely, Ometauhtli and Omezihuitl. After this she (the midwife) handed the baby to the mother to nurse. Before the second washing, which was like a christening, on the fourth day after birth, the parents of the child called one of their wizard-astrologers and gave him the hour of the birth . . . ."

On the fourth day, or the day designated by the astrologer, a feast was prepared to suit the wealth of the father, and relatives, friends and children were invited, who all lighted numerous torches, and after sunrise they put a glazed earthenware tub with water in the middle of the court. The midwife brought the baby out, undressed it and bathed it as the first time, again blowing water into its mouth, breast and on the head, offering it to the gods; then raising it upwards, they offered it to the sun . . . ."

Chapter XXXVI.

About the Festivity Celebrated on Account of Christenings, the Order of Service, and the Hard Drinking Done on Such Occasions.

We continue the description of such baptismal feasts. On the day of the feast the guests gathered in the house of their host and were seated in their order; that is, each one had his place according to his rank. At once those who were in charge began to serve the food that had been selected for the occasion. With the plates they first put smoke-sticks (canes) in front of each of the guests, gave them flowers to hold in their hands, placed wreaths on their heads and garlands of roses around their necks. At once all the guests began to inhale the smoke of the canes and to smell the perfume of the flowers, then the servants entered with the food and served each one according to his appetite, placing it in front of him wherever he sat. The first order was a sort of willow baskets containing various kinds of bread, and next to these chiquihuites as many little square boxes (generally of paper), with different kinds of meat- or fish-stews. Before the guests began to eat the food placed before them, each one took a mouthful to throw into the fire (of the hearth) in honor of the god Tlaltecutli; after this they all ate. At the end of the dinner they gave the left-overs to their own servants as also the little paper boxes and the baskets, called chiquivites (or chiquihuites). Then came those who served the cocoa or chocolate, placing before each guest a xicara (bowl) of it, and at the same time they gave each a little stick, which they call aquavitl. The left-over cocoa was also given to their servants (by the guests).

After having satiated themselves with the cocoa, they remained a little while seated, resting, but some, displeased with the food and drink offered, would rise at once in anger and, murmuring against the feast and their host, would go home cross (angry). If anyone on the part of the host noticed it he would tell the latter at once, and he would then invite these people to dinner on the next day in order to appease them. This second day invitation was called apealo because this was the end of the feast.

The women, who were eating in another part of the house, were not given cocoa to drink, but a certain kind of gruel powdered over with various kinds of chilmolli. The old men and women gathered (again) that night to drink pulque and they got drunk. In order to produce this drunkenness, they placed before them a large pitcher or jar of pulque, and the one who served them poured from it into a jicara and gave each one according to his rank until there was none left. Sometimes they served the kind of pulque called iztacuctli, which means white pulque, which is (made of) the sap of maguey; at other times they served imitation pulque of water and honey boiled with the root of maguey and which they called ayuctli, meaning pulque made with water, and this the host had prepared and in readiness several days before the feast. When the servant found that his charges (the old men and women) did not become intoxicated, he began to serve again, this time from the left or opposite side on, beginning with those lowest in rank. Once they were all intoxicated they began to sing; some sang and cried, others sang to give pleasure. Each one would sing whatever he liked and in the key he fancied best, and none of them harmonized; some sang out loud, others softly, merely humming to themselves. There were some who, instead of singing, talked and laughed, told funny stories, and they would laugh out loud if they heard a good joke.

In this manner private festivities were celebrated upon invitation from a host, for one reason or another.

Chapter XXXVII.

About the Celebration of Baptismal Festivities of Today Which Are Very Similar to the Ancient Customs. About the Way Banquets Were Offered in Ancient Times and in Our Era, among Chieftains, Prominent Men and Merchants. Also about the Rest of the Days of the Sign Cequauhtli.

The manner in which today christenings are celebrated is the same as it was in ancient times with the exception that then the chiefs, prominent men, merchants and the wealthy people made their invitations each one after his own taste and fashion. All, however, invited a great many guests, and they had head waiters and servants to serve their guests; the first named were to see to it that all were honored according to their rank, in giving them flowers as well as in serving the meal and presenting them with blankets and belts. For this purpose a large amount of food was prepared, a great number of blankets, of belts, flowers and smoke-canes were assembled, so that all the guests would be provided plentifully with everything. No guest was to be insulted or affronted, neither was the host to be ashamed of his banquet, but rather be praised and honored on account of the order in which it was conducted and the great abundance of viands and presents offered his guests. As these latter knew this, they had hopes that they would partake of all the things at the banquet, but they also wished that there would be no lack of anything, so that their host might not fall into disgrace, and that nobody would have cause for complaint of the host nor of the banquet itself.

As the day of the banquet approached, all the servants and the overseers and head stewards hired for this occasion were solicitously preparing all the necessary items, adorning the courts and roads with reed-mace and flowers, sweeping and levelling the said courts and entrances to the house where the banquet was to be held. Some carried water, some swept and sprinkled the grounds or strew them with sand; some hung up the reed-mace where the dance was to be held. Many were busy dressing chickens or killing and singeing dogs, some roasted and others boiled chickens, still others filled the little canes with perfume (for the so-called smoke-canes). Old women and girls were busy making the many varieties of tamales, for some of these were made of bean-flour, others with meat. Some of the women washed the boiled corn, others peeled off the eye of it which is hard, in order to make finer bread. Still others carried water or cracked cocoa beans or ground them and mixed the cooked maize with the cocoa, and many were cooking soups and stews. As soon as the day dawned they spread petates (mats) everywhere and also seats, and they also piled hay on the floor entwining the edges of it so that they looked like blankets of soft herbs. Thus they prepared everything as required, and it was not even necessary for the master to give orders or to see what they were doing, for it was all done by the servants, or rather, waiters, and their officials (head waiters), who were also the ones who distributed the smoke-canes, the flowers and the food. Also by those who make the cocoa and lift it into the air (to cool it?) and serve it to those who are (entitled) to drink it. There were also special people detailed to personal service of the guests customary among chiefs, prominent men, merchants and the wealthy in general. The poorer classes made their feasts as they were best able, in a poor, rustic way, for they have little and do not know much about manners. They give flowers that cost little, and the smoke-canes they give their guests usually have already served once.

The rest of the days of the sign Cequauhtli are lucky according to their numeral. The second day is called Umecozeaquauhtli; the third, Ciollin; the fourth, Navitecpatli; the fifth, Macuiltquiavitl; the sixth, Chiquacenxuchitl; the seventh, Chicomecipactli; the eighth, Chicueyecatl; the ninth, Chiconavicalli; the tenth, Matlactlicuetzlpalli; the eleventh, Matlactliocecoatl; the twelfth, Matlactliomomemiquiztli; the thirteenth, Matlactliomeimacatl.

Chapter XXXVIII.

About the Twentieth and Last Sign, Called Cexuchitl.

The twentieth sign, Cexuchitl, is the last of all, and they said it was quite lucky, because those born under it would be prosperous, even wealthy, and have an abundance of all necessities. But this was only because they were great workers, diligent harvesters, making good use of their time, and always looking ahead. They were, moreover, said to be great hoarders for their children, very careful to guard their honour and property. If the one born under this sign became a land tiller, he was very diligent in cultivating his land, sowing all sorts of seeds and taking care of them, and he would thus harvest all sorts of vegetables to fill the bins in his home; he would gather many kinds of corn, the ears of which are suspended after the harvest from all the rafters in the home in long strings and bunches (of corn-ears). They used every part of the maize plant, such as the leaves, the corn-stalk, the husks and the after-bloom, and with all these endeavors and their industry they became wealthy.

Chapter XXXIX.

(This chapter is omitted as useless.)

Chapter XL.

About the Days of This (last) Sign.

For the time being, this volume closes with the enumeration of the remaining days of the sign Cexuchitl, and there is nothing more to add.

If future data, which today is hidden, should come to light concerning those signs, the reader will have to make his own deductions.

The second day of Cexuchitl is Umecatl; the third, Eyetzcuintli; the fourth, Naviocumatl; the fifth, Macuillimalinali; the sixth, Chicuacenacatl; the seventh, Chicomeocelutl; the eighth, Chicueyquauhtli; the ninth, Chiconavicozcaquauhtli; the tenth, Matlactliolin; the eleventh, Matlactliocetecpatl; the twelfth, Matlactliomomequiavitl; the thirteenth, Matlactliomeyxuchitl.

BIBLIOGRAPHY

Bibliography of Fray Bernardino de Sahagun's Writings

Señor Joaquin Garcia Icazbalceta, in his "Bibliografia del Siglo XVI (published in Mexico in 1886) states that "the bibliography of Father Sahagun is perhaps the most difficult one in Mexican literature, for not only did he write a great number of books, essays and articles on many different subjects in almost half a century, but he changed, rearranged and often extracted them for publication in so many diverse ways that they were often taken as parts at least of different books."

He wrote constantly in three languages, to wit: Spanish, Mexican or Latin, and to his Aztec or Mexican texts he, moreover, gave two different interpretations. As we have gleaned from the biography, he even made use of the Aztec hieroglyphs, having his Indian assistants paint them and then explain them to him. This he did especially at the beginning when he planned his history. It was a very safe, perhaps the safest way, to write about a people whose ancient history was laid down in such signs in part at least, and we must admire his genius, which found so unusual a mode of obtaining true source material. Surely he was the only historian of his time to hit upon such an ingenious method.

The "History," however, was so often changed, modified and rearranged, and even title pages altered, that confusion ensued in cataloguing it.

If we were only considering printed and generally known books in our bibliography, the task would be comparatively simple, but on the other hand would in no way do justice to so prolific a writer as Father Sahagun, neither would we give even remotely an idea of him as an author.

Mr. Alfredo Chavero, Secretario perpetuo de la Sociedad de Geografia y Estadistica de Mexico, published, in 1877, in Mexico city, a book called "Sahagun," a sort of biographical study, in which on p. 7 he mentions as the first work by Fray Bernardino a Ms. in quarto containing the "Epistolas y Evangelios de las Dominicas" in Mexican. It consists of 74 folios and an index of 1 fol. This latter is not in Sahagun's handwriting, while all the rest seems written by him. The titles and capital letters are in red ink, some of them adorned with figures of birds and monsters in various colors and gold, as was customary in those times. The letter itself was still firm and clear, a sign that the translation was made shortly after the good missionary's arrival in Mexico, certainly before 1563, when the writing already showed traces of fatigue. Mr. Chavero is of the opinion that this Ms. is not only unpublished but was unknown and was doubtlessly the first work of Sahagun preparatory to the "Evangeliarium, Epistolarium et Lectionarium." This Ms. belonged to Mr. Chavero and later became the property of Mr. Fernandez del Castillo, who later on ordered the entire collection of books he had bought of Mr. Chavero and most of which had formed part of the library of Sr. Don Josè F. Ramirez, to be sold at public auction in London. In the catalogue of this sale the above mentioned Ms. appears without naming its author, with the following title:

"524. Mexican.—Epistles and Gospels in Mexican, Ms. 4°, seventy-four leaves. It commences: Incipiunt Epistole et Evangelia que in Diebus Dominicis per Anni Totius circulum leguntur, Traducta in linguam Mexicanam."

It was bought by Mr. B. Quaritch for £15.10 and he later put it on sale for £20.

In "Notes for a Catalogue of Writers of Native Languages in America" (No. 103) by Señor Icazbalceta he entered this Ms. without knowing that it was by Sahagun. But even admitting that the "firm and clear" letter shows that it was written in his younger years, is that sufficient proof to assert that it was his *first* work?

In the "Biblioteca Nacional" there is a Ms. in 4° also containing the Epistles and Gospels, etc., in Mexican, but it bears no name of an author, nor any other indication to help us to discover by whom it might be.

II. Sermonario, which belonged to Señor Ramirez and Señor Icazbalceta, gives the following description of it:

"It is written on thick maguey paper, size large folio. On the first page, the lower part of which is missing, it bears the following title:

✠ Siguense unos Sermones de Dominicas y de Santos en lengua mexicana: no traducidos de Sermonario alguno sino compuestos nuenamente a la medida de la capacidad de los indios: breues en materia y en lenguaje congruo venusto y llano facil de entender para todos los que le oyeren altos y baxos principales y macegales hombres y mujeres. Compusieronse el año de 1540, anse comenzado a corregir y añadir este año de 1563 en este mes de julio infraoctava visitationis. El avtor los somete a la correccion de la madre sancta yglesia romana con todas las otras obras que en su lengua mexicana a compuesto. fray bernardino de sahagun."

This entire title is written in Sahagun's hand, signed by him, and provided with the scroll he uses in his signature. Immediately following this title page several pages are missing, then come two loose leaves written evidently by a scribe. At the head of the following page is a note, written by the author, as follows: "Siguense unos sermones breves en la lengua mexicana: el autor dellos los somete a la correction de la madre sancta yglesia con todas las demas obras suyas son para todo el año de dominicas y santos no estan corregidos. fray Bernardino de Sahagun."

There remain to the manuscript 95 folios with wide margins on which the author wrote in his own hand many corrections.

After Sr. Ramirez this Sermonario was owned by Sr. Chavero; it then went to Sr. Fernandez del Castillo, who sold it in London. In the catalogue Ramirez it is listed under No. 762, Mr. Quaritch bought it for £210, and put its price at £360 when announcing it for sale.

There is hardly any doubt that this was one of the two volumes Eguiara saw in the library of the Franciscan convent in Tlaltelolco, and which he describes as follows: "Sermones varios de Dominicis et Defunctis idiomate Mexicano pro Indorum captu formatos, é nulloque Sermonario ut dicitur traductos; quos Authographos vidimus Tomis duobus Regia charta in Bibliotheca ad S. Jacobi de Tlaltelolco Franciscanorum." Eguiara, however, must have written Defunctis instead of de Sanctis, as is previously given in the same title. What the other volume contained we do not know. It might have been the Evangeliarium.

This Sermonario gives us the first indication of a definite date of the beginning of Sahagun's literary activities. No doubt he wrote it when he found himself with free time on his hands after leaving the chair of Latin of the college of Tlaltelolco in that same year of 1540.

In the National Library in Mexico city there is a manuscript in quarto of Sermones mexicanos, the title of which is as follows: "Tabla de los sermones que se trata en el presente libro primeramente un aviento y sermones de la natividad del Señor y las dominicas lxx^{a}, lx^{a}, y l^{a} y una quaresma y Resurreccion lo qual es compostura y lengua del pe. frai Bernardino de Sahagun.

"Item se trata luego otro aviento çon los demas que son fiestas y dominicas del señor y es lengua del pe. fray Alonso de Escalona."

Outside of the titlepage it has 263 numbered folios and one at the end containing the rest of the index started on the titlepage. Several of the letters are in the style of the sixteenth century; the titles are in red ink.

On the reverse of folio 116 one reads the following note, written also in writing of that epoch, but different from the rest of the volume: "hasta aqui me parece no ser de los padres fray Bernardino de Sahagun ni del padre Escalona porque no lleva el frasis lengua y espiritu que las obras de los dichos padres suele tener comunmente, porque es mas y mejor su orden de proceder en su escriptura y ansi yo siento no ser suya sino de otro padre que no sé quien es."—

The reader will have to choose between the assurance of the one who wrote the titlepage and the doubt expressed by the author of above note, both of whom are anonymous.

III. Evangeliarium Epistolarium et Lectionarium Aztecum sive Mexicanum ex Antiquo Codice Mexicano nuper reperto deprompum cum Praefatione Interpretatione Adnotationibus Glossario Edidit Bernardinus Biondelli. Mediolani. Typis Jos. Bernardoni Qm. Johannis. MDCCCL VIII.

A beautiful edition in large quarto XLIX preliminary pages, one folio of a faccimile of the original codex, 425 pages of text in double columns, Latin and Mexican.—Glossarium Azteco—Latinum, pp. 427-453.—Index totius Voluminis, pp. 565-574.—Errata 1 folio.—According to Sr. Chavero, the handwriting of the Codex is identical to that of the Sermonario, and both volumes are very similar in appearance to judge from the description the editor of the Evangeliarium gives of his volume.

This manuscript was obtained in some rather obscure way by the traveller Beltrami, who published a notice of it filled with errors, irrelevancies and vulgarisms, in "Le Mexique," published in Paris 1830, 2 vol. in 8^0, in vol. II, p. 167. Upon the death of Beltrami in 1854 it was acquired by Biondelli from the former's heirs. This latter editor utters the belief that the Ms. was written in 1530, which is absolutely impossible, since Sahagun arrived in Mexico the previous year. It certainly was written much later, probably in 1563, at the same time as the Sermonario.

Sr. Orozco y Berra, in his "Bibliografia inédita," says that this book is the famous "Postilla," mentioned by Torquemada, or rather Mendieta. The noun postilla is not a Spanish word in the sense it is given here, but rather a low-Latin expression meaning "notes," especially "marginal and perpetual notes referring to the Bible," and it is in this sense rather that we ought to understand Mendieta's reference to this "muy elegante Postilla sobre las Epistolas y Evangelios dominicales." The Evangeliarium contains no notes at all, but is merely a translation of the sacred texts. Beltrami had fallen for this same error, and Biondelli remarked on it. Señor Chavero surmises that Manuscript No. I might have been the first draft of the Evangeliarium.

IV. "Vida de S. Bernardino de Sena" as it is written up in the Chronicles of the Order and which was translated by Sahagun into Mexican on petition of the Indians of Xochimilco. It is mentioned by Torquemada lib. XIX cap. 33. It has not been found so far.

This translation was probably made before the year 1551.

V. "Exercicios Quotidianos" in Mexican, Ms. in 4^0. It consists of 43 folios and on the first page we read:

"Comienza un exercicio en lengua mexicana sacado del sancto Evangelio y distribuido por todos los dias de la semana contiene meditaciones devotas muy provechosas para cualquier christiano que se quiere llegar á Dios."

At the end is the following note: "Este exercicio halle entre los indios, no se quien lo hizo ni quien se le dio tenia muchas fallas e incongruidades mas con verdad se puede decir que se hizo de nuevo que no se enmendo. Este año de 1574. fray Bernardino de Sahagun."

This article is No. 764 in the Ramirez catalogue. It was sold to Quaritch for £14 and he put it on sale at £20.

It was for a time the property of the library of the College of San Gregorio and Beristain saw it there, and he is the one who transcribed the final note by Sahagun. Sr. Chavero did not number it among the Ms. in the possession of Sr. Ramirez, neither does he ascribe it to Sahagun, and the note at the end of it might well bear out this belief, for in translation it reads: "this exercise I found among the Indians. I do not know who composed (made) it, nor who gave it to them. It contained (had) many faults (deficiencies) and incongruities, but in truth it can be said that it was made anew but not corrected." This may mean that Fray Bernardino copied it for the natives perhaps because it was soiled or worn out, but he did not correct it or add to it. While it is true that he signed the final remark, that does not mean that he was the author of the manuscript.

VI. Manual del Cristiano.

This is not mentioned by any author on Sahagun, and its existence is only known by a few loose leaves which belonged to Sr. Chavero and later were sold in London. In the Ramirez catalogue they are listed under No. 544. According to Chavero they are octavo, while the catalogue Ramirez lists them as 4^{0}. They are in Sahagun's hand, or at least in the same writing as the Evangelios, the Doctrina, the apostillas del Sermonario and the first page of the Trilingüe. The title is as follows:

"Izcatqui yn innemiliz yn teniutica omonamitique. Inic ce Cap.^{0} uncan mitoa, etc. The chapter covers about two folios and at the end of the second fol. (i.e., p. 4), another begins under the following heading: "Inic. 6. Cap.^{0}, etc. At the end of the next page it says: Inic 7. Cap.^{0}, etc. The last folio bears the following paragraph without a beginning: . . . . para que libremente pueda hacer imprimir el dicho Manual del Christiano a qualquiera ympressor a quien señalare y fuere su voluntad lo haga, por tiempo de diez años primeros siginentes, imprimiendolo todo en un cuerpo conforme al original que a recibido, o por partes y tratados como el dicho autor quisiere, y dentro de dicho tiempo otro ninguno ympressor ni persona particular lo imprima ni haga imprimir sin permission del dicho Fray Bernardino de Sahagun, so pena de quinientos pesos de oro para la camara y fisco de su magestad y de perder los moldes y aparejos de la enprenta y perdidos los libros que se hallaren auer ymprimido sin la dicha licencia y cumpliendo esto mando que en ello por ningunas justicias y otras personas no se le ponga embargo ni ynpedimento alguno: fecho en Mexico a dieziseis de Hebrero de mill y quinientos y setenta y ocho años.—Don Martin Enriquez."

This fragmentary document certainly is a puzzle on account of the enormous gap. If chapter I covers two folios and is followed immediately by chapter VI, there are four chapters missing, unless there were, in between, the pages containing them. At the end of the next folio, that is, the third, we read the summary of chapter VII, and on fol. 4 the paragraph, without a beginning, which embodies the permit for the printing of the book. The general description of the Ms. fails to mention whether these four folios were found bound together or loose, in which case we would not be sure that the three first ones ever formed part of the volume for which the permit was granted.

Mr. Chavero is of the opinion that this was the draft of a work by Sahagun ready for print, in which case we not only have here a third printed volume by the Franciscan friar, but one until now completely unknown, the "Manual del Christiano." It is true that such a work is unknown and was never mentioned as from the pen of Sahagun, but it could not have been a rough draft with the official permit for printing appended, or rather, written on one of its pages, for the simple reason that such permits were never granted on drafts, but only on neatly copied manuscripts. Once a manuscript had been sent in for examination and approval it was illicit to make even the slightest change, or ever so small and insignificant corrections. It is therefore quite evident that the few pages of this Ms. were intended for the press, because they had received official recognition and a permit for printing, but this does not mean that they were ever actually printed. Beristain came across a great many Mss. provided with permit and privileges required for their printing and yet they remained unpublished. We have above all the explicit and often repeated declaration by Mendieta concerning Sahagun's published works, to wit: "This friar (Sahagun) was particularly unfortunate in the sense that of all the books he wrote only a "Cancionero" was printed, which he composed for the Indians so they might sing at their dances songs that were edifying. All the rest of his works (with the exception of the "Historia"), which remained here (in Mexico) he could not print." Torquemada, also one of Sahagun's contemporaries, copied the above passage without correction, with only a few slight changes.

VII. Doctrina cristiana en mexicano.

Original Ms. in folio, which begins as follows:

"Nican vnpeoa yn nemachtliliz tlatolli . . . .
oquichiuh fray Bernardino de Sahagun."

It contains 27 folios, and the end is missing.

"Syguense veynte y sois addiciones de esta Postilla: las quales hizo el auctor della despues de muchos años que la ania hecho, ante que se imprimiese. Es lo mismo que está al principio debaxo de titulo de declaracion breue de las tres virtudes theologales."

On the reverse is a prologue in Spanish which recommends the usefulness of the book, and winds up as follows:

"Este mismo año de 1579 se puso por apendiz desta Postilla en lo ultimo un traslado que contiene siete Collationes en lengua mexicana, en las quales se contienen muchos secretos de las costumbres destos naturales: y tambien muchos secretos de las costumbres destos naturales: y tambien muchos secretos y primores desta lengua mexicana: y pues que este volumen no a de andar sino entre los sacerdotes y predicadores, no hay porque tener recelo de las antiguallas que en el se contienen, antes darán mucha lumbre y contento á los predicadores del sancto Evangelio."

This treatise does not exist in the Ms.; there are only 24 additions on 16 folios, poorly bound, since the last seven come before the nine first ones.

This Ms. was property of Ramirez, later of Chavero and, like the others, found their way to London. It is listed in the Ramirez catalogue with No. 763, and was sold to Quaritch for £24.10, who announced it for sale at 32 Pounds Sterling.

The Postilla went through the same vicissitudes as the Historia. It was commenced at Tepepulco when Sahagun took the first interrogatory to that town in 1558. It was corrected and copied in 1567-69, while its author was in Mexico city, and then was forgotten for some ten years, until 1579, when the corrections spoken of in the prologue were made. A possible reason for this long delay may be found in the fact that Fray Bernardino had gone to the city principally to work on his historia, as we have seen elsewhere. About its purpose we may glean an idea from a passage in the Historia: "Si bien se considera la predicacion evangelica y apostolica, hallarse ha muy claro que la de los catolicos predicadores ha de ser de vicios y virtudes, persuadiendo lo uno y disuadiendo lo otro; y lo mas continuo ha de ser el persuadirlos á las virtudes teologales y disuadirles los vicios á ellas contrarios. De esto hay mucha materia en los seis primeros libros de esta Historia, y en la Postilla sobre las Epistolas y Evangelios de los domingos de todo el año que hice. (III. prologue.)

As Sahagun himself calls this book "La Postilla," this possibly solves the doubt about which one should be thus called, although the title "Doctrina cristiana," goes somewhat against it. It may, however, be assumed that Sahagun perhaps interspersed his doctrinal teaching with explanations of texts from the Epistles and the Gospel. Betancurt owned the "Libro de las Postillas," and he says: "He wrote, (meaning Sahagun) a Postilla of the Gospel and the Epistles in very pertinent and beautiful language, where I found very elegant passages. In this volume he gives an account of the arrival of the first priests together with all their talks, and questions and answers they held with the satraps and so-called priests of the idols concerning the mysteries of the faith, in Spanish and Mexican. This is contained in two books, one of 30, the other of 21 chapters."

Señor Chavero is of the opinion that this book was printed, because the 26 additions were made before printing it "ante que se imprimiese." This sentence might of course mean that such was the case, but we might also take it to mean simply that these additions were made in order to prepare it for print, but that in reality this never came to pass. In fact, Mendieta himself assures us that Sahagun was "very unfortunate as far as printing of his books was concerned, and while alive only saw the "Psalmodia" printed.

VIII. Tratado de las Virtudes Teologales en mexicano.

Beristain saw this Ms. in the College of San Gregorio. It might be a fragment of the Doctrina or Postilla, the more so because here he, Sahagun, says that the "additions" were the same as mentioned here at the beginning under the caption of explanation of the three theological virtues. If this treatise was at the beginning of the Gospel, it is very probable that what Beristain saw was the Gospel itself, which he named then after the first title he found in the Ms.

IX. "Libro de la venida de los primeros padres, y las platicas que tuvieron con los sacerdotes de los idolos."

While this Ms. cannot be found, or at least had not been found at the time Sr. Garcia Icazbalceta wrote the "Bibliografia Mexicana del Siglo XVI" its existence in times long past cannot be doubted. Betancurt had it, and Mendieta made an extract of the first talk in libro III, chap 13. One difficulty, however, arises in the fact that Mendieta states that these talks with the Indians took place directly upon arrival of the first twelve Franciscans in Mexico, when they talked to the caciques (chiefs) and prominent men, and that they did so by using Jeronimo de Aguilar or some other interpreter in the services of Cortés. Naturally they did not master the language from the very first, nor had they brought an interpreter of their own. The context—extracted by Mendieta—shows clearly that they were held upon their arrival, but Sahagun says that he compiled these conversations as auricular witness, that is to say, that he was present, and here lies the snare—these talks were held in 1524 and Sahagun arrived in Mexico in 1529. It seems to me that his learned bibliographers lose sight of the fact that the title of his book or Ms. mentions such conversations held with the "priests of the idols," not with chiefs, etc., so that it is well possible that while he recorded in it the talks held by the first arrivals with the chiefs, he only becomes a "testigo de vista" when they talk with the priests, i.e., shamans. And he may even have witnessed repetitions of those first talks, the more so that even in 1529 the conversion of the Aztecs was not yet widespread, and there surely were large provinces and districts in full sway of their ancient idolatry.

D. Nicolas Antonio was of the opinion that these conversations had been printed: editum quidem formis typographicis, so does Pinelo-Barcia, but none says where nor when. This belief originated, no doubt, in the "Psalmodia," the printing license for which includes another book entitled: "Colloquios de Doctrina con que los primeros doce frailes de la dicha orden que vinieron á esta Nueva España instruyeron y enseñaron á los Naturales de ella." In the prologue, however, Sahagun only speaks of the Psalmodia without mentioning the other book, so that in all probability this latter never was printed with it. It may have been left out to be printed later on, and then for some reason or other never got into press.

X. "Catecismo de la Doctrina Cristiana en Lengua Mexicana, Imp. por Ocharte, 1583. 4°."

Sr. Garcia Icazbalceta is of the opinion that this Catecismo is really the Coloquios de Doctrina mentioned in the prologue of the Psalmodia, but under a disfigured title. Beristain very frequently got titles wrong or mixed up. The reason for believing that this is the case is that it follows as a continuation of the Psalmodia and the printer and date are the same.

XI. Psalmodia Cristiana.

Description of this work has been given above. It is noteworthy that of the only book printed in the lifetime of Father Sahagun only one copy should be known to exist—up to 1886, when Icazbalceta published the Bibliografia, and this copy belonged to the author of this bibliography. Betancurt tells us that among other things Sahagun also taught music at the College of Tlaltelolco, and that many of his students did so w el that some were appointed to the choir of the Cathedral of Mexico.

XII. Arte de Lengua Mexicana.

Today this Ms. cannot be found. Sahagun composed it while in the big Franciscan Convent of Mexico city in 1569. Later on, in 1585, he rearranged and edited it again, as he says himself:

"Tambien me movi á enmendar este tractado, porque tengo proposito que en acabando el Arte y Vocabulario de la Lengua Mexicana (en que ahora voy entendiendo), leer á nuestros Religiosos el Arte de esta Lengua Mexicana, y tambien el Vocabulario y esta conquista."

The Arte composed in Mexico had as supplement a vocabulary both of which were transcribed in 1569. Mr. Rémi Simeon, in the foreword of the French translation of the "Historia" asserts that the "Arte y Vocabulario" were used as complements throughout the twelve books of the "Historia." They would certainly have been in their proper place in that great Mexican encyclopaedia, but we must not forget that in 1585 the author, Fray Bernardino, still was adding to the old copies of "Arte y Vocabulario" and copying them anew.

XIII. Vocabulario Trilingüe; castellano, latino y mexicano.

Mendieta never mentions this Ms., and we owe our first knowledge of its existence to the other great bibliographer of Father Sahagun, Torquemada, who possessed it, moreover. He says: "He, Sahagun, also wrote another Vocabulary which he called 'Trilingüe' because it was in Mexican, Spanish and Latin, and showed great erudition in the Mexican language. . . . He, Sahagun, says in his prologue: 'Va en romance toda esta Gramatica Historica, ne dedisse videamur ansam Rabinis qui saepe expugnaverunt me a juventute mea.' " Betancurt repeats all this in his "Menologio," and he, too, owned a copy of the book, although by then very much worn. Chavero owned a copy of this Ms., which he thinks once belonged to Fray Bernardino. He says about it: "The vocabulary in question was believed to be lost, for after Betancurt (1871 about) no one had seen it, and there were even such as denied its existence altogether. Yet, besides the unimpeachable testimony by Torquemada as well as Betancurt, there is the obvious fact of its existence, for it formed part of the Chavero library, which later passed into the hands of Manuel Fernandez del Castillo.

It is a thick volume in small Spanish 4^0, written in magnificent semi-Gothic writing on Genoese paper. On each line the first word is in Spanish, followed by its Latin translation and, written in red ink above the line, the Mexican equivalent, although in some places this latter is not given. The dictionary is disposed in two columns, first come two independent leaves of the vocabulary and on them and on the last page there are, in different writing, several names with their translation in Aztec. One of these writings on the first page is Sahagun's hand. These additional pages which look very much like corrections of or additions to the original copy, together with the fact that there is no known other author of the epoch who wrote a trilingual vocabulary, are ample proof that this manuscript was the one owned by Sahagun himself. In the Codex of Santiago there are several signatures of his disciple (student), Martin Jacobita, and by comparing them with the handwriting in the Vocabulario, one at once perceives that this student was the copyist of the magnificent work of the master.

Garcia Icazbalceta described this volume as "anonymous" in his "Apuntes" (No. 169). It has 155 fols. and was recorded in the Ramirez catalogue under No. 545. It was sold to Quaritch at £48, and he announced it on sale for £50.

Ramirez in his Suplementos Mss. to the Beristain library also mentions it among Anonymous Mss., and gives it the following title: "Dictionarium ex bismensi (sic) in latinum sermonem interprete Aelio Autonio Nebrissensi. Lege foeliciter, MS. en 4° de 310 paginas, en mi biblioteca."

He supposes it to be by Sahagun, but does not say that there is any of the friar's handwriting in it. He also believes it to be the Ms. once belonging to Torquemada and to Betancurt later, because he says: "I acquired it through the favor of the Superiors of the same convent which they once inhabited," namely, San Francisco of Mexico city.

Thus this volume, either original or copy, might very possibly have belonged to Sahagun at one time, but there are indications of a Trilingual Vocabulary which do not very well agree with the above mentioned.

Fray Juan Bantista, in his "Advertencias para los Confesores de los Naturales" (published in Tlaltilulco in 1600) copies a large portion of the Vocabulario, giving it the following title: "Siguense algunas Abusiones antiguas que estos naturales tuvieron en su gentilidad, segun que escribe el P. Fr. Bernardino de Sahagun en el libro segundo de su Vocabulario Trilingüe. Y es bien que los confesores las adviertan, para que si alguno se acusare dellas las entienda bien."

He then copies twenty-five paragraphs and arranges them in the same order as they are found in the appendix of book V of the Historia, where we find twelve more. Among the fragments mentioned further on, the author speaks of a Vocabulario Trilingüe he was writing in 1585, in which he mentions the secular feast of the Mexicans as he does in book VII, chap. 9 of the Historia. In order to avoid repetitions we shall mention this last Vocabulario when we treat of the History. The volume, which had once belonged to Messrs. Ramirez and Chavero, and which in July, 1885 was still in the hands of Quaritch, was a simple lexicon which did not nor could it contain the references made by the author and later, by Fray Juan Bantista.

XIV. Sahagun wrote a great number of small pamphlets, all of which appear to be lost. Torquemada gives us a few titles of part of them: 1. Declaracion parafrástica y el Simbolo de Quicumque vult (de S. Atanasio). 2. Otra declaracion del mismo Simbolo por manera de Diálogo. 3. Pláticas para después del bantismo de los Niños. 4. Lumbre espiritual.

5. Leche espiritual. 6. Bordon espiritual. 7. Espejo espiritual. 8. Espiritual y Manjar sólido. 9. Escalera espiritual. 10. Regla de los casados. 11. Fruta espiritual. 12. Impedimento del Matrimonio. 13. Los Mandamientos de los Casados. 14. Doctrina para los Médicos.

Let us see whether we can trace one or the other of these writings. In his "Camino del Cielo" (fol. 40) Fray Martin de Leon copies the declaration of the Quicumque vult of San Atanasio in Mexican, but he fails to mention that he copied it from Sahagun's pamphlet (1). However, since he also copied Fray Bernardino's calendar and several other things without giving him due credit, it surely is not too far fetched to accuse him of the literary theft of the "Declaracion del Simbolo, etc.

Chavero seems to think that in the loose sheets belonging to the "Manual de los Casados," there are parts of the essays Nos. 10, 12, and 13.

It would not be strange if Sahagun had written a special treatise called "Doctrina para los Medicos," for the simple reason that medicine was taught at the college of Tlaltelulco, and he himself was very fond of experimenting with indigenous remedies. If he wrote the Doctrina he no doubt incorporated it later on in book X in part, and a few chapters in book XI of the Historia, which was his favorite work, and into which he embodied many loose tracts, such as the "Apologia sobre el Calendario," which appears as a loose treatise in 1585, while in the history it forms the appendix to book IV. Boturini attributes to him a "Doctrina" of 11 folios, on European paper, in figures and ciphers, and calls it "cosa de ver muy curiosa." This seems to be the one which Aubin obtained, if we may deduce it from what Mr. Rémi Siméon says about it, to wit: "Mr. Aubin possède de cet auteur (Sahagun) onze feuilles de Doctrina en figures et en chiffres, sur papier européen."

We are probably safe to refer in regard to the "Doctrina" as well as the other articles mentioned above, to the following paragraph of Sahagun's monumental work, where he says: "For more than forty years I am now preaching in these parts of Mexico and on what I have persisted most myself and many others with me, is to convert them to the catholic faith by many means (in many ways), trying different opportunities to attain it; by means of pictures as well as with sermons, demonstrations and elocution experimenting with adults as well as with children; and in this I have insisted even more in the past 5 years, giving them the necessary means to attain Faith in a very short time and in clear words." By the date when this was written we glean that these five past years were those between 1571-75, within which time Sahagun also composed the Exercicios Quotidianos (1574). In referring to "demonstrations," he no doubt means the Autos, so commonly used at that time. It is wholly probable that Sahagun cultivated that sort of literature, and he possibly even instructed Valericano and others among his pupils in it.

Orozco y Berra (in Tezozomoc, Cronica Mexicana, Mexico 1878, p. 175-177) attributes the "Historia de los Mexicanos por sus pinturas," called the Códice Zumarraga, although it ought to be called rather Códice Fuenleal to Sahagun. The original of this work is incorporated in the Libro de Oro y Tesoro indico which belonged to Señor Icazbalceta, and was published by him in vol. II of the Anales del Museo Nacional, p. 85. The reason for attributing it to Sahagun was that Don Manuel Antonio de Lastres, who was one of the owners of the Códice, wrote at the foot of the report: "Fr. Bernardino de San Francisco, franciscano," and consequently Mr. Orazco supposed this friar to be Sahagun. In the Codex itself there are further proofs of this erroneous belief, and even above the "Memoriales" by Fray Toribio de Motolinia, Lastres again wrote: "by Fray Bernardino de Sahagun y el Señor Zumarraga." These annotations have no value whatever but, although the man may have been quite honest though hasty in attributing them both to Sahagun, he was accused by Franckenau (that is, Don Juan Lucas Cortés) in his "Biblioteca Heraldica" as a forger and simulator of authors. The curious fact is that Lastres obtained the Libro de Oro from his accuser's library.

In "Suplementos MS. á la Biblioteca de Beristain (art. Bantista)" Mr. Ramirez conjectures that in the compilation of the "pláticas antiguas de los mexicanos" which Fray Juan Bantista published under the title of "Huehuetlatolli," Sahagun had his hand in; others attribute a possible assistance in the work to Father Olmos. The true Huehuetlatolli written by Fray Bernardino is incorporated in Book VI of his Historia and concerns rhetoric, philosophy, morale and theology of the ancient Mexicans. There are indications that originally this book was more extensive than it is today. In order to be able to say whether or not Sr. Ramirez supposition had any justifiable foundation, it would be necessary to know the full text in Mexican of Sahagun's Huehuetlatolli and to compare it with the one of Fray Juan Bantista, a task most difficult if not impossible, since up to the present time no complete copy has come to light. In an index of documents referring to the Tercer Concilio Mexicano we find among many other clauses which Dr. Hernando Ortiz de Hinojosa, councellor, proposed to that assembly, the following: "(g.) That the book on the Life of Jesus Christ in Mexican and in verse, written by Fray Bernardino de Sahagun, Franciscan, be introduced among the Indians so that by means of this book they might forget their pagan songs." It is not stated whether the book was printed or in manuscript, nor do there remain any signs of it.

XV. Calepino.

All of Sahagun's bibliographers mention the above work; some of them confuse it with the "Historia"; others consider it as a separate book, but none of them ever saw it. So they do not help us any, and the best we can do is to recur to what little information we find in original sources. The first one is Mendieta, who speaks of the book or Ms. in two places. In one instance he says: "he composed a Calepino (thus he called it) of twelve or thirteen very superior volumes, which I had in my hands, wherein he explained all the different ways of the Mexicans, in their manner, religion, education, mode of life and conversation. These, for the reason of being so lengthy, could not be copied. One of the viceroys took it away from him by cunning, and sent it to a certain chronicler who had begged him most insistently for written material about customs of the Indians. These probably served his purpose about as well as the verses of Gaiferos." A little later he states: "I had in my keeping eleven large folios—books containing in the quaintest Mexican idiom, translated into Spanish, all manner of material about ancient customs the Indians had in their paganism; about their gods, idolatries, rites and ceremonies, as also in their government, polity, laws and customs of their superiors and of all manner of conversation and human intercourse used among them before the advent of the Spaniards. He wrote these books also because he intended later to use them for the composition of what he called a Calepino, in which he would give a minute description of the Mexican language (which is marvelously intricate) in all its uses and ways such as the Indians (at that time) still spoke it, but which was already beginning to get corrupted. . . . The good father had, however, such poor luck with his writings that these eleven books I just mentioned (like so many others), were taken from him with great cunning by a governor of this country, who sent them to Spain to a chronicler who asked for papers about the Indians. These papers may have been used over there to wrap up spices."

We find that in these two statements by Mendieta there are several discrepancies, not to say contradictions. First, he mentions twelve or thirteen volumes and later eleven. In one place he says that Fray Bernardino composed a Calepino, in another that he had written those volumes in order and with the intention to make a Calepino. There is quite a difference between having made one such Calepino and having the intention to make one. The matters treated in that great work are the same that are contained in his History, and even the number of volumes is the same, so that here the Calepino is identified with the history.

Let us look up Torquemada and his "Monarquia Indiana." He wrote after Mendieta. We find likewise two paragraphs with reference to the Calepino, in fact, he copied them from Mendieta's work with slight variants to fit the particular aim of the new author. He says that he only had seen and consulted the volume about the "conquest of this country, (Mexico) which has helped me a great deal in what I mention about it." This confirms us in the conviction that this Calepino was the "Historia," that is, the preparatory sketch for it to which Fray Bernardino gave that collective name. The author of the Monarquia Indiana knew and freely used almost all the books of the Historia General, some of them completely, some in parts, others in abstracts with the exception of only three, according to Sr. Troncoso, who made out a list of contents of the two works.

About 80 years later Betancurt wrote regarding this: "He wrote a book which he called Calepino, a masterpiece consisting of twelve volumes, in which he put down a description of nature, animals and herbs of the land, its boundaries, the manner of speech, customs, religion and politics of those natives." This identifies the Calepino still more definitely with the history. Betancurt did not see any of these tomes, and, in fact, saw only the second edition of the volume describing the Conquest of Mexico.

The word "Calepino" indicates at once a vocabulary. It originated from the Latin vocabulary by Ambrosio Calepino, which later on became so enlarged by his successors as to contain eleven languages. Its use in the various universities all over the southern part at least of the old world became so general that the generic name of Calepino was identified with vocabulary. It is even today mentioned in Spanish dictionaries as: "Latin dictionary." The many different subjects treated in Sahagun's Calepino are not, properly speaking, material for an ordinary vocabulary, but as we know not whether there existed in the 16th. century any such works as historical Dictionaries or some such titles, Sahagun probably had no idea of compiling a similar work and simply called it by the then familiar title of Calepino.

However, Sahagun himself explains the reason why he called that work Calepino in a "warning to the reader" in his Historia. Although it is rather lengthy, it is well worth copying here: "When this work was started, I began by saying to those who knew about it that I was making a Calepino, and even today there are many who will still ask me 'how goes the Calepino.' It certainly would be of great advantage to write such a useful book for those who wish to learn the Mexican language as Ambrosio Calepino did it for all who wanted to learn Latin and the significance of its expressions. But I have not had the same opportunity, for, while Calepino took his words and their meaning, their errors and metaphors from poets, orators and authors of the Latin tongue, verifying whatever he wrote by comparison with the ancient authors of Latin,

I have no such foundations, for there are no writings among those people (the Mexicans); thus it was impossible to write a Calepino proper; but I put down the ground-work for whoever should wish to do so might learn it with ease. Through my industry 12 books were produced of the proper and indigenous language of the Mexicans, where, besides its being of very pleasing and profitable reading, one also finds all manners of speech and all the words used in this tongue, as well authorized and certain as those Virgil and Cicero and other Latin authors ever wrote. These twelve books are arranged in such a way that each page bears three columns, the first one Spanish, the second Mexican, and the third the explanation of the Mexican words marked with their ciphers on both sides. All of the Mexican part is copied by now in all the twelve books, the Spanish part and the commentaries are not done because I could not finish that for lack of assistance and favour. If I could obtain the help I need I could finish it all in about a year, and most assuredly if it could get done it would prove a treasure for the knowledge of many things worthy to be known, and to learn easily this language with all its secrets. It would be a thing of great value in Old and New Spain."

This shows clearly that Sahagun himself did not call his chief work a Calepino, that people began calling it such, but that he considered a vocabulary backed by authors as a very useful thing, and that had he received sufficient means and the opportunity to carry out the idea in full he no doubt would have finished it. Ambrosio Calepino had found more than ample material for his work in the treasure-house of Latin literature, whereas the Mexicans had neither literature nor even letters with which to write their language. Nevertheless, he considered what he had set down in those twelve tomes as a good basis for learning pure Mexican. His genius had found a way to commit to modern language a native tongue that had never been written, and he used as his authorities men who knew well all the expressions and idioms before their language had become even slightly corrupted through intercourse with the Spaniards. These twelve volumes were intended to supply the ancient Mexican with a literature, and they furnished him material in the linguistic field when he wrote the "Historia," which in part he also divided into three columns, the last one providing explanation of expressions in Aztec. The Mexican Codex in four volumes of the Historia General, now in the library of the Real Academia de la Historia in Madrid, presents in a part of book X an example of this division into three columns. The author's advanced age may have been the reason why a work of so great an importance as were these commentaries could not be finished, or else, and this perhaps is the main reason, when all his historical papers were taken from him, he did not have time to finish them. At all events, the Calepino as a separate work never existed.

XVI. Historia general de las cosas de Nueva España.

The first bibliographer to mention this work was Leon Pinelo, in his Epitome (1629, p. 101) quoting Torquemada, because he himself had not seen it. Then, under the title of "Diccionario" and giving added explanation, it was mentioned by the Franciscan analyst, Wadding, in his Scriptores Ordinis Minorum (Romae, 1632). Don Nicolás Antonio did not know more about it than Pinelo. Barcia, in the second edition of the library of Pinelo, is equally unable to locate the manuscripts. Fray Juan de San Antonio was the first to announce that the work, divided into four volumes, was preserved in the Franciscan convent of Tolosa of the province of Cantabria. Eguiara simply copied the above notice. So did Clavijero do likewise, and he, moreover, attributed to Sahagun, as a separate work, a "Diccionario Universal de la Lengua Mexicana" in twelve volumes, in "Storia Antica del Messico" (vol. 1, p. 8). Beristain mentioned a "Diccionario Historico Mexicano" and mixed up Betancurt's notes on book XII; then he separated the four volumes mentioned in the Biblioteca Franciscana and supposed them to be part of the twelve volumes of the Diccionario, in the "Bibliotica Hispano-Americana Septentrional (vol. III, p. 92).

Thus far we obtain from these early bibliographers only one important fact given by Fray Juan de San Antonio. Neither do the early chroniclers shed any light on Sahagun's many writings, and it was necessary that the "Historia" itself be published to reveal its origin and its many vicissitudes, and even so we do not obtain as precise information as we would like.

Ever since 1547 at the latest, our Fray Bernardino busied himself with historical research among the Mexicans, according to an annotation at the end of book VI, which states: "It was translated into Spanish by the said Padre Fray Bernardino de Sahagun, after it had been written in the Mexican tongue, thirty years before, in this year of 1577."

Ten years after that date, in 1557, when Fray Francisco de Toral was appointed as provincial of the Franciscans in Mexico, this latter ordained that Sahagun was to write, by sacred obedience, and in the Mexican language, whatever to him would seem "useful for the instruction, culture and support of Christianity among these natives of New Spain, and to help the workers and ministers who instructed them." In compliance to this mandate, Father Sahagun prepared a number of notes or memorandums of the subjects that were to be treated, "which was what is written in the twelve books, the marginal notes and the canticles," that is to say, that he traced a plan for the work to be done and even of subsequent books. He took this sketch with him to the pueblo of Tepepulco. The selection of this latter place as the operating field, if we may say so, was a very wise move, because, according to ancient documents, the chiefs of Teotihuacan and of Tepepulco were married to the daughters of the late Ixtlilxochitl II, the last king of Tetzcoco, consequently in those places it might be easily possible to collect from the last servitors of the last king the Acolhua version of Mexican ancient history. He called together the chieftain and prominent men of the village and told them what he intended to do, and he asked them to send him skilful and experienced men with whom he might talk and obtain what he wanted to know. After deliberating awhile, they brought him ten or twelve old men prominent in the town, who, they said, would be able to inform him on the subjects he wished to know. To these were added four Latin students whom he had taught at the college of Tlaltelolco. With this group of Indians he worked for almost two years (from 1558-1560) on all the points contained in his memorandum-book or questionnaire. The old men gave their answers by means of paintings, as was their custom, and the students explained them, writing down the explanation underneath each picture. Even twenty years later the author still preserved this precious manuscript, which may well be considered as the first one of the "Historia."

In 1560 Sahagun returned to Mexico city to attend the sessions of the Chapter of the Order when Fray Francisco de Bustamante was elected Provincial. He did not return to Tepepulco, but was sent to Santiago Tlaltelolco, and there he again gathered some eight or ten principals of the town "said to be very well versed in their language and things concerning their antiquities." With these men and four or five of the college students who knew the three languages, Mexican, Spanish and Latin, he locked himself in at the college, and for over a year they examined, corrected and added to, what had been done at Tepepulco. A copy was made of it all, although poorly written, because it had to be made in a hurry. At this examination or re-writing of it, the one who did the most work was Martin Jacobita, principal of the college.

As soon as the work was done, Fray Bernardino returned to the convent in Mexico city where, alone, he examined and re-examined the work done so far, in the course of three more years; he re-arranged them and then divided them into twelve books, each book into chapters, and some of these latter he subdivided into paragraphs. He nowhere speaks of a new copy of the work in these three years, so he must have simply revised the one made in Tlaltelolco. This, of course, could be done in three different ways: by adding marginal notes, by writing between lines, or by making pertinent annotations on separate sheets.

"After this," Sahagun says, "while Fray Miguel Navarro was Provincial and Fray Diego de Mendoza local Superior of Mexico, through their assistance all the twelve books were copied in good, clear handwriting." And while this copy was being made the Mexicans added and corrected many of the things contained therein. This was the third manuscript or text of the history, as Sahagun says himself: . . . "the first strainer through which my works were pressed was made up by the Indians of Tepepulco, the second by those of Tlaltelolco, and the third by those of Mexico, and at all those different corrections there were present students of grammar." Since Sahagun has preserved the names of some of his assistants, we might as well mention them here: "The principal and most learned one was Antonio Valeriano, of Azcapozalco; another one almost as good was Alonso Vexarano of Cuauhtitlán; another was Martin Jacobita, and still another Pedro de San Buenaventura of Cuauhtitlan." The copyists, Indians, of course, were Diego de Grado, Bonifacio Maximiliano and Mateo Severino, who copied all the books in good, clear handwriting, and it cost a goodly amount of pennies.

This manuscript was finished in 1569, and appears to have been the definitely corrected copy and the one which contained exact the Mexican text such as Fray Bernardino accepted it as correct. It is a pity that at least in notes or some other way the previous manuscripts of Tepepulco nor of Tlaltelolco were preserved so that we might have the three versions: acolhua, tlaltelolca and mexicana. Today, of course, this can no longer be remedied; there is no news of the whereabouts of the codex of Tepepulco; there appears to be something left of the codex of Tlaltelolco, as we shall see later.

When the work was finished, its author asked the commissary, Fray Francisco de Ribera (1569-1573) to ordain that three or four monks should examine it and then give their opinion of it at the meeting of the next Chapter in 1570. Who were the censors? Possibly Father Mendieta was one of them, because in his "Historia Eclesiastica" he mentions the fact twice that he had had in his keeping the monumental opus in eleven, twelve or thirteen volumes, and this could not have been the manuscript copied (anew) in 1575, for this one was assembled in only four volumes. Thus it must have been the copy prepared in 1569, which, as is quite natural, was turned over for the verdict of the censors in its original state. It is doubtful that Mendieta could have seen it again in its newer form, since very shortly after the above mentioned meeting of the Chapter the volumes were dispersed and later when gathered again remained in the hands of the author.

The censors, whoever they may have been, declared the work to be of great value and that the author should have the necessary assistance in order to finish them. As the Mexican text was complete, the above observation must have been meant for the Spanish translation which at that time had probably only been started. Despite the favorable judgement of the censors, there arose voices in the governing chapter of the Franciscan Order against the increase of expenditure on this score because, they pretended, such was in direct opposition to the professed poverty of the order. This vote being adopted, the author was ordered to dispense with his copyists, granting him, however, complete liberty to do the work himself if he so desired. Fray Bernardino could not obtain a revocation of this order, the result being that the work remained in statu quo for over five years because the author being more than seventy years old at that time, was unable to write on account of the trembling of his hands. This is clearly visible in his signatures in the Codex Tlaltelolco.

After the meeting of the Chapter (1570) he no doubt made a summary of the contents of the books, giving thereby an idea of the trend of his work; adding the prologues, he sent this to Spain in the same year in care of the Fathers Miguel Navarro and Jeronimo de Mendieta. In one of the prologues there is a "note to the reader," the ending of which may give us a clue as to the motive of sending it across the water. It says: "The Spanish part and the commentaries are not done because I could not do it for lack of assistance and support; if I were given the necessary help, in a year or a little more it could all be done. And to be sure, if it were finished it would prove to be a treasure, for the knowledge of all things worthy to be known and to learn the Mexican language and all its secrets. It would be a precious thing for New and Old Spain." This evidently was written after the Chapter had refused further assistance and the cooperation of copyists, with the idea to obtain, by mediation of the two friars, Navarro and Mendieta, some help from those in power in the old country.

Very shortly after this Fray Alonso de Escalona was appointed as Provincial of the Order, and he took away all of Sahagun's books and dispersed them throughout the province of the Franciscans so that they were seen and approved by many monks, and they even got into the hands of seculars who took advantage of them. Fortunately, in 1573 Father Navarro returned to Mexico with the title of Commissary of the order (higher than Provincial) and upon petition from Sahagun and with a reprimand, he ordered the dispersed books to be brought back. They were all returned to Sahagun himself within a year, but nothing more was done, for still there was no one ready to help him finish the translation until towards the end of 1575 or the beginning of 1576 the new Commissary, Father Rodrigo de Sequera, arrived. He saw the work, liked it so much indeed that he told the author to finish it, and saw to it that it was copied again, this time in two columns, one in Mexican, the other in Spanish. (This was the first manuscript in two languages and the fourth of the History.)

As a matter of fact, Fray Bernardino did not owe this good fortune entirely to the munificence of Father Sequera, but to the President of the Council of the Indies, the Licenciate Juan de Ovando who, having seen the summary, wished to see the entire work, and commissioned Father Sequera to send him a copy. And, if we go still more deeply into the matter, we find indications that it was Mendieta, one of the bearers of the summary who, being on intimate terms with Ovando, probably enthused him to get it done. Ovando and Mendieta corresponded frequently in matters concerning the colonies, and Icazbalceta owned an unpublished correspondence between these two men. As Mendieta knew the "Historia" by Sahagun, had doubtlessly revised it before leaving for Spain, he used his influence with the official to favor his friend. Ovando in turn was a man of superior intelligence; he had great influence with the king and, in fact, accomplished so much in his life-time that it is rather surprising that not more is known about him. He took great pains that the "Descripcion é Historia general de las Indias" be finished, and he dictated pertinent orders to that effect, and to this may be due the request to Sequera to send him a complete copy of the manuscript of Sahagun. To please that gentleman, who most assuredly did not know the Mexican language, it was imperative to finish the Spanish version. It is equally true that we glean from the glowing expressions of gratitude by Sahagun towards the Father Commissary that even though the latter was willing to do all in his power to please Ovando, he took also a personal interest in the author once he had seen his books in Mexico.

When Father Sequera ordered a separate copy made for Ovando he did not know that the latter had died in Spain on September 8th of 1575, an event which explains two things: the slowness with which this copy was made, and the order of the Council of the Indies to gather and send to Spain all the originals and copies of the history. This we learn from a paragraph in the letter of Archbishop Moya de Contreras to the king, dated Mexico, March 30th. of 1578. It reads: "La Historia universal de estos naturales y de sus ritos y ceremonias," composed by Fray Bernardino de Sahagun, of the Order of Saint Francis, which Your Majesty ordained to be sent in the original and that no copy either printed or manuscript remain over here, for justified considerations, the author has told me that he gave it, together with all his original papers, in Spanish and Mexican, as well as certain copies, to the Viceroy. I pray Your Majesty to value the Mexican language written by this friar, because it is the most elegant and genuine of these parts, and as time goes on it will become even more valuable, because in time the genuineness and antiquity of the language becomes less and less. Therefore the careful manner of this friar to collect it will some day become a great emolument especially for the Inquisition, for it gives this institution a clear insight into the rites of those indians so that it may judge their sins."

The same Archbishop, in another letter of December 16th, 1578, says: "The 'Historia Universal de las Indias,' written by Fray Bernardino de Sahagun, Franciscan, together with the copies and originals left with the latest fleet, as the author told me, and Your Majesty has probably received them by now."

This second letter was probably an answer to a royal decree addressed to the Archbishop and dated at San Lorenzo el Real, July 5th of the same year (1578), and which said in part: "If the Historia Universal de las Indias by Fray Bernardino de Sahagun has not yet been sent, you will entreat the Viceroy to send it at the first opportunity."

The first of these two letters was accompsnied by one from Sahagun to the king, conceived as follows:

"The Viceroy, Don Martin Enriquez, received a royal decree from Your Majesty ordering him to send some manuscripts in the Mexican language and in Spanish which I wrote, as soon as possible to Your Majesty. The Viceroy and also the Archbishop of this city told me. I finished copying these said manuscripts this past year and I handed them to Fray Rodrigo de Sequera, Commissary General of our Order of Saint Francis so that in case he should go to Spain he might take them to Your Majesty and in case he did not go himself to send them by someone, so that when the decree (order) came, he had them already in his care. I understand that the Viceroy and the Commissary will send these manuscripts to Your Majesty. They are divided into twelve books (bound) in four volumes, and they are on the fleet sailing now, if they have not been sent on the despatch-boat which sailed a short while ago. If they do not send them I humbly entreat Your Majesty to be pleased to advise me so that the manuscripts may be copied again and thus the opportunity to bear in mind the remarkable events of the new world may not be lost. The man who carries those manuscripts, Custodian of this Province, and who goes to Spain to attend the General Chapter, will be able, if Your Royal Majesty should so please, to inform You about me and my work. May God guard Your Royal Majesty with increase of estates for his holy service. Mexico, March 26th, 1578. Sacra Caesarea Real Magestad. Your Majesty's least vassal and chaplain who kisses Your royal hands. (signed) Fray Bernardino de Sahagun."

Very innocently Fray Bernardino believed that his manuscripts were wanted because his work was appreciated and was perhaps going to be printed. This is the only reason why he said that in case the manuscripts did not reach the king to let him know so that he could make another copy. All the king did was to send the poor friar's letter to the Council of the Indies, and this body very laconically decided, on September 18th, "that by decree the Viceroy be ordered to gather all papers or manuscripts, copies and originals that might remain there (in hands of Sahagun) and to send it all to Spain, without leaving a scrap."

Mendieta in his "Historia Eclesiastica Indiana" mentions twice the fact that one of the Viceroys took away Sahagun's books, by cunning or with precaution, to send them to Spain to a certain chronicler who asked insistently for manuscripts on the Indians, and he adds "these will about further his purpose (as he knows nothing concerning the natives of America) as would the verses of Gaiferos; and they will probably be used over there to wrap up spices." The expression "by cunning or precaution" might mean that the manuscripts were asked for with the pretext of sending them to the chronicler, hiding the fact that the Council had sent for them. If the Viceroy really acted in this manner, and it is not merely a supposition of Mendieta (which might well be the case), he perhaps only tried to spare the feelings of the already aged monk, who was so highly deserving the highest respect. It remains a fact, however, that at that time a renewed effort to obtain "histories of the Indies" was being made, as can clearly be gleaned from a Royal Decree, dated at San Lorenzo, June 25th, 1578, in which Philip II ordained that all authorities in his dominians across the seas should send to Spain, in the original or authentic copies, all such documents referring to history that they were able to find in the archives of those countries.

Sahagun's letter is confusing and contradicts those of the Archbishop. In the latter's first letter there is the assurance "that Sahagun told him that he had given the Viceroy the 'Historia' with all of its originals and copies." In the second letter he repeats that everything had been sent on the preceding fleet, that is to say, towards the middle of 1578. The author himself states that he gave the manuscripts to the Commissary, not to the Viceroy, "because when the decree arrived, the former had them already in his keeping." If the Commissary received the clean and clear copy and also the other copies (which would explain what Sahagun told the Archbishop, and it would fully attest for the truth), perhaps it was Fray Rodrigo who gave the Viceroy only what he thought best (the copy made in 1569 and perhaps another original or copy), keeping all the rest. It is very likely that when Sahagun spoke to the Archbishop he was of the belief that the Commissary had delivered everything to Don Martin, "even the recent copy in Spanish and Mexican," and that it was on account of that belief he assured it so positively. However, later on he must have found out the truth, and that it was for this reason that in his "reformed" book on the conquest, he distinguishes very distinctly two deliveries, one to the Viceroy and another to the Commissary. He says in this respect: "Our Lord, King Philip sent for the books, twelve in number. I sent them to him in care of Don Martin Enriquez, who was then Viceroy of this land, and I do not know what became of them, nor in whose hands they are now. After that Father Rodrigo de Sequera took them over after having been Commissary in this country. He never wrote me what had become of those books he took along and which were in Spanish and Mexican and excessively adorned (with paintings, made by the Indians, as we know). I do not know who has them now." As for the new copy which he offered to the king, we may surmise that to do so he counted with some papers he had kept back, perhaps carefully hidden, for it looks as if the good Franciscan monk always rather feared that either the Viceroy or the Commissary were going to keep the manuscripts instead of turning them over to His Majesty, and that was why, in his letter to the king he said that he would replace the books given to both "if they do not send them." He harboured the same mistrust in 1585 when he says that he did not know the whereabouts of the books. It is not known for certain whether the manuscript of Tlaltelolco was sent with the remittance of 1578; however, even if it went, the Tepepulco manuscript remained in Mexico as well as several copies or parts of copies in the hands of different people throughout the province ever since Escalona had so recklessly dispersed them. Sahagun was perfectly cognizant of the fact, and says so very clearly in the "reformed copy of the book on the Conquest: ". . . those who hold this treatise in Mexican only are to know, etc. . . ." This can only refer to the loose copies, distributed so promiscuously. Seven years after the date of his letter to the king, when most of these copies had become completely lost, he was still able to replace a part at least of the work in what he called "Vocabulario, de las tres lenguas."

The mere offer that a new copy would be made if those sent across the ocean should not arrive was an indication to the Council that there remained in Mexico still some material for them to gather, and this fact no doubt caused the resolution of the 18th of September, 1578. It is not quite clear whether anything was obtained from the Commissary or Sahagun himself on account of this resolution or not. We are forced to believe that the copy sent by the Viercoy in 1578 reached Spain and the Council, because the order came back to the Viceroy "to take all that might still be there." If it had not been received, the order would enclose the manuscripts announced by Sahagun and the Archbishop. It is quite evident that Father Sequera took the copy in Spanish and Mexican made, as ordered by him, in 1575-77, but it was no longer possible to hand it to Ovando, the President of the Council who, as we know, had asked for it, because he had passed on in the meantime. What became of that manuscript? It seems to have finally landed in Florence, Italy.

Thus Don Martin Enriquez obtained and sent a copy in 1578, which was not the one of Father Sequera, but was in all probability the one which Fray Miguel Navarro had asked Sahagun to prepare after the text had been corrected by the Mexicans and which, moreover, was the same that had been presented before the Franciscan Chapter in 1570. As the translation into Spanish had not been finished, Father Mendieta had considered them as useless for a chronicler who did not know the Mexican language. For a time it was believed that the chronicler was Antonio de Herrera, which is not possible, since the latter received his appointment as such much later, in 1596.

Betancurt, in Escritores no. 12 speaks of the remission of manuscripts to Spain, but he or else his printer committed the great error to create a new Viceroy, completely unknown, by making of the name of Don Martin Enriquez, who was the one who sent the papers, a Don Martin de Villamanrique, and also changed the title of Don Alvaro Manrique de Zuñiga into Marqués de Villamanrique. But elsewhere Betancurt gives the correct name of the Viceroy (Catálogo de Autores, plana 3). Unfortunately, Clavigero and others after him repeated the erroneous name, paying no heed to the correct one which of courrse led to the supposition that it was the Marqués de Villamanrique who took Sahagun's last manuscripts away from him, a thing quite impossible, since that gentleman arrived in Mexico in 1585, when everything was over and Sahagun was busy reconstructing his great work.

A long time after the "Historia General" was finished, Fray Bernardino thought it convenient to rewrite the book of the Conquest, which in former copies formed book 9 and in the last one was the twelfth. He gives as reason that, when it was written first "they put in it some facts that were wrong, while others were not mentioned that should have been stated." The specific title of the new book was: "Relacion de la Conquista de esta Nueva España como la contaron los soldados indios que se hallaron presentes. Convirtióse en lengua española llana é inteligible y bien enmendada, este año de 1585." It was written or rather edited in three columns. "The first is in the Indian language, coarse (or uncouth) such as they pronounced it. The second column is a correction of the first one, in words as well as whole sentences. The third column is in Spanish, translated according to the corrections of the second. Whosoever has a copy of this treatise in Mexican only, is herewith told that there are many corrected items in the copy of the three columns."

Torquemada had a corrected copy; nevertheless, his citations are not always in accord with the printed form we have today. The differences, which would take up too much space here, appear to come either from a perusal of the second column in Mexican or else from a Spanish text, we do not know. It is not known where Torquemada's copy went, but long afterwards a certain manuscript appeared in Mexico which was copied by Fray Esteban Manchola, in 1668 and published. (Florencia, La Estrella del Norte de Mexico, chapt. 28.) The original was signed by Fray Bernardino and belonged to Dr. Juan Francisco de Montemayor y Cuenca who, in 1679, took it to Spain with intention to have it published. It is possible that the copy of Father Manchola might be the one Betancurt used later on. Carlos Maria de Bustamante, editor of the Historia General, mentions the fact that during the upheavals of the month of May, 1808, in Madrid, Spain, a robbery was committed in the "Secretaria" of the Academy of History and several bundles of manuscripts by Sahagun were stolen; one of these was the history of the conquest. He copies a sales certificate which states that in 1828, when the Conde de la Cortina was in Madrid he bought this manuscript from Señor Don Lorenzo Ruiz de Artieda, through mediation of Don José Musso y Valiente. Count Cortina probably brought it to Mexico when he went there in 1832 and facilitated it to Bustamante almost at once, for the latter was already at work on the copy in 1833. He assures us that the codex was written entirely by Sahagun and bore his signature. Don Joaquin Garcia Icazbalceta doubts that, because being written only in Spanish, it was not the original which Sahagun himself states to have been written in three columns. Bustamante however even tries to make that plausible by saying in a note (p. 20) that the Mexican text was appended to the manuscript but that as those who stole it in Madrid did not understand that language, they discarded that part and sold Count Cortina only the Spanish text. The mere fact of the arrangement of the manuscript in three parallel columns annuls such a supposition. Nor is it admissible to suppose that the author wrote an autographed copy of only the Spanish version, for if already in 1570 the tremor of his hands made it difficult for him to write, how much less able would he have been in 1585 or later, to do so. In the Boletin de la Real Academia de la Historia, vol. VI, p. 122, issued in 1885, Señor José F. Ramirez declares emphatically that the manuscript in question is not an autograph of Sahagun. It might be, at best, a copy signed by Sahagun and perhaps the one Montemayor took to Spain.

It is quite natural to suppose that in order to co-ordinate a work of the great importance of Sahagun's history of Mexico many statements, essays, notes, partial copies, and even adaptations like the one of book XII were made. At the time all his manuscripts were distributed throughout the Province, many had occasion to see them, and many a one made extracts for his own use. Muñoz Camargo had them before him when he wrote the Historia de Tlaxcala and Suárez de Peralta made many notes from their contents for his own use. Dr. Francisco Hernandez, the famous Spanish physician, was the one who profited the most, not only by the text but by the pictures as well.

In short, the author himself mentions only four complete documents:

1. The manuscript of Tepepulco, with drawings and their explanation in Mexican under each picture.

2. The one of Tlaltelolco, corrected later at the Convent of San Francisco in Mexico by the author himself. It was written entirely in Mexican without any division into columns in a very poor handwriting, with many corrections and interlinear writing.

3. The copy made with the kind assistance (financial) of the Provincial Father Miguel Navarro in 1569, the text of which was later on corrected by the Mexicans. This manuscript, approved by the Franciscan Chapter in 1570, was written in a clear letter, in three columns, the center one bearing the Mexican text, the one to the left the Spanish translation, and the one to the right the comments. It is probable that these last two columns were only partly done, a small part even at that. This clean copy may also have been used as rough draft for the new copy of 1575, reduced to two columns. The 1569 copy was divided into twelve books, which facilitated their dispersion throughout the Province.

The "Sumario" which the Fathers Navarro and Mendieta took to Spain must not be considered as a new copy of the manuscript.

4. The copy made in 1576 and 1577 for Fray Rodrigo de Sequera, divided into four volumes and written in two columns, in Spanish and Mexican, and enhanced by many pictures.

There is no clear notice of any other copies.

Two of the manuscripts seem to have gone to Spain. Viceroy Enriquez sent one, presumably number three of the above mentioned, and Fray Rodrigo took number four. If the second request of the Council of the Indies had any effect, it is probable that number two was sent, but number one remained in Mexico and cannot be traced any more.

There is almost as much uncertainty concerning the whereabout of the codices as of the text. It is difficult to identify the codices on hand in Mexico with those that were made for the purpose at Sahagun's suggestion, nor with the ones which were sent to Spain.

Sahagun's great historical work rested in oblivion for two centuries, in fact, until on July 17th, 1779, Don Juan Bantista Muñoz was appointed as Historiographer of the Indies. He at once set about with great zeal to assemble whatever manuscripts could be found to accomplish the work his difficult commission called for. He naturally was very anxious to acquire the complete set of manuscripts and codices pertaining to Sahagun's work, but, being convinced, no doubt, that none of the bibliographers or chroniclers of the epoch would offer information of their whereabouts, he began a personal search everywhere, particularly in the archives of Sevilla and Simancas. He found nothing; later he was told of a copy of the work at the Franciscan convent of Tolosa. This proves that he did not examine the bibliographies which might have given him clues; had he done so, he would have found the annotation by Fray Juan de San Antonio, and that would have saved the tedious search in the above mentioned archives. The existence of the manuscript at Tolosa once known, he found no difficulty to obtain it by means of a royal order which read:

"The king having decided that Señor Don Juan Bantista Muñoz, Chief Cosmographer of the Indies, who is herewith presented to your Reverence, should go to that convent to examine the 'Historia del Reino de Nueva España,' written by Fray Bernardino de Sahagun, and all similar manuscripts that might exist in that archive and might prove useful to the commission he has received from His Majesty to write a General History of America, of which I herewith inform your Reverence by Royal Order, that you may facilitate him the said documents. And if the said commissioner should consider it necessary to retain in his keeping any one of those documents for any length of time, he will give the corresponding guarantee for their return. May God preserve your Reverence for many years. El Pardo, April 6th, 1783. Joseph de Gálvez. To the Rev. Father Superior of the Convent of St. Francis of Tolosa."

On the 30th of that same month (April) Muñoz presented himself at the convent with the order, and by virtue of it "he took and carried off with him one folio volume which contained the Historia original de Nueva España." Muñoz never returned the codex (contained therein) to the convent. In the year 1800, seventeen years later, the monks of San Francisco de Tolosa gave a power of attorney to Don Antonio Uguina, of Madrid, to claim it. The latter did so and "was given to understand that His Majesty would be extraordinarily pleased if they (the monks) would let him keep the original" in exchange for which they were offered an authentic copy. The attorney called a meeting of the friars and explained the king's wishes; they unanimously declared themselves satisfied, and a formal deed of transfer was set up, dated March 27th, 1801, before the notary public Manuel Joaquin Purundarena. Of course, the Order was duly thanked for this act, but that authentic copy met with many difficulties, especially because there seemed to be no special appropriation of funds provided for said copy. After having reclaimed on several occasions, Uguina finally, on the 16th of September, 1802, succeeded in the obtaining devolution of six of the books, but had to wait until July 4th, 1804, to obtain the other six.

The above passage is obtained from a Ms. extracted by Fernandez Duro, called "Expediente sobre la copia de la Historia de la Nueva España, escrita por Fr. Bernardino de Sahagun." These proceedings are open to suspicion, or at least create confusion, for we must ask, did the four volumes of which Fray Juan de S. Antonio speak really exist in the convent of Tolosa? If so, then either the monk hid the three with Mexican text, or else Muñoz, although he saw them, did not want them, for being useless to him (being in Mexican). If they did not exist there, then what had become of them? In any case, to which of the copies mentioned as being by Sahagun did that codex, written all in Spanish, belong?

Icazbalceta is of the opinion that the Tolosa manuscript was not one in four volumes, and that the extract made by Muñoz did not come from one of these four volumes, the other three having remained at the convent, because they were in Mexican, which the cosmographer of the king did not understand. Upon examining the announcement of Fray Juan de San Antonio we find that this bibliographer always added the word "vidi" to any notice of a document he had seen; the supposed Sahagun copy does not bear this sign in the list. In an appendix to the bibliography he says that the author of the "Historia" had belonged to the province of Cantabria: "Alumnum fuisse ex Cantabricae prov. dixi ex relatione ejusdem Provinciae;" and this seems to explain it all. This bibliographer spoke about Sahagun and probably mentioned his historical work from a report that had been sent to him from the Province of Cantabria. In this report the monks probably included—to make it more impressive—a copy of the title page of Sahagun's book, and on this title page four volumes are mentioned and Fray Juan accepted this as a fact that the copy at Tolosa consisted of these four volumes, while there really existed only one, namely, the Spanish part. In the "Boletin de la Real Academia de la Historia," vol. VI, page 86 (February, 1885) appears the following note, which had been written in the book at the time it was copied in 1804: "this book, although it is called an original, is only a copy, nor has it any other merit than its having been written in the ancient handwriting of the time of the conquest of New Spain, or a few years later." It has no connection with any one of the manuscripts mentioned by Sahagun, because it bears none of their marks, nor the signature of the author who was in the habit of signing all copies made either by himself or one of his copyists. It is in all probability a contemporary copy, as the writing indicates, made, perhaps, by order of the author, although this is doubtful because of the lack of his signature. The original from which this copy of the Spanish part was made might very well have been the manuscript of Father Sequera, which is doubtless the one now at Florence, the more so that the Spanish of the Florentine codex is identical with the one of Tolosa. A further proof that it is the copy of an original which was more explicit is the following passage of Par. 10 of chap. 2, book XI, which says: "The text of the 10th paragraph, which speaks of the various parts of birds, internal as well as external, are all synonyms, and in the translation they are given in the Mexican language, explaining in Spanish only to which part of the bird they are to be applied, or in which part they are used, and so I did not put any of this down, because it applies more to the Mexican language than to anything else." This no doubt means that the author, Fray Bernardino, put the nomenclature of the various parts of birds (wings, head, body, feet, etc.) in the Mexican column and translated it for the Spanish part, but with the native names, but the copyist of the Tolosa manuscript, when he found that this was rather a linguistic than a historical matter, simply left it out and replaced it by above note. Mr. Jourdanet, the French translator of Sahagun, however, believed that the note was by Sahagun himself, left it out altogether, contenting himself with a note of its contents (p. 710). The existence of this copy in the (Franciscan) Province of Cantabria without any indication concerning its origin no doubt led to the erroneous supposition that Sahagun had been a member of that Province. It is not known how that copy ever got there, but it is well to remember that Sahagun's principal supporters, Fathers Mendieta and Navarro, were both from Cantabria and belonged to that Province. The first named returned to Spain after the historical work of Fray Bernardino had become known in Mexico, and he had possibly examined it himself; the second, Father Navarro, returned to Spain to die in his old convent, presumably because nothing is known of his later life after leaving Mexico, and he may have taken a copy with him, or may have had one made in Spain to leave it later in Tolosa. At any rate, this copy of Tolosa seems to have been the matrix of the editions of today.

After Muñoz' sudden death, July 19th, 1799, all his writings and documents were sent to the "Secretaria del Despacho de Gracia y Justicia de Indias," and from there to the library of the "Real Academia de la Historia," for the reason perhaps that since 1755 the office of Chronicler of the Indies had been incorporated into that learned society. So when the king asked the convent of Tolosa for the codex, this latter was already in the library of the Academy. Quite naturally, as soon as it was obtained it went into the private library of the king, and it appears to have been there in 1807 when Don Antonio Capmany wrote his "Questiones Criticas sobre varios puntos de Historia Economica, Politica y Militar (Madrid, 1807). On page 177 this author cites some utterances made by Sahagun, which he says he took from a codex "of a handwriting of the beginning of the reign of Philip II, which codex, after having been kept in the library of a certain monastery, is today the property of His Majesty in his private Royal library." The allusion to the Tolosa codex is clear. Why and how it went back to the library of the Academy is unknown. It is possible that because it belonged to the collection of Muñoz' papers, the king donated it to the Academy in 1815, as we find in "Memorias de la Real Academia de la Historia, vol. VI, p. XII: "Although the donation had been made on the cited date, it was not delivered until March, 1816."

Señor José F. Ramirez saw it there, and he gives us the following description: It is a volume in folio, a clean, clear copy with wide margins. The writing is clear of the XVI century, in modern Dutch binding, entitled, on the outside: Coleccion de Muñoz.—Sahagun.—Historia de las cosas de Nueva España. Num. de orden, 50, Marca, A77. The codex has 682 pages, recently numbered, and it contains the twelve books of the history, in Spanish only. Although various pictures are mentioned, this volume only contains the one of the Mexican Olympus in book III, p. 396. At end of book I are the texts of the Scriptures which Bustamante translated into Spanish while Kingsborough omitted it. Sr. Ramirez adds that "the author renders them more or less extensively, making precise and interesting allusions and applications to the pagan rites of the Mexicans." This is not included in the three editions extant in Mexico, but as Señor Garcia Icazbalceta adds it to his Bibliografia Mexicana it might be wise to add it either to this volume or publish it in vol. II, to follow soon, we hope.

Ramirez then continues with a description of a Mexican codex in the same library. It is bound in an old parchment cover on which, in black ink, is the following strange title: "Obras de Sor Maria de la Antigua." On the inside of this same vellum cover we find, effaced, an old mark: S. 2. XXII. C. n. 3: today it bears the same number, 103. With but a slight exception, the entire codex is in Mexican. "Its aspect shows still that it was originally a clean copy, although in various handwritings, and later converted into a rough copy. There is no doubt that it belongs to the sixteenth century, because near the center and again at the end it bears the signature of Father Sahagun." The manuscript begins with two empty folios on the first of which the above strange title is repeated, followed by 342 folios of text, without numbering of folios, but today all numbered, which constitute books VIII, IX, X, and XI of the Historia. There is no title-page.

We repeat here the most notable parts of the careful copy Ramirez made of the codex, which still can be obtained in printed form:

Book IX begins on folio 26 and continues to the end in accordance with the Spanish Codex, but differs in chapters 16, 17, 20 and 21 (last of the book). The difference is very serious. These chapters treat of silversmiths, lapidaries, and of implements used in the manufacture of objects in precious metals and feather-work. The Spanish codex limits itself to less than four lines, simply mentioning the various industries, while the Mexican one covers several pages of from 41-45 lines closely written for the discussion. Book IX concludes on folio 50 with the signature of the author.

Next come 35 folios which contain many colored pictures representing the symbolic effigies of the Mexican kings and governors, the latter succeeding the kings after the conquest in Mexico, Tetocuco and Huexotla. There are also figurative representations of a judicial court, of the meting-out of justice, of armour, flags, helmets, spears, drums, military devices and ornaments, with long nomenclatures of proper names belonging to nutritious substances, objects for the wardrobe, devices, distinctive emblems and instruments and implements for art work, public buildings, seats, mats, etc., etc., all these items being related to matters treated in book VIII, of which this part appears to be an illustrated reproduction. Much of this is written in ink of a gorgeous red color. This part concludes on page 81.

The next part begins with a (so-called) chap. 4 divided into seven large sections called paragraphs. These paragraphs contain the proper names of people, relationships, offices and professions, many of which are accompanied by short explanations. This chapter ends on page 85, and is followed by two blank ones. The contents tally with the first chapters of book X of the Spanish codex.

Book X, which begins on folio 88, also tallies as far as the subject is concerned, but all the pages are divided into three vertical columns; the one on the left contains the Spanish text, the center one the Mexican. This central column bears, moreover, over each sentence or word a progressive number until the end of the corresponding paragraph. The right hand column, also numbered, is the translation of each one of the Mexican words or phrases with their synonyms, etymologies and variants according to the way they are used, that is to say, when speaking to men or women, to relatives, persons in authority or distinguished otherwise, or else to inferiors. The Mexican language is exceedingly rich. This same distribution or division continues up to paragraph 4 of chapter 3, which speaks of the "mujer moza" (the unmarried woman), and fills the rest of folio 96. The reverse and the seven following folios are blanks, no doubt reserved for a conclusion of the chapter.

"Then follow six folios, in the same form, and reproduce, in rough draft, the preceding folios to the end of chapter 3. On folio 111 continues chapter 4, again in three columns, but only the right side of the page, the reverse of each folio and all the following until the end of chapter 26 contain only the Mexican text in the central column, the other two remaining blank. Folios 146-48 of the Mexican text represent personal names written in two and three columns, which are not found in the other.

"Chapter 27 of the Spanish codex consists of barely four lines, confined to the notice 'that the author did not translate any part of this chapter into Spanish,' substituting it by a narrative. Then follows chapter 28, disposed again in three columns, only the central one being filled in with the Mexican text. The book ends on folio 197, with chapter 29 and the signature of Father Sahagun, continuing in accord with the Spanish codex. Then two blank folios.

"On folio 200 begins book XI, which is dedicated to natural history, conserving the expressed form and also bearing only the Mexican text. Its narration is in concordance with the Spanish codex, but not in the sequence of subjects. In many places the Mexican text is more abundant. At the end of the book there is again the signature of the author, and with it the volume ends."

The origin of the codex is entered in the proceedings of a meeting of the Academy of History, celebrated on July 30th, 1762, as follows:

"Habiendome avisado el Señor Don Felipe de Samaniego, que en poder de un librero habia un tomo en folio, manuscrito, en lengua mexicana, de letra, al parecer, de tiempo poco posterior á la conquista de aquel Reino, y con algunas pinturas de Indios, armas y adornos militares, fui á verle, y pareciéndome ser digno de comprarle para la Academia, di cuenta de ello al Señor Director, con cuya orden le ajusté y compré en precio de ciento y cincuenta reales. Hice presente el librero en la junta, y habiéndose reconocido, se aprobó lo ejecutado.—Eugenio de Llaguno Amirola."

Señor Ramirez heard of another Mexican codex, very similar to the one of the Academy; however, he did not pay any attention to it, be it that he never saw it or had not been able to make sure that it belonged to Sahagun's work. And, indeed, there is no absolute certainty about it. However, as there is no doubt about its being an ancient Mexican document, we might as well state here what is known about it, for in some way there is a certain relation between this and the manuscript at the library of the Academy. Whatever is known about it is due to the efforts of a Benedictine monk, Fray Martin Sarmiento, who was appointed

Chronicler of the Indies in 1750 and remained as such for five years, but we know of no special work in his field that he accomplished in that time.

After his retirement from office and once more in his convent, he received one day an interesting call, and he tells it himself in the following paragraph:

"On August 1st of 1762 there came to visit me, in my cell, Señor Antonio Sanz, well known printer of Madrid. He showed me an old memorandum-book in folio, paper-bound, the writing of which consisted of Spanish characters, but the language was strange to me. It contained several painted pictures of animals, birds, etc. To the questions of Mr. Sanz to tell him the merits, contents and author of said badly worn volume, I did not delay long to answer that I did not understand a word because, without a doubt, the text was in Mexican in its square and its rounded forms as well. Also I told him that although I owned the Vocabulario Mexicano by Fray Alonso Molina, in order to look up one or the other single word, this was not sufficient to give him an idea of the text of this volume. I told him merely by guessing that the volume probably contained notes made by some quaint Mexican who intended to write a Natural History of New Spain in the Mexican language."

It so happened that the same afternoon Señor Don Felipe Samaniego also came to visit me in my cloister and he, upon seeing the notebook of Señor Sanz, told us that it looked very much like other books, also in the Mexican language, and which formed a Mexican Codex owned by the Academia de la Historia. Not without a certain amount of justification I suspected that the book Sanz had might be some stolen part of the said manuscript codex. Señor Samaniego promised me on the occasion to send the said codex to my cloister so that I might examine it and give him my verdict."

Father Sarmiento continues by saying that on the very next day the codex of the Academy was sent to him; that, although he was unable to read it, because it was in Mexican, some of the marginal notes in Spanish, and the signature of a monk which occurred twice, once in the middle and again at the end of the book, made him recognize it as the work of Fray Bernardino de Sahagun. He then gives an account of the author and of his writings, which he extracts from Torquemada's work. Among the writings (by Sahagun) he mentions some songs (cantares), the only part printed and, he adds: "It is true that in the book owned by Sanz one sees columns in larger type of letter and with lines that rhyme." A little farther on he says: "In conclusion I would say that the present codex owned by the Academy is very valuable, useful and quaint for anyone who knows Mexican, but also deserves appreciation from those who do not know that language. I am, therefore, of the opinion that the Academy should purchase the book owned by Sanz and add it to the codex. One of the former owners of this codex made it ridiculous by binding it in a cover with the title on the outside: 'Obras de Sor Maria de la Antigua.' This cover was, no doubt, picked up at random and with no other intention than to bind a lot of loose books into a good solid cover, and they got hold of the one with a very misleading title." He then gives a short description of the codex by stating that "it (the one of the Academy) has no illustrations, while on the contrary the book of Sanz contains many pictures of objects of natural history." He finally proposes that someone should translate the codex of the Academy into Spanish, as well as the one owned by Sanz, or at least book XI, which contains the notes on natural history.

At the meeting of the Academy of August 6th, 1762, Don Felipe Samaniego reported the existence of the book owned by Sanz, and it was agreed that the former should try to purchase the book by whatever means he considered best or, in case this could not be done, he was to obtain permission to copy it. At the following meeting of August 13th, Samaniego presented the report of Father Sarmiento, which was read and put away with the codex (of the Academy). The proceedings are as follows:

"And bearing in mind that in order that this work may be useful it is necessary to search someone who knows the Mexican language and who can translate it. We are informed by Messrs. Diéguez and Marcos that there is a Tlaxcaltecan priest in Madrid who, so we are told, is capable to do this work and therefore Mr. Diéguez has been commissioned to propose it to him." A week later, on August 20th, Samaniego informed the meeting that Sanz refused absolutely to sell the book, but that he would allow it to be copied as soon as a friend to whom he had lent it, would return it. On the other hand, Señor Diéguez reported that the Tlaxcaltecan priest had seen the codex of the Academy and "found some difficulty in understanding it on account of its ancient and forgotten language;" that notwithstanding this difficulty, he said he would study it slowly and Diéguez would report on the results of this study.

It is not known what became of the book of Sanz or whether the codex of the Academy was ever translated. The Mexican priest mentioned as possible translator may very well have been the one mentioned by Robertson with reference to a letter from a Spanish gentleman. This letter says: "There is now in Madrid an aged priest (monk?) native of Tlaxcala, whose name is Don Juan Cerilo de Castilla Aquihual Catehutle (sic), descendant of a cacique converted to Christianity shortly after the conquest. . . . He came to Madrid more than thirty-four years ago for the sole purpose to solicit admission of the Indians to colleges and seminaries of New Spain (Mexico)." This had been written about 1788, and it is said that the Tlaxcaltecan priest arrived in Madrid in 1754, so that he was certainly there when a translator for the codex was sought. The Mexican names have been misspelled by Robertson in his History of America, but the name of Castilla was that of a noble family of Tlaxcala.

Ramirez mentions another codex by Sahagun, although very slightly; he says: "Señor Don Manuel de Goicoechea had the good fortune to discover another fragment of Sahagun in the library of His Majesty. From the intelligent and interesting notes he made of it and which he showed me, I think it is also a rough draft which probably belonged to the second copy of 1569. It is somewhat more explicit than the one of the Academy, and is at least the duplicate of one of its books." Señor Garcia Icazbalceta, upon receiving this information, wrote to Madrid asking for particulars, and received the following information from Señor Fernandez Duro:

"Private library of His Majesty, the King (Madrid, Royal Palace) 2, F. 2—manuscript in folio, bound in a mottled cover, entitled: Sahagun. Historia de Nueva España. And, in another small (binder's) title in red in an upper corner, MS. After the flyleaf and two blank pages, we read the following inscription in a flowing Spanish hand: "En este volumen se contienen seis libros del original de los libros historiales de las cosas desta Nueva España tocantes á lo espiritual y temporal, que son todos doce libros."

"The words in the fifth line, 'de las cosas desta Nueva España,' are written in the German Gothic style. On the first page of the manuscript proper is the title:

" 'Historia uniuersal de las cosas de la nueua españa repartida en doze libros en lengua mexicana y española, fecha por el muy reuerendo padre, fray bernardino de Sahagun, frayle de sant francisco de obseruancia.

" 'libro primero en que se trata de los dioses: que adoravan los naturales desta tierra, que es la nueua españa.

" 'Capitulo primero, que habla del principal dios: que adorauan y á quien sacrificauan los mexicanos, llamado vitzilubuchtli.

" 'Este dios, llamado vitzilubuchtli, fue otro hercules: el qual fue robustissimo de grandes fuerzas, y muy belicoso: gran destruydor de pueblos, y matador de gentes.

" 'En el folio 19 está el

" 'Capitulo veyute y dos, que habla del dios llamado tezcatzoncatl: que es uno de los dioses del vino.

" 'Segundo libro que trata del calendario, fiestas y cerimonias, sacrificios y solenydades: que estos naturales desta nueua España, hacian: a honvra de sus dioses.

" 'Libro quinto, que habla de los agueros: que esta gente mexicana usaua.

" 'Capitulo primero del aguero que tomauan cuando alguno oya de noche aullar alguna bestia fiera, ó llorar como vieja: i de lo que dezian los agueros en este caso.

" 'Capitulo treze, en que se trata de otras fantasmas que aparecian de noche."

Thus far the notes of contents of the manuscript which are quite insufficient to enable us to classify this codex. No mention is made as to the language in which it is written or whether it is both in Spanish and Mexican, as the flyleaf tells us. We know not to what epoch the handwriting can be ascribed, while the orthography is of the 16th century. This latter, however, might have been simply copied in a later issue. To judge from the flyleaf, the volume should contain the first six books of the "Historia," but the descriptive index stops at book V. It appears disconnected, truncated and, as Señor Ramirez says, it is not a duplicate of any of the books in possession of the Academia. Not even the notes tally, thus do not, seemingly, refer to the same codex.

Another exceedingly important codex is the one in the Biblioteca Laurenziana of Florence, Italy, known for almost a century and a half. It was described minutely already in 1793 by Bandini in his work, Bibliothecae Mediceae Palatinae in Laurentianam translatae Codices I-CCXLIV. Bibliotheca Leopoldina Laurentiana, seu Catalogus Manuscriptorum qui nuper in Laurentianam translati sunt. Sub auspiciis Fernandi III Arch. Austr. Magni Etr. Ducis, Angelus Maria Bandinius eiusdem Bibliothecae Reg. Praefectus recensuit, illustravit, edidit. . . . (Florence, 1793). The learned Franciscan monk, Fray Marcelino da Civezza, mentions it in his Saggio di Bibliografia Geografica, Storica, Etnografica Sanfranciscana. (Prato, 1897, p. 525) and Bandini, above quoted, gives a lengthy description of the contents of all the books.

Señor Cayetano Rosell, towards the end of the 19th century, proposed to the Real Academia de la Historia a plan to publish the great work of Sahagun by making use of the Florentine codex together with the one at the Academy in Madrid and whatever else might be gathered or discovered here and there, but his death put an end to such a highly commendable undertaking.

Up to the time Señor Joaquin Garcia Icazbalceta published his "Bibliografia Mexicana del Siglo XVI," in 1886 the following Codices by Sahagun were known.

1. The one which passed from the hands of the Franciscans of Tolosa into possession of Señor Juan B. Muñoz in 1783; and which later went to the Secretaria del Despacho de Gracia y Justicia de Indias, to remain

finally in the library of the Royal Academy of History in Madrid. It consists of just one volume containing the Spanish text of the twelve books with only one illustration, and does not correspond with any one of the manuscripts mentioned by Sahagun, nor does it bear his signature. It is possibly an old copy of the Spanish text in the Ms. of Father Sequera.

2. The Mexican Codex of the Academy of History, which comprises books VIII-XI, with a few additions. This is an original bearing in several places the author's signature. It appears to belong, however, to two distinct manuscripts and contains, moreover, parts of copies. The first original fragment contains books VIII and IX (folios 1-50 of the codex), and belongs to the Tlaltelolco manuscript. It is written in full lines and only in Mexican, with exception of the headlines or titles, and a few additions which the author inserted in his own handwriting and in Spanish. In order to justify the assumption that it is the Tlaltelulco manuscript we find the following indications: first—in chapter 1 of book VIII he only speaks of the Mexican chieftains "before the arrival of the Spaniards," that is, until 1519 and not until 1560, as it appears in print where this particular chapter is divided into two parts, the second one entitled "Continuación de la historia de los reyes mexicanos." The first part no doubt was written in Tlaltelolco, the second (which does not seem to exist in the manuscript, to judge from the title) may well be one of the many additions the Mexicans made upon copying the original again in 1569. Second—in the manuscript chapters 3 and 5 of book VIII are missing and this book in the printed copy speaks mainly of the Acolhua chieftains. This omission can be explained by the fact that the Tlaltelolcos probably only knew the Alcolhuas of Tepepulco and, as the manuscript was composed in a great hurry ("con mucha prisa"), they did not care to copy the above two chapters to which they had nothing new and important to add. The Spanish notes which the author added to this manuscript in his own hand were written most certainly after the clean copy had already been sent to Madrid. By examining them very carefully one could almost fix the time when our missionary still retained the manuscript at Tlaltelolco.

The second fragment containing books X and XI is undoubtedly part of the manuscript of Mexico made in 1569. This copy was the only one made in three columns per page, and so it appears on the copy of the Academy from folio 103 to the end of the book. Notwithstanding the fact that now it appears more like a rough draft, it once was a clean, clear copy, and this was the fate of all or most of Sahagun's writings, because he constantly made corrections, additions, or notes, and consequently what today was a neat copy tomorrow looked like a rough draft. This happened to the copy of 1569. Between folio 50, where the original one of Tlaltelolco ends, and folio 103, where the original copy of Mexico begins, three fragments are interpolated which look like transcripts. The first one of these is of 35 folios and tallies with book VIII; it contains many images. It is not very well described, so that one remains in doubt whether to ascribe it to the codex of Tepepulco or whether it should rather be considered as a transcript of the manuscript of 1575-77, or is, perhaps, some rough draft of the same. A comparison with the Florence codex might elucidate this point. Ramirez is of the opinion that the above mentioned fragment may have belonged to the 1569 copy; however, as he fails to state whether or not it is written in three columns (as was that of 1569), it is still doubtful. The second transcript has 7 folios and bears no clear connection with the rest; the third has 8 folios followed by 7 blank ones. It seems to be a clean copy, unfinished though, of the manuscript of 1569. These two last transcripts treat of matters corresponding to book X.

The Academy acquired this codex in 1762, and at that same epoch the printer Sanz owned another part of a Mexican document. The only indication, however, that it might be by Sahagun consists of a very short description of it by Father Sarmiento, who had owned the manuscript a very short while and, moreover, did not know the language in which it was written. He expresses himself as follows: "some annotations made by a quaint Mexican who intended to write on the natural history of New Spain (Mexico) in the Mexican language." It was enhanced or illustrated by paintings of birds and other animals, and in the written text there were columns "of a larger type (of letter) and in versified lines."

The idea that this codex might be by Sahagun occurred to the learned Benedictine monk only after he had seen the one owned by the Academy, but it is best to be more guarded of opinion. Sahagun was not the only author of natural history in Mexico of the 16th century. Dr. Francisco Hernandez also had at least part of his great work on Mexican Natural History translated into Mexican and also furnished adequate illustrations. It is quite likely that when he returned to Spain he took part of this with him, so why might not the book owned by Sanz be from the pen of Hernandez?

Even supposing that it was part of Sahagun's work, it could only belong to book XI, and would simply be one of the many copies made in the 16th century.

The Academy tried to acquire this volume from Sanz or at least to obtain permission to copy it, but did not succeed either way. Today the whereabouts of it are unknown.

3. The fragment in the private library of the king. There is no clear nor ample enough description of it, and there is no primitive codex to

which it might correspond. It is even doubtful whether the notes copied above refer to the same manuscript as those of Ramirez.

4. The great Codex of Florence, Italy, complete in both languages and enhanced by many illustrations. For these two reasons it is the most important of all known so far. The description tallies with the well illustrated copy of Fray Francisco de Sequera, notwithstanding the fact that the latter is divided into four volumes, while the codex consists of only three. The first volume consists of the five first books, the sixth more voluminous than any one of the others makes a volume by itself, a fact even more credible if it is true, as Kingsborough indicates, that this sixth book has come down to our era greatly decreased. The six remaining books form volumes 3 and 4. It is easy to surmise that later on the four original volumes of the copy were reduced to three of equal size.

5. The ancient copy of the second edition of book XII, which belonged to Conde de la Cortina, who lent it to Bustamante for publication. It is not known so far what became of it.

6. As sixth codex we may consider the small but interesting fragment in the Mexican National library, which will be mentioned later.

The modern copies of the great work of Sahagun present no less confusion than the old ones. In the catalogue of the Muñoz collection Fuster says: "There is another volume in black binding, paper-lined, the label of which is 'Sahagun,' and on the flyleaf it bears the following inscription: 'Historia Universal de las cosas de Nueva España, en doce libros y cuatro volumenes, en lengua española, compuesta y copilada por el M. R. P. Fr. Bernardino de Sahagun de la Orden de los frailes menores de la Observancia. . . .' A bundle of loose sheets in folio which are copies of the above mentioned volume, but only as far as chapter 13 of book III, and even so there are missing the beginning, dedication, prologue and summary of the five first books. Mr. Muñoz was working on this copy when death overtook him." The first of these two items is the Códice Tolosano, the second its copy which Muñoz was making.

Ramirez mentions also a fragment of a modern copy in the library of the Real Academia de la Historia (Madrid), which must be the one alluded to by Fuster (above), although while the latter states that it only went as far as chapter 13 of book III, Ramirez says it goes to chapter 12 of book IV, and adds that it is very defectively bound, so much so that it is almost illegible.

Col. Diego Panes, who was himself a learned collector and writer of Mexican lore, as well as a friend and correspondent of Muñoz, obtained from the latter the loan of the Tolosa Ms. And here we stumble upon a new difficulty, for Panes assures us that this codex consisted of "two large volumes of very close, ancient script," while the Tolosa Ms., when it came from the convent of Tolosa, was in one volume, as is manifest from the deed of delivery to Muñoz. Moreover, there is no trace of another old copy in the hands of the latter, and still less is there any trace of his having obtained another copy in two volumes from the same convent; and yet the one he lent Panes consisted of two volumes! It is difficult to solve this problem unless we accept a supposition made by Garcia Icazbalceta to the effect that Panes possibly considered the fact that there were two different dedications to Father Sequera, one in Spanish and the other in Latin, in this codex, to mean that they belonged to two different volumes, albeit bound in one, which might have been merely an accidental error by the book-binder. Still, why should Panes mention two separate volumes instead of one? At any rate, he made his own copy in 1793, and to facilitate perusal he divided it into three volumes with the odd coincidence of an identical distribution of the Codex of Florence. Panes brought his own copy to Mexico with intention to have it printed there and, although he did not accomplish that, at least his copy became the original of Bustamante's edition, herewith translated.

In 1802-1804 a copy of Panes' Ms. was made for the Franciscans of Tolosa, which went there through the mediation of the well-known collector, Antonio Uguino, and if the latter delivered it at once to the monks it probably perished when the convent was burned down during the war with the French, according to Father Mier.

Lord Kingsborough is said to have had another copy made "in the handwriting of Muñoz, some forty years ago," which makes us go back to the last decade of the 18th century. It is more than doubtful that Muñoz who had not even been able to finish his own copy before he died, should have done this one, so that when Lord Kingsborough says in his "Antiquities of Mexico, vol. VI, pp. 265-66 . . . which was transcribed about forty years ago by the hand of the Spanish librarian Muñoz . . . it . . . consists of two folio volumes," there is a mistake somewhere.

Sacchi, who wrote the biography of the Italian painter, Aglio, employed by Kingsborough to collect the material for the great work, "Antiquities of Mexico," speaks of the discovery by Muñoz of Sahagun's work and adds: "with his customary energy Muñoz copied in his own writing the entire work, thereby enriching his valuable collection of manuscripts, etc., but which, unfortunately, he was not allowed to enjoy fully. Later Aglio, commissioned by his wealthy patron (Kingsborough) obtained towards the end of 1828 a transcript of that copy, which was published in 1830." The biography of Aglio was published in 1868 at Cremona.

Although here a complete copy of Sahagun is mentioned, made by

Muñoz, we may be allowed to doubt its ever having existed, for above mentioned reasons. It is very probable that Kingsborough's copy was made from the Tolosa Ms. directly which, being among the manuscripts of the Muñoz collection, was erroneously thought to have been made by him. Garcia Icazbalceta believes that the copy Aglio purchased was one sold about that time by the distinguished Spanish marine officer Felipe Bansá to a London bookdealer for 135£. Bansá was then one of the Spanish emigrants residing in London. The copy in question had been made when the Ms. already formed part of the library of the Spanish Royal Academy, that is, after 1816, and could not have been the one given to Uguina in 1802 or 1804 for the convent of Tolosa.

Although this copy was then already in the library of the Academy, and there existed several copies of it, the literary world did not know the "History" by Sahagun. The first to call attention to it were the editors of a monthly journal published in London under the title "Ocios de Españoles emigrados." On pp. 369-380 of the first volume these men gave quite an extensive extract of the work for which they no doubt used the copy of Bansá who may even have been the author of the article. A few years later the same publication was published almost simultaneously in Mexico and London.

Truly unlucky was our great missionary Sahagun to the very last, his valuable data being in part exploited by foreign editors and in part by Bustamante, which was almost worse.

Kingsborough included Sahagun's History in his great collective work, called "Antiquities of Mexico" (London 1830-48, in 9 large volumes). Strangely enough, he had the odd idea to divide the history into two distinct parts; the 40 first chapters of book VI are in vol. V of his work, and all the rest of it is gathered into vol. VI. There are no notes of any kind.

Although Col. Panes brought his copy of Sahagun back to Mexico with him when he returned from Spain in 1795, he told no one of it, nor showed it to his friends, so that upon his death 16 years later (1811) nobody knew of the existence in their midst of this important work on the ancient history of Mexico. His motive may have been the desire to publish it himself. Mexico at that time went through her war of independence, so no one had either time nor the desire to look over historical documents, but with the declaration of independence accomplished in 1821, the family of Panes decided to offer the papers of the late colonel to the first Mexican Congress, and did so through intermediary of Congressman José Ignacio Esteva of Veracruz. However, as this happened early in August, 1822, when that assembly was about to be dissolved, the commission appointed to examine those papers never reached a decision. Amid the many political disorders of that epoch, several of the manuscripts were lost or perhaps stolen, and the valuable donation was buried in the archives of the Chamber of Deputies; nobody seemed to care. This prevented Esteva to deliver another "large case" of books which Panes' heirs had sent him, and it is not known what became of it.

It was only in 1825 and 1826 that Dr. Felix Osores made a list of the Panes donation of Ms. and at the time added many manuscripts to the Beristain library, but the Sahagun Ms. is not among the number. Perhaps it remained in that "large case" the family sent to Esteva, or else it was still retained by them. Bustamante tells us that when Panes' books were sold, Mr. Miguel José Bellido purchased the Sahagun Ms. for one hundred "pesos" Mex. This sale must have been one made by the heirs, and could only have comprised papers or books they still retained, or at the most the contents of that large case. The Sahagun Ms., however, reposed in possession of its new owner as ignored as before, so much so that when the publication called "Ocios de Españoles Emigrados" arrived in Mexico, the article referring to it caused great surprise. It was at once reproduced by the periodical "El Sol" in the numbers corresponding to the 16th and 17th of May, 1825, without mentioning the source. At once Bustamante began to call attention to the great work by the Franciscan missionary, by either copying entire paragraphs of the History in his editions, taking them from the periodical, "Ocios de Españoles Emigrados," and also by entreating Congress to acquire the London manuscript, all of which amply proves that the existence of another copy in Mexico was unknown to him. He only learned of its existence at the beginning of 1829.

In no. 10, vol. I of "Voz de la Patria," a periodical published by Bustamante, there is a report by the second financial Commission of Congress dated March 4th, 1829, which in art. 5 proposes that the Government of Mexico authorize forthwith its Chargé d'Affairs in London to purchase there the Sahagun Ms. and send it at once to Mexico. As this document was published in a newspaper, thus became known to everybody, Bellido, owner of the Panes copy, decided to offer it to Bustamante, who was commissioned by Congress to publish several historical works in Mexico. He, Bellido, offered it at the same price he had paid, i.e., one hundred pesos, deducting twenty as his contribution towards its publication. The Chamber of Deputies at once accepted formally the proposal of publication and agreed in a formal document dated May 31st, 1829, to defray the edition. However, when under the same date the proposition was sent to the Senate, the negotiation became somehow entangled, and for the time being nothing further was done.

On account of the second ordinance of expulsion of Spaniards, enacted

March 20th of that year, there existed a certain antagonism between the two Houses (Senate and House of Representatives), which may account for the comparative indifference with which the project was received by the Senate. The government, on the other hand, adopted several severe methods against the Spaniards, which disgusted even its partisans, and Bustamante, an honorable and grateful man despite his facitious opinions, undertook, like others, the defense of the persecuted, partly in the House of Representatives and partly by means of the press. Passions ran exceedingly high, so much so that Bustamante even feared for his life. With this idea in mind he planned to place the manuscript in care of the library of the Cathedral and, not content with this measure, he even donated it to that library in the case that he should die, "as was probable," with the stipulated condition that it was to be published. The act of donation is dated April 14th, 1829, and is included at the beginning of vol. I of the manuscript.

When animosities ceased later on he reclaimed his manuscript, and it was probably at that time when he separated book XII from the rest and failed to incorporate it later, for it still is missing in vol. III. The Spanish expedition which appeared in Mexico towards the end of July of that year may have been the reason why Bustamante published *first* and in a separate volume this last book which treats of the Conquest. By presenting this lamentable picture to his readers he intended to revive the patriotism of the Mexicans and cause them to repel a renewed invasion of the Spaniards. He gives it clearly to understand in the preface. Towards the end of May the edition was almost ready, and by June 15th it was on sale, in "Voz de la Patria," vol. I, no. 21.

By publishing this XII book first, no doubt Bustamante opened the way for the rest of Sahagun's historical epic and, although an official edition could not be obtained because both Senate and House of Representatives remained indifferent, ecclesiastical bodies came to his assistance with liberal donations. On May 15th, 1830, Bustamante announced that "after eleven months of untold hardships and considerable expenditure the edition of the eleven books was finished and would be on sale early in June at the price of nine pesos." Bustamante deserves great credit for his efforts for, despite the fact that he had no money, no credit, and was forced to go around soliciting donations, he succeeded in publishing the great work in eleven months, while Kingsborough, who had obtained the original long before and was not hampered by any lack of funds, took much longer to get his edition out. It is to be deplored that the Mexican editor should have given to the world an even more incorrect edition than the English by Kingsborough, omitting such parts that to him appeared "indecent," for by so doing he lost some of the credit due him.

The work once accomplished, Bustamante returned the original to the library of the Cathedral, with the exception of book XII. In 1867 this latter belonged to Señor José F. Ramirez, and later it was purchased by Señor Alfredo Chavero. When the library of the Cathedral was confiscated by the government, the manuscript went to the National library of Mexico city, department of manuscripts.

Bustamante appears to have been satisfied that the eleven books of Sahagun's History were all his readers should want, leaving them to hunt for book XII, printed previously as stated above, if they wished to add it for completion of the series. He added to the edition of the eleven books a wealth of notations of his own, which prove useless if not impertinent, and none of them are included in the present translation, for, as Señor Ramirez very justly remarked, not one of them helps to explain the text. But then, it was a habit, perhaps a weakness of the editor, to write supplements to everything he published!

In 1880 the "Historia" by Sahagun was published in French under the following title:

"Histoire Générale des Choses de la Nouvelle Espagne par le R. P. Fray Bernardino de Sahagun. Traduite et annotée par D. Jourdanet. Anteur de divers Ouvrages sur la Climatologie du Mexique et traducteur de la Chronique de Bernal Diaz del Castillo, et par Rémi Simeon, Éditeur, avec Commentaires, de la Grammaire Nahuatl, du R. P. Fray Andrés de Olmos.—Paris, G. Masson, Éditeur, Librairie de l'Académie de Médecine, 120, Boulevard Saint Germain, 1880. En 8^{0} jésus.

This translation includes book XII from its original text, not the reformed one. It seems strange that while the translator confesses on page IX of his introduction that the edition of Bustamante is less true to the original than the one by Kingsborough, he nevertheless uses the former for the greater part. The real value of the French translation consists in the valuable linguistic studies by Mr. Rémi Siméon.

At the time Garcia Icazbalceta published his Bibliografia Mexicana (1886), none of the original manuscripts of Sahagun remained in Mexico with the exception of two fragments of old copies included in a codex at the library of the University, later transferred to the National library. The original was a volume in Spanish 4^{0} entitled: "Cantares de los Mexicanos y otros opúsculos." It begins with a collection of songs, in Mexican, not of their primitive, pagan tunes, but of the Christian era. It is quite probable that Sahagun himself made the collection of songs, because he refers to it when he says: "They sing the ancient songs they used to sing in the times of idolatry, not all, but many of them, and nobody understands what they say, their words being incomprehensible. If they do sing some of the songs they composed after their conversion, speaking of God and the saints, these songs are full of irrelevancy and heresy." Sahagun evidently had seen and had studied these songs as far as this was possible. He, moreover, cited the two songs Huexotzincaiutl and Cuextecaiutl, which were the ones the ancient Mexicans used in their rites, and which are contained in the collection of the National library. It is to be hoped that if some day a complete edition of Sahagun's work is published, these two songs may be included.

This collection of songs is followed by the two fragments by Sahagun, the principal merit of which is that in part they are still inedited. They are not originals, but contemporary copies. The first one bears the title of "Calendario Mexicano, Latino y Castellano," preceded by a short prologue, also inedited, as we shall see later. It is arranged very similarly to the insertion in book II of the History, but somewhat different in substance. While in the Buntamante edition the Mexican months follow in their order, and the Christian months are so arranged as to correspond, in the manuscript our calendar comes first and the Mexican one is subject to it in its sequence. Thus the latter begins with the 11th day of Tititl, corresponding to January 1st. Both agree in placing the beginning of the Mexican year on February 1st, but Sahagun, in the manuscript, conceived the singular idea, "in order to eradicate superstition," as he says, to distribute the five "unfortunate" or left-over days, the "nemontemi" of the Ancient Mexicans, throughout the months as best it seemed to him. To each one of the months of Atleahualo, Tozaztontli, Toxcatl, Tecuilhuitontli and Panquetzaliztli, he assigned 21 days, thus changing as may be imagined, the entire original sequence of the ancient Mexican count. Thus, in the manuscript, January 1st corresponds with 11, and in the printed edition with 14 Tititl. With each month the corresponding feasts and sacrifices are annotated, although much more briefly than in the "History." At the end, on five folios, there are ten pictures of as many months which form two separate groups; the first group represents the images of the months of Tlacaxipehualiztli, Tozoztontli, Hueytozoztli and Toxcatl, then comes a lapse of eight months, followed by the second group of Quecholli, Panquetzaliztli, Atemoztli, Tititl, Izcalli and Quahuitlehua. On another folio is the image of the nemontemi, or last days of the Mexican year. This calendar was no doubt prepared in 1585, at all events after 1584, because he speaks of the Gregorian correction of the Christian calendar, which in Mexico was only made in the latter year, and not, as in Europe, in 1582. The change was made in the colonies only after the reception of a Royal Decree, dated May 14th, 1583, which, by the way, brought about a certain amount of confusion in the lives of Spaniards living in Spain and Mexico or traveling back and forth, because for two years there was a difference of ten days in their day count.

The new Calendar by Sahagun, with its weird system of intercalation, was adopted by Fray Martin de León in his "Camino del Cielo," published in Mexico in 1611 (fol. 96), with only the difference that he begins the Mexican year on February 2nd, then, by allowing to the month Atlcahualo twenty days only instead of twenty-five, he made the rest agree with the above distribution. Fray Martin fails to say—positively—where he obtained his information, and this is the more surprising because at that time (1611) Sahagun's work, at least part of it, still was in the hands of brethren of the same religious Order; some of his contemporaries, such as Torquemada, were still alive, yet no one raised protest against such shameless literary plagiarism.

The second fragment refers to the "Arte Divinatoria," which is found in book IV of the History, although this latter is not accompanied by the interesting prologue, nor by the "Notice to the Reader" and chapter I. The II chapter of the manuscript corresponds to chap. I of the History, and so on successively with exception of one, up to the XXXII of the manuscript (the XXXI of the edited version), which was cut down to about one-half, not on account of a mutilation of the (original) codex, but because the copyist failed to proceed, leaving one sentence cut in half at the top of one folio, the reverse of which is blank. Comparing both texts they show a good many variations.

Fray Martin de León had this manuscript before him when he wrote on the idolatries of the Mexicans, and it even appears that it was then more extensive on certain points than what is now preserved at the National library, and we may be sure that these points would not have escaped Sahagun's great talent of observation, so that we are safe to surmise that in some way or other several folios, perhaps, of the original, were lost or wilfilly taken out. In one place he refers that Demon told the Indians "that this subjection to the Spaniards he had permitted by his own carelessness and also on account of the lack of respect and consideration they (the Indians) paid to the cult and sacrifices of their (own) temples; that they were to be patient, because after eighty years he would again give them their liberty, and that therefore he ordained that they should obey them (the Spaniards) forcibly and all they could, because later he would reward them." At any rate, it is most remarkable to notice the opinion the author formed about the conversion of the Indians as contained in this fragment. Previously he had not been quite so rigorous, because in his "Postilla" he states that "for the first twenty years the fervor of the natives was great, but that later on they again inclined towards idolatry." Thus the first predicants were safe from criticism, since it was rather a matter of apostasy than of a feigned conversion; but in 1585 he revokes that restriction and does not vacillate in declaring that these first missionaries were deceived because they lacked "the prudence of the snake," and that the Indians at no time abandoned their idolatries, but always accepted in their pantheon the gods of nations subdued by them, and did the same with the Christian God, granting Him a place among the idols, without changing for the rest their ancient religion, although they practiced it secretly for fear of the Spaniards.

Such notions must not only have been very shocking to the Order of St. Francis, in as much as it hurt the memory of holy men who had given their lives in the effort of converting the Indians to Christianity, but it forcibly would disturb the peace of mind of active priests who administered the Sacraments "indiscrimination" to a mass composed of few Christians and a great many idolaters. Although this prologue or notice was never printed and was not even included in the copies of the History, but appears to have been written after the last copy had been made, it no doubt was known by the monks, because it was handled by transcribers, as it is not very likely that the copy at the library of Mexico was the only one. And, moreover, if Father Sahagun was of that opinion he no doubt expressed it also by word of mouth.

He based this opinion principally on his discovery of the Tonalamatl or Calendar of 260 days, which surprised him because such a day count could not be so easily adjusted in a computation of time, and he therefore failed to understand its object. He thought that it was purely superstitious and, perhaps, a modern invention of the Indians to palliate idolatry, and thus be able to continue their prognostications under the protection of this new Calendar. In the History he had already shown that the Tonalamatl was really apart from a chronological use, the basis of prognostications of a sort of judiciary astrology (vol. III of Bustamante's edition, p. 339, et seq.).

Father Sahagun knew a great many of the secrets of the Indians, and he was a severe persecutor of idolatry, even saw it everywhere. He condemned the game of the "volador," and obtained its prohibition, as we see in "Torquemada's History" (book XX, chap. 43). Even in certain Christian ceremonies, if practiced by Indians, he discovered or suspected an idolatrous background.

But where is the truth in all this? Was Sahagun endowed with greater perspicacity than all his companions of the Franciscan Order, or did he, perhaps, see evil where it did not exist? In primitive conversions the humble classes, the common people, generally accepted the teachings of Christianity more readily because of a hope that thereby they might rid themselves of the enormous weight of human sacrifices and of the des-as compared with his contemporaries, laymen as well as ecclesiastics, who through jealousy or a spirit of obscurantism tried to dim the light which the writings of this great missionary spread. It is quite true that Fray Bernardino's life was full of opposition; that he was obliged more than once to obey orders imposed by his superiors, but there seems to be a good deal of exaggeration for, even if there were men who antagonized him, he had on the other hand also great and staunch friends.

Perhaps Sahagun's own complaints were responsible for these exaggerations when he stated that only through the great assistance granted him by Father Sequera his books were being brought to light again, after having been all but forgotten. Like all authors he loved his books, children of his brain; he frequently praises them, believing them to contain great lessons for other missionaries. He is certain that no one knows the secrets of the ancient Mexicans as well as he, declaring that his books are worthy to be presented to a king. This, however, cannot be called vanity; he speaks of himself only incidentally, but freely gives the names of his Indian informants and collaborators; he is merely the expounder of what they tell him. Aside from the affection of the author for his work, he also felt sorry that such great efforts should fail to produce the benefit he hoped for. He had worked hard and faithfully among the Indians to Christianize them, so surely his sorrow upon seeing all his efforts frustrated was justified.

This is all very true, but was there really a systematic persecution? There existed a general opinion among the missionaries that it was not wise to write anything concerning native lore, idolatries as well as superstitions, in the Mexican language, simply in order to avoid that the Indians themselves should read what was not meant for them or that they should, by so doing, remember things the monks were trying to make them forget. That was the reason why Sahagun wrote the "Postilla" and the so-called "Gramatica historica" in Spanish; he was himself anxious to avoid controversies. Both these works contained plenty of material for discussion, and it should not be considered as a matter of personal persecution if some of the friars were of a different opinion and voiced it.

It was the venerable Father Toral himself who adjusted the differences by an act of authority. He ordered Sahagun to write the "History" in the Mexican language and granted him all sorts of assistance. He and his successors allowed him to go wherever he pleased; he was free to consult at length, on three different occasions and at various places, the Indians and the students of the College; he was allowed to go over his notes gathered at these places as many times as he deemed necessary for their perfection; several copies were made at a considerable expense, for all these copies were made by copyists. Thus so far there appeared to be nothing but very decided protection on the part of the Order of St. Francis.

When Sahagun found nothing more to add to the History he himself asked that it should be read and examined before the Chapter. It was approved, and yet right at this point complaints began, because this body refused to spend any more money for copyists. Now, if we examine the decision impartially, we must agree that it was quite justified. The Mexican copy which the Father Superior had ordered to be made at the expense of the Franciscan Order was finished, but now its author proposed to write the Spanish version, and it was this new expense the assembly refused to incur in. Father Escalona, the newly elected Father Provincial, was exceedingly zealous to preserve the vow of poverty which he practiced on himself with extreme rigour. He was of the opinion that money gathered from alms should not be spent for the translation into another language of a work already finished in a tongue almost all the friars understood. Moreover, the resolution was neither against the author nor his finished work, but merely against an extra expenditure. He had full liberty to finish the Spanish version if he so desired. True, he was no longer able to write it himself, but it seems impossible to believe that he would not have found among his students of Tlaltelulco one or the othe· who would have been glad and willing to help him at odd moments, because they all loved him. There was, for instance, Martin Jacobita, a good penman and his foremost friend and collaborator.

It is not easy to understand the reason why the Father Provincial took the books away from the author and dispersed them among the convents of the Order. At first sight this looks like a grave injustice, but let us try to trace it. It must be said that Fray Bernardino was not always the humble and submissive monk as represented. He had a temper of his own (but who would blame him?). He was greatly annoyed by criticism and contradictions voiced often at Tlaltelulco, on the part of people who did not approve of the instruction given the Indians, and he bitterly resented the opposition of the monks to his studies of the antiquities of that part of the country which, it appears, he began long before he was given the order of Father Torral to do so. It is surprising, for instance, that not only once, but several times, he spoke against the first twelve missionaries in Mexico, accusing them of lack of "serpentine prudence or wisdom" in their work and of having made fake conversions. We do not know what may have brought about such deep resentment on the part of Sahagun, for there are no positive data, except the fact that he and Motolinia had absolutely opposite ideas about the conversion of the natives to the Christian faith. The latter considered it unwise to alarm the Indians by searching for idols which, he said, they had so completely forgotten, "as if a hundred years had gone by." Sahagun assured the contrary, and while Motolinia warned against bringing back into their minds the idolatry of their fathers, Fray Bernardino was tireless in tracing it. In this controversy the latter naturally lost, in the eyes of the Order, even if it were only on account of the general respect in which Fray Toribio was held and for the great work he had done as a missionary.

The decision to scatter the books naturally hurt the author's feelings, as he states himself, but if this was done in order to injure them, the result was quite the opposite, because they were read by many of the monks and even by laymen, so that they really were given greater publicity, and a great many copies were made. If it was the intention of Father Escalona to destroy them, he would have succeeded better if he had burned them, or kept them under lock and key. Of course, they ran a great risk to get lost (and maybe he meant them to become lost), but, as a matter of fact, they all were sent back when Father Navarro ordered that they be returned to the author. The latter had, meanwhile, prepared an abstract which he sent to Spain, as stated elsewhere. It has been said that this was considered as an act of insubordination, but no proof exists to that effect.

The abstract called the attention of no less a personality than the President of the Council of the Indies, who wished to see the entire work and, as we know, Father Sequera brought back to Mexico an order for a complete copy in both languages. These are certainly signs of appreciation rather than of indifference. It would be difficult to point out a work of that epoch which was so often copied or transcribed in part, and which was used by so many authors without ever having been printed.

The statement that the Marqués de Villamanrique had taken away the Ms. is, as previously stated, a misstatement, erroneously made first by Betancurt and inadvertently repeated by others, but there is no doubt that the Council of the Indies ordered the seizure of all the copies, not leaving either original nor transcript in Mexico. We can only guess at the reason for such an act; the Archbishop speaks of "justified considerations" in his letter. Ramirez is of the opinion that Sahagun himself killed his works by the means he employed to spread knowledge of them, but we cannot quite agree that the arrival of the "Sumario" in Spain in 1570 should have been the reason for the order of 1577 (to collect all manuscripts); a span of seven years is too long a time for any plausible relation between the two events. All the summary obtained was the order of a copy of the book for Ovando. The decision to gather all of the books must have obeyed some other reason, and the most probable one is that one or the other of the many Franciscan monks who returned to Spain many have been of those who had opposed the publication of ancient rites and idolatries of the Mexicans, and gave unfavorable reports to the Council. This latter, upon receipt of this report or accusation, which as it often happens in similar cases, may have been grossly exaggerated, feared trouble if such a work remained free of access, and therefore wished to examine it for qualification. Nothing else is apparent in the few data we have; there is not the slightest indication of ill will against Sahagun, In Mexico he was greatly esteemed, and civic and ecclesiastical authorities did all they could for him; the Archbishop recommended him personally and indirectly also his literary abilities. Sahagun's own letter proves that he considered the demand from Spain as a sign of appreciation and that he was far from thinking that it was one of disapproval, so that he did not see it in the light of persecution, and he even made every possible effort to speed the invoice. The Franciscan Order always considered Fray Bernardino as an honored member; he was given prelacies, special commissions of importance, such as director of the College of Santa Cruz de Tlaltelulco, and even in the last years of his life, after having spent all the time he wished in his literary pursuit, he still held the position of chief definer (member of the governing assembly of the Order of St. Francis).

The only reason for complaint Sahagun might have had was that none of his books was ever printed in his lifetime, but this he shared with a great many others. The conquest and colonization of the Indies originated an enormous amount of histories and reports on the innumerable provinces and the Spanish government could not possibly master all that, the more so because printing in those times did not count with the facilities of modern times. To suspect that the government left these works, often of the utmost value, inedited on purpose, is stupid. The vast amount printed even in foreign lands proves the contrary.

The "Historia General de las cosas de Nueva España" by Sahagun is, without a doubt, one of the most complete sources of information concerning the Ancient Mexicans. It contains every phase of life of those people, and students in the same field will always occur to its pages for information.

The peculiar method Fray Bernardino pursued to obtain his facts is curiously clear throughout; we always feel that, although the diction is his, one hears the Indians themselves speak in their own way. He gave them complete liberty to express all their ideas as they best could; he did not change their mode of speaking in any way; he was even afraid to do so, and only wrote down his own opinion in notes or prologue, when the horrible rites and customs called for protest of a Christian mind. It is in every sense of the word an aboriginal history, for he cites no other writer or collaborator of his own race, mentions no one else but his native informants. Thus it is a true history of the Mexican Indian, told in Indian fashion.

Of course, it would be dangerous to only consult this work by Sahagun and his Indians, were we to write an exhaustive work on ancient customs and beliefs, for there may have been many misstatements. After all, the author had occasion to compare his data only in the three different places where he gathered them, and he put the last touches to this great work more than fifty years after the Conquest, when, perhaps, Spanish ideas had already in a measure permeated the native mind.

The language, being a literal translation from the Mexican idiom, is forcibly often crude and heavy and tiresome to read, and few may be the students who will read even the Spanish version from cover to cover.

We may truly say that Fray Bernardino de Sahagun is one of the most venerable and most learned figures of Spanish American history, an honour to Spain, where he was born, and a glorious memory for Mexico, where he spent the greatest part of his life and in whose soil the weary body found its last resting place.

INDEX